CONTESTED CANONIZATIONS

CONTESTED CANONIZATIONS

The Last Medieval Saints, 1482–1523

†RONALD C. FINUCANE

The Catholic University of America Press
Washington, D.C.

Design and typesetting by Kachergis Book Design

Library of Congress Cataloging-in-Publication Data
Finucane, Ronald C.
Contested canonizations : the last medieval saints, 1482–1523 / Ronald C. Finucane.
p. cm.
Includes bibliographical references and index.
ISBN 978-0-8132-1875-5 (cloth : alk. paper) 1. Canonization—History.
2. Christian saints—History. 3. Church history—Middle Ages, 600–1500.
4. Church history—16th century. I. Title. II. Title: Last medieval saints, 1482–1523.
BX2330.F56 2011
235'.2409024—dc22 2011014811

Contents

Preface

At the time of the author's death in August 2009, the main text and footnotes were complete and had been submitted to the press for peer review. The book lacked only a bibliography and an index. Ronald C. Finucane, with the scrupulous care and attention to detail that was the hallmark of everything he wrote, had substantially finished the manuscript almost a year previously. When not distracted by failing health, he spent the intervening period revising his text in response to comments by the numerous scholars with whom he was in regular touch (and whom he generously acknowledged in the footnotes). In an e-mail to me of July 30, 2009, the author had written: "I believe I can add nothing more to the ms at this point." Now, precisely one year later, it gives me great pleasure to submit the edited text to the publisher. Ron Finucane's widow, Claudia Voit, kindly sent me a disk with the final versions of the author's files, but they confirmed the truth of Ron's final e-mail to me, and the text you have before you is substantially as he left it in July 2009. I have limited my interventions to correcting a few minor errors and then to bringing the referencing conventions into line with that of the Catholic University of America Press. I have also compiled the consolidated bibliography and the index.

In the course of bringing this volume to press, I would like to thank David McGonagle, until recently director of the Catholic University of America Press, for his solicitous interest in the project, as well as Theresa B. Walker, managing editor, for her practical editorial work and advice on the manuscript. It is also a genuine pleasure to acknowledge the helpful thoroughness and eagle eye of my copy editor, Carol Kennedy, for improving the text in so many ways. I am also very grateful to David Collins for his helpful reader's report and to Claudia Voit for her interest and support at a difficult time. Ron had barely begun his own acknowledgments, and since he was scrupulous in acknowledging the work of other scholars in his detailed footnotes, the attentive reader will see where his gratitude lay. However, I know that he did want to say a special thank you to the archivists and librarians of the Congregation of the Causes of Saints, the Vatican Library, and the Vatican Archives.

Finally, Ron's sisters have told me that he would surely have dedicated this book to his beloved dogs, Stella Bella and Ziggy, who "remained by his side while he was writing and kept him company during breaks when they would sit in the sun, play ball, and nap together."

Simon Ditchfield
York, England
Feast of Abdon and Sennen

Abbreviations

AASS	*Acta sanctorum quotquot toto orbe coluntur,* 65 vols. Antwerp-Brussels-Tongerlo-Paris, 1643–1940.
ACCS	Archivio della Congregazione per le Cause dei Santi, Rome.
ASV	Archivio segreto vaticano, Vatican City.
BAV	Biblioteca apostolica vaticana, Vatican City.
BNP	Bibliothèque nationale, Paris.
Di Fonzo, "Il processo"	Lorenzo Di Fonzo, "Il processo di canonizzazione di S. Bonaventura da Bagnoregio O. Min (1474–82)," *Miscellanea Francescana* 75 (1975): 227–89.
Ludwig	Vinzenz Oskar Ludwig, "Der Kanonisations-prozess des Markgrafen Leopold III des Heiligen," *Jahrbuch der Stiftes Klosterneuburg* 9 (1919).
PC	Cosenza trial for the canonization of Francesco di Paola in Mario M. Pinzuti, ed., *I Codici Autografi dei Processi Cosentino e Turonense per la Canonizzazione di S. Francesco di Paola* (Roma: Curia Generalizia dell'Ordine dei Minimi, 1964), 4–233.
PT	Tours trial for the same case, ibid., 237–402.
Sposato, "Fonti"	Pasquale Sposato, "Fonti per la storia di S. Francesco di Paola: La sua canonizzazione attraverso il 'Diarium' di Paride De Grassi prefetto delle ceremonie pontificie sotto Leone X, Introduzione," *Calabria Nobilissima* 10, nos. 31–32 (Giugno, 1956): 1–32.

Vauchez, *Sainthood*	André Vauchez, *Sainthood in the Later Middle Ages,* trans. Jean Birrell (Cambridge: Cambridge University Press, 1997).
Volkmar, *Die Heiligenerhebung*	Christoph Volkmar, *Die Heiligenerhebung Bennos von Meissen (1523/24)* (Münster: Aschendorff, 2002).
Wetzstein, *Heilige vor Gericht*	Thomas Wetzstein, *Heilige vor Gericht. Das Kanonisationsverfahren im europäischen Spätmittlalter* (Cologne: Böhlau Verlag, 2005).

CONTESTED CANONIZATIONS

Introduction

Popes canonized only five saints between 1482 and 1523, following well-established medieval procedures; there were no more official canonizations until 1588, long after the Protestant and Catholic reformations began and more than twenty years after the final meeting of the Council of Trent. When saint-making resumed, the atmosphere was very different, even if, to begin with, the rules and procedures for making saints remained the same.[1] Though other medieval figures were canonized centuries later—one thinks of Joan of Arc—these elevations occurred in totally different contexts. Secondly, not one of the five saints considered in this book achieved sainthood without slips in procedure or varying degrees of hostility expressed by one party or another. These facts determined my choice of title for this book. We'll deal with Bonaventure, Leopold, Francis of Paola, Antoninus of Florence, and Benno of Meissen. Our five became saints in a tumultuous period, troubled by discordant religious ideologies within Christendom, the Turkish threat, Italian city-state rivalries, a politicized papacy and college of cardinals, and, especially, the rise of French and imperial superpowers that would significantly alter European life and politics. The twists and turns of their canonization processes reflect this unsettling background, as each one of

1. See Finucane, "Saint-Making at the End of the Sixteenth Century: How and Why Jacek of Poland (d. 1257) Became St. Hyacinth in 1594," *Hagiographica* 9 (2002), 207–5. For the wider context, see Simon Ditchfield, "Tridentine Worship and the Cult of Saints," in *The Cambridge History of Christianity*, vol. 6: *Reform and Expansion 1500–1660*, edited by R. Po-chia Hsia, 201–24 (Cambridge: Cambridge University Press, 2007).

them was affected by these transformative, exciting two decades either side of 1500.

There is plenty of medieval and later evidence about the procedures for saint-making at the local level, that is, the gathering of testimony—for example, in England, France, or Germany—about the lives and miracles of particular individuals. However, we're less well informed about what happens next. Records of these local inquiries were sent to the papal curia, where they were examined in many stages by several different sets of eyes. Information about this curial phase is almost nonexistent for the Middle Ages, becoming more abundant after 1500. One of the aims of this book is to examine curial attitudes and procedures at this crucial period when—to use the traditional terms—the "Middle Ages" slides into "Reformation." Even so, the data for our five saints—a secular prince, a hermit, a friar, a bishop, and an archbishop—are incomplete, so that the chapters will not follow exactly the same narrative lines. Another goal of the present work is to determine how far practice matched theory. As we'll see, in every case there were disjunctions between what was supposed to happen in a canonization process—the procedural flow—and what actually occurred. For example, anyone hoping to gain a place in late-medieval and early-modern princely or royal courts, apart from an acceptable résumé, needed patronage, a network of supporters; in other words, reputable backers. Would-be saints (some of whom themselves became "patron" saints) similarly needed patrons pushing their cause, their entrée into the papal and then heavenly courts. Our case studies will reveal that this patronage wasn't always easily obtained or maintained. Many other factors were involved: no one became a saint without performing miracles, but there were disagreements about specific examples; a whiff of unorthodoxy might be enough to quash a candidate's hopes; lackluster papal or curial interest, even outright hostility, was always a possibility, for whatever reasons; and insufficient funding was a constant concern.

Each our saints (a Saxon, an Austrian, and three Italians) spanning the late-medieval and early-modern eras has been well studied by scholars whose works are the foundation for this book. However, this the first attempt in English to consider them as a group, and to compare their careers and sometimes endangered progress through the curial bureaucracy.

Saint-making was a time-consuming, expensive, and messy business in the late fifteenth and early sixteenth centuries. In our exploration of five case studies we'll encounter a pope who warmly supported, then bitterly rejected, a saint-candidate; another pontiff who tricked his cardinals into a canonization; a cardinal too preoccupied with worldly affairs to work on a report needed for a candidate; another cardinal on a canonization committee who didn't bother to attend. There was the bishop who didn't carry out a preliminary investigation as ordered, and another bishop who publicly supported a candidate, but told friends he'd like the process delayed for one hundred "or at least eighty" years; and so the list goes on, including a complaint about "improper" canonization ritual raised almost as soon as the candles were snuffed out, worries about a collapsing stage where pope and VIPs sat during the ceremony, fears that props used in a canonization would be stolen, saint-lobbyists forced to sell their horses just for food and lodging in Rome, and, at the grassroots level, witnesses whose testimony wandered right outside neatly scripted lists of interrogatories set by the lawyers. Even though procedures for testing candidates' sanctity and miracles were in place well before 1300, and canonists and theologians had produced commentaries and guidelines in plenty by 1400, things seldom (probably never) played out according to plan.

The aim of this unashamedly narrative study is quite limited: rather than drawing sweeping conclusions about "sainthood" and so-called models of sanctity from so few examples, I'm interested mainly in how internal problems (within the curia for instance) and external influences (such as political changes) affected saint-making.[2]

Before proceeding, I must address a semantic issue: the distinction between people thought to be holy ("saints") and those officially canonized (also "saints"). The ambiguity lies in the medieval Latin *sanctus,* which can be either adjective or noun—"holy," "holy object," "holy person," or "canonized person." At all times in this book the word "saint" and "canonized person" are interchangeable. Though Thomas Wetzstein points out the pitfalls of such usage, I employ the alternation merely to prevent constant repetition of the word "canonization"; when I write "saint" or "saint-making" I refer to the canonized person, or the process of creating one.[3] People crowd-

2. The concept of a "model" often meant different things to the upper clergy, who pushed for imitation, and most laypeople, who sought only intercession (miracles) and "a vague moral guidance." John H. Arnold, *Belief and Unbelief in Medieval Europe* (London: Hodder/N.Y.: Oxford University Press, 2005), 83–84.

3. Thomas Wetzstein, *Heilige vor Gericht: Das Kanonisationsverfahren im europäischen Spätmit-*

ing round a tomb can "make" a saint in the sense of fostering the cult of a holy person; that is not the usage followed here, though a local cult was normally the prelude to a canonization process. Another point to clear away is the need to acknowledge the complexity of contemporary politics, which I have described in generalizations that may at times seem far too broad for specialists of the period; for this I ask their indulgence.

It may well be, as the history textbook cliché has it, that every age is an age of transition; but some transitions are more significant than others. Lauro Martines notes that "the political earthquakes of the late fifteenth and early sixteenth centuries"—the very period covered in this book—had profound social and cultural effects extending into practically all aspects of life.[4] The creation of new saints, too, was deeply affected by these tremors. For example, years ago André Vauchez suggested that political influences on canonizations became marked from about 1270, and by the fourteenth century "became supreme."[5] Was this still, or even more, true of the late fifteenth and early sixteenth centuries? This is but one theme to explore in the following chapters. We'll examine various individuals and groups that supported or resisted those who eventually succeeded to sainthood in that crucial era of transition from the late medieval to the Reformation periods, when many forces pushed and pulled papal policies as His Holiness grew into and expanded his role as territorial sovereign. We'll look back to medieval modes of canonizing and forward to 1523, when the saint-making machinery at Rome shut down for sixty-five years: our five saints would be

---

telalter (Cologne: Böhlau Verlag, 2005), 205 nn. 6 and 211. This magisterial work will rank with Vauchez's study (below) of medieval sanctity; Wetzstein includes a very useful list of primary sources for late-medieval processes, including Bonaventure's and Leopold's, in his appendix I. For a later period, Simon Ditchfield's *Liturgy, Sanctity and History in Tridentine Italy* (Cambridge: Cambridge University Press, 1995) is unsurpassed; see also Stefan Samerski's *"Wie im Himmel, so auf Erden"?: Selig- und Heiligsprechung in der Katholischen Kirche 1740 bis 1870* (Stuttgart: Kohlhammer, 2002).

4. Lauro Martines, *Strong Words: Writing and Social Strain in the Italian Renaissance* (Baltimore: John Hopkins University Press), 254–55. While not denying continuities between medieval and early-modern societies and cultures, Robert Bireley reprises the historical tradition of a "meaningful break" around 1500 in "Early-Modern Catholicism as a Response to the Changing World of the Long Sixteenth Century," *Catholic Historical Review* 95, no. 2 (2009): 219–39, at 221.

5. André Vauchez, *Sainthood in the Later Middle Ages,* trans. Jean Birrell (Cambridge: Cambridge University Press, 1997), 77, 82. Michael Goodich, in "The Politics of Canonization in the Thirteenth Century: Lay and Mendicant Saints," republished in *Saints and Their Cults,* ed. Stephen Wilson (Cambridge: Cambridge University Press, 1983), writes that while "the Christian idealism and *imitatio Christi* embodied in the life of the saint of course remained paramount, the immediate aims behind papally confirmed sainthood were specific, and limited by the political interests of Rome" (83).

the last to be elevated to the altar, as it was termed, until 1588. For some scholars, this hiatus was the result of a papal "loss of nerve" in the face of Protestant criticisms. However, in the longer view the slowdown that ended in temporary stoppage in 1523 had been a long time in coming: using Vauchez's figures, between 1198 and 1304 (106 years) twenty-four individuals were canonized, the high point in official sainthood during the Middle Ages; but between 1305 and 1500, a period (195 years) nearly twice as long as the first, only nineteen were made saints.[6] There was a total of five during the sixteenth century.[7] Vauchez attributed this decline to increasing costs and the growing length of curial processes, with a consequent need to replace defunct curialists and promoters as a result, as well as bringing new popes on board. Furthermore, Vauchez claims that as a glut of saint-candidates threatened to inundate the Holy City by the late thirteenth century, curialists were deliberately attempting to discourage processes and their supportive suppliants.[8] Many scholars, as noted, also posit the Protestant Reformation, and Catholic sensitivity to criticisms of saints, cults, and relics, as a factor in declining numbers of canonizations. We'll examine this contention in the concluding chapter.

The mechanism slowly revived as the work of the new Congregation of Rites (1588) was augmented by changes effected by Urban VIII (1623–44). When he could find the time to disengage from the confusion of the Thirty Years' War, for example, or the annoying obstinacy of his old friend Galileo, in the 1630s Urban introduced more exacting qualifications for sainthood, which remained in place until the twentieth century. Changes introduced by John Paul II (1978–2005) greatly simplified and accelerated the process, producing a shower of canonizations that threw Rome's saint-making institution (the Congregation for the Causes of Saints) into high gear. John Paul beatified more individuals (1,341) and made more saints (482) in a single papal reign than had been created, in total, in all the centuries since the

6. Vauchez, *Sainthood,* 61, 252–55.

7. In addition to Francis, Antoninus, and Benno, there were Diego (cd. 1588) and Hyacinth (cd. 1594).

8. Vauchez, *Sainthood,* 62–77; in n. 45, the martyrs of Morocco (1481) were incorrectly included; they did not receive universal *cultus.* Ghost canonizations of the next century included "St." Bruno in 1514, "St." Casimir, supposedly canonized in 1521, and "St." Norbert, presumably made a saint in 1582. There are many such examples of what usually turn out to be papal authorizations for a local community or order, etc. The question of *beatus* versus *sanctus* was not yet at issue during this period.

beginnings of the official canonization process in the Middle Ages. Renaissance Rome witnessed no such mass production.

On any given day, usually in the morning, litigants, lobbyists and proctors, prelates and their clergy, the laity and their servants swarmed the streets of the City heading for cardinals' palaces or judges' and curial bureaucrats' homes or offices, hoping for an audience and the granting of favors of all kinds; Rome, "theater of all the world," attracted business from all over Christendom. Many of those lobbyists came armed with letters supplicating for canonizations. In the minds (and hopes) of their supporters, attention to would-be saints ought to have been among the top priorities of curial officials and cardinals. Viewed from France or Germany, even Italy, failure to canonize a favored candidate might easily be blamed on bureaucratic laziness, indifference, or hostility (which sometimes was the case, as we'll see). However, this criticism—sometimes aimed at particular cardinals—was not wholly justified. To balance the picture, let's glance at the routine of Rome's cardinals, which encompassed much more than saint-making. We'll choose an admittedly unusual example, the brother of Florence's republican leader Piero, Francesco Soderini (cardinal from 1503 to 1524). His being out of favor with one pope (Julius II), exiled by another (Leo X), and imprisoned by a third (Adrian VI) certainly makes him unusual, but also has attracted interest, giving us insight into cardinals' lives.[9] Three of our saints were canonized during his membership in the college of cardinals. On an almost daily basis most cardinals, including Soderini, attended ceremonies or directed liturgical observances and sat on various ad hoc committees and in congregations or consistories (secret, semipublic, or public). They received petitioners lining up at their *palazzi* gates, including those sent by their secular patrons, and entertained important guests or ambassadors; they served as judges on various tribunals, were curial administrators, and of course elected popes. Occasionally they went on legations, even to places where they understood the native language; a few led troops into battle. Soderini did many

9. For the following, K. J. P. Lowe, *Church and Politics in Renaissance Italy: The Life and Career of Cardinal Francesco Soderini, 1453–1524* (Cambridge: Cambridge University Press, 1993); another view of the busy life of a later cardinal including many useful tables of expenses is Mary Hollingsworth, *The Cardinal's Hat* (New York: Overlook Press, 2004), a study of Hippolito d'Este (d. 1572), esp. chap. 8, "The New Cardinal," 229–63. See also Marco Pellegrini, *Ascanio Maria Sforza* [d. 1505]: *La parabola politica di un cardinal-principe del rinascimento,* 2 vols. (Rome: Istituto storico italiano per il medio evo, 2002).

of these things and more, ranging from attending *sponsalia* (betrothals of important people) to acting as governor of bandit-infested Campagna and Marittima, serving on many concurrent and successive committees, and attending the Fifth Lateran Council. By the end of his life he'd been named dean of the college and had also been assigned to deal with the "Luther problem." Clearly, conscientious cardinals had to master the art of multitasking. William Hudon neatly sums it up: they "worked amid competing commitments. The interrelationships they established were varied, multifaceted, and rather fluid. The positions they took and tactics they used were anything but uniform. Individual lives, groups of friends, political entities, and long-lasting institutions filled with contradictions" were the stuff of their lives.[10] On the other hand, some cardinals shirked their responsibilities, which happened in a few cases involving our holy candidates. (This included popes: Leo X, reported one ambassador in 1519, was neglecting business while enjoying Carnival festivities.)[11] Committees of three cardinals were assigned to each of our five canonizations.

As we'll see, apart from all the routine activities indicated above, sometimes these men received papal orders to drop everything and concentrate on other issues; occasionally the entire college was distracted by extraordinary developments. During such times a saint's cause might be temporarily shelved. In fact, without renewed impetus, it could become permanently "pending." There were as yet no standing committees of cardinals assigned to specific administrative duties, no Congregation for the Causes of Saints as there are now. Until this Congregation (in its earlier form as the Congregation of Rites and Ceremonies) established its own archive in 1624, there was always the chance that important documents might be misfiled or taken home by one of its members, never to be seen again.[12] In 1620, for instance, the Congregation noted that a letter in the king of Spain's own hand had

10. William Hudon, reviewing Paul V. Murphy's book on Cardinal Ercole Gonzaga (1505–63) in *The Catholic Historical Review* 95, no. 4 (2008): 827.

11. *Letters and Papers Foreign and Domestic,* Henry VIII, vol. 3, part 1, 1519–21, March 29, 1519, Silvestro de Gigli, Bishop of Worcester, to Wolsey.

12. Ditchfield, *Liturgy, Sanctity and History,* 48, 98–99; on the 1588 Congregation, see Giovanni Papa, *Le cause di canonizzazione nel primo periodo della Congregazione dei Riti (1588–1634)* (Città del Vaticano: Urbaniana University Press, 2001). On the history of the archive see Jaroslav Nemec, "L'archivio della Congregazione per le Cause dei Santi," in *Miscellanea in occasione del IV centenario della Congregazione per le Cause dei Santi (1588–1988),* 339–52 (Rome: Ministero per i Beni Culturali ed Ambientali, 1988).

been mislaid by one of the cardinals or his secretary, though it was "diligently" looked for.[13] Such an event was probably even more common before the Congregation was established in 1588. In 1857 a bundle of forty-two documents was turned over to Pius IX by someone who'd acquired them "from private hands," namely the descendants of an apostolic protonotary who'd kept them in the family archives for about 250 years. The bundle included autograph, sealed documents from Polish royalty of the 1580s supplicating for the canonization of Hyacinth (cd. 1594).[14]

Another aspect that affected the saint-making process was the fact that the college of cardinals, which discussed and voted on canonizations, was a relatively small body, numbering perhaps three dozen or so in Rome at any given time, often fewer that this. By about 1500 this small ecclesiastical elite had developed political factionalism that became more evident as Spain and France battled over Italy and as pontiffs became more "politicized" in ruling their Papal States while dealing with Europe's superpowers.[15] Moreover, although the college was becoming more "Italian," other *nationes* were represented as well. In this complex mix, it was sometimes possible for popes to impose their authority, but changing circumstances might shift the balance of power to factions among the cardinals. As yet the college wasn't that worldly, powerless group of "idols in appearance" that some claimed it had become by the end of the sixteenth century; it still had authority.[16] Since votes were taken in consistories made up of competing factions, a canonization might be blocked until agreement could be reached. For the most part the promo-

13. Process of Isidore, report of December 12, 1620, in Archivio della Congregazione per le Cause dei Santi (henceforth ACCS), *Decreta servorum Dei,* 1:170.

14. ACCS, the seventh document I found in a box made up to resemble a large book, on the spine the words "Documenta Autographa canonisationis B. Hyacinthi Poloni Ord. Praed," and the designation "R53." Among the forty-two documents, including the 1857 letter and several autographs, was a large drawing of Hyacinth's shrine as it was at the end of the sixteenth century. My thanks to Monsignor Sarno for providing access to the archives in 1998.

15. Marco Pellegrini, "A Turning-Point in the History of the Factional System in the Sacred College: The Power of Pope and Cardinals in the Age of Alexander VI," in *Court and Politics in Papal Rome, 1492–1700,* ed. Gianvittorio Signorotto and Maria Antonietta Visceglia, 8–30 (Cambridge: Cambridge University Press, 2002).

16. "Idoli in apparenza," Venetian ambassador's report of 1598, quoted in Gigliola Fragnito, "Cardinals' Courts in Sixteenth-Century Rome," *Journal of Modern History* 65, no. 1 (1993): 26–56, at 36; this opinion illustrates Prodi's thesis that as popes became princes, their cardinals became more subservient, a "courtly aristocracy dependent on the pope as prince," Paolo Prodi, *The Papal Prince,* trans. Susan Haskins (Cambridge: Cambridge University Press, 1987), 84. See also Jennifer Mara DeSilva, "Senators or Courtiers: Negotiating Models for the College of Cardinals under Julius II and Leo X," *Renaissance Studies* 22, no. 2 (2008): 154–173.

tion of any given candidate to sainthood was a matter of negotiation involving patrons (religious orders, princes, cities), the college, and popes.

On a more mundane level, there is the cost. Saints weren't made for free; their causes were supported by emperors, kings, princes, the secular and ecclesiastical nobility, religious orders, towns (even small ones) and cities, and indirectly by the ordinary laity, whose contributions came in as offerings at tombs or purchases of indulgences on the candidate's behalf. Without significant financial backing, mediated by bankers, it's not likely that even the holiest of individuals would gain entrance to the exclusive circle of saints. If funds dried up, so would the cause: at one point in a fourteenth-century case the local examiners nearly quit because the saint's promoter hadn't paid them.[17] Osmund of Salisbury's proctor wrote a begging letter from Rome in 1452, complaining that as soon as coins ceased to clink, so did curial activity; a few weeks later he was begging again, this time in his native language: "For goddess love pray for us and send us sylver." In 1465 a bishop ordered his proctor for a would-be German saint to "ask around" the curia for the best deal, while the proctor suggested cutting costs by paying curial advocates not in cash but in honorary titles of nobility and, for the local hearings, calling upon friends and others willing to do the job on the cheap; alternatively, money might be saved by teaming up with two other pending German processes. Sometimes the anticipated expenses discouraged would-be supporters: in 1471 the Bordeaux canons decided they couldn't afford a defunct bishop's canonization.[18] The vexed question of cost will be considered in the concluding chapter; among the few indications that have survived, we know that the ceremony itself in St. Peter's basilica ran to more than 2,000 ducats, a figure that in one case—as we'll see—amazed the pope himself. A canonization ceremony, then, was very costly—and this was in addition to the years, even centuries, of expenditure that went into promoting a candidate. Our five saints took between 12 (Francis) and 417 years (Benno) to move into the heavenly ranks.

Even with enough financial backing and the greatest of goodwill on all sides, saint-lobbyists were faced with further hindrances: geography, war-

17. "Canonisation et politique au xive siècle. Documents inédits . . . de Charles de Blois," ed. A. Vauchez, in *Miscellanea in onore di Monsignor Martino Giusti*, 2 vols. (Vatican City: Vatican Archive, 1978), 2:381–404, at 385–86.

18. Wetzstein, *Heilige vor Gericht*, 358, 368, 371–72: "quamdiu sonitus pecuniarum in curia cessat, negotiorum expeditiones omnino cessant."

fare, and the weather. The sending and receiving of popes' and cardinals' mandates and letters to distant committees investigating a cult, and the return of written findings from those committees to Rome, along with letters to and from supporters of the cause, were of necessity part of the process. Agents carrying reports from a cult site to Rome, often clerical proctors, faced a variety of hindrances—foul weather, difficult terrain, insufficient funds, hostile armies; regarding canonization papers for Peter of Luxembourg, reports the bishop of Avignon in the fifteenth century, "I did not send them because of the dangers of the roads."[19] And when proctors finally reached Rome, they might find that pope, cardinals, and curia had moved off to cooler regions. We'll encounter an epic example of such struggles in Leopold's case, but all our canonizations, depending on the written word that must be examined only in Rome, were affected by these issues. Communication was anything but straightforward or reliable. Travel, as the classic studies of Braudel and Delumeau have shown, was slow, sometimes dangerous, often arduous, in the sixteenth century, as it was throughout the Middle Ages. Couriers might make the Rome to Florence trip in a day for important matters, but up to four days otherwise; four or five days to Venice, twenty to Paris, from a month to seven weeks to London or Toledo for "ordinary" letters: "The viceroy of Naples is without instructions, the government of [Philip II] does not know what is happening in the Netherlands."[20] And when the mail pouch finally arrived its jumbled contents might exasperate even an emperor: Charles V wrote to Adrian VI (who canonized two of our saints) on January 10, 1523, in reply to four of the pope's letters written in September and October 1522; later on the same day, he sent yet another response to three more letters he'd just received from Adrian, from October and November of 1522; on February 8, 1523, Charles replied to three of Adrian's letters, all dated January 16.[21]

Finally, as popes of necessity became more involved in politics and warfare, starting in particular with the network of concordats worked out af-

19. *AASS* July I (Antwerp, 1719), 605.

20. Fernand Braudel, *The Mediterranean and the Mediterranean World in the Age of Philip II,* 2 vols., trans. Siân Reynolds (New York: Harper and Row, 1972), 1:356–358; Jean Delumeau, *Vie Économique et Sociale de Rome dans la seconde moitié du XVIe siècle,* 2 vols. (Paris: De Boccard, 1957–59), 1:49–55.

21. Louis-Prosper Gachard, *Correspondance de Charles-Quint et D'Adrien VI* (Bruxelles: M. Hayez, 1859), pp. 144–153, 158.

ter the Council of Constance and continuing with a consolidation of power by most European governments, Rome became *the* stage for "international" politics: between 1490 and 1500, about 243 diplomats were accredited to the Holy See, 161 to the imperial and 135 to the French courts, and 100 to Milan.[22] Conflicts involving Italian and European states, an important, but not the only, part of the saint-making process, will be discussed fully in each of the following chapters. In come cases the political elements might seem to dominate the process, but it's important to bear in mind what Simon Ditchfield has recently written: saints cannot be explained away by invoking the idol of politics alone, which has been the case with some earlier studies. "Saints could be produced and consumed for a variety of ends and purposes and . . . these ends transcended the interpretative limitations imposed by earlier historiography."[23] As we'll see, our five subjects before and after their canonizations were variously used: inter alia as political bargaining chips; to highlight the importance of regions at the boundaries of Christendom, heresy, and the Turks; to emphasize dynastic legitimacy; as resources for individual and communal physical and mental well-being and protection; to embody papal authority; as opportunities for liturgical invention and literary polemic; as economic resources for their "possessors"; to bolster communal, conventual, or episcopal prestige; as ways to think of the natural and supernatural worlds; and as sources of entertainment, art, music, poetry, and pageantry.

22. Henry Dietrich Fernández, "The Patrimony of St. Peter: The Papal Court at Rome c. 1450–1700," in *The Princely Courts of Europe,* ed. John Adamson, 141–63, at 142 (London: Weidenfeld and Nicolson, 1999).

23. Simon Ditchfield, "Thinking with Saints: Sanctity and Society in the Early Modern World," *Critical Inquiry* 35, no. 3 (Spring 2009): 552–84.

CHAPTER 1

Saint-Making at the End of the Middle Ages

For most of the medieval period, particular individuals were honorably buried by local authority—abbot, bishop, lord, or commune for instance—because of their nobility, charity, exemplary piety, or healing powers. They might subsequently become the center of a local cult. Eventually they might be reinterred in a more honorable location (the process known as "translation"). Their devotees communicated with them through prayers that could result in miracles performed by God through their intercession. By the end of the twelfth century, however, the papacy began to take control of this process, removing recognition of individuals as saints from the periphery to the center. From that point forward, saint-making became a long, arduous business involving repeated supplications to the pope, local hearings into a candidate's life and miracles, examination of these at the curia, and further commissions of inquiry. The next phase brought curial advocates, judges of the Rota, and others into the process, with the appointment of a team of cardinals to oversee the affair. After several discussions in consistories, successful applicants were honored in a ceremony of canonization. The routine has been described by many scholars, with plenty of primary and secondary references.[1] Although this lessens the temptation to reinvent the wheel,

1. In addition to Vauchez, *Sainthood,* for medieval processes see Roberto Paciocco, *Canonizzazioni e culto dei santi nella christianitas (1198–1302)* (Assisi: Edizioni Porziuncola/Società internazionale di studi francescani, 2006), with bibliography updating Vauchez; Eric W. Kemp, *Canonization and Authority in the Western Church* (London: Oxford University Press, 1948); an older but nicely composed study is by Margaret R. Toynbee, *S. Louis of Toulouse and the Process of Canonisation in the*

an overview of the procedures that gave us the last medieval saints will set the scene. During the thirteenth century, as more aggressive popes built up their bureaucracy and enhanced their role as the focus of authority, canon lawyers found themselves with plenty of opportunities to exercise their craft, producing commentaries on collections of decrees and on other commentaries. The Church adapted Roman (civil) legal processes—*ius commune*—such as inquisitorial procedures to a variety of situations, including canonizations.[2] By c. 1300, saint-making was a well-articulated process, as was the analysis of associated miracles, which continued to be almost daily occurrences: about 1400 some English nuns, preparing for the inevitable, established a litany to chant "whenever a miracle" might occur in their midst.[3] Just before 1500 a canonist was wondering whether a person raised from the dead was "the same" person, whether a will he'd made should be revoked, and whether he could take a different wife.[4]

Although Innocent III summed up the official approach in declaring that both a holy life *and* miracles were needed, and this remained the standard line, determinations about miracles seem to have taken up more time and cerebral energy at the curia than the investigation and discussion of a candidate's life. By the thirteenth century the possibility was generally accepted that an apparently saintly person might secretly be engaged in sinful behavior or harbor evil, heretical thoughts; by their nature, such ugly tendencies weren't immediately obvious. Miracles, however, those attributed to the candidate when alive and, especially, after death, were events open to investigation. Because of this, miracles (or their lack) were essential elements

Fourteenth Century (Manchester, UK: University Press, 1929). More recently, Thomas Wetzstein has produced a masterpiece in *Heilige vor Gericht;* for lighter fare, see Kenneth L. Woodward, *Making Saints: How the Catholic Church Determines Who Becomes a Saint, Who Doesn't, and Why* (New York: Simon and Schuster, 1990).

2. On distinctions between inquisitions as examination procedures developing from the late 12th century, and later inquisitions into heresy, see H. A. Kelly, "Inquisition and the Prosecution of Heresy: Misconceptions and Abuses," *Church History* 58 no. 4 (1989): 39–451; idem., "The Right to Remain Silent: Before and After Joan of Arc," *Speculum* 69 no. 4 (1993): 992–1026, and Lotte Kéry, "Inquisitio—denunciatio—exceptio: Möglichkeiten der Verfahrenseinleitung im Dekretalenrecht," *Zeitschrift der Savigny-Stiftung für Rechtsgeschichte, Kanonistische Abteilung* 87 (2001): 226–268.

3. J. Tolhurst, ed., *The Ordinale and Customary of the Benedictine Nuns of Barking Abbey,* 2 vols., Henry Bradshaw Society 65–66 (London: Henry and Sons, 1927–28), II, 348.

4. Troilus Malvetius, "Tractatus non Infestius de sanctorum canonizatione," in *Tractatus Illustrium in utraque tum pontificii, tum Caesarei iuris facultate Iurisconsultorum* (Venice, 1584), vol. 14, fols. 97r–103v at 99v–100r. Aquinas, of course, had discussed this issue relative to the resurrection of bodies at the last judgment.

in managing the process. Popes and cardinals could more easily manipulate their acceptance or rejection, and thus a candidate's canonization prospects. A Salisbury proctor at Rome complained in 1453 that "nearly thirty years ago" Osmund's case was "examined in the curia and set aside" because of purported failure to show continuous miracles. A new commission was in the offing to reevaluate the matter, but "in my opinion" this was done only "to prolong the case."[5] Vauchez's opinion seems to be that even by the end of the thirteenth century—as mentioned in our introduction—popes were trying to discourage mounting numbers of canonization requests, thus avoiding decisions they "did not want to have to take." For Vauchez the process could be employed as a "blocking mechanism," a barrier against an inundation of supplications to the curia, a way "to slow things down and protect the pope from having to make a decision."[6] He doesn't follow up these interesting suggestions, but they would seem to demand further exploration. In any case, there's no doubt that during the thirteenth century many processes were sent back to be redone, sometimes repeatedly, almost always because of alleged procedural defects in testimony about miracles. For some reason or other, the curialists, having examined the reported wonders, might claim that they were not satisfied with what they'd found. But what had they found? Some of our five saints' causes nearly failed because of doubts about miracles—raised *pro forma* or for real.

MIRACLES

Medieval collections of sworn depositions about miracles attributed to would-be saints exist in abundance. These (originally local) miraculous cults were spread right across Europe. Thousands of folios of testimony have been used by modern historians interested in what peasants, townsfolk, and the more privileged among clergy and laity can tell us about contemporary society, culture, and especially belief in the miraculous. Reading these collections against (and with) the grain has proven to be rewarding, especially now that we appreciate their multivalence: though examiners scripted their questions in Latin beforehand, witnesses responded usually in the vernacular to what *they* believed was pertinent, sometimes creating

5. *Nisi pro negotii protelatione;* Wetzstein, *Heilige vor Gericht,* 470, citing Malden's ed. of Osmund's process.

6. Vauchez, *Sainthood,* 68, 74–75.

messy disjunctions between questions and answers. Paradoxically, it's even more difficult to get into the minds of the upper echelons—the lawyers, medical doctors, judges, cardinals, and other curialists at Rome. There are plenty of clues about attitudes toward miracles at the grassroots, out on the peripheries (as viewed from Rome): miraculously touched folk were called before local inquisitorial committees and if "cured" of paralysis made to walk about (sometimes crashing into obstacles), or if of blindness to name colors, or to speak if dumb or even tongueless prior to their saintly encounters, or to show the examiners their life-threatening scars or deformities (in one case a pointed head over which a cartwheel had trundled) or facial discoloration (green) after lying about dead in a pond. But few indications of subsequent, upper-level analysis at Rome have survived (apart from theological tracts) before the late medieval and early modern periods.[7] Ideally, we'd like to listen in on the discussions of the clerical intellectuals surrounding the pope who received and analyzed these lists of miracles that had been gathered, perhaps hundreds of miles away; to learn how the reported wonders fit in—or not—with their preconceptions and how they made their decisions about whether or not specific miracles were acceptable as proven. Unfortunately, our cases provide only glimpses of this process, which begins opening up in the seventeenth century, when extensive arguments pro and con about particular cures are reported.

There was no dearth of theoretical treatments. In his *Summa* of the 1240s Geoffrey of Trani claimed that miracles had to fulfill four conditions: they had to (1) be performed by God; (2) be *contra naturam;* (3) be accomplished through a person's merit, not the power of words alone; (4) and corroborate the faith.[8] These four defining points came to be repeated by later com-

7. Finucane, "Authorizing the Supernatural: An Examination of Some English Miracles around 1318," in *Aspects of Power and Authority in the Middle Ages,* ed. Brenda Bolton and Christine Meek (Turnhout: Brepols, 2007), 289–303, at 296–97. See comments by Wetzstein, *Heilige vor Gericht,* 464–466.

8. Aviad M. Kleinberg, "Proving Sanctity: Selection and authentication of Saints in the Later Middle Ages," *Viator* 20 (1989): 183–205, at 201. On Geoffrey/Goffredus, cf. *Dictionnaire de Droit Canonique,* 5, col. 952: Geoffroy de Trani or de Trano. Born in Trani, in Apulia, he studied at Bologna under Azo, then taught civil law at Naples, canon law at Bologna. Auditor of *litterarum contradictarum* (a papal court where legal matters were considered, sometimes in an adversarial manner) for Gregory IX in 1244. Made cardinal; died April 1245. For a comprehensive, general overview see the late Michael E. Goodich's *Miracles and Wonders: The Development of the Concept of Miracle, 1150–1350* (Aldershot: Ashgate, 2007).

mentators including, for example, Hostiensis.[9] Also during the thirteenth century, Aquinas noted that a miracle must have a manifest effect, evoke wonder in the observer, and occur by occult means but ultimately through God, who might, however, allow sinners or demons to perform pseudo-miracles. Some miracles were greater than others, and they could be ranked in three grades depending upon how far they exceeded nature's powers: miracles of the highest rank surpassed nature substantially, as when two bodies occupied the same space, or the sun went backward; second-tier miracles involved supernatural events, for example, changing a corpse to a living being; while the lowest of the three were miracles that went beyond nature in the order or rate of action, as in sudden cures.[10] As for the *vita* and lists of purported miracles sent to the curia on a would-be saint's behalf, preliminary procedures entailed reading, analyzing, and rubricating the reports, then sending them on to auditors or cardinals and consistories (discussed below). However, before the sixteenth century we have very little documentation indicating what was *thought* about the miracles as they shuttled through these high-level committees, *how* they actually were analyzed and discussed. In fact, according to Kleinberg, there are only two significant medieval examples, "probably the most important documents among the few surviving critiques of miracles (in the context of canonization) from the Middle Ages."[11] These involved the miracles of France's Louis IX (d. 1270, cd. 1297) and an English bishop of Hereford, Thomas Cantilupe (d. 1282, cd. 1320). Vauchez found the Cantilupe document so important that he transcribed in *Sainthood in the Middle Ages.*[12] Peter of Morrone, Pope Celestine V, was a third interesting case. He died in 1296 and was canonized in 1313. Miracles attributed to these three

9. Diego Quaglioni, "La prova del miracolo spunti dalla dottrina di diritto comune," in *Notai, Miracoli e Culto dei Santi,* ed. Raimondo Michetti (Milan: Giuffré, 2004), 99–114, at 110–11.

10. *Summa Theol.* I, Q. 105, arts. 7–8; Q. 114, art. 4. In Thomas's *Scriptum super Libros Sententiarum Magistri Peter Lombardi,* ed. Pierre Mandonnet, Tom. 2 (Paris, 1929), 456, Thomas correlates the three levels, respectively, to miracles done *supra naturam, praeter naturam,* and *contra naturam,* the lowest grade. Interestingly, raising the dead was a second-, not a first-, level miracle.

11. Kleinberg, "Proving Sanctity," 201.

12. Vauchez, *Sainthood,* 540–54 at 488–98. It has also been examined by Patrick H. Daly, "The Process of Canonization in the Thirteenth and Early Fourteenth Centuries," *St. Thomas Cantilupe Bishop of Hereford: Essays in His Honour,* ed. Meryl Jancey (Hereford: Friends of the Hereford Cathedral Publications Committee for the Dean and Chapter, 1982), 125–35. For Saint Louis, Louis Carolus-Barré, "Consultation du Cardinal Pietro Colonna sur le IIe miracle de Saint Louis," *Bibliotheque de l'école des chartes* 117 (1959): 57–72 and H. F. Delaborde, "Fragments de l'enquête faite a Saint-Denis en 1282 en vue de la canonisation de Saint Louis," *Mémoires de la société de l'histoire de Paris et de l'ile-de-France* 23 (1896): 1–71.

were examined by curialists between about 1280 and about 1320, giving us interesting perspectives on how intellectuals dealt with supernatural wonders in the decades around 1300. It should be borne in mind that documents for these three reflect different phases (i.e., are different types of document) in canonization investigations. They will be taken up chronologically.

Witnesses described Louis IX's miracles during a hearing in 1282–83 at Saint Denis. The record was sent to the curia, where the wonders were organized and analyzed. Sometime between 1285 and 1287, the results of the analysis were presented in consistory before Honorius IV. Delaborde edited a "memorandum" read on that occasion, concerning just one of the curative miracles. The testimony of several witnesses was compared. Evidently the only discrepancies noted in the memo had to do with timing: the alleged day and hour of the cure. Apparently the "miraculous" core of the cure itself was not at issue. Between 1295 and 1297 on Boniface VIII's orders, Cardinal Pietro Colonna prepared a *consilium* on another of Louis's wonders—not the same one analyzed in the 1280s, as Delaborde wrongly believed. Again, the report seems to concentrate on reconciling or explaining witnesses' discrepant statements about what might seem (to us) to be "secondary" issues. Colonna set out his report in scholastic fashion, raising then responding to various objections.[13] He claims that even though witnesses may disagree as to details, if they agree as to substance their statements can be accepted, as in the following example. A paralyzed woman was said to have been miraculously cured. There were contradictions among witnesses about how her paralysis was verified: some said by using a pin, others hot water, or fire. Colonna responded that each witness proved the debility, though in a different fashion, as in paying tithes: some pay in wheat, some beans, others barley. Yet tithe is paid; and whether a criminal is sentenced to be decapitated or hanged, this affirms the judge's capital jurisdiction regardless of mode of execution. Aquinas, among others, had dealt with this issue, stating that if witnesses disagreed in certain principal circumstances relating to the substance of the fact, for example, in time, place, or persons, their evidence was of no weight. However, disagreement as to circumstances not touching the substance of the fact, for example, whether the skies were clear or cloudy, or a house painted or not, "does not weaken the evidence."[14] Having bol-

13. *In hoc responderi potest* or *Ego respondeo . . .*

14. *Summa Theol.* II.II, Q. 70, art. 2.

stered his responses with more than forty citations from canon and civil law—but only one biblical reference—Colonna concluded that the case at hand seemed proven, after which he appealed to the pope for a definitive ruling.[15] Yet, to our way of thinking, perhaps, the central issue—was this a "real" miracle—seems to have been ignored.

Our second example, Celestine V, was canonized on May 5, 1313. The same Cardinal Pietro Colonna involved in Louis IX's case also played a role here, as did his uncle Giacomo Colonna. Accounts of Celestine's miracles were examined at the curia. In one case, a witness didn't seem to prove a miracle because he hadn't been present at the cure, didn't specify whether the cure was instantaneous, or might have been effected with medication, and was too vague when commenting on Celestine's *fama.* Besides that, the notaries seem to have fallen down on the job, for they didn't set out the testimony of the next witness *per extensum,* but merely noted that it was the same as that of the previous witness. In another case—Philippa, unable to walk until touched with a relic of Morrone—the statements of several witnesses were compared. One deposed that Philippa had applied the relic to herself, another, that a follower of Morrone had done this; a witness who stated that Philippa couldn't move from one place to another was contradicted by someone who claimed that she could, by scuttling along on her posterior; and a witness failed to say how long she'd been crippled and how long after her cure she was seen to walk.[16] Once again, concentration seems to be placed on the circumstances of the miracle rather than its substance. But this was bound to be the case, given contemporary understanding about the human body, and because, as canonists and theologians recognized, theoretically one couldn't actually testify about miracles per se, since by definition they were supernatural, that is, beyond humanly observable nature; testimony was not about a miracle but about "that from which it could be shown to be a miracle."[17] Proof of both Louis IX's and Celestine V's mir-

15. *Videtur . . . miraculum esse probatum.*

16. Bernard Schimmelpfennig, *Die Zeremonienbücher der römischen Kurie im Mittelalter* (Tübingen: M. Niemeyer, 1973), 174. There are interesting marginalia in another collection of Morrone's miracles, e.g., *Sufficienter deponit de miraculo secundum auditores,* a reference to curialists, later known as auditors of the Rota, having examined the material, in *Die Akten des Kanonisationsprozesses in dem Kodex zu Sulmona,* in Franz Xavier Seppelt, *Monumenta Coelestiniana: Quellen zur Geschichte des Papstes Coelestin V* (Paderborn, Germany: F. Schöningh, 1921), 211–331, at 314.

17. Malvetius, *Tractatus de sanctorum canonizatione,* fol. 101v, 102r: *non deponit de eo, prout est miraculum . . . sed prout ex eo probatur miraculum.*

acles was, and could only be, circumstantial. In the dead pope's case, however, we find an additional, mundane factor at work at the final stages, when cardinals had to vote on a short list of miracles that seemed "true." Between December 1312 and May 1313 at a secret consistory in Avignon, twelve of Celestine's miracles were considered. Here we glimpse the inner tensions among the cardinals as they sat before the pope ostensibly discussing miracles, while actually wrangling over their personal, familial, and political animosities; such clashes—often quite unedifying—occurred in many consistories, just as they enlivened conclaves. In this case, the lines were pretty clearly drawn, between the anti–Boniface VIII, pro-Celestine faction on the one hand, and on the other, those trying to protect Boniface's memory by resisting Celestine's canonization. Boniface had deprived both the Colonnas of their cardinalates in May 1297. They were reinstated by Clement V in 1305. Celestine's cause began soon afterward, pushed by Philip IV of France. In the 1312–13 consistory, then, as Clement V looked on, the Colonna cardinals and their allies consistently voted in support of Celestine's miracles, while the other faction voted just as adamantly against them. Pietro Colonna made his position clear at the start: in the five prefatory questions put to each of the cardinals, when Pietro was asked whether Morrone's holy life had been proven, he replied "yes," and added that Clement could have canonized him a year earlier. When the other Colonna was asked whether witnesses had proven Morrone's life to have been holy, he replied that since he was convinced of his holiness, he wasn't going to weary himself by reading the depositions.[18] Asked the same general questions, other cardinals, particularly Francesco and Giacomo Caetano (Boniface VIII was a Caetano) naturally disagreed with the Colonnas. This was made clear when it came time to vote on the twelve miracles, one by one. The Caetanos voted that most were not proven: of their twenty-three votes (one was not recorded), a "no" was registered sixteen times, with six "doubtfuls" and a single "yes." The two Colonnas, on the other hand, only once voted "no."[19]

The third example, taken from Thomas Cantilupe's canonization, removes us from the consistorial hothouse of personal animosities. Testimony on Cantilupe's life and miracles was gathered in England during 1307 and

18. *Nec in legendis huiusmodi fatigare.*

19. "Procès-verbal du dernier consistoire secret préparatoire à la canonisation de Pierre Célestin," *Analecta Bollandiana* 16 (1897): 389–92, 475–87; voting on 477ff.

sent to Avignon. Some time between 1318 and 1320, a document analyzing some of his miracles appeared. In an Oxford manuscript it runs to eleven folios.[20] The version transcribed by Vauchez from a less-legible French manuscript takes up fifteen printed pages.[21] This important, anonymous document was also discussed by Daly and Kleinberg. Each of these three scholars has attributed it to a different author: (Vauchez) high-ranking curialist, perhaps a cardinal; (Daly) junior curial cleric; and (Kleinberg) theologian (a status that could also apply to either of the two preceding figures). The two dozen or so miracles include one about a child, Roger, who fell from a bridge into a ditch at night, was found "dead" in the morning, though without any evident serious injuries. He was soon resuscitated through prayers to Cantilupe.[22] The writer raises two issues. First, why was Roger's body, falling from a height onto stony ground, not seriously mangled? In the margin is the word *Dubio.* A few lines down appears *Solutio,* which refers to the (Aristotelian) explanation: as Roger's body was very light, he hit the ground with little force. Moreover, the disposition of his limbs suggested that he had flailed about while falling, probably moving himself out of a vertical line of descent. It has been shown "from experience," the writer notes, that falling objects deviating from the vertical will land less forcefully.[23] A second *dubium* follows: If he was apparently uninjured, what had killed him? Was he actually dead? The *solutio* emphasizes that death had occurred, since the signs of death (coldness, rigidity, absence of breath, etc.) were present. It is suggested that he may have died from internal injuries, or the movement of the air while falling, or the shock of fear. In sum, the child had truly died, and through Cantilupe's intercession, been revived. The circumstances are very carefully analyzed, their physical attributes established (including such things as the composition of the dirt underneath under the body and the precise location of bruises on his limbs and face), as context for the

20. Exeter College, Oxford, ms. 158, fols. 48v–59v. Testimony about this alleged miracle (as opposed to its analysis) taken from witnesses gathered in Hereford during 1307, is best read in BAV, ms Vat. lat. 4015, fols. 188r–203v; the *AASS* transcription is not to be trusted.

21. From BNF, ms lat. 5373 A, fols. 66r–69v, 540–54 in the English ed. of Vauchez, *Sainthood.* For my emendations of Vauchez's readings, see Finucane, "Authorizing the Supernatural," 290 n. 1.

22. Testimony of 1307 about the miracle in MS Vat. Lat. 4015, fols. 188r–203v; I have discussed this case in "The Toddler in the Ditch: A Case of Parental Neglect?," in *Voices from the Bench: The Narratives of Lesser Folk in Medieval Trials,* edited by Michael Goodich (New York: Palgrave Macmillan, 2006), 127–48. See also Vauchez, *Sainthood,* 547–48.

23. *Experimentaliter probatur.*

subsequent miracle of revival. Following a line taken by many canonists, the writer observes that disagreement among witnesses didn't vitiate a miracle "as to the substance of the thing that happened."[24] As in the Colonna analysis of Saint Louis's miracle, in the Exeter manuscript contraries are established and then resolved, with authorities cited along the way. But that's the extent of the similarity: the Colonna report deals mainly with discrepancies in testimony, but the Cantilupe writer is interested in the physical setting. This led Kleinberg to suggest that Roger's case represents "one of the first signs of the influence of scientific thought on the process of canonization."[25] The Colonna legalistic analysis, on the other hand, does not exhibit such interests. Kleinberg may be right, but until other documents come to light, the fourteenth-century Cantilupe report is unique, which is precisely why Vauchez printed it *in extenso.* With no other similar, subsequent analyses surviving from the medieval period, there's no way to test Kleinberg's claim. What we may actually be witnessing with the Cantilupe writer is a concentration on points of fact (which would thus appear to be a "scientific approach") rather than aspects of canon law surrounding the miraculous, somewhat analogously to the distinction between medieval advocates' interest in theoretical fine points on the one hand, and proctors' more practical analyses of events on the other, or modern jurists' divorcing matters of fact from matters of law.[26] In any case it is not until the late fifteenth and sixteenth centuries that detailed reports (*relationes*) have survived from auditors of the Rota and others that go into similar analyses of miracles. Sixtus V's institution of the Congregation of Rites in 1588 (when canonizations resumed) increased the chances for documentary survival. By the end of the century, we're more fully informed about miracle investigations at the top, as in the case of Raymund of Peñafort (d. 1275, cd. 1601).

The unpublished *Relatio* of the three auditors of the Rota (who were the top judicial body apart from the pope and consistory), who examined Peñafort's cause between 1596 and 1601 includes, inter alia, discussion of eight

24. *Quantum ad substanciam facti quod evenit,* Exeter Coll. ms 158, fols. 54v–55r.

25. Kleinberg, "Proving Sanctity," 205.

26. James Brundage, "'My Learned Friend': Professional Etiquette in Medieval Courtrooms," in *Readers, Texts and Compilers in the Earlier Middle Ages: Studies in Medieval Canon Law in Honour of Linda Fowler-Magerl,* ed. Martin Brett and K. G. Cushing (Aldershot: Ashgate, 2009), 183–96, at 184: "Some judges in fact commanded advocates to confine their arguments to legal issues alone, and called on proctors to address the factual evidence involved in a dispute."

posthumous miracles. In working through their deliberations, they drew upon a broad range of legal and theological sources (and prior canonizations), with some 206 references to about seventy authorities. They prefaced their analysis with extensive commentary on the validity of the process itself, the characteristics of miracles, and that way they are proven.[27] On this last point, once again, (citing Aquinas) they note that "miracles cannot be proven directly, since direct proof occurs through the principles of things and pre-existing causes. Miracles do not have these, as they occur through divine power and will alone."[28] One of the miracles, mentioned in the canonization bull of 1601, occurred about 1589, during a pestilence in Barcelona. A nobleman, Michael, became infected and was deserted by his doctors.[29] He took extreme unction and then, near death, prayed to Raymund. At that instant, Peñafort's spirit appeared to him, touched him, and removed the cloth that Michael's confessor had put over his face. He improved immediately, and rose from his bed that same day. Michael himself, the auditors wrote, proved this as a witness in the process, along with his confessor, Bartholomew. Thus, "without any difficulty," the authors noted, "we came to the opinion that this was a true miracle, considering the circumstances." They set out reasons for their opinion: (1) the quality of the illness from which, as Celsus (first century AD) claimed, no one could be safe; (2) since Michael had been given up by his doctors, and couldn't be cured by medications, the requisite qualities were present for a true miracle; and (3) the miracle was divinely wrought specifically through Raymund's merits because the sick man was cured after commending himself to him, who in that instant appeared to Michael. As if anticipating objections, the auditors noted that it should not detract from the miracle that some said that marks of the illness remained after Michael's recovery, or that some medications had been used; the essence of the miracle was the overcoming of the pestilence. They concluded that it was also clear from other canonization records that cures could be miraculous even though human remedies were involved. To follow the story of miracle-investigations further

27. *Quomodo probentur miracula*, ASV, Congr. Riti, Processus 4216, fols. 73v (alt. 53v)–88 (68).

28. ASV, Congr. Riti, Processus 4216, fol. 83 (alt. 63): *Miracula non posse probari directa probatione, quia directa probatio fit per rerum principia, et causas praeexistentes, quales non habent miracula, que fiunt ex sola voluntate, et virtute divine.*

29. Idem., fols. 105 (alt. 85)–106 (86), and ASV, Congr. Riti, Processus 224, fols. 199, 286v–287r.

would take us into the seventeenth century and well beyond the limits of this book. We may observe in passing, however, that in Carlo Borromeo's canonization (1610), in addition to citations to criminal and canon law, theology, and the works of Galen, Hippocrates, Celsus, and Avicenna, the testimony of "modern doctors" of Rome's Gymnasium was part of the investigation into supernatural cures.[30] By this time, too, further refinement had crept into the process in an increasing tendency to distinguish "miracles" from "graces," which were of a lesser significance.[31]

PROCEDURES

Just as miracles were being dissected, analyzed, and domesticated by theologians such as Thomas Aquinas, thirteenth-century canonists were laying down rules for the canonization process. About 1270 one of the most famous of these, Henry cardinal of Ostia, or Hostiensis (d. 1271), formulated a commentary on the 1,971 chapters of the collection of decretals, or *Liber Extra* by Peñafort, commissioned by canon lawyer Gregory IX (d. 1241). In his commentary Hostiensis outlined twelve stages in the canonization process, a "veritable synthesis of thirteenth-century traditions" that was echoed by later canonists.[32] Fourteenth-century composers of such

30. *Medici moderni,* ASV, Congr. Riti, Processus 1681, fols. 124r–130r. Doctors had testified in medieval cases as well, though usually as participants rather than "expert witnesses": see Joseph Ziegler, "Practitioners and Saints: Medical Men in Canonization Processes in the Thirteenth to Fifteenth Centuries," *Society for the Social History of Medicine* 12 (1999): 191–225. In addition to Nancy Siraisi's works on sixteenth-century medical history and the Church, see for a later period Giovanna Pomata, "Malpighi and the Holy Body: Medical Experts and Miraculous Evidence in Seventeenth-Century Italy," *Renaissance Studies* 21 (2007): 568–586.

31. Aquinas dealt with "miracle" and "grace" in *Summa Theol.* IIa IIa, Q. 178, art. 1, 2, though only hinting at a clear distinction, referring for instance to the "grace of healing" as a species of miracle; see also Fernando Vidal, "Miracles, Science, and Testimony in Post-Tridentine Saint-Making," *Science in Context* 20 (2007): 481–508, esp. 489–90; in the fourteenth century the two seem equivalent, as in *Acta et Processus Canonizacionis Beate Birgitte,* ed. Isak Collijn (Uppsala, 1924–31), 611; in the early sixteenth century distinctions are still less clear-cut, as in ASV, *Congr. Riti, Processus 2177* of 1625/26, fol. 504v, where a "miracle" is a "grace" done supernaturally by God. However, the distinction was developing particularly from the later sixteenth century, when "miracle" was considered to be instantaneous, by God, "grace" less so, through his saints; in 1665, for instance (process of John of Capistrano) a priest, asked to define the difference, testified that "la gratia stimo che sia . . . non instante, ma col concorso della causa seconda, mai il miraculo si fa instante, e si fa solo da Dio," ASV *Congr. Riti, Processus 77,* fol. 27r–v.

32. *Le Cérémonial papal de la fin du moyen âge à la renaissance,* vol. 2: *De Rome en Avignon ou Le cérémonial de Jacques Stefaneschi* [ceremonial of cardinal Jacques Stefaneschi, d. 1341], ed. Marc Dykmans (Brussels: Institut historique Belge de Rome, 1981), 226–27 and n. 228. For Hostiensis see J. F. von Schulte, *Die Geschichte der Quellen und Literatur des canonischen Rechts,* 3 vols. (Stuttgart:

guides, constantly looking back to Hostiensis, included Johannes Andreae and Augustinus de Ancona; in the fifteenth century the leader was Giovanni Francesco Pavini (discussed in the next chapter).[33] By the sixteenth century a routine was well established, drawing heavily on trial procedure common to criminal and civil cases; by 1596, for instance, in Raymund of Peñafort's process, the Spanish king's proctor appeared "on the one part," against an apostolic proctor fiscal "on the other part," as an adversary.[34] Apart from some formal changes initiated in 1588, the procedure would not see substantive revisions until the 1630s; the process then remained more or less unchanged until John Paul II's reign. Beatification became a necessary

F. Enke, 1875–80), 2:123–29, and references in James Brundage, *Medieval Canon Law* (New York: Longman, 1995), 214.

33. E.g., Dykmans, *Le Cérémonial papal,* 2:458–66. The following steps are referred to by Pavini in Bonaventura's canonization, ASV Congr. Riti, Processus 4216, fols. 161v–166v (see chap. 2): (1) The papacy should repeatedly be asked to canonize someone, because in such serious matters, the pope is not accustomed immediately to set up an *inquisitionem,* but waits to see whether a cult becomes established. (2) Establishment of an investigative commission follows, and (3) an inquisition by the commission. It is obvious, Pavini notes, that these things were properly carried out in Bonaventura's case (literally in "our" case, *in casu autem nostro*). (4) A report, *relatio,* summarizing the (general) inquiry is produced; the commissioners are to write up *(describant)* what they find, stating whether they think that there should be a second inquisition. (5) Diligent examination of the *relatio* follows. Pavini explains: if upon completing their *praeambulam inquisitionem* the *inquisitores* find that there should be a further investigation, this time into the truth of the allegations, the pope takes counsel with his cardinals regarding this second, "solemn inquisition." If warranted, he appoints at least three cardinals to oversee the process from Rome. As for the onsite investigation, the pope orders the original commissiaries, or other prelates *in partibus,* to inquire specifically into the truth of statements about the candidate's *fama,* life, faith, death, and miracles. The findings are to be returned, under seal, to the pope. Next, a curial commission of papal chaplains (or other suitable persons) examines the documents and produces a rubricated summary of points to be considered by the three cardinals, who determine whether there is sufficient evidence for canonization. (6) Discussion of the examination in consistory follows, with a (7) decision or judgment of the case. (8) After this, keeping the first decision secret, the pope invites the bishops and other prelates then in Rome, and cardinals and other curial officials, to a second consistory, where an advocate or promoter of the faith (*promotor fidei*) narrates the history of the case. The pope requires the advice and vote of all present whether or not to canonize. (9) If the second group of prelates votes for sainthood, the pope sets a date for the ceremony. Pavini briefly describes the decorations of the church and other aspects of the ceremony. (10) During the ceremony the pope and assisting prelates, on their knees, ask God not to let his Church err or be deceived, followed by the *Veni sancte spiritus,* or a suitable alternative. (11) There is a recitation of the saint's life and miracles, and a declaration of his or her inclusion in the catalog of saints; the ceremonies conclude with (12) the pope celebrating a solemn Mass in honor of the new saint, with appropriate liturgy, concluding with a *Te Deum.* Three notaries should always be present, along with the three cardinals and three chaplains (papal clerks/advocates) who were directly involved in the process.

34. ASV, Congr. *Riti, Processus 224,* fols. 1v, 5v, *Procuratorem Ser.mi. D. Philippi Hispaniarum Regis . . . ex una, et Mag.cum virum D. Johannem Jacobum Nerottum sanctitatis suae . . . generalem procuratorem fiscalem ex adverso in dictis literis principaliter nominatum partibus ex alteram . . .*

preliminary to canonization only during the seventeenth century, though the concept of the *beatus* or *beata* was established before then. Since 2005 beatification is overseen by a papal representative (usually the prefect of the Congregation for the Causes of the Saints) and, normally, no longer takes place in Rome but in the home diocese of the candidate.

The "official" medieval canonization process began when the pope was informed that there was an individual in Austria, perhaps, or Florence, France, or Saxony, around whom a posthumous reputation (*fama*) had grown (though it might recognize living individuals as "holy," the Church canonized only the dead). A summation of this reputation and sometimes a list of the candidate's miracles written up by the keepers of the holy dead accompanied supplications from various supporters begging the pope to initiate a canonization investigation. His Holiness might then refer this request to his curialists and cardinals. Although it was always possible for a pope to accelerate the process for a favored candidate, normally he had to be asked repeatedly, and over a long period—usually years, even centuries. Raymund of Peñafort's case, for instance, was brought to the curia four times in the thirteenth and fourteenth centuries, with no results.[35] In most cases, dozens of letters would pile up to gather dust in some curial office as the years went by and one king or bishop succeeded another, the newcomers sending yet further requests on behalf of their candidate. Newly elected popes who might never have heard of the candidate needed prompting, so the whole campaign of letter-writing and lobbying might have to start over. Sometimes, a particularly active and interested agent managed to collect several supplications to present to the pope, a bundle of sealed—even signed—letters boosting a process. During a papal audience these might literally be handed over to the pontiff, who then handed them on for appropriate action. If supporters complained to a friendly cardinal, perhaps, or to their curial proctors or representatives kept on retainer, about what seemed to be a sluggish response in moving a process forward, the official reply was that such an important matter could not be hurried; it was incumbent upon His Holiness to make certain of the continued repute and miracles of the candidate before any further moves were made.

Delay was built into the system, a "let's wait and see" principle that Vauchez saw as a way to control supplications. Canonist Johannes Andreae

35. Vauchez, *Sainthood*, 72–73 (table 4).

(d. 1348) wrote that it wasn't customary for the pontiff to move at once to set up a commission of inquiry, but rather he would consider the case over a period of time, ostensibly to test whether the candidate's following would lose interest as his *fama* declined, and to see whether miracles continued. Though some say, Johannes notes, that fraudulent miracles can scarcely continue beyond forty days, he wasn't quite sure of that.[36] The canonists' and theologians' interest in, and definitions of, miracles were noted above; it was up to the curialists to decide whether the supernatural claims for a candidate were "proven." The curia could always find ways to put off potentially risky political moves—would the king of France welcome this or that German saint?—or controversial candidates—were her visions from the devil, as some believed, rather than God? Some canonizations were delayed for centuries, as in Benno's case: he died c. 1106 but didn't become a saint until 1523; the cause of Saint Osmund, bishop of Salisbury, lasted from 1099 to 1451, while Joan of Arc hovered at heaven's gate from 1431 to 1920. On the other hand, there were occasions when speedy elevations occurred: Thomas Becket, murdered in late 1170, was canonized in 1173.

If pope and cardinals agreed, on the basis of information and letters received, that a case might be worth investigating, the pontiff appointed a committee of two or three bishops or other suitable individuals, in the place where the person called holy (or a "saint") lay buried, to inquire into his or her repute, and the people's devotion, as well as the miracles and "other things that had been intimated to the curia." This was the general inquisition, that is, examination (*inquisitio,* a judicial procedure misleadingly linked in the modern popular mind only with heresy) that took place out in the areas (*in partibus*) associated with the dead; in a fourteenth-century canonization process the examiners were called "apostolic inquisitors."[37] The examiners were to deal with general claims, without trying to ascertain the truth about the candidate's purportedly holy life or apparent miracles.[38] A late-fifteenth-century ceremonial even specified that this inquiry was not to in-

36. *De quo tamen certi non sumus,* Johannes Andreae, *In Quinque Libros Novella Commentaria,* vol. 3 (Torino, 1963, a facsimile of the Venice, 1581 ed.), 230r, "De reliquiis, & veneratione sanctorum," cap. I. Cap. II has to do with the selling of holy relics and abuses such as taking them from reliquaries and sending them around to raise money, "just as a silly woman, a lawyer or a boxer offer themselves anywhere, for cash" (*sicut mulier fatua, advocatus, & pugil, qui pro numis passim se offerunt*), 230v. On the famous Johannes see the long entry in von Schulte, *Die Geschichte,* 2:205–74.

37. Schimmelpfennig, *Die Zeremonienbücher,* 211: *inquisitoribus apostolicis*

38. *In genere et non in specie, et quoad ad famam non quoad veritatem.*

volve (sworn) witnesses.[39] At this stage the local commission was merely to determine whether a further examination into the truth of the allegations should follow. The preliminary findings were written up and sent to the curia.

If curialists decided that the case merited further investigation, the pope again consulted his cardinals in consistory as to authorizing a second, special examination into the truth of the case. If the college agreed he once again notified the distant commissioners (who might be the same people heading the first hearing) to gather witnesses again, this time as to the truth about a candidate's allegedly pious life and wondrous miracles. Claims about miracles required the testimony of at least two witnesses who swore on a Bible, as they do today, "to tell the truth, the whole truth."[40] The examiners were to dig into the claims "exactly, diligently, truthfully and prudently," following a list of questions or articles *(articuli)* and interrogatories *(interrogatori)* sent along with the papal authorization. These lists were already a feature of secular as well as ecclesiastical hearings of all types by the early thirteenth century. Normally in canonizations they numbered perhaps 20 or 30, but in 1351 an officious proctor formulated a barrage of 170 articles to put to witnesses (though not all of them were put to them); even this was surpassed in a case from 1390 that included 285 questions.[41] These preset questions were intended to discourage witnesses from verbose wandering, to focus on the essentials; the papal commissioners might also ask their own questions.[42] In spite of articles, however, sometimes witnesses were allowed

39. *Sine testium iuridica examinatione facere debent,* Agostino Patrizi Piccolomini, *Caeremoniale Romanum* [completed in 1488] (Venice, 1516, repr. Ridgewood, N.Y.: Gregg Press, 1965), fols. XXXv–XXXIIv, edited by Marc Dykmans as *L'Oeuvre de Patrizi Piccolomini ou le Cérémonial Papal de la Première Renaissance,* 2 vols. (Vatican City: Biblioteca Apostolica Vaticana, 1980–82), 1:128*–130* for discussion and comparison with earlier ceremonials; canonization process on 118–24. An appendix in Dykmans sets out the ceremonial of Jean Burckard (Jakob Burchard or Burchardus, papal master of ceremonies and diarist who worked with and then succeeded Patrizi). Patrizi (bishop of Pienza 1483–96) claimed that his book was the fruit of twenty years and more of labor at the papal curia.

40. Ecclesiastics could take such an oath merely by placing their hands over their hearts, or touching a crucifix.

41. Jacques Cambell, "Le Sommaire de l'Enquête pour la canonisation de S. Elzear de Sabran, TOF d. 1323," *Miscellanea Franciscana* 73 (1973): 438–73, at 443; Elzear was canonized in 1369. The second instance is from Peter of Luxembourg's, with 285 *articuli quasi interrogatoriis* in *AASS* I July (Antwerp, 1719), 490.

42. Cf. e.g., Master Damasus/Damasius/Damascus who, c. 1210–15, composed a *Summa de Ordine Iudiciario,* ed. L. Wahrend, *Quellen zur Geschichte des Römisch-Kanonischen Processes im Mittelalter,* IV Band, Heft IV (Innsbruck: Wagner, 1926), 49, Tit. LXVII, *Qualiter testes deponere debeant: [I]lle, contra quem recipiuntur,* [in non-ecclesiastical cases] *consuevit ponere in cartula articulos illos, super quibus vult, quod testes interrogentur*... Cf. the brief note in Linda Fowler-Magerl, *Ordines Iudiciarii* and

to ramble on rather than giving straightforward replies.[43] Indeed, Troilus Malvetius, a canonist writing in the later fifteenth century, repeated the traditional assumption that a too-quick response to a question suggested that a witness was lying.[44] By the early seventeenth century, the investigating commissioners granted that a witness should not be prohibited from talking about miracles outside those specified in the articles.[45]

The second onsite committee seeking "the truth" gathered witnesses at a specified time and place; some probably were vetted by the candidate's local promoter before being sworn in. Some may already have appeared at the preliminary exam; the promoter might also seek out particular witnesses, and the papal commissioners could call or recall witnesses on their own initiative, ex officio. The number of individuals interrogated varied from day to day, month to month—in Peter of Luxembourg's process, the figures ranged from twenty-four witnesses in March to four in June.[46] The hearings were recorded by two or three notaries, who later transcribed their notes into Latin, thereby altering what most witnesses, speaking their vernaculars, had said.[47] As I found when examining testimony to a fourteenth-century English miracle, the reconstruction of events was affected by the witnesses' primary personal, political, social, and emotional makeup: in this case church, castle, town, and parents each represented the "same" event differently.[48] This is only to be expected in a highly emotional context involving an infant (whose mother may have been drunk) known to townspeople, discovered in a ditch by Conwy castle officials one frosty September morning. The notarial record of the subsequent inquisition reflects these different perceptions as well as the scripting of testimony through preset interrogatories and the

Libelli de Ordine Iudiciorum, Typologie des Sources du Moyen Âge Occidental, Fasc. 63 (Turnhout: Brepols, 1994), 65–66.

43. Matthew Hale (d. 1676) noted that "formal Interrogatories . . . preclude . . . the best Method of searching and sifting out the Truth" by not allowing witnesses to speak freely: Sir Matthew Hale, *The History of the Common Law of England,* ed. Charles M. Gray (Chicago: University Press, 1971), 164.

44. "Tractatus . . . de sanctorum canonizatione," fol. 101v, citing Martin de Laude (Martinus Caratti de Laude, fl. 1438–1445). Malvetius's work probably dates to between 1457 and 1487. On Malvetius, see von Schulte, *Die Geschichte der Quellen und Literatur des Canonischen Rechts,* 2:310 n. 31.

45. Process of Isidore "Agricola" (cd. 1622) interrogatories of 1612, *ASV Congr. Riti, Processus 3192,* fols. 8v–9r. The commissioners were also told to ask nothing further if a witness answered "no" to a question.

46. *AASS,* July I, 565–567: Jan., 5 witnesses; Feb., 13; Mar., 24; Apr., 9; May, 10; June, 4, July, 6.

47. For examples of this aspect of the process, see Quaglioni, *Notai, Miracoli e Culto dei Santi.*

48. Finucane, "The Toddler in the Ditch," 144–45.

movement of vernaculars (English and Welsh) into formulaic Latin, alluded to above. My observation in this case that "the apparently calm, rational atmosphere of the judicial tribunal where truths are supposed to be revealed is an inviting, useful but unstable forum" applies to all the batches of neatly ordered depositions that underpinned our five saints' cases. As the Cohens put it, "The industry of the faithful notary does indeed afford us a very accurate transcription of words said.... But the truth behind those words is another matter."[49]

Apart from these problems inherent in acquiring and interpreting "legal testimony," as we'll see, local inquiries into sanctity didn't always (ever?) follow the neatly constructed lines of procedure hatched in canonists' heads in Rome. On completing this second examination, that is, into the truth (*quoad veritatem*), the local committee remitted their sealed findings, with notarial transcripts of witnesses' depositions, to the pope.[50] In theory. In fact, the distinction between the two local hearings, the first one general, the second more specific, is not always apparent. Once the onsite investigations were completed, the curial phase began at Rome—though sometimes, as we'll see, only after further delays caused by any number of obstacles.

Assuming that such hindrances were absent or overcome, the report sent to the pope was turned over to papal chaplain-secretaries or other "suitable individuals," who analyzed the dossier and arranged its contents under appropriate rubrics. By the mid-fourteenth century, the auditors of the Rota (who, as we have seen, became the top judicial body apart from the pope and consistory at least until the end of the sixteenth century) took the matter to the next stage: as described in 1488, they were to make sure that legal formalities had been followed in the examination and to evaluate the quality of the evidence about a would-be saint's life and miracles, reporting all this in consistory. If everything seemed in order, with the cardinals' agreement the pope assigned the formally correct inquisition with its diligently

49. Thomas V. Cohen and Elisabeth S. Cohen, *Words and Deeds in Renaissance Rome: Trials before the Papal Magistrates* (Toronto: University of Toronto Press, 1993), 5. See also Peter Brooks, "The Law as Narrative and Rhetoric" in *Law's Stories: Narrative and Rhetoric in the Law*, ed. Peter Brooks and Paul Gewirtz (New Haven: Yale University Press, 1996), 14–22, at 19: "Against what may often appear as the fragmented, contradictious, murky unfolding of narrative... stand formulas by which the law attempts to impose form and rule on stories." My thanks to Simon Ditchfield (and, indirectly, Lu Ann Homza) for this reference.

50. Dykmans, *Le Cérémonial papal,* 2:460–61; Hostiensis's points five through eleven are found at 461.

organized rubrics and summarized depositions to a three-cardinal committee for further examination. Again, this was the prescribed procedure. In fact, the cardinals might be appointed even before the completion of the onsite investigations. From the mid-fourteenth century popes usually assigned such triads (or sometimes groups of six) from the different ranks—bishop, priest, deacon—to deal with a great variety of issues, not only canonizations. This seems to have been a normalization of variable thirteenth-century procedure. Having examined the auditors' dossier, the committee reported what they had found in several meetings, beginning usually with a secret consistory.[51] Pope and cardinals decided whether the holiness of the candidate's life was fully proven or not. If it was, then depositions about the miracles were presented. After hearing the testimony under each article, consistory decided whether to accept some or all the miracles as proven.[52] (Further onsite investigation could be ordered if needed, the whole process being repeated.) Finally, the pope sought a consensus as to whether claims about the candidate had been sufficiently proven to the point that a canonization might occur.[53] This examination and discussion in which the candidate's proctors and advocates had their say continued in subsequent consistories variously called "secret," "semi-public," "public," according to their composition.[54] By the fifteenth century if not earlier, an official known as the *promotor fidei,* promoter of the faith, also took part, raising theoretical objections along the way (although his role was formalized only in the seventeenth century at the time of Urban VIII's reforms). Here again the flow could be interrupted at any point, as we'll see in our five examples, by unconvinced or reluctant cardinals, sudden papal preoccupation elsewhere or

51. Dykmans, *Le Cérémonial papal,* 2:462; cf. Schimmelpfennig, *Die Zeremonienbücher,* 168. Malvetius writes that what is called "secret" is what is known to as many as are in the college of cardinals, which, in his day, numbered between twenty-five and thirty-five. Actually, the loquacious Malvetius adds, there could be as many as 236 cardinals, as in the time of Pope Pontianus (AD 230–35). Malvetius goes on to define "secret" as what is done in a private place. But it might be argued, he continues, that among so many cardinals nothing could be kept secret. The word means, Malvetius concludes, what is not known among the common folk: Malvetius, *Tractatus,* XIV, fol. 103r, col. 1.

52. Early-fourteenth-century directions for the canonization of Celestine V (cd. 1313), refer to the pope marking the better-proven miracles with some sort of sign (*manu vestra fuerunt signate*): Schimmelpfennig, *Die Zeremonienbücher,* 168.

53. Dykmans, *Le Cérémonial papal,* 2:462: *sit canonizatio . . . facienda.*

54. For details, Toynbee is good, and see the Patrizi ceremonial, ed. Dykmans, 129*, for the observation that "public consistory" *eo nomine* was a novelty of the later Middle Ages: "est nouveau, le texte emprunté à l'*Hostiensis* parlait seulement d'un consistoire où le pape parlerait publiquement" to all the curial prelates.

illness, political changes that abruptly made a candidate less appealing to His Holiness, or questions about funding.

Eventually, if all went well, the canonization day arrived, and a high wooden stage was erected in St. Peter's to display the dramatic ritual in the midst of rich hangings, torches, candles, and pictures of the new saint.[55] Among the many symbolic acts and prayers of that solemn occasion, the pope asked God to keep him from error. Originally, these prayers were not merely pro forma. Both Hostiensis in the thirteenth and Johannes Andreae in the fourteenth centuries were of the opinion that error in canonizations was possible. In those same two centuries, however, theologians and lawyers found rebuttals to such a possibility.[56] By the fifteenth century it was claimed that no one could be canonized in error since the pope was guided by the weight of Church tradition and doctrine on the one hand and the Holy Spirit on the other, as well as the archangel Michael, his special helper. At another point in the ceremony, as we'll see, the pope also pronounced a formal protestation, disavowing any intent do to anything contrary to the faith, the Catholic Church, or the honor of God. Following a formal declaration of sainthood and papal *Te Deum,* additional prayers were offered, then a Mass in honor of the new saint. At its conclusion the pope, having received gifts from the new saint's promoters, authorized indulgences and then processed out of the basilica.[57] This highly orchestrated ceremony was well established by the early fourteenth century, used for instance in Celestine V's canonization (1313). It will be followed, generally, for our own five saints as well.[58] We'll examine how far the procedures and assumptions described above actually worked out in canonizing our five, and the degree to which external factors played a role in creating the last medieval saints, beginning with Bonaventura.

55. A convenient summation of medieval to modern canonization ceremonies is Ferdinando Dell'Oro's *Beatificazione e Canonizzazione. «Excursus» storico-liturgico* (Rome: CLV, 1997).

56. Kemp, *Canonization and Authority,* 151, shows that Hostiensis takes his argument from two decretals of Innocent III; Vauchez repeats the observation about Hostiensis and Andreae, adding that Aquinas and Augustinus Triumphus provided theological and legal argument why in a canonization *papam . . . errare non posse,* Vauchez, *Sainthood,* 102 n. 53.

57. Schimmelpfennig, *Die Zeremonienbücher,* 170–71.

58. For the diplomatics and developments in canonization bulls, see Otfried Krafft, *Papsturkunde und Heiligsprechung* (Cologne: Böhlau Verlag, 2005). My thanks to David Collins for this reference.

CHAPTER 2

The Embattled Friar

Bonaventure (c. 1220–74, cd. 1482)

Saints usually don't behave as "normal" people do. Take Bonaventure our first example. Sporting razor-sharp iron fingernails, he "impetuously leaped down" from his perch at the top of a tree to attack an enemy, but Christ "sent Francis with a stone to grind down Bonaventure's nails."[1] Hardly pious behavior; yet that's how an enraptured Franciscan envisioned the man who was canonized about two centuries later. This bizarre image of an iron-taloned, tree-climbing Bonaventure sums up the anxieties felt throughout the entire Franciscan Order that found expression in the troubled mind of one of its members. Problems within the order will have a significant impact upon Bonaventure's long journey to sainthood.

EARLY LIFE AND ENTRY INTO THE FRANCISCANS

Giovanni, son of Giovanni da Fidanza and Maria, was born about 1220 in Bagnoregio near Lake Bolsena, some sixty-five miles north of Rome.[2]

1. *Angeli Clareni Opera,* vol. 2: *Historia Septem Tribulationum Ordinis Minorum,* ed. O. Rossini (Rome: Istituto storico italiano per il Medio Evo, 1999), 182, with references to Dn 7:9 and Ez 5, quoted in David Burr, *The Spiritual Franciscans: From Protest to Persecution in the Century after Saint Francis* (University Park: Pennsylvania State University Press, 2001), 33. This vision experienced by a thirteenth-century friar, well known to scholars of the medieval Franciscans, was described by Angelo Clareno c. 1323–26.

2. Bonaventure, *Opera, Sixti V pont. max iussu diligentissime emendata,* 7 vols. (Rome: Ex typ. Vaticana, 1588–96), VII. following p. 844, "Acta Canonizationis S. Bonaventure" by JUD Octavianus

Very little is known about the childhood and youth of the person who came to be known—we don't know when—as Bonaventure. He himself tells us that "when I was a boy, as I still vividly remember, I was snatched from the jaws of death by his [Saint Francis's] invocation and merits. . . . I recognized that God saved my life through him. . . ."[3] Around 1240 he joined the Franciscans. Being sent to study at the university of Paris, during the later 1240s he would have come under the tutelage of the famous Franciscan philosopher-theologian Alexander of Hales (d. 1245) and his ponderous, unfinished, Aristotle-based *Summa Theologiae.*[4] Bonaventure came to the university at a particularly eventful time: by mid-century the Dominican and Franciscan friars, newly founded and papally approved only a few decades earlier, began competing with the established teachers of theology, which led to internal university squabbles, threats, appeals to the pope, even bloodshed as non-mendicant clergy defended their professorial chairs against the popular friars. Having lectured on the Bible and Peter Lombard's *Sentences* for several years, by 1254 Bonaventure was master in theology and the leading Paris Franciscan. He had little time to enjoy this honor, however, since the mendicant-secular conflict finally exploded, and from 1255 to 1257 academic life at Paris was decidedly difficult for the friars. Meanwhile, at a general chapter in Rome in 1257, 350 Franciscans elected Bonaventure (in his absence) minister general, the top post among the Franciscans, after Pope Alexander IV talked the incumbent, John of Parma, into resigning.[5] John had become too sympathetic to the eschatological tendencies of the twelfth-century Cistercian abbot and mystic Joachim of Fiore, whose teachings appealed to some members of the variegated groups of otherworldly Franciscans eventually known as "Spirituals." Bonaventure (John of Parma himself had recommended him for the job) would spend much of his life trying to

---

Martinis Suessanum, consistorial advocate of the Apostolic Palace; unpaginated, twenty-eight double-column pages in length; see also ASV *Congr. Riti, Processus 4216* and *AASS* July III (Antwerp, 1723), 811–60. For documentary sources see Wetzstein, *Heilige vor Gericht,* 517–18.

3. "Life of St. Francis (Legenda Maior)," in *Bonaventure: The Soul's Journey into God; The Tree of Life; The Life of St. Francis,* ed. Ewert Cousins (New York: Paulist Press, 1978), 182.

4. The *Summa* "weighed more than a horse," according to an acerbic Roger Bacon, a later thirteenth-century Paris Franciscan with anti-scholastic tendencies: Hastings Rashdall, *The Universities of Europe in the Middle Ages,* ed. F. M. Powicke and A. B. Emden, vol. 1 (Oxford: Oxford University Press, 1936), 364 and n. 1.

5. Nicholas Glassberger, *Chronica,* in *Analecta Franciscana,* vol. 2 (Quaracchi; Ex typ. Collegi S. Bonaventura, 1887), 74. Glassberger's chronicle, especially important for Franciscans in Germany, was compiled c. 1506 and 1508, when he died. He became an Observant Franciscan in 1472.

end Franciscan civil wars, with little success; the ugly conflicts between the less strict "Conventuals" and more strict Spirituals, or "Observants," seriously disrupted Franciscan life to the end of the Middle Ages. In 1274, Bonaventure resigned as minister because of poor health. He was succeeded in May of that year—a few months before his death—by Jerome of Ascoli, later the first Franciscan pope, Nicholas IV (1288–92). Gregory X made Bonaventure a cardinal (Albano) in 1273, charged with important responsibilities at the Second Council of Lyons (1274). There he died (July 15), "to the consternation of the whole Council," Glassberger writes, and he was buried at Lyons, where "the glory of many miracles gleamed."[6] The ceremony was attended by, inter alia, Gregory X and the king of Aragon. An arm bone, apparently, is Bonaventure's sole surviving bodily relic, kept in Bagnoregio's church of San Nicola, still revered every April 14 (in addition to the saint's July 15 feast day).[7] In spite of many administrative distractions, Bonaventure managed to produce some of the most moving spiritual literature of the thirteenth century, such as the famous mystical work *The Soul's Journey into God,* a *Commentary on the Sentences,* various exegetical works, *On the Mystery of the Trinity, The Tree of Life, On the Governance of the Soul,* and several other writings, including the definitive *Life* of Saint Francis.

Recent scholarship is reluctant to slice the order into neatly opposing segments, Conventuals versus Spirituals/Observants, preferring to imagine a central force or core surrounded by numerous satellites that seem to have begun their spinoffs not long after Francis was dead, accelerating their flights especially from the 1270s, following Bonaventure's death.[8] And, as the decades passed, even the core itself changed. For instance, Francis's personality and inspiration "could hardly be intelligible" to Bonaventure, a product of the "refined academic and scholastic thought" of the university.[9] Such discordances are hardly surprising. The friars of Bonaventure's day,

6. Glassberger, *Chronica,* 87.

7. Bonaventura Marinangeli, "La canonizzazione di S. Bonaventura e il processo di Lione," *Miscellanea Francescana* 17 (1916), 65–86, 105–20, 164–74; 18 (1917), 125–35, at 74: "è la solaveramente *insigne* che sussista ai nostri giorni." Marinangeli's article includes an edition of the testimony given at the second Lyons hearing in 1480, discussed below.

8. Nicholas III's bull *Exiit qui seminat* (1279) helped to perpetuate the controversy by emphasizing Franciscan poverty individually and communally, in this apparently following Bonaventure's thinking. Patrick Nold, *Pope John XXII and His Franciscan Cardinal: Bertrand de la Tour and the Apostolic Poverty Controversy* (Oxford: Clarendon Press, 2003), 55.

9. Rosalind B. Brooke, "St. Bonaventure as Minister General," in *San Bernardino francescano,*

hoping to follow Christ-Francis into a life of simple poverty, had somehow to accommodate these hopes to the world in which they found themselves. Not only was that world in constant flux, but according to some, influenced by Joachim of Fiore, it was about to come to an end. To what degree should one compromise?[10] For example, if Francis wanted his followers to preach, they must have something to preach about; but if so, they must learn, which required books, a basic training—things that, some Franciscans would say, Christ and his followers hadn't needed. The situation was complicated by Francis's own ambiguous if not contradictory messages that appealed in certain ways to some friars, in other ways to others. In short, different Franciscan groups had their own take on managing times past, present, and future on both spiritual and mundane levels. The confusion continued well beyond Bonaventure's term as minister general. Although the fourteenth and fifteenth centuries witnessed similar moves toward "observance" or "reform" in other orders (Dominicans, Carmelites, Augustinian Hermits), the conflict was most serious, and visible—or, as Denys Hay puts it, "most celebrated and most productive of good and ill"—among the Franciscans.[11] The forceful Pope John XXII (1316–34) tried to settle the Franciscan controversies, realizing that claims about Christian perfection and poverty involved larger issues affecting the institutional, hierarchical Church and its possessions. Firing up his chain saw, as Burr puts it, John began to trim away the crooked branches of the Franciscan tree: "It isn't pretty, but it's terribly effective."[12] At least for much of John's reign. Spirituals and radical offshoots of the Spirituals, clusters of groups known generically as Fraticelli, were swiftly condemned; in Marseilles during May 1318, four of them were burned to death. Concurrently, Observants, often with the aid of civic leaders or princes, were throwing the presumably more relaxed Conventuals out of their convents and taking them over for themselves. Meanwhile the Dominicans, by now traditionally anti-Franciscan, contributed to the

Centro di Studi sulla Spiritualità Medievale, Convegni, 14, October 14–17, 1973 (Todi: Accademia turdertina, 1974), 77–105, at 104.

10. Of course, the same problems disturbed the monastic life as well, which, significantly, was in decline as the friars' popularity was rising.

11. Denys Hay, *The Church in Italy in the Fifteenth Century* (Cambridge: Cambridge University Press, 1977), 60.

12. David Burr, "John XXII and the Spirituals: Is Angelo Clareno Telling the Truth?" in *Franciscan Studies* 63 (2005), 271–87, at 280: the pope trims "a few unruly branches off the Franciscan *arbor vitae*."

fray whenever possible.[13] Their efforts were made easier by a flowering of fourteenth-century satire directed against money-grubbing, lascivious friars—usually Franciscans.[14] The troubles continued: a de facto recognition of irreconcilable differences occurred in 1446;[15] this became de jure in 1517 when the order's bifurcation was made official, the Medici pope Leo X declaring the two groups independent of each other; and in 1528 under Clement VII the Observants themselves split, divisions that have continued into the twenty-first century's Conventuals, Observants, and Capuchins.

From all this it's clear that when Bonaventure became minister general of the Franciscans in 1257, he walked onto a minefield. Whatever he did was criticized by one faction or other (or others). His efforts, despite later claims by some Observants, seem to have been aimed more at fighting laxity in general, if his letters of 1257 and 1266 are taken into account, than actively trying to pull "radicals" of spiritualist ilk back into the fold.[16] He had to face criticisms from outside the order as well. In 1269, for instance, Gerard of Abbeville preached a university sermon at Paris attacking the Franciscan doctrine of poverty as a threat to Church property generally. He followed up with a treatise on this theme, which Bonaventure answered with his *Apologia pauperum,* defending the mendicants as followers of the pauper Christ. Burr puts the matter bluntly: Gerard charged that "the Franciscan claim to superiority was hollow and pretentious, that they had in fact been living a lie."[17] Regardless of Bonaventure's strategies, such as promulgating a constitution for the order at Narbonne in 1260, superseding others developed since 1239, and his rewriting of Francis's life—with the destruction of all earlier versions, as ordered at the general chapter at Paris in 1266—he was unable to effect unity.[18] As it turned out, no one ever did.

13. Thomas Turley, "John XXII and the Franciscans: A Reappraisal" in *Popes, Teachers, and Canon Law in the Middle Ages,* ed. James Ross Sweeney and Stanley Chodorow (Ithaca, N.Y.: Cornell University Press, 1989), 74–88.

14. Michael Robson, *The Franciscans in the Middle Ages* (Woodbridge, UK: Boydell Press, 2006), 151: "Franciscans are singled out more than the other groups" and chap. 13 ("Giovanni Boccaccio, Satire and the Friars") passim; cf. Chaucer's "The Summoner's Prologue" and "Summoner's Tale."

15. Raphael M. Huber, *A Documented History of the Franciscan Order, from the Birth of St. Francis to the Division of the Order under Leo X, 1118-1517,* (Milwaukee: Nowiny Publishing Apostolate, 1944), 369.

16. Burr, *Spiritual Franciscans,* 35–37.

17. C. H. Lawrence, *The Friars* (London: Longman, 1994), 158; Burr, *Spiritual Franciscans,* 270.

18. The *Life,* commissioned in 1260, was presented to the thirty-four provincials at the general chapter of Pisa in 1263, and formally approved at Paris in 1266: Cousins, *Bonaventure,* "Introduction," 37–40. John Moorman called this decision to destroy earlier Lives a "rash decree"; Bon-

FIRST EFFORTS TOWARD CANONIZATION

In the longer view, such an untenable position meant that those who pushed for his canonization later on faced more than the usual hurdles outlined in the previous chapter. Normally, saint-candidates from a religious order benefited from its financial backing and networks within secular and ecclesiastical society, kings, princes, towns, bishops, cardinals, and heads of religious orders who solicited the pope. In Bonaventure's case, however, there was no unified Franciscan campaign on his behalf, and distracted popes often disagreed with their predecessors' handling of the friars' civil wars, firing recalcitrant or "schismatic" ministers;[19] canceling earlier papal decrees regarding the Franciscans;[20] executing or throwing too-spiritual individuals into prison.[21] Everything hinged on their own prejudices. When a pope was also a Franciscan, this obviously affected his approach (as with the pro-Conventual Sixtus IV).

Bonaventure died in 1274 but wasn't canonized until 1482. His long-deferred case was not unique: other saints canonized in the fifteenth century had waited centuries for their promotions.[22] However, Bonaventure's two-century delay is striking in view of the fact that another Franciscan, the Observant Bernardino of Siena, who died in May 1444, was canonized only six years later. The Sienese had received an encouraging letter from a sympathetic cardinal as early as February 1445. By mid-April 1445, a pro-Observant Eugenius IV (1431–47) had begun the process.[23] The emaciated

aventura's *Life* of Francis, as far as the Spirituals were concerned, was "something of a disaster." *A History of the Franciscan Order from Its Origins to the Year 1517* (Oxford: Oxford University Press, 1968), 287–88. Brooke, "Bonaventure as Minister," while acknowledging the weaknesses of the cleaned-up *Life*, soft-pedals Bonaventure's role in obliterating earlier versions, claiming that his *Life* was "scrupulous by medieval hagiographical standards," 85–89. Further on Bonaventure's reinterpreting Francis's life is William R. Cook, "Fraternal and Lay Images of St. Francis in the Thirteenth Century," in *Popes, Teachers, and Canon Law in the Middle Ages*, ed. James Ross Sweeney and Stanley Chodorow (Ithaca, N.Y.: Cornell University Press, 1989), 263–89, at 267–69. The destruction order was not universally implemented.

19. E.g., Boniface VIII and the Spiritualist Raimondo of Provence; Urban VI and Leonardo Rossi.

20. Clement V reversing Benedict XI, who reversed Boniface VIII, or Martin V abrogating John XXII's decree on property ownership; Pius II withdrawing a bull of Calixtus III.

21. Apart from John XXII's propensities, cf. Clement VI and Gentile da Spoleto.

22. For the long-delayed canonization of Osmund see Wetzstein, *Heilige vor Gericht*, 366–70.

23. Ludwig von Pastor, *The History of the Popes from the Close of the Middle Ages*, trans. F. Antrobus, 40 vols. (London: Kegan Paul, 1899–1953) 2:79–82. Eugenius IV (1431–47) was a "firm

Bernardino was a high-profile charismatic, a very popular preacher whose sermons attracted huge crowds and who ended up entombed in central Italy (at l'Áquila); Bonaventure was a teacher, theologian, and administrator of his order, practically invisible to the general populace, buried in France.[24] In addition, his attempts to reconcile the warring groups within his order generated little enthusiasm among his brethren, especially those associated with the Spirituals, or Observants. In Leff's opinion Bonaventure's efforts only accentuated "the opposition between the extremes by fostering both."[25] One problem that may have provoked misunderstandings and animosity was that sometimes Bonaventure's preferences were as opaque to his contemporaries as they seem to be to some modern scholars.[26] In any event, a Florentine Franciscan wrote in the margin of one of his tracts, about the time of the canonization process (1475–80), that his sainthood was delayed by the passions he'd aroused as minister general.[27] Though Di Fonzo (a twentieth-century Conventual Franciscan) minimizes internal squabbles as

---

supporter of the Observants," Duncan Nimmo, *Reform and Division in the Medieval Franciscan Order: From St. Francis to the Foundation of the Capuchins* (Rome: Capuchin Historical Institute, 1987), 619; C. Piana, "I processi de canonizzazione su la vita di S. Bernardino da Siena," *Archivum Franciscanum Historicum* 44 (1951), 87–160, 383–435, at 92. Even Bernardino's half-hearted participation in the Franciscans' squabbles earned him "some odium within his own party," Nimmo, 627–28.

24. M. D. Lambert, *Franciscan Poverty: The Doctrine of Absolute Poverty of Christ in the Franciscan Order, 1210–1323* (London: S.P.C.K., 1961), 113, asserts that the earliest extant biography of Bonaventure was the work of Peter Galesino, apostolic protonotary to Sixtus V (1585–90). An earlier biography, by the Spaniard Franciscan Zamorra (c. 1300), does not seem to have survived.

25. Gordon Leff, *Heresy in the Later Middle Ages*, 2 vols. (Manchester, UK: Manchester University Press, 1967), 1:83–4. As C. H. Lawrence puts it in *The Friars*, 57, Bonaventure "had of necessity to face both ways at once." See also Lambert, *Franciscan Poverty*, 124: "It is difficult to avoid the conclusion that the Bonaventuran settlement failed through inherent defects."

26. For example, Lambert, *Franciscan Poverty*, 103–40; at 115: "Bonaventura was himself not immune from Joachimite influences." In Andre Vauchez, however, we read about "those who could not be suspected of Joachimism, such as St. Bonaventura," *Sainthood*, 113. Brooke, "Bonaventure as Minister," 91, quoting Marjorie Reeves, agrees that Bonaventure's "attitude toward Joachimism . . . was ambivalent." Review of the debate in E. R. Daniel's somewhat apologetic "St. Bonaventura a Faithful Disciple of St. Francis? A Reexamination of the Question," *S. Bonaventura 1274–1974*, 5 vols. (Grottaferrata: Collegio S. Bonaventura, 1973–74), 2:171–87, and discussion of background to the poverty issue and John XXII's part in Nold, *Pope John XXII*, passim.

27. Stanislao da Campagnola, "Le vicende della canonizzazione di S. Bonaventura," in *San Bernardino francescano*, Centro di Studi sulla Spiritualità Medievale, Convegni, 14 (Todi: Accademia turdertina, 1974), 211–55 at 246–47, quoting Francesco Micheli, OFM Conv. with spiritualist leanings: Bonaventure, though perhaps *beatus*, was not canonized *propter animas* that broke out *dum foret generalis minister;* and see Rosalind B. Brooke, *Early Franciscan Government* (Cambridge: Cambridge University Press, 1959), 284: "The Spirituals did not appreciate [Bonaventure's] services." See also Rona Goffen, "Friar Sixtus IV and the Sistine Chapel," *Renaissance Quarterly* 39, no. 2 (1986), 218–62 at 226–28.

a reason for the delay, another modern Franciscan is in no doubt that this was a cause.[28] It's also suggested that a dearth of miracles may have retarded pilgrimages and the growth of a cult.[29] It seemed, a sixteenth-century curialist reflected, that memory of Bonaventure had been buried along with his corpse.[30]

There are other possible causes for the 208-year gap between Bonaventure's death and canonization. Perhaps one of them was John XXII's problems with the Franciscans, which set the general tone for most of the Avignon popes as dissension continued over apostolic and institutional poverty; another may have been the Franciscan-associated apocalyptic rumblings that continued through the fourteenth century. Little enthusiasm for Bonaventure is evident in two fourteenth-century versions (1330s, 1380s) of a catalog of Franciscan saints: he merits mention as a sinless cardinal, theologian, and minister general, buried at Lyons by pope and cardinals; the only inkling of a heavenly connection is the story about a bit of Eucharist miraculously popping into his mouth during a Mass.[31] At the end of that century, the Great Schism's splintering of the papacy into two and then (in 1409) three "obediences," each with its own pope, certainly threw Christendom and the Franciscans—who now had three ministers general—into greater than usual disorder.[32] When Pius II canonized Catherine of Siena in 1461, some eighty years after her death, he claimed that the delay arose out of fear that, during the schism, she'd be celebrated as a saint by one part of the Church, but mocked by another.[33] Something of the sort may well have inhibited Bonaventure's advancement, at least for part of the time.[34] As in the fourteenth, during the fifteenth century quarrels and failed compromises among relaxed, moderate, and strict elements of the order continued

28. *Dubium non est:* L. Spätling, "Tractatus pro canonizatione divi Bonaventure a Fr. Antonio de Vercellis conscriptus," *Archivum Franciscanum Historicum* 48 (1955), 381–426, at 382–83; 49 (1956): 166–90; cf. Lorenzo Di Fonzo, OFM Conv., "Il processo di canonizzazione di S. Bonaventura da Bagnoregio, O. Min (1474–82)," *Miscellanea Francescana* 75 (1975), 227–89 at 228, 240–41. This article has proven extremely useful in reconstructing the canonization process.

29. Di Fonzo, "Il processo di canonizzazione," 228–29.

30. Spätling, "Tractatus pro canonizatione," 383, from Galesino's *Vita* in AASS (see below).

31. Roberto Paciocco, *Da Francesco ai "Catalogi Sanctorum": livelli istituzionali e immagini agiografiche nel ordine Francescano (secoli 13–14),* Collectio Assisiensis 20 (Assisi: Porziuncola, 1990), 148.

32. Moorman, *Franciscan Order,* 388.

33. *Oggetto di scherno,* Campagnola, "Le vicende," 238.

34. Wetzstein, *Heilige vor Gericht,* believes that Pius's reasons veiled his desire to canonize a fellow-Sienese, just as Sixtus desired Bonaventure's elevation as a fellow-Franciscan, 495.

to cause upheaval, especially from about 1430. In 1443, for the first time ever, with Eugenius IV's backing an Observant was put forward as Franciscan minister general. At the general chapter at Padua where he expected to be confirmed by vote of the Observants and Conventuals present, as he began to read a papal letter, a crowd of Conventuals shouting, "'Liberty! Liberty'... surged forward, tore the missive from his hands, and dragged him bodily from the chamber, while delegates of the two factions came to blows." After Bernardino of Siena restored calm, the Conventuals installed their own candidate.[35]

SIXTUS IV BEGINS THE PROCESS

In the midst these unrelenting and unedifying battles, the Franciscan Pope Sixtus IV (1471–84)—an ex–minister general of the order—began Bonaventure's process. Answers to the question in whose interest was his canonization, and why now, include the suggestion that the canonization of Bernardino (one of the "four pillars of the observance") in 1450 stimulated interest in Bonaventure; elements of the latter's teachings have been detected in Bernardino's preaching. Some of the Siena saint's followers—such as another of the four pillars, John of Capistrano (d. 1456)—also supported Bonaventure's cause.[36] Interestingly, given internal rivalries, a few decades later yet another Observant pillar, James of the Marches (d. 1476), wrote to Sixtus offering to assist in Bonaventure's process. The pope politely declined, saying (in January 1475) that the matter was still under consideration; James could assist by providing comments on Bonaventure, and coming to Rome for the ceremony at a later time—but James had died by then.[37] These are exceptions to the consensus among the Observants, who continued to ignore Bonaventure, in their eyes a defender of the Conventuals. As late as 1472, for example, Sixtus cited the Constitutions of Narbonne (1260) in a bull against a group of brothers of the order "who are called *de Observantia.*"[38] Moreover, Sixtus, himself a Conventual, enacted pro-Conventual legislation that "inevitably drove the Observants into more determined op-

35. Nimmo, *Reform and Division,* 629–30.

36. Di Fonzo, "Il processo di canonizzazione," 267; Campagnola, "Le vicende," 238–39.

37. Moorman, *Franciscan Order,* 374–77; *Bullarium Franciscanum,* nova series, vol. 3 (1471–84), ed. Joseph Pou y Marti (Quaracchi: Ex typ. Coll. S. Bonaventure, 1949) (hereafter, *Bull. Franc.*), #673, 304.

38. *Bull. Franc.*, #324, 134.

position."[39] The pope found that Observants were drawing support from some secular authorities—on one occasion he heatedly blasted lay leaders who sullied themselves with "lousy, begging friars."[40]

From whatever impulses, and in spite of all the bickering, there is evidence of a nascent Bonaventure cult by at least 1455, when his body was translated to a new location in the Lyons Conventual church. On that occasion his tongue, purportedly, was "as in life" (discussed below).[41] On November 2, 1474—two hundred years after his death—Sixtus IV issued what seems to be the first official mandate opening the process However, Campagnola continues, it's difficult to identify who or what impulses were behind this papal order.[42] Nevertheless, the process was finally under way. We saw in chapter 1 that from the thirteenth century the curia continued—in general—to follow established rules for canonizations. In Bonaventure's case, a near-contemporary *Ceremoniale* by the papal master of ceremonies Agostino Patrizi Piccolomini, published in 1488, reflects the theoretical course that his process would or should have taken.[43] We'll compare his directives with what actually happened as Bonaventure's supporters pushed him toward sainthood. In the November brief, Sixtus ordered the archbishop and prelates of Lyons to assist an Observant, Gervasius de Salis, sent to inquire into Bonaventure's miracles so that a decision as to further action could be made by the Apostolic See, which was urged to canonize him. No further reference is made to who was doing the urging.[44] The initiation of a formal process is in stark contrast to the case of Saint Francis (d. 1226, cf. 1228), for whom Gregory IX saw no point in going through the usual procedures.[45] Two elements in the 1474 brief are somewhat problematic. First, the pope directs an investigation of miracles only, without mentioning Bo-

39. Moorman, *Franciscan Order,* 488; see also von Pastor, *History of the Popes,* 4:391.

40. Luke Wadding, *Annales Minorum seu Trium Ordinum a S. Francisco Institutorum,* 3rd ed., vol. 14 (Florence: Ad Claras Aquas [Quaracchi], 1933), 2.

41. The translation has been variously dated; Di Fonzo agrees there may have been an earlier one.

42. "Il primo documento che... avviava una procedura di verifica della sua santità"; "Permane difficile indicare la provenienza di queste pressioni." Campagnola, "Le vicende," 241.

43. *L'Oeuvre de Patrizi Piccolomini* (ed. Dykmans), vol. 1: for Patrizi's life and works including the *Ceremonial* see 1*–32*; for the editor's analysis of Title VI on canonization, 128*–39*; Latin ed. of this section is on 118–24.

44. *Bull. Franc.* #644, 284: "Quo sancta apostolica Sedes, apud quam pro illius canonizatione instatur."

45. Vauchez, *Sainthhood,* 337.

naventure's life, merits, teachings, and so on. Does this reflect an uneasiness about his thaumaturgic abilities (especially during his lifetime), a requirement for sainthood? Second, once again the Observants, in the form of Gervasius de Salis, play a role in the process. One scholar has suggested that an Observant was sent into the nest of Lyons Conventuals to give an appearance of impartiality. Another, more positively, implies that Gervasius indicates ongoing Observant interest in the cause.[46] What Campagnola calls the first formal supplication from the *Conventual* Franciscans themselves is dated May 15, 1475, some six months after the papal brief, following rather than preceding the official opening of the case.[47] Normally, as we saw in chapter 1 and as Patrizi's Ceremonial indicates, repeated requests, from a variety of supporters, over a long time—sometimes many years—were needed to budge the papacy toward initiating an investigation. In Bonaventure's case, however, the Franciscan ex–minister general Sixtus IV was himself the primary agent in setting the machinery in motion.[48] Wetzstein finds no similar example in the fifteenth century of such a clearly papally initiated process.[49] In the canonization bull of 1482, the pope drew parallels between his own life story and Bonaventure's, whose works, he admitted, had always delighted him.[50] As children, he proclaimed, they'd been rescued from serious illnesses after vows to Francis. Then, after dedicating themselves to theology and the religious life, both he and Bonaventure came to be ministers general of the order, and cardinals; thus by entirely similar steps one arose to be pope, the other, a saint. And lest it be thought that he'd canonize Bonaventure simply out of affection, Sixtus continues, he opened a formal process, as matters of such magnitude required.

There's no doubt that individuals were canonized as a direct result of papal initiative—and that sometimes even pontifical efforts came to nothing.

46. *Bull. Franc.* #644, 284; Di Fonzo, "Il processo di canonizzazione," 234–38; Campagnola, "Le vicende," 239–40.

47. *La supplica formale,* Campagnola, "Le vicende," 241.

48. Ibid.; the author also suggests that probably there was cooperation between pope and order prior to the November 1474 mandate, but documentation of this is, so far, unnoticed.

49. Wetzstein, *Heilige vor Gericht,* 376: "Das 15 Jahrhundert kennt kein weiteres Beispiel, in dem die Eigeninitiative des Papstes bei einer Kanonisation ähnlich deutlich zutage träte"; cf. also 380.

50. The following in Pastor, *History of the Popes,* 4:205–7, and *Bull. Franc.,* #1562, 798: "Sed memores Nos eumdem Minorum ordinem ex voto ingressos, in quo . . . in sacris litteris et religiosis moribus utcumque profecimus, eademque ministeriatus officia exercuimus, atque inde ad cardinalatus dignitatem, ita ut per consimiles gradus."

Although Innocent III published four documents praising the "martyr" Peter of Castelnau, murdered in the course of his duties in 1208, no canonization resulted. The disappointed pope blamed the locals, whose weak faith "made it impossible for miracles to occur at his tomb"; without these, as Innocent himself acknowledged elsewhere, canonizations could not occur.[51] The same thing happened in a later epoch when another Franciscan pope, the fiery Sixtus V (1585–90), tried to canonize his friend the Capuchin Felix of Cantalice, who died on May 18, 1587. Two days later the pope had a biography written up, and on May 25 he tried to open a process. Felix's superior blocked this on procedural grounds, which, naturally, infuriated His hot-headed Holiness, who claimed that the will of the pope was enough. Eventually there was a hearing (June to November 1587), the pope declaring himself ready to testify to eighteen miracles he'd seen the friar perform. (Since canon law prohibited judges from acting as witnesses in cases brought before them, it would seem that the pope, as ultimate ecclesiastical judge, overstepped the line here.)[52] Sixtus V's enthusiastic bombast and disregard of canon law was wasted effort; Felix was canonized only in 1712.[53] Most of the time, however, when a pope wanted someone canonized, for instance at the urging of some political ally, this was done.[54] In Bonaventure's case, however, Sixtus's political preoccupations, and squabbles within the Franciscan Order, frustrated his designs.

Although he'd spent most of his life as a Franciscan, when Francesco da Savona/della Rovere became a cardinal in 1467, then pope in 1471, Sixtus IV turned to a life of nepotism, extravagance, and political intrigue, a Becket in reverse, perhaps. Consequently, it's not difficult to imagine him starting a push for the canonization of someone he personally admired, who might represent a virtuous *alter Sixtus* in response to criticisms of his reign; what Lee calls "the multivalence" of Sixtus's character easily allows for this.[55] Whatever the impetus, in the process he set in motion on November 2, 1474, as noted above, the pope's mandate directed the Lyons arch-

51. Vauchez, *Sainthood,* 37.

52. James A. Brundage, *The Medieval Origins of the Legal Profession* (Chicago: University of Chicago Press, 2008), 382, for Gratian's and other canonists' opinions on this subject.

53. *Processus Sixtinus Fratris Felicis a Cantalice,* ed. M. ab Altari, *Monumenta Historica Ordinis Minorum Capuccinorum,* vol. 10 (Rome: Istituto storico dei Capuccini, 1964), xii–xxx, 369–74.

54. See discussion in Vauchez, *Sainthood,* 77–81.

55. Egmont Lee, *Sixtus IV and Men of Letters* (Rome: Edizioni di storia e letteratura, 1978), 41.

bishop and prelates to help de Salis collect information about Bonaventure's miracles.[56] Di Fonzo writes that this clearly established a general informative process.[57] According to Master of Ceremonies Patrizi, a general hearing should be executed without formal (juridical) examination of witnesses, followed by a report of findings to the pope.[58] By early February 1475, the papal command had been read during Sunday Mass in many Lyons churches, with an call for anyone wishing to testify.[59] As a result, de Salis examined nineteen sworn witnesses, including four Lyons Conventuals, from February 14 to 17. About the same time five other lesser processes were executed elsewhere in France.[60] The findings (including testimony about Bonaventure's head and tongue at his 1455 translation) were duly sent to the pope. The next phase, according to Patrizi, writing in the 1480s, was for the pope to refer the issue once again to the cardinals and, if it seemed warranted, to inquire further as to the *truth* of things by properly examining sworn witnesses.[61] This dossier, Patrizi continued, after examination by auditors of the Rota, who put it in rational order and made sure that the hearing had been legitimately carried out, was then committed to three cardinals, who went over everything again.[62] In Bonaventure's case, however, the pope seems to have skipped most of these intermediate steps. It seems, according to Di Fonzo, that in reality Sixtus, convinced of the worth of the cause, went directly to setting up the three-cardinal committee to oversee Bonaventure's case at a secret consistory on May 29, 1475. The cardinals were Angelo Capranica (d. 1478), who had worked on Bernardino of Siena's canonization; the papal nephew and (new) protector of the Franciscans, Giuliano della Rovere (later pope Julius II, d. 1513); and Francisco Gonzaga (d. 1483).[63]

56. Di Fonzo, "Il processo di canonizzazione," 236–44, for the following.

57. *In termini lucidissimi,* ibid., 234.

58. *In genere et sine testium iuridica examination,* Piccolomini's *Ceremonial* (ed. Dykmans), 118.

59. Di Fonzo, "Il processo di canonizzazione," 236: "Furono notificati al popolo in molte chiese della città la domenica seguente (12 febbr)."

60. Di Fonzo, "Il processo di canonizzazione," 237–38 lists the sites.

61. *Inquirant de veritate rei . . . testes examinent.*

62. Piccolomini's *Ceremonial,* 118–19.

63. Capranica was elevated by Pius II in 1460, title of Cardinal S. Croce or Rieti; Gonzaga too was created cardinal by Pius II, in 1461. The papal nephew della Rovere, created cardinal in the first year of his uncle's pontificate, 1471, took the title of S. Pietro in Vincolo, was named bishop (1474) then archbishop (1475) of Avignon; sent on many embassies, as in 1480–81, when he was in France and Flanders. Giuliano was elected pope Julius II in 1503, d. 1513. He left the Franciscan Order as a novice.

The papal nephew's appointment would seem to emphasize Sixtus's personal interest in promoting Bonaventure's sainthood.

Several days before this secret consistory, a Conventual chapter general at Urbino elected Francesco Nanni (d. 1499), whom the pope nicknamed Samson or Sansone for his strength in debate, as their minister general. He would be a firm Bonaventure supporter. On May 15, 1475, the chapter agreed to collect information on Bonaventure's miracles and send petitions (evidently, as suggested above, for the first time) to the pope and Cardinal Protector della Rovere. In the meantime, however, Franciscan fratricide continued as always: two groups of Observants in separate chapters general also held in May (at Naples and St. Omer) ignored Bonaventure and put up their own candidate for sainthood, the Observant John of Capistrano (cd. only in 1724). Although Di Fonzo claims to find this "curious," clearly it makes sense given the ongoing strife within the order.[64]

While these internecine battles raged, letters supporting Bonaventure arrived in Rome between July 1475 and April 1476 (again, only after the pope opened the case), where they were exhibited by Franciscan proctor Giovanni da Trevi to Promoter of the Faith Ardicino della Porta.[65] Meanwhile in February 1476 the other lesser processes from various French Franciscan convents came to the proctor fiscal's attention.[66] Another batch of supplications arrived in early 1479. The list of suppliants, as normally the case in proposed canonizations, reads like a *Who's Who* of contemporary leaders, bringing together some who were mutual enemies and occasionally at odds with popes. The absence of particular names is just as noteworthy. The letter-writers of 1475–79 included the archbishop of Lyons, Ferdinand (Ferrante) of Naples, a few sympathetic Observants, the duchess and duke of Calabria (Alfonso II, Ferrante's son), Hippolita Maria, Don Giovanni of Aragon (later cardinal), Filibert I of Savoy, the duchess and duke (Giovanni II) of Bourbon. Emperor Friedrich III's (1440–93) name also appears, although during this very period he was also (somewhat unenthusiastically) pushing for a rival candidate discussed in the next chapter, Leopold of Austria. Other supporters were Friedrich's rival king Matthias Corvinus of Hungary, Ferdinand II of Aragon, Louis XI of France (though at this time Louis was threatening Sixtus

64. Di Fonzo, "Il processo di canonizzazione," 228, 240–41.

65. Ibid., 242 n. 36: "Promotore della Fede."

66. Ibid., 237–38.

with a general council), the doge of Venice (Mocenigo), the duke of Milan (Giangaleazzo Sforza) and Florence's Lorenzo de'Medici, as well as the cities of Lyons, Siena, Perugia, and Bonaventure's hometown, Bagnoregio, which sent its own representatives to the curia.[67]

Sixtus IV moved things along, on October 9, 1475, officially appointing a subcommittee of two bishops (Louis Bertrand of Bergamo and Ardicino della Porta) as "promotors, judges and commissaries" of the case, joined by Antonio da Gubbio as procurator fiscal and second promoter of the faith.[68] By early 1476 this committee had assembled various documents, including the Lyons process of 1475 and a list of fifty-one points (*articuli*) that the procurator fiscal intended, as he stated, to put to this body of documentation. After notice was posted in Rome (March 1476) in St. Peter's and the Campo dei Fiori inviting anyone objecting or opposing the process to come forward, the documents were officially accepted. Then, for the next fifteen months (April 1476 to July 1477), nothing happened.[69]

Di Fonzo suggests two reasons for the delay: plague, which forced Sixtus out of Rome from June 1476 to October 1476, and controversy over the Immaculate Conception (January and February 1477). The first reason seems realistic, given Rome's many encounters with pestilence, although one suspects that delay of curial business "because of the plague" sometimes was, or became, a convenient cover for bureaucratic stalling. The second reason is less convincing, since the Conception debate ended in late February. In any event, Sixtus approved the cult of the Immaculate Conception, which in general was supported by the Franciscans (although, as it happens, Bonaventure never accepted the idea). By July 1477, the canonization process was restarted when cardinal Capranica and da Gubbio requested a hearing at Orvieto on local miracles. This was carried out in January 1478, with a report sent to Rome in March. Toward the end of 1477, in response to continued Franciscan interest and prompting by secular notables, Sixtus indicated that he expected to canonize by Pentecost (May 10) of 1478. In yet another instance of bipartisan interest in Bonaventure's cause, the vicar general of the cismontane Observants, Peter of Naples, anticipating that this would

67. Campagnola, "Le vicende," 242.

68. *Promotor fiscalis et Fidei,* Di Fonzo, "Il processo di canonizzazione," 243 n. 40, quoting from the process. For the appearance of this officer in canonizations, see my "Saint-Making at the End of the Sixteenth Century," 240 n. 122.

69. For the following, Di Fonzo, "Il processo di canonizzazione," 244–49.

happen, hoped to schedule a chapter general so that his Observants would be able to participate in the ceremony. However, as Luke Wadding writes, none of this occurred, because of pestilence and war—*hinc peste, illinc bello.*[70]

The process stalled once more, perhaps because Sixtus was preoccupied with the Pazzi conspiracy that exploded in bloodshed on April 26, 1478, leading to the excommunication of Lorenzo, a papal interdict against his city, and war between the pope and Florence. Evidently, the attempt to kill off the Medici brothers had been engineered by (inter alia) papal nephew Girolamo Riario; Sixtus was fully aware of the planned attempt to overthrow the Medici, and sanctioned it.[71] In the midst of this in July a member of the canonization commission (Capranica) died, and another (Gonzaga) resigned. The pope didn't set up a second commission until late December of 1478. He reappointed his nephew Giuliano della Rovere. To assist him Sixtus chose Cardinal Giacomo Ammanati. This may have led to some uncomfortable committee meetings, given Ammanati's belief that Sixtus's elevation of Giuliano (and another cardinal-nephew, Pietro) in December 1471 had disgraced the college of cardinals; it was a papal "act of imbecility."[72] The third member of the commission was the pope's grandnephew, the young Raffaele Sansoni Riario, a worldly princeling who didn't care to participate in the committee's work.[73] Perhaps his recent experiences in Florence left him temporarily without much energy or ambition, understandably. In the wake of the Pazzi conspiracy he was imprisoned, though apparently unaware of the plot. Lorenzo refused the pope's requests to release the young man. On the day Raffaele finally returned to Rome, June 20, his face bearing a "deadly pallor," Sixtus placed Florence under interdict, following up his excommunication of Lorenzo (on June 1). Moving closer to outright war with Florence, in July because of plague the pope left Rome for Bracciano, twenty-five miles to the northwest, where in August 1478 he met with several ambassadors involved in the Florentine issue. By early De-

70. Wadding, *Annales,* 223, s. a. 1478; Campagnola, "Le vicende," 244; Huber, *A Documented History of the Franciscan Order,* 439.

71. Lee, *Sixtus IV,* 39 and cf. 43 n., where Lee refers to Pastor's "device of transferring all blame from Sixtus to his nephews."

72. Pastor, *History of the Popes,* 4:35–36; Lee, *Sixtus IV,* 219, records another comment by Ammanati: "Nonne ignominiosum est nostro collegio?"

73. Sansoni Riario (d. 1521) became a cardinal in 1477; Ammanati-Piccolomini—he'd been adopted by Pius II—elevated by that pope in 1461, was known as the "Cardinal of Pavia"; he died on September 10, 1479.

cember he was sending two nuncios to Friedrich III asking for aid against Florence and their ally Louis XI.[74] In January and February of the new year, ambassadors from both France and the Empire were in Rome. These preoccupations suggest that the canonization of even a favorite long-dead friar might not occupy the forefront of the papal mind, for the time being anyway. And, in general, they stand for the multitude of hindrances that might derail a canonization process as papal and curial energies were focused elsewhere. As for the commission finally reestablished on December 28, 1478, in effect Ammanati was the only cardinal on the job.[75] On the same December day Sixtus appointed another procedural subcommittee, this time of four jurist-theologians, Johannes Baptista de'Giudici, Ardicino della Porta (reappointed), Giovanni Francesco Pavini, and Paolo da Roma, and he confirmed Antonio da Gubbio as promoter of the faith and procurator fiscal.

Only now, more than four years after the first preliminary examination, did Sixtus establish a hearing into the *truth* of claims regarding Bonaventure. In a brief of August 7, 1479, he directed Edward de Messiaco, abbot of Insulebarbare, the dean of Lyons cathedral chapter, and John de Fayeta, canon of St. John's church of Lyons, to inform themselves "generally and then specifically" about Bonaventure's life, merits—here in the margin of the Lyons process someone wrote, "this should rather speak of miracles"—piety, and teachings.[76] Di Fonzo terms this the "true" remissorial trial of Lyons (1479–80), whereas the first one of 1475 was merely an exploratory preamble. He suggests that a second, more convincing inquiry was desired by the pope, implying that the first was defective. However, his comment that the two Lyons hearings were "in opposition" goes too far.[77] Sixtus's brief of 1479 and the 1482 canonization bull's claim of insufficient "solemnity" at the first inquiry was a *topos* often used in setting up later hearings.[78] Di Fon-

74. Pastor, *History of the Popes,* 4:308, 315–27.

75. Ibid., 412, and Di Fonzo, "Il processo di canonizzazine," 248 n. 52.

76. *Alias ad supplicationem* in *Bull. Franc.,* #1201, 609, *in genere et demum in specie;* cf. Marinangeli's ed. of the hearing, 79.

77. *Un più persuasivo processo,* Di Fonzo, "Il processo di canonizzazione," 249–51 and n. 57 ("l'opposizione tra le due *Relazioni* . . . è evidente"). Perhaps he was influenced by the terminology in Sixtus's mandate establishing a second Lyons process to bring out matters *clarius et apertius,* "more clearly and openly"; in addition, Di Fonzo further faults Gervasius for not using a list of interrogatories, and for improperly questioning the witnesses.

78. Vauchez, *Sainthood,* 70. The expression was "quia non videbatur in procedendo tanta, quanta requiritur, observata solemnitas, illum reiterari jussimus": *Bull. Fran.* #1562, 798.

zo suggests that defects in the first hearing included vagueness of testimony about miracles, more depositions about miracles than the life (though the pope's original brief mentioned only miracles), confusion as to events at the translation, and possible bias in the four Conventuals' depositions. However, for Campagnola, the surviving documentation of that first hearing doesn't justify the claim of insufficiency.[79] What all of this does show, however, is that the difference between the neatly distinguished categories of a first, on-site general process and a subsequent, more specific investigation as described in papal ceremonials, might reflect canonists' theories better than procedural facts.

In any case, a second Lyons process began.[80] In the absence of one of the papally nominated commissaries (the dean of the cathedral chapter), the two remaining prelates selected two expertly trained assessors to replace him and added two apostolic notaries, Lyons citizens. On January 26, 1480, the procurator appointed by the Lyons Franciscans, the Conventual Giovanni de Vallibus (de Vaux), formally requested the opening of proceedings and handed over several documents to the papal commissioners.[81] A list of eight *articuli* propounded by the Franciscan brethren and the warden of the Lyons convent was also presented.[82] The record then sets out the depositions of thirty-seven men and seventeen women of all classes, ranging from cloth worker to theology professor and medical doctor, as well as some religious (though no Franciscans were called to testify, or they did not volunteer), recorded between late January and late February of 1480. Of these fifty-four witnesses, seven had also testified at the 1475 hearing.[83] Although there are eight articles, witnesses seem to have responded to nine points (two being contained in article five). In any event, the answers sometimes deviated from the questions. When we examine the articles it's immediately

79. Campagnola, "Le vicende della canonizzazione," 246.

80. For the following see Marinangeli's edition of the hearing, "La canonizzazione di S. Bonaventura," 77–84.

81. These included his notarized letter of procuration, the papal brief, and a letter from Louis XI to the seneschal of Lyons allowing the papal mandate to be executed. His Highness notes that the investigation will delve into Bonaventura's "bonne vie, doctrine et miracles"; miracles are mentioned two more times in the royal command.

82. On the injunction (January 8, 1475) against publishing papal decrees in France without royal approval, Pastor, *History of the Popes,* 4:321; the February 1475 hearing would thus technically have required royal approval as well. Di Fonzo, "Il processo di canonizzazione," 253 n. 6, comments on the vagueness of *articuli* numeration: the order was "non sempre . . . rispettato."

83. Marinangeli, "La canonizzazione di S. Bonaventura," 77–82.

evident that witnesses couldn't possibly have discussed some of them in any meaningful way:

> (1) [Ask the witness about] the common assertion that Bonaventure was a holy and devout man... [Each article ends with the phrase "thus it was and is true"]. (2) A particle of the consecrated host miraculously flew into his mouth during a Mass. (3) At a conclave at Perugia Bonaventure, Minister-General of the Franciscans, was proposed as the next pope or at least his advice was taken as to the next pope, and he suggested the man who became Gregory X who made Bonaventure a cardinal and also called the Council of Lyons where he died. (4) At Lyons his exsequies were celebrated by Gregory X and cardinals, the body being buried in the sacristy of Lyons church. (5) [This fifth article comprised two different aspects:] Bonaventure's commentary on Luke was divinely inspired; and when the Franciscans translated him to their new Lyons church, though the corpse had turned to dust his tongue appeared to be almost alive. (6) Bonaventure was famous as a Master of Theology at Paris. (7) He performed miracles after his death [the only article about which witnesses could offer firsthand testimony]. (8) All the foregoing is well-known and true, as is clear from common or public knowledge or notoriety.

Testimony of the first two witnesses is summarized below, to give some idea of responses to the procurator's *articuli.*[84]

The first witness was Humbert Randery, Carmelite provincial prior, a professor of sacred theology, age fifty-five, who could remember forty years back, as he claimed. He (and all other witnesses) was individually and secretly examined on the articles by the papal commissioners in the presence of the assessors and notaries. "First he was asked whether he had seen Bonaventure; he had never seen him because he'd been dead for a long time now. When did he die? Witness didn't know."[85] What about his fame? Humbert had always heard, and it was widely held, that Bonaventure was a great theologian and devout man, which still was claimed in the schools of theology. In the schools Humbert often heard that he'd commented on the *Four Books of Sentences,* which he, Humbert, frequently read and heard read, to his and others' great edification. Bonaventure was reputed a devout, scholarly, and saintly man whose many books were held in great esteem by faculties of theology. Was he a member of a religious order? Witness heard that he'd been a Franciscan. What about his way of life? Humbert had always

84. Ibid., 84–86, 105.

85. This curious passage (84) is: "Et primo interrogatus si viderit dictum dominum bonaventuram dicit se non vidisse: quia jamdiu est obitus. Interrogatus quo tempore obierit dixit se nescire."

heard that he was devout and of good life and religious reputation; about particulars Humbert couldn't testify. Was Bonaventure persecuted? Humbert didn't know. Did he perform any miracles when living? Humbert didn't know how or what to testify about this.[86] Did he know by sight or hearing of any posthumous miracles? Humbert had heard many say that his tongue was as if he'd only recently died, and this was held to be a miracle. Did this happen long after his death? He didn't know. From whom had he heard this? The Carmelite responded that it was common knowledge among the people of Lyons. Moving on to the second article (the host miracle), Humbert knew nothing about it. On the third, he knew nothing except that Bonaventure had been a cardinal, but he didn't know which pope had promoted him. He knew nothing about article four (the Lyons funeral). Article five, the duplex one about the commentary on Luke and the preserved tongue, Humbert knew nothing more than he'd already stated. When asked about the sixth article, the witness said he'd heard of many miraculous cures at the tomb, though he couldn't name names. In the list of articles, however, number six had to do with Bonaventure's fame as a Paris theologian—were the commissioners deviating from the procurator's plan? Perhaps they felt that Humbert had already responded to this issue. In any case, his testimony jumps from article six to eight; the deposition ends with article nine "and other articles following," with the witness claiming that he knew nothing further. Finally, in response to the standard question, whether his testimony was influenced by outside factors, he said no, "he spoke only to tell the truth."[87] Humbert's testimony illustrates how a jumble could be made of neatly formulated interrogatories prepared by saint-candidates' promoters or procurators fiscal. Nor did papal commissioners feel bound to follow such lists down to the letter, but asked ex officio whatever they wished by adding to, rearranging, or ignoring the preset queries. They asked their own questions—as well as those on the procurators' lists—if they recognized new issues, or confusion, in the testimony calling for further examination; and witnesses just as freely ignored the script.

The second to testify, Michael de Chiel or de Geminas, was a Lyons shoe-

86. *Et super hoc deponere nesciret.* Simon Ditchfield, "Thinking with Saints," 567, contends that as a result of the Protestant Reformation and touchiness about miracles, canonization witnesses testified about them with "care and circumspection," many claiming that "they did not know of any." Here we have an example of such (pre-Reformation) caution.

87. *Pro sola veritate dicenda.*

maker. An "honest man" of about fifty, Michael belonged to a parish that included the Franciscans' convent. As for the first article, he'd always heard that Bonaventure was a good man, a Franciscan of great sanctity and learning. Asked if he'd been a cardinal, Michael didn't know; regarding his fame, he'd heard his high reputation often praised in sermons in the cathedral and in his parish church. For miracles Bonaventure performed during his lifetime, the witness—wandering off the mark—claimed that he'd often heard from many that he was reputed a devout man who wrote many notable books. He knew nothing about the second, third, and fourth articles. Concerning the fifth article (the commentary on Luke and almost-living tongue), Michael testified that about twenty-six years earlier the body was transferred from the old to the new Franciscan church (in 1455), when he, Michael, kissed Bonaventure's head, as did many others. The commissioners dug deeper, asking whether he'd done this because he'd thought of him as a saint. Michael's answer was a muddled repetition of his earlier comments. Then: had he seen the tongue? No, but he'd heard from many others that *they'd* seen it, inside his mouth. They told him that the tongue was preserved because Bonaventure had made many fine sermons—and wrote notable books. Article six, the university career, was answered by the witness with tales of miracles at the tomb. He himself, after a horse injured his ribs on his left side, heard a sermon in the Franciscan church about Bonaventure's miracles. This encouraged him to vow a pound of wax shaped like ribs, at which he was immediately healed. About articles seven, eight, and nine, Michael knew nothing beyond what he'd already stated.

In general, most witnesses' testimony concentrated on that essential ingredient in the saint-making recipe, miracles before and after the death of the candidate. Not much is said of the living Bonaventure's wonders, obviously because the witnesses knew of these only by tradition. In fact, one of the deponents, an Augustinian Hermit master of theology, had heard that the candidate performed one single miracle while alive, but even he couldn't say what it had been. Posthumous wonders of the usual curative genre, on the other hand, make up the bulk of the testimony, starting with the translation of the body from the "old" Franciscan convent of Lyons to the new one. This took place in 1455 according to Di Fonzo, though Marinangeli mentions a date of 1434. Examination of the sworn statements shows that witnesses who could remember the event claimed that it happened "about thirty years earlier," that is, about 1450, with a few others suggesting dates between 1440 and 1460. The reasons witnesses gave for the translation seem to have been that (1) the old Franciscan church was in a ruinous state, and (2) since Bonaventure was considered holy (or a saint, *reputabant eum sanctum*), he deserved a more honorable burial site. At the translation the bones were carried in procession from the old to the new church, the archbishop taking advantage of the opportunity to remove a shoulder bone (translations were often marked by the furtive or public removal of parts of the deceased). The remains, in a wooden container, were placed in the choir of the new church for viewing. The skull, separated from the body, was on top of the box. And here we return to the miraculous tongue. The following reconstruction is based on responses scattered through the depositions—though many witnesses knew nothing of the translation or the tongue.[88]

One witness claimed that the crowds were so great that he couldn't get a clear view of the skull, which—according to another witness—contained a fresh tongue. Another said that she, being just a little girl, could see only the top of the skull. Among those who did get a full view, however, one claimed that a tongue was inside the skull; another that a tongue (inside the skull) was displayed on the altar in the convent's chapel of St. Louis; a third that it had been taken out of the skull on the translation day; a fourth that the tongue was removed from the skull by the convent warden, John Bertheti, who showed it to everyone; a fifth deponent—probably referring to the same incident as the fourth—testified that Warden John while preaching in the convent (very likely on the same day) held a man's tongue in his hand, claiming that it was Bonaventure's; a sixth witness saw, near but separate from the rest of the bones, a pyx containing the fresh tongue of a man "they said" was that of the dead Franciscan. Finally, another witness remembered that the tongue had been put into an ivory box and placed in Bonaventure's new tomb by the convent's friars. Some witnesses offered reasons for the tongue's miraculous preservation: it was due to the wonderful sermons preached by the dead friar; to the many accurate predictions he had made; and to his reluctance to pass by an image of the Virgin without pausing to say an *Ave Maria* and other prayers.

Many said this fresh tongue was "beautiful." We cannot refrain from exploring this a little more. Most interesting is the testimony of a master mason

88. Marinangeli, "La canonizzazione," 17 (1916), 84–86, 105–20, 164–74; 18 (1917), 125–35.

who swore that on the translation day he had his men open Bonaventure's tomb (in the old church), in which he saw the bones and skull. However, he "specifically" stated that he didn't remember noticing any tongue. Yet he'd heard that many claimed to have seen such on object on that day. There's a further twist to the tale. Testimony about the events of 1455, as noted, was provided to papal commissioners in January and February in 1480. A few years later, in April 1482, consistorial advocate Ottaviano de Martinis da Sinuessani gave an oration (discussed more fully below) before pope and cardinals prefatory to Bonaventure's April 14th canonization. He referred to a situation that sheds some light on the fresh tongue. In 1263, Ottaviano states, the body of the Franciscan Saint Antony was translated at Padua (d. 1231, cd. 1232). Bonaventure assisted. When the bones were inspected, it was found that Antony's tongue was red and fresh, even though he'd been dead thirty-two years. Bonaventure, who greatly esteemed Antony, took the tongue in his hands and prayed, noting that God had preserved the "blessed tongue" because of the saint's merits and wonderful preaching.[89] Presumably this event was known to the order's members. It's not unlikely that it suggested a similar preservative "miracle" to the Franciscans at Bonaventure's own translation of 1455. Since Antony was already canonized, wouldn't the same miracle improve Bonaventure's chances? Mendicant sanctity had centered on their dedication to preaching the Word to the laity as well as providing models of moral and spiritual virtue. Though by the fourteenth century new elements had appeared, such as greater emphasis on the intellect and defense of orthodoxy, these earlier core values persisted.[90] A tongue-relic would be eminently appropriate as symbol of Franciscan sanctity. Whether fraudulently produced in 1455 by warden John in imitation of Antony's translation or not, the tongue became such a sought-after item that one witness heard that it had been "lifted" by a Franciscan.[91] The mystery deepens: some time after the translation, another witness heard from a Lyons citizen who "truly" knew that the tongue was no longer in the Franciscans' convent, "but he knew where it was." When asked to reveal the secret, the reply was that the tongue was in the hands of the mother of a certain Francis Bucleti, doctor of laws of Lyons, but—the informant added—for a long time he hadn't seen it in her

89. *AASS*, July III, 826.

90. Vauchez, *Sainthood*, 343–47, for mendicant sanctity.

91. *Per unum ex fratribus dicti ordinis sublata et furata est.*

possession. There, at least as far as the Lyons process was concerned, the trail ends. We'll examine the fate of Bonaventure's other relics below. For now, it's clear that publicity surrounding the translation and lifelike tongue had the desired effect: miraculous cures occurred at the tomb in the new church, where pilgrims left wax votives, crutches, and other offerings. Before leaving this topic, it should be noted that evidently the motif of the "living tongue" was hardly peculiar to Franciscans: some time after the burial of Bohemian priest John of Nepomuk, murdered in 1393, his preserved tongue was said to have been found among his entombed bones. He was canonized in 1729.

After all fifty-four people had given evidence in early 1480, a record of their testimony was notarized, sealed, and sent to Rome.[92] Before the data could be reviewed by the cardinal-commissioners, Sixtus IV again—around May 20, 1480—reconstituted this committee, whose head, Ammanati, had died in September of 1479. The group now consisted of one survivor from the original or first committee, Giuliano della Rovere, named new leader of the triad; the reappointed papal grandnephew Raffaele Sansoni Riario from the second committee, with the well-known jurist Stefano Nardini, doctor of civil and canon law (JUD), as the new member.[93] Since as usual neither papal relative was keen to serve (the titular head of the group, Giuliano, "wasn't exactly the sort" to sit on boring committees) they authorized Nardini to act for them.[94] As it turned out, the pope sent Giuliano on embassy into France, where in August 1480 he and (future consistorial orator) Ottaviano de Martini spent a day praying at Bonaventure's tomb. Meanwhile the archbishop of Naples, Oliviero Carafa, stood in for Giuliano on the committee. In May 1480 Nardini and procurator fiscal da Gubbio received the Lyons dossier with its fifty-four depositions of January and February; three months later the Turks captured Otranto, once again diverting papal energies from Bonaventure's canonization. We lose sight of the process until April 1482, though most of its intervening stages can be conjecturally reconstructed.

92. For the following, Di Fonzo, "Il processo di canonizzazione," 255–57, correcting Marinangeli's introductory comments on various points.

93. Sixtus elevated Nardini, archbishop of Milan, in 1473; he died in 1484.

94. Sixtus recognized this delegation of authority on September 13, 1480, Di Fonzo, "Il processo," 257. Of Giuliano, Di Fonzo writes, "non era proprio il tipo da sedere in tribunale ad ascoltare e registrare atti," 256.

ENTERING THE FINAL PHASE

The next step would have been for Nardini and Carafa to pass on the Lyons dossier to the several *revisores,* such as auditor of the Rota Pavini, who examined and reordered the materials; this would then have been summarized by Nardini for discussion by the pope and cardinals in consistory.[95] Evidently Nardini's *Relatio* has not come to light, but, by analogy with later procedures, it would have set out Bonaventure's life, virtues, writings, and miracles. In addition, from December 1479 three scholars, at the cardinal-commissioners' request, were bolstering the case with theological and legal dissertations. Di Fonzo believes that this was something new in the saint-making process.[96] Giovanni Battista de'Giudici, a Dominican theologian already involved from 1478, examined Bonaventure's excellence of life, doctrine, and miracles.[97] Although de'Giudici exhibited certain antihumanistic characteristics, Di Fonzo claims that his and the others' tracts, for the first time in the history of canonization processes, were written in humanistic prose, products perhaps of what John D'Amico has identified as the golden age of Ciceronian humanism in Rome (c. 1475–c. 1520).[98] In de'Giudici's case, however, this judgment must be tempered since the tract reads much like countless other scholastic exercises, with division, subdivision, and sub-subdivision, as opinions are put forward only to be analyzed and refuted (*respondeo quod, sed contra,* etc.) one by one. Though Cicero is referred to a few times, most citations take us to the Bible, Augustine, Aquinas, Alexander of Hales, even Antoninus of Florence (one of our five saints), and several popes, theologians, and a few canonists. As an example of his style, here's his treatment of the miraculous:

> A miracle . . . is whatever is difficult or unusual, beyond the faculty of those admiring it. We admire however an effect the cause of which we are ignorant. We are ignorant of the cause since it is greatly removed from our senses. However, the most removed from our senses is nothing else than divine power (*divina virtute*).

95. For the following, ibid., 258–66.

96. Ibid., 276.

97. Giovanni Battista de'Giudici, *De canonizatione B. Bonaventure,* in two books in *Miscellanea,* ed. E. Baluze, 4:471–87 (Lucca, 1764); on this canonist see Wetzstein, *Heilige vor Gericht,* 313–16.

98. Di Fonzo, "Il processo," 259; John F. D'Amico, *Renaissance Humanism in Papal Rome* (Baltimore: Johns Hopkins University Press, 1983), passim; see also Alison Knowles Frazier, *Possible Lives: Authors and Saints in Renaissance Italy* (New York: Columbia University Press, 2005), for humanists as hagiographers.

Therefore it's necessary that the true reason for a miracle is its being done by divine power only; anything caused by an inferior power . . . is more properly called trickery, portent, monster or prodigy, or other similar things.

He then follows Aquinas in distinguishing the three levels of the miraculous and the three alternative categories of miracle: above (*supra*), against (*contra*), and beyond (*praeter*) nature, and so on. In the preface (he dedicated the work to Sixtus IV) de'Giudici admits that he's a theologian and no canonist, so he will analyze issues in the theologians' manner.[99] We're left in no doubt about that: when it comes to the traditional four elements required for a true miracle (done by God; *contra naturam;* not through power of words but merits of the doer; for corroboration of the faith), our theologian agrees with the first condition only, then questions the last three, concluding that "truly it should be held that judgment about miracles pertains more to the theologian than the canonist, and their opinions considered more certain and true."[100] Generally, however, de'Giudici's work is derivative, actually referring to Bonaventure in only a few places. One of these is particularly noteworthy, as it emphasizes Bonaventure's lack of miracles. Having earlier remarked that "everywhere these days multitudes of miracles are talked about, in most of which there is a suspicion of fraud," de'Giudici turns to Bonaventure's living and postmortem miracles. In two short paragraphs he notes the bit of Eucharist flying into the saint's mouth and the "living" tongue, nothing more since "the rest will be recited abundantly in the processes."[101]

A few days after submitting his tract to the pope and "other learned men," de'Giudici composed a second, shorter essay to answer objections from "dull individuals" who'd misunderstood what he'd written. They asserted that he'd silently suppressed some things pertaining to Bonaventure's canonization that should have been considered. His detractors, presumably anti-Bonaventurans, noted that eight candidates for sainthood had been proposed to Sixtus IV, evidence that "everyone these days wants to canonize someone in whom slight vestiges of sanctity appear." Although we'd expect de'Giudici to defend his earlier work, what we find is an almost inconsequential response, in four parts: whether the Church ought easily to move to a canonization, the quality of the candidates, whether baptized children

99. *Theologorum more,* De'Giudici, *De Canonizatione,* 471.
100. Ibid., 480.
101. Ibid., 474, 481.

should be canonized, and whether children killed by infidels out of hatred for Christ ought to be made saints. Presumably the last two points are linked to the fact that in 1477 de'Giudici had voted against canonizing Simon of Trent, the child killed in 1475, supposedly by the Jews.[102] In any case, his essay abruptly ends with our theologian commending himself to the pope.

The second scholar, Antonio da Vercelli (d. September 1483) was an Observant Franciscan theologian, a well-known preacher, and a friend of Sixtus as well as Lorenzo de'Medici. Vercelli's is a rather peculiar piece of work. Although its editor, Spätling, titles it "Essay for the Canonization of Holy Bonaventura," the incipit to Antonio's work is actually "Essay on Canonization or Certitude of Eternal Life," advertising itself as a study of how we can be certain that an individual has merited eternal life among the blessed. An examination of this long disquisition subdivided into twelve components reveals that it really doesn't concern Bonaventure. Spätling notes that it was commissioned by Stefano Nardini, the newest member of Bonaventure's cardinalate committee (appointed in November 1480). Nardini had heard or had learned about a sermon that Antonio had given "on the certainty of eternal election, or the canonization of the blessed to eternal life." Since the pope wanted scholarly input, Nardini asked Antonio for a written version of the sermon to use in Bonaventure's cause. However, in haste or indifference Vercelli merely tacked on a reference to the would-be saint at the end of the last six (but not the first six) major sections of the work; a slipshod performance, to say the least. The editor admits, "We wouldn't be truthful were we to call father Antonio's tract a work of profound theology; yet it would be wrong to call it unlearned." Nevertheless, it contributes nothing to our understanding of Bonaventure's case.[103]

PAVINI'S *RELATIO*

The charge of insubstantiality cannot be leveled at the last of our trio, canonist Pavini. His *Relatio* of 1482 sums up canonization procedures that had evolved over the previous two and one-half centuries. It became a template for other canonizations for the next two and one-half centuries; as the

102. Spätling, "Tractatus pro canonizatione divi Bonaventure," 48: 381–426, at 389 and n. 2.

103. Ibid., 397: "Veritatem non servaremus, si tractatum Fr. Antonii opus profundae scientiae theologicae diceremus; sed et nefas esset illud ineruditum vocare." The tract itself is split between two issues of *Archivum historicum Franciscanum*, vol. 48 and vol. 49, 166–90, containing sections six through twelve of the work.

Bollandists put it, Pavini's lucid exposition of Bonaventure's process applied to later saints as well.[104] Giovanni Francesco Pavini (Pavinus, d. May 26, 1485), doctor of theology and of canon and civil law, taught canon law before Paul II (1464–71) called him to the Roman Rota. One of the most respected and productive of papal judges, he also worked for the next two popes, Sixtus IV and Innocent VIII.[105] He was assigned by Sixtus to Bonaventure's case in December 1478; his *Relatio* drew upon depositions, previous canonizations processes, biblical sources, and Roman and canon law citations spanning the years from Innocent III's time (1198–1216) to his own. Pavini's expertise, and his privileged position as an auditor of the Rota who was also involved in other canonizations, turned his tract, as noted above, into a blueprint for later processes. The *Relatio* is in two parts, each subdivided into ten topics.[106] The first part deals with Bonaventure's life and works, the second with miracles.[107] Doubts about Bonaventure's miracles may lie behind this extended examination. The first article of the second section raises a fundamental issue: whether miracles are necessary in canonizations.[108] Pavini begins by defining miracles, distinguishing them from wonderful events that are not miraculous, namely, prodigies, related

104. Di Fonzo, "Il processo," 259–60 on Pavini; he was also involved in the processes of Catherine of Vadstena, d. 1381—not canonized—and Leopold of Austria, d. 1136, cd. 1485. Interestingly, in the matter of the Jews' alleged murder of the child Simon of Trent in 1475, whereas de'Giudici opposed Simon's canonization, Pavini tended to favor it; cf. also Wetzstein, *Heilige vor Gericht,* 299–313.

105. *Dictionnaire de Droit Canonique* (Paris, 1953), vol. 5, cols. 899–901: "Francois de Pavini," canonist and Italian theologian, born in the first third of fifteenth century; by 1448, a canon at Padua, where he taught canon law for several years. He left many writings. One, especially praised, was his *Relatio circa canonizatione Bonaventure,* addressed to Sixtus IV. He also wrote *Oratio . . . S. Leopold Marchionis,* pronounced in 1484 in public consistory in Rome, before Innocent VIII and Emperor Frederick III. Another work was an *Oratio* to Sixtus IV (1483), *De expedienda canonisatione.* His *Defensorium canonisationis* (Hain, 12532, 12535, 12536), reappeared as *Defensorium canonisationis sanctorum* (Barcelona, 1618). His name is associated with a gloss on *Extravagantes* and commentary on *Regulae Cancellariae.* He also produced *Decisiones* of the Rota, Rome, 1472, 1475; Pavia 1485.

106. The printed ed. (S. Bonaventura, *Opera,* vol. 7, Rome, 1596) has been used in conjunction with a manuscript of the *Relatio* in ASV *Congr. Riti, processus 4216,* fols. 115r–172r; *Relationes* for Raymund of Peñafort and Francis of Paolo are also included in the same trial document.

107. ASV, *Congr. Riti, processus 4216,* fols. 148r–172r; the list of topics on fols. 115v–116r. An excellent study of fifteenth-century processes and their miracles is Thomas Wetzstein's "*Virtus morum et virtus signorum?* Zur Bedeutung der Mirakel in den Kanonisationsprozessen des 15. Jahrhunderts," in *Mirkel im Mittelalter: Konzeption, Erscheinungsformen, Deutungen,* ed. Martin Heinzelmann et al., Beiträge zur Hagiographie 3 (Stuttgart: Franz Steiner Verlag, 2002), 351–76.

108. ASV, *Congr. Riti, processus 4216,* fols. 148r–152r; Dddd 2, recto, in 1596 ed. The unpaginated section following page 844 of the 1596 ed. is titled "Acta Canonizationis S. Bonaventure" of 1482 by Ottaviano de Martinis, consistorial advocate; it includes much of Pavini's *Relatio* verbatim.

to the heavens; portents, to the earth; unnatural or monstrous things, referring to the present; and omens, to the future.[109] He then refers to the four conditions of Geoffrey of Trani's *Summa* that we encountered in the last chapter.[110] Geoffrey's scheme thus reappears two hundred years later in Pavini's *Relatio.* Indeed, most of Pavini's work is derivative, but useful to later canonists because he discussed the issues with great clarity. He continues: using herbs for apparently miraculous effects would not satisfy the four conditions, whereas old women of no virtue might seem to perform miracles and predict the future because God can grant these abilities to anyone. Diabolical tricks can also appear to be miracles, worked through incantations and signs. By such means some pretend to cure the sick and even raise the dead and compel them to eat. Furthermore, the power of fervent prayer or the imagination can cause things to seem what they are not. The main reason why miracles are necessary in canonizations, however, is that without them we can't know whether the candidate led a truly virtuous life. Pavini claims that Bonaventure's miracles were especially remarkable because they took place when heresies were not a problem, as they were in the era of saints Dominic and Francis. Evidently Pavini has in mind the assumption, forcefully stated in various canonization bulls, that whenever heresies arose, God provided saints and miracles to counteract them.[111] Ironically, the sixteenth century would abound in Protestant "heresies," and yet this was precisely when canonizations came to a sixty-five-year halt—as some historians claim, because of the Reformation itself.

Pavini then deals with the frequency, diversity, and continuation of miracles.[112] Although he often cites Johannes Andreae approvingly, here he dis-

109. Pavini's citations include Augustine, Justinian's *Code,* Aquinas, Hostiensis, and the "Archdeacon" (Guido de Baysio, c. 1250–1313).

110. Kleinberg, "Proving Sanctity," 201. Kleinberg notes that the power of words refers to the miracle of the Mass; it is worked by the sacred formula regardless of the celebrant's merit; see ch. 1, above, for discussion of this point.

111. E.g., the 1594 canonization bull of Saint Hyacinth of Poland, where at the end of the first paragraph and again toward the end of the document Clement VIII claims that the new saint will overcome great heresies and enlighten blind heretics; in G. Fontanini, *Codex constitutionum quas summi pontifices ediderunt in solemni canonizatione sanctorum a Johanne XV ad Benedictum XIII* (Rome: Ex typ. Rev. Cam. Apostolicae, 1729), 248–59, at 248 and 259. Vauchez refers to similar comments in thirteenth-century bulls, specifically mentioning Francis and Dominic along with two others in *Sainthood,* 112 and n. 13.

112. ASV, *Congr. Riti, processus 4216,* fols. 152r–153v. Printed version has *adversitatis* for *diversitatis.*

agrees, finding no reason to stress frequency of miracles as a criterion. Article three balances in-life versus postmortem miracles: are both required; are both equally significant?[113] After referring to part of a consecrated Host *miraculose* leaping into Bonaventure's mouth, Pavini glides over Bonaventure's lack of *in vita* wonders and decides that they were less important than his postmortem miracles. In the canonizations of Homobonus (1199), Wulfstan (1203), and Osmund (1456), only posthumous miracles, Pavini claims, were significant. The examination of witnesses is dealt with in the next article.[114] Pavini claims that they should be examined only by papally appointed commissioners, not their deputies. However, he acknowledges that other canonists claim that commissioners can delegate.[115] Pavini then turns to procedures for interrogation and proof, reviewing guidelines established long before his day. Canonical and civil procedure (the *ordo iudiciarius*), already complex and technical, became increasingly sophisticated during the thirteenth century.[116] Several manuals on testimony and proof were available; for canonizations, Pavini often refers to Augustinus de Ancona's (d. 1328).[117] In claiming that Innocent VI's directions for examining witnesses (1358), didn't differ from other common forms used in civil or criminal cases, Pavini emphatically acknowledges the absorption of saint-making procedures into the legal structures of Roman law.[118] Turning to another issue, Pavini sets aside the opinion of Vincent (of Spain, d. 1248), who claimed that miracles should be attested by the same witnesses throughout,

113. Ibid., fols. 153v–154v; Dddd 2v–Dddd 3r in 1596 ed.

114. Ibid., fols. 155r–159r; Dddd 3r–3v.

115. *Dict. de Droit Canonique,* vol. 2, cols. 976–80: "Boatinus," Bovetino de Bovettini, Boetinus or Boventinus, an Italian canonist of the second half of the thirteenth century, from Mantua, was also known as Mantuanus.

116. James A. Brundage, *Medieval Canon Law* (London: Longman, 1995), 129.

117. Augustinus de Ancona's (d. 1328), *De Modo Canonizationis Sanctorum:* in Augustini Triumphi Anconitani Catholici Doctoris *Summa de Potestate Ecclesiastica* (1320; Rome: Ex typ. Geo. Ferrarii, 1582), 104–5 (Question 16, article 1). Augustinus, also Aug. "Trionfo" was born in Ancona in 1243, and died at Naples April 2, 1328. His *Summa* on ecclesiastical power (dedicated, appropriately, to John XXII), composed in the 1320s, went through several editions, e.g., Augsburg 1473, Venice 1487, Rome 1582. The 1582 edition used here consists of 563 pages plus indexes of about 50 pages, covering 112 *quaestiones.* See Wetzstein, *Heilige vor Gericht,* 277, where Augustinus's work on canonizations is characterized as "extremely creative."

118. "Non discrepat ab aliis communibus formis examinum aliarum causarum civilium, vel criminalium"; Augustinus of Ancona stated that canonization processes began with repeated *denunciatio* to the pope, followed by *inquisitio, Triumphi,* 104–7, Q. 16, a.1, "Utrum papam in canonizatione debeat ordinem iudiciarium servare."

rather than the usual two or three witnesses for individual miracles. Pavini rejected this, for otherwise, he claimed, the same group of witnesses must perpetually accompany the saintly person (or be constantly present at the shrine, presumably), noting his or her miracles. This would encourage collusion, Pavini explained, and exclude the poor from ever becoming saints, since (an acute comment on the sociology of sainthood) they couldn't be expected to attract constant followers.[119] "I reflected this opinion in my vote," he writes, against the Jews of Trent who martyred the infant Simon.[120] Next, Pavini denies that miracles must be instantaneous.[121] After a brief discussion of this topic, he concludes somewhat peremptorily that it would be impious to denigrate Bonaventure's posthumous miracles. He then moves to the question whether supernatural healings accompanied by pain could be considered miraculous.[122] He asserts not only that it is reasonable that they could, but they can occur with some natural assistance (though he earlier questioned the use of herbs); sinners can experience them; there may be some delay in effecting them; one saint can perform a miracle that another cannot; and a miraculously cured person might relapse. It suffices that good health resulted, even temporarily. Pavini rounds off this article by remarking that even critics of miracles may be blessed with cures.

The longest, seventh article covers canonization procedure and ceremonies.[123] Pavini's contemporary Troilus Malvetius published a similar exposition, both following a list of twelve steps outlined during the fourteenth century by Johannes Andreae and Augustinus de Ancona; these in

119. The poor, in fact, did not supply many saints until much later in the Church's history. Of course, being "poor" was a variable concept, as the destructive Franciscan battles show.

120. This manifestation (one of many during the Middle Ages) of the charge of "ritual murder" brought against the Jews was related to the death of the child Simon of Trent in 1475, just seven years before Pavini wrote this *Relatio.* Troilus Malvetius, a contemporary of Pavini, when discussing indirect proofs of miracles, noted that he himself witnessed the skin of Simon of Trent secrete very clear oil. Malvetius's "On the Canonization of Saints," in *Tractatus* XIV, fol. 101v–102r, section 3, #53.

121. ASV, *Congr. Riti, processus 4216,* fols. 159r–160r; Dddd 3v in 1596 ed. Pavini cites the Bible and canonists, particularly Martin of Lodi (Martinus Caratti de Laude/Martinus Laudensis, fl. 1438–45) in his *allegationes* in Bernardino of Siena's canonization of 1450, though the contrary seems supported in Acts, Luke, Matthew, John, and Ambrose.

122. ASV, *Congr. Riti, processus 4216,* fols. 160v–161v; Dddd 3v in 1596 ed. The title would be better translated "about things that do not seem to be miracles," as is clear from the content of art. 6. References include biblical passages, saints' lives, canonists, Gregory's *Dialogues,* and Vincent of Beauvais (*Spec. Hist.* book 21).

123. ASV, *Congr. Riti, processus 4216,* fols. 161v–166v; Dddd 4r–4v in 1596 ed.

turn looked back to the thirteenth-century work of Hostiensis, mentioned in chapter 1. Pavini concludes with a reference to the canonization of England's Saint Osmund in 1456, only about a generation before he composed this *Relatio* on Bonaventure. All our five cases would follow these procedures—in theory. Article eight pertains to Bonaventure's process per se: Pavini notes that Franciscan chronicles can be accepted in evidence even though anonymous.[124] In his next article he denies the possibility that anyone could be canonized erroneously, since the pope cannot err, guided as he is by the weight of Church tradition and doctrine on the one hand and the Holy Spirit on the other.[125] The pope's guardian angel helps out in these matters, and the archangel Michael assists as well.[126] The final, tenth, article raises the question whether opponents of a canonization should be heard.[127] For Pavini, because it doesn't proceed against anyone in particular, or to anyone's prejudice, a canonization isn't strictly speaking a judicial act—for there are no contending parties—and litigants aren't summoned extrajudicially.[128] Pavini admits that a judge might want to hear what someone has to say, for his own information. This, he notes, is what the cardinals investigating the canonization of Charles of Blois (d. 1364) concluded in 1371–72.[129] As for those who might oppose a canonization, although it might be expedient to hear them, they aren't to be admitted as litigants or parties, but solely as extrajudicial sources of information. On the other hand, if anyone takes exception to a proposed saint not out of positive zeal for the Church and the faith, but rather from hatred of the dead person or members of the dead person's class or kin, then he is to be totally rejected, unheard. Pavini concludes his *Relatio* by claiming that the pope should proceed to Bonaven-

124. Ibid., fols. 166v–167v; Dddd 4v in 1596 ed., referring to a main source of information on Bonaventure.

125. Ibid., fols. 167v–169r; Dddd 4v–next fol., which has no sig/gathering designations. Pavini cites, inter alia, Johannes Andreae and, particularly, Augustinus de Ancona, questions 14 and 17; as usual, he includes citations referred to by these canonists as well.

126. *Papa habet Angelum personalem.*

127. ASV, *Congr. Riti, processus 4216,* fols. 169v–172r, at which point the *Relatio* ends.

128. "Non fore necesse vocare illos quorum interest . . . quai talis actus non potest dici iudicialis. . . . Nec est negotium illud iudiciale." He cites the example of a pope who inquires about the suitability of a candidate seeking nomination to a cathedral office; he doesn't summon anyone, or hear anyone, except by grace, because the business is extrajudicial.

129. On Charles of Blois, see Andre Vauchez, "Canonisation et politique au xive siècle. Documents inédits des Archives du Vatican relatifs au procès de canonisation de Charles de Blois, duc de Bretagne (†1364)," 381–404, esp. 393–404.

ture's canonization, with a duplex feast day (the highest liturgical level), as is the case with the Four Doctors of the Church. He suggests further liturgical options, citing canonization bulls for saints Bridget (cd. 1391), Bernardino of Siena, Osmund, and Catherine of Siena (cd. 1461). With pious reflections on the value of saints and the danger of denigrating their merits, Pavini closes with a "Thanks be to God."

About the time that Pavini was completing his work, yet another external conflict was brewing that must have diverted papal and curial thoughts, slowing the canonization's progress yet again. From March 1482 the Dominican Andreas Zamometič was threatening to revive the Council of Basel. Sixtus had to counteract this potential threat, which took up the rest of the year and involved Emperor Friedrich III. (The details of this conflict and papal-imperial relations will be considered in the next chapter, because they directly affected Leopold's sainthood.) In an interesting conjunction of ideas, immediately following his description of Bonaventure's canonization ceremony the chronicler Glassberger launched into a tirade against Zamometič and his "impious, false, sacrilegious, blasphemous, horrid and detestable words" against Sixtus and God himself; the word "insane" appears four times.[130]

CANONIZATION ACHIEVED

According to Patrizi Piccolomini and Pavini, a cause was to be discussed first in a secret, and then in a public consistory. The case for Bonaventure's sainthood having been bolstered by the works of de'Giudici, Vercelli, and Pavini, on April 10 and 12, 1482, consistorial advocate Ottaviano de Martinis da Sinuessani read a summation in two consistories. At the first, Giacomo da Volterra reported that there was so much chatter in the room that hardly anyone understood Ottaviano's presentation, although it was greatly commended by those who could hear it.[131] During the second, larger public consistory attended by cardinals and other prelates, auditors of the Rota, proctors general, abbots, and the like, more attention was paid to de Martinis's eloquence. Di Fonzo rather naively remarks that it's odd that the bab-

130. Glassberger, *Chronica,* 482; cf. Pastor, *History of the Popes,* 4:358–61.

131. Ludovico A. Muratori, *Rerum Italicarum Scriptores,* vol. 22, part 3: *Il Diario Romano di Jacopo Gherardi da Volterra,* ed. Enrico Carusi (Città di Castello, 1905), 95–96: "propter strepitum frequentissimi senatus audir ivix potuit."

ble level among the smaller group of cardinals was greater than in the larger assembly.[132] Piccolomini noted that a "lengthy oration" on the candidate's life, deeds, and miracles was to be declaimed in a public consistory.[133] Perhaps Ottaviano's speech in the secret consistory was generally ignored as a mere formality subsequently to be repeated. As for content, Ottaviano reviews Bonaventure's life, dilating on the problems facing the minister general: he managed to reform some of the friars through "warning, insisting, chastising, and actively laboring" toward that end. Ottaviano takes aim at the "extremely pernicious" book against the Franciscans by Master Gerard of Abbeville (mentioned above), eloquently and subtly refuted by Bonaventure in his *Apologia pauperum*. Not long afterward, the advocate claims, Gerard—by God's judgment—died paralyzed and leprous.[134] After Bonaventure's life and virtues, death and burial, a recounting of miracles ensues, including the leaping eucharistic particle along with a few other in-life wonders; but the vast majority were posthumous (arranged by type), taking up more than a third of the oration, including the names of those cured, their particular ailments, the mode of cure, and votives at the tomb. Ottaviano refers to Bonaventure's translation, when it was found that although part of the body had decayed, the head remained, with its hair, lips, teeth, and tongue. Since he dates this to 1434, this translation, not that of 1455, may have been the first. The advocate ends by naming those who had sent in supplications. With a rhetorical finale he asks why His Holiness defers matters; why the delay? Along the way, he manages to slip in references to Ulysses, Homer, and of course Cicero.

At the conclusion of the April 12 consistory the assembled prelates were asked to give their opinions; most of them—or the greater part, *pars maior*—agreed to Bonaventure's sainthood. However, Giacomo da Volterra notes, some agreed only on condition that the merits and miracles related by Ottaviano "were true." Glassberger notes that, further suggesting that the candidate was not wholly acceptable to everyone in the assembly, a decision was reached only, it seems, after a certain amount of disagreement.[135] The pope set the canonization date for just two days later, an unusually

132. Di Fonzo, "Il processo," 263 n. 90: "Alquanto strano . . ."

133. Piccolomini's *Ceremonial* (ed. Dykmans), 118–19.

134. *AASS*, July III, the *Oratio* on 824–30, and Wadding, *Annales*, 329–41; Di Fonzo, "Il processo," 262, for various editions of the oration.

135. *Post aliqualem discrepantiam*, Wadding, *Annales*, 341.

short period when compared with other processes (Antonino of Florence will be an exception). This strongly suggests that Sixtus had already made his decision prior to the consistories of April 10 and 12.

According to Master of Ceremonies Patrizi Piccolomini, a platform was to be built in the basilica, with altars and chairs placed on it in hierarchical order. The stage was to be decorated with herbs, flowers, and images of the new saint. About eighty torches were to burn throughout the church during the event; he specifies the weight of candles given to each participant, varying with ecclesiastical status.[136] After the processional entry and seating of pope, cardinals, and prelates, from the stage the pontiff delivers a short sermon referring in general to the life and miracles of the holy one, ending with an exhortation to pray that the Church not err in deciding on sainthood. After further prayers the proctor of the cause asks that the blessed one (*beatum N.*) be ascribed to the catalog of saints. At this point, writes Piccolomini, the pontiff used to pronounce a protestation, which "we found" had been used by many popes. However, he continues, some very eminent men say that this was introduced because of a particular reason that's now irrelevant. It's thought that at some (earlier) time a pope was forced to canonize someone, so he protested. Now, however, although this protestation doesn't seem fitting, Piccolomini says, he gives us its wording: "We publicly protest before all of you here present that by this act of canonization we do not intend to do anything that is contrary to the faith or to the Catholic Church or the honor of God." This protestation is not in the early fourteenth-century ceremonial of Giacomo Stefaneschi (d. 1341), but is found in Peter Ameil's (d. 1404) for Bridget of Sweden's canonization in 1391.[137] It seems that Sixtus pronounced it, in any event. The proctor fiscal asks notaries and others to record the papal protestation; the saint's proctor in turn asks the same as to the solemn pronunciation of the canonization, also requesting the pope to issue appropriate bulls. The pope scribes the holy one to the catalog of saints, intones a *Te Deum* followed by prayers for the new saint and the announcement of indulgences. Referring to Bridget's ceremony, Piccolomini has the pope or a cardinal leading the first com-

136. Piccolomini's *Ceremonial*, 120–24.

137. *Le Cérémonial Papal de la fin du moyen âge à la renaissance*, vol. 2: *De Rome en Avignon ou Le cérémonial de Jacques Stefaneschi*, ed. Marc Dykmans (Rome: Institut Historique Belge de Rome, 1981), 458–65; cf. also vol. 4: *La retour à Rome ou le cérémonial du patriarche Pierre Ameil* (Rome: Institut Historique Belge de Rome, 1985), 236–37.

memorative Mass for the new saint. The offerings are presented to the pope during the chanting of the *Credo:* first, the cardinal bishop brings two large candles, and with him the first orator offers his candle along with two turtle-doves in a gilded cage; the cardinal priest carries two large loaves, with napkins, while the second orator bears one candle and a silver cage containing two white doves. Finally the cardinal deacon offers two flasks of wine, the third orator, his candle, and a multicolored cage enclosing various birds.[138] The cardinals kiss the pontiff's knee, the others his foot, and then the Mass continues to its conclusion and recessional.

To what extent did Bonaventure's canonization reflect the master of ceremony's guidelines? The ceremony took place in St. Peter's, still under reconstruction, on April 14, 1482. Giacomo da Volterra claimed that the stage, a man's height, was surrounded by crowds drawn to the spectacle, "eager to see something novel" on the religious scene. It had been more than twenty years since the last such ceremony (Catherine of Siena, in 1461), so this was indeed a novelty for many.[139] Ambassadors, proctors, cardinals, and other prelates entered in solemn procession, carrying candles of appropriate weight; and at last the pope, seated on stage, opened the theatrical proceedings. During the ceremony, after preliminaries the Franciscans' proctor general de Rodulfi stood up and, in his and other suppliants' names, asked Sixtus to canonize Bonaventure *instanter, instantius et instantissime,* a phrase that Di Fonzo considers an innovation.[140] Finally, the pope ascribed Bonaventure to the catalog of saints among the Confessors, Bishops, and Doctors, with appropriate liturgy and indulgences, and urged the clergy to publicize this new saint. The remaining ritual acts occurred in due order.

On April 20, 1482, the pontiff informed the order generally of the canonization, once again describing himself as a fellow-Franciscan, an admirer of Bonaventure's writings; he also emphasized the roles played by "our neph-

138. See chap. 1; *canistellum diversorum colorum cum variis aviculis,* Piccolomini's *Cérémonial,* 124.

139. At Catherine's canonization, her home-city staged a magnificent celebration, with poems, song, music, and very likely the hoisting of an effigy of the saint from a stage up to "heaven" on top of the Cappella Pubblica as had been done for another city-saint, Bernardino, in 1450. Hidden rings, ropes, and pulleys were the usual mechanisms behind such spectacles, common also in Rome: Andrea Campbell, "A Spectacular Celebration of the Assumption in Siena," *Renaissance Quarterly* 58 (2005), 435–63, at 443, 445; and cf. Barbara Walsh, "Keys to Success: Propriety and Promotion of Miraculous Images by Roman Confraternities" in *The Miraculous Image in the Late Middle Ages and Renaissance,* ed. Erik Thunø and Gerhard Wolf, Analecta romana instituti danici, supplementum 35 (Rome: "L'Erma" di Bretschneider, 2004), 161–84, at 174.

140. Di Fonzo, "Il processo," 276.

ew" (Giuliano della Rovere) the order's protector, and its minister general Francis Sansone, who "for many years zealously pursued" the case for his canonization.[141] In October 1482, the pope granted an indulgence for those helping to build a chapel to the new saint in the Franciscan church of his home town, Bagnoregio.[142] The canonization bull notes that Bonaventure's life, writings, and miracles deserved praise in themselves, although—unlike in many other such bulls—there are no references to specific miracles, nor to the details of the ceremony. In addition to lauding the saint's merits, the document acknowledges that several powerful interests had lobbied on his behalf.[143] Given the stormy relations between Sixtus and Louis XI, one might not expect to see his name among the supporters, but in fact it is there, perhaps out of diplomatic tact and because from 1480 Louis seemed willing to participate in the pope's anti-Turkish crusade. On the other hand, although Ferrante of Naples is listed among the suppliants, ironically, his forces were attacking the papal states around mid-April 1482—just about the time Bonaventure was being canonized.[144] As was the normal procedure in canonization bulls, His Holiness authorized notarized copies of the bull, commanding that anyone contravening or questioning it (the usual *si quis* clause) would incur the indignation of God and the Apostles Peter and Paul.[145] No doubt the heavenly powers were moved to high indignation when Bonaventure's shrine was desecrated by Huguenots in 1561 or 1562. His head, having been hidden, escaped destruction (it vanished for good during the French Revolution).

Bonaventure's case illustrates several points that recur in the following chapters, for example, that procedures "on the ground," so to speak, didn't always follow contemporary canonists' programs. In addition, although historians used to think that testimony was a guide to the inner thoughts of participants, we now understand that depositions are no more foolproof than any other historical source, are just as manipulable and potential-

141. *Bull Franc.*, #1564, 802: "Qui plurimis annis causam huius canonizationis summo studio prosecuti sunt."

142. *Bull Franc.*, #1650, 838.

143. Papal bull in Fontanini, *Codex constitutionum*, 189–94, in *AASS*, III July, 830–33, and Wadding, *Annales*, 341–46.

144. Pastor, *History of the Popes*, 4:352–55. As early as April 2, 1482, the pope was beefing up his border defenses, and as late as April 18 he warned Ferrante to take his troops out of Roman territory.

145. For further discussion of the bull, see Krafft, *Papsturkunde*, 988–93.

ly misleading. Even the seemingly logical arrangement of interrogatories, on the surface an indicator of inquisitors' intentions, reflects only some of what occurred during depositions. We learn from Bonaventure's case, too, that a canonization could involve conflict, even a great deal of it, as well as consensus. While an order would normally back its candidate with financial and diplomatic resources, factionalism within the Franciscans clearly hindered Bonaventure's cause. Sometimes controversy centered on the candidate himself, his life, teachings, or miracles. Part of Bonaventure's problem, linked to the factiousness of his order, lay in his attempts to end Observant-Conventual disputes that were, in the end, ineffectual. A great spiritual writer he may have been, acknowledged in the canonization bull and by his subsequent elevation as a Doctor of the Church (1588); but he was unable successfully to resolve this internal squabbling, and his journey to sainthood suffered for it: the elevation of the Franciscan Bernardino of Siena took six years, but Bonaventure's more than two centuries. As we've seen, another difficulty was his lack of miracle working while alive, though there were plenty of wondrous examples reported after his death (though not in the bull). Pavini's raising and attempting to smooth over the issue, and the conditional approval of his canonization even at the final consistory—"if his miracles were true," suggests that some cardinals were uneasy about this.

That a canonization occurred at all depended in the first place on the existence of a cult, a tomb-become-shrine and pilgrimage to that holy place. The inconspicuousness of such a cult in Bonaventure's case was balanced by patronage at the highest levels, including kings and emperors. However, in the end it's unlikely that Bonaventure would have succeeded without the encouragement of the Franciscan pope, Sixtus IV, and the presence of the papal nephew Giuliano as a (somewhat disengaged) member of the committee. However, if it was hoped that his canonization would be useful in calming disputes within the order, this did not happen. Our next saint will face other difficulties, of a more political (papal-imperial) nature, as he slowly climbs to a place among the heavenly host.

CHAPTER 3

The Good Duke

Leopold of Austria (c. 1073–1136, cd. 1485)

"You know," the pope grumbled, "that in canonizing saints, requests should be made frequently; [but] since the emperor disdains writing to us, we scorn to please him." Leopold's canonization commissioners continued to plead. Sixtus IV replied that unless Friedrich III responded to him, "neither in this nor in any other cause do we wish to satisfy him."[1] Canonizations—as well as "other causes"—could hinge on such stubbornness at the top of the hierarchy, in this case because of a political-ecclesiastical fight over an anti-papal refugee living in an imperial city. The intertwined links of sainthood and dynastic politics grew even tighter after Leopold became a saint. The first sight to strike visitors walking toward the shrine of Saint Leopold around 1500 would have been a gigantic triptych some twenty-four feet wide and twelve high, painted between 1489 and 1492 by at least three artists. It depicted the Babenberg family tree, of which Leopold was a component. Just in case the pilgrims missed the point—that the current emper-

1. Vinzenz Oskar Ludwig, "Der Kanonisationsprozess des Markgrafen Leopold III des Heiligen," in *Jahrbuch der Stiftes Klosterneuburg* 9 (1919): 111, document #CXXV, n.d., n.p. (hereafter referred to as Ludwig), a report from Rome by proctor Thomas List: "dnus. imperator dedignatur nobis scribere et nos dedignamur sibi complacere. . . . Quod nisi imperator eciam sibi scriberet, neque in hac neque in aliqua alia causa sibi complacere vellet." Ludwig's study is quite comprehensive, with extensive introduction and 151 documents. Citation is not exactly straightforward, because Ludwig's introductory text is paginated in capitalized Roman numerals, whereas his collection of documents is paginated in the usual way with Arabic numbers, but each document is given a capitalized Roman numeral. Ludwig is a main source for this chapter. Wetzstein, *Heilige vor Gericht,* lists manuscripts and printed editions about Leopold, 525–26.

or, the Habsburg Maximilian, was related to the Babenbergs and thus to the saint—eight magnificently illuminated parchment leaves hanging nearby explained the genealogical artwork. There was more to admire in the painting: apart from the individuals portrayed in their roundels, Austrian topography was laid out before the pilgrims' eyes, the states and towns of the archduchy, the domains over which Saint Leopold (and Maximilian) spread their protective mantles. The huge triptych was itself almost a holy thing, radiating assurance that Austria had powerful patrons in this world and the next; Austria becomes sanctified. It's not surprising that when Maximilian arrived for the saint's translation in 1509, first he led a "history seminar" in which his dynastic credentials were discussed and chronicles and old documents were passed around. Then, when the moment came for the unveiling of the holy bones, Maximilian found yet another way to emphasize his links with the saint (below).[2] Yet he came to the game late, reaping the benefits of others' work. The impetus, the stamina, came not from Maximilian or his insouciant father Friedrich III, but from the Klosterneuburg canons, their prior, and a proctor in Rome whose efforts can only be described as heroic. We'll have ample opportunity to follow him back and forth to the Eternal City.

The bones being washed before their relocation in a silver reliquary in 1509 belonged to a man who in 1095 became margrave at age twenty-two in what, for convenience, we'll call Austria. He found himself in the midst of political and ecclesiastical storms, raised to a great extent by an ambitious emperor Heinrich IV (d. 1106), whose battles with pope Gregory VII have found a niche in history textbooks under the rubric "Investiture Controversy." That Leopold wasn't blown away probably was due more to a reluctance to choose sides than to his political skills. A nighttime withdrawal from a confrontation between Heinrich and his son, a rejection of the imperial crown when it was offered because—Leopold claimed—of "old age" (fifty-two) and the demands of a large family, have led some historians to characterize this member of the Babenberg line as rather disengaged from the political issues of the day. On the other hand, he founded religious houses and sired among his brood of eighteen children (apart from Heinrich and Leopold, who succeeded him in power) the historian Otto of Freising and

2. Floridus Röhrig, *Leopold III. der Heilige: Markgraf von Österreich* (Vienna: Herold Verlag, 1985), 137–39; cf. BAV *Vat. lat. 4023, 4024.*

Conrad who became bishop of Passau and then archbishop of Salzburg. Leopold's dedication to his own *patria* is beyond question (the first known document definitely referring to the margravate as "Austria" was Leopold's charter for Heiligenkreuz monastery, 1136).[3] His most famous foundation was Klosterneuburg, about eight miles from the center of Vienna. Originally established as a college of secular Augustinian canons, in 1133 it changed to regular canons and was placed under papal protection. When acknowledging this, Innocent II called Leopold a "son of saint Peter."[4] The (probably) illiterate margrave came to be considered Austria's founder—the first person to take the title "duke" was his son Heinrich.[5] Leopold died, perhaps in a hunting accident, on November 15, 1136, having lived through the reigns of five popes, two anti-popes, and three emperors.[6] He was buried at Klosterneuburg. By the 1170s a Klosterneuburg chronicler memorialized him as the "pious," godly margrave.

No documentation has come to light suggesting a Leopold cult during the next century, when the direct male Babenberg line died out, eventually replaced in the Austrian duchy by the Habsburgs. However, by the fourteenth century the margrave's tomb was becoming a holy site. There were prayer requests, candles, and a new altar at the tomb, as well as indications of relics and pilgrimage. An Avignon indulgence of September 15, 1326, referred to "many miracles" at the site. Albrecht, Habsburg duke of Austria, was among the pilgrims. On November 15, 1339, he gave thanks at the grave for the birth of a son. Albrecht was related to the Babenberg line—and thus to Leopold—through his mother; tradition has it that he applied to Innocent VI for Leopold's canonization in 1355. However, the first documented moves in this direction were made by his son Rudolph IV (1358–65), considered a second founder of Austria's greatness and its first archduke.[7] In 1358 at his urging Innocent VI established a commission to investigate

3. Alexander Leeper, *A History of Medieval Austria* (Oxford: Oxford University Press, 1941), 231.

4. Karl Lechner, *Die Babenberger: Markgrafen und Herzoge von Österreich 976–1246* (Vienna: Hermann Böhlaus, 1976), 129.

5. Heide Dienst, "Werden und Entwicklung der babenbergischen Mark" in *Österreich im Hochmittelalter (907 bis 1246)*, ed. Anna M. Drabek, 94 (Vienna: Verlag der Österreichen Akad. der Wissenschaften, 1991). The margrave "konnte hochwarscheinlich weder lesen noch schreiben."

6. On January 8, 1137, Innocent II, writing to Leopold's wife Agnes, granted him absolution by apostolic authority, normally accorded people of Leopold's class who had died suddenly, without last rites.

7. Röhrig, *Leopold III. der Heilige*, 131–34.

Leopold's possible sainthood. It is not known whether the commission ever met; in any case with Rudolph's death in 1365 the canonization was shelved. On a popular level, however, interest in the cult seems to have continued throughout the fourteenth century: there were further bequests for candles at the grave, iconic pictures of the margrave and his wife, a biography, and pilgrims reporting miracles and donating votives.[8] The activities that finally culminated in the canonization on January 6, 1485, began some twenty years earlier, during the 1460s. Why did it take so long—even longer than Bonaventure, over three hundred years after Leopold died—and why, more generally, was he canonized at all?

To start with the first issue, by the later fifteenth century Leopold's partisans explained his delayed canonization with some justification by referring to dynastic strife within Austria, Hungarian and Hussite conflicts, Turks, recurring plague, difficulties of travel, and especially, Pavini claimed, the painful schism of the church.[9] In short, many issues affected relations linking eastern Europe and the papacy between the 1350s, when an attempt to canonize came to nothing, and the 1460s, when the process revived and finally succeeded. No doubt there were additional reasons for the hiatus.

A frightful aspect of contemporary life, as reexamined by each new generation of medieval historians, was the plague. From mid-fourteenth-century central Asian–Mediterranean beginnings, the Black Death had spread throughout the rest of Europe within a few decades. It wasn't just the first major attack of 1347–48 that struck fear into Europeans of whatever status; it was, as Petrarch wrote, the fact that it never was really over—it kept returning, perhaps just as people were beginning to hope that it was gone for good. The plague affected European and Italian life through the later medieval and early modern periods, continuing to force popes, cardinals, prelates, and curialists out of Rome (and other cities) "on account of the contagion." Naturally, this disrupted curial proceedings of all kinds, not just canonization causes. Church leadership also was affected by self-inflicted wounds as well as natural disasters. We saw that apart from the controversy within his order, Bonaventure's delayed canonization could be blamed on the schism with its dual papacy, and the subsequent confusion of three popes; in addi-

8. Ibid., 135–37.

9. Pavini, *Summarium* of Leopold's cause (1483) in Hieronymous Pez, *Scriptores rerum austriacarum veteres ac genuini*, 3 vols. (Leipzig: J. F. Gleditschii, 1721–45), 1:col. 604.

tion, various conciliar movements challenged papal authority even into the sixteenth century. Although councils themselves might take up canonization causes (as at Constance), nevertheless from the 1370s it became more difficult to pursue established procedures until a single pope was settled once again in the Eternal City, surrounded and bolstered by a curial routine and officials. The schism disrupted more than just papal officialdom; it caused many, Petrarch included, to criticize the papal machinery, even the papacy itself, the source of validation and approval of would-be saints.

Perhaps the most pressing problem for eastern Europe was the advance of the Ottoman Turks from Anatolia through the Balkans until only Hungary stood between the Muslims and Friedrich's empire; and Austria was at the eastern edge of that loosely governed empire. The aggressive Turks had moved into the Balkans as early as the 1360s. After the fall of Constantinople in 1453 Mehmet II (1451–81) sent his army into Bosnia, Herzegovina, and Albania during the 1460s; by the 1470s Turks were raiding southern Austria. During this period Venice and Genoa saw their overseas possessions fall to Turkish forces, while even mainland Italy was not safe: launching themselves across the Adriatic from Albanian bases, the Turks captured the port of Otranto in 1480, causing panic throughout Italy and especially Rome. Only Mehmet's death in 1481 and subsequent Ottoman withdrawal from the port ended the threat and, for now, this phase of Ottoman westward expansion. Though no one knew it at the time, Europe was to be relatively free from Turkish incursions for another forty years. Nevertheless, it's obvious that from the 1350s to the 1460s Europe and Italy became increasingly, and justifiably, anxious about eastern-front security. The papal mantra evoking a crusade against the infidel became more insistent after 1453, though European, but less so Italian, powers tended to ignore the call except for Hungary on the front lines. Undeterred by Pius II's fruitless efforts, Paul II (1464–71) attempted a general pacification of the Italian states for the sake of common defense; Sixtus IV (1471–84) almost immediately responded to the Turkish threat. In consistory just three weeks after his election he discussed a possible congress of European leaders who would coordinate efforts against the common enemy, but the idea died in squabbles over where this grand conference should be held.[10] In the back-

10. Pastor, *History of the Popes*, 4:180–81, 217–21.

ground to these ineffectual moves, the presence of the Turk, sometimes ally, usually enemy, constituted a major element in later fourteenth- and all of fifteenth- and sixteenth-century European life. Everyone from popes to peasants felt the anxiety, to a greater or lesser degree; and this included cardinals and curial officials trying to go about their business—such as making saints. Apart from Turks, curial anxieties were stirred by the highly unstable conditions in eastern Europe. Papal crusades against the Hussites led to invasions of Bohemia by imperial forces in the 1420s, and in the 1430s to Hussite counterattacks into Saxony, Bavaria, and other imperial territories. During the 1460s Hungarian king Matthias Corvinus (d. 1490) took up the crusading cause. The Hussites successfully resisted under their "king" George Podiebrady (1457–71). Paul II (1464–71) claimed that Podiebrady's "pestiferous venom that spread gradually, as a cancer, was to be cured by the antidote of apostolic authority."[11] Declaring him a deposed heretic, he called for a crusade.[12] Obviously Bohemia was a source of military, religious, and political confusion, which demanded curial attention. Hungary, an independent kingdom, shared a common border with the empire, and on occasion emperors claimed to be kings of Hungary, though their rule seldom was effective. Hungarians, not emperors, were more effective against Turkish advances. Friedrich III, Hungary's western neighbor, had not offered much assistance to Corvinus, perhaps reluctant to help a potential enemy whom the pope lauded as Europe's "bulwark." Having stabilized relations with the Turks, Corvinus, in fact, did turn against his weaker neighbors. In the 1470s and in 1480 he attacked Austria (Sixtus's attempts to patch up a peace between king and emperor to create a united front against the Ottoman "perfidious dogs" who took Otranto in 1480 were, as usual, ineffectual).[13] The king took Vienna in 1485 and the imperial residence at Wiener Neustadt by 1487. He will play an interesting role in Leopold's canonization, which he supported financially. This may seem paradoxical since Leopold's cause was theoretically to the advantage, as well as being the responsibility, of Corvinus's enemy Friedrich III.

11. Adolf Bachmann, ed., *Briefe und Akten,* in *Fontes Rerum Austriacarum,* zweite Abtheilung: *Diplomataria et Acta,* 44 Band (Vienna, 1885), 593 (February 10, 1465): *venena pestifera.*

12. Bachmann, *Diplomataria et Acta,* 42 Band (Vienna, 1879), 418–20, 489–90, *arma sumere.*

13. Bachmann, *Diplomataria et Acta,* 46 Band (Vienna, 1892), 444–67, *perfidissimi canes;* Karl Nehring, *Matthias Corvinus, Kaiser Friedrich III, und das Reich* (Munich: Oldenbourg Verlag, 1975), 132–33, noting Sixtus's first impulse to flee to Avignon because of the Otranto outrage.

Leopold's canonization process began in earnest, and ended successfully, during the reign of an archduke of Austria who reluctantly accepted election as king of the Romans in 1440 and became the last emperor to be crowned in Rome (March 1452).[14] Throughout most of his long reign Friedrich III (1415–93) faced numerous enemies, as noted above. He preferred to avoid hostilities through negotiation or inaction (rather like Leopold). In addition to external conflicts (Hungary, Bohemia, the Turks), he had to contend with disunity within his sprawling empire, as well as among his own turbulent Austrian subjects. After returning from his Roman coronation, the emperor devoted much of his time (until around 1471) to his south Austrian homeland, Styria. Partially as a result of his Austrocentrism and concomitant neglect of broader imperial issues, Friedrich's reign was punctuated by occasional attempts to dethrone him. Friedrich managed to survive and somehow, as archduke, king, and emperor, to live through the reigns of eight popes, the fourth of whom, Aeneas Piccolomini, later Pius II, served at his court (until 1455). Generally, imperial-papal relations were proper and cooperative. With the 1448 Concordat of Vienna Nicholas V gave Friedrich control over the selection of bishops in Austria, though reserving many traditional papal prerogatives.

THE PROCESS BEGINS

In 1465 in the midst of these political, dynastic, military, religious, and ethnic confrontations, the final push for Leopold's cause began. The mainly French and Italian stages on which Bonaventure's story played out had episodes of high drama and violence, Fraticelli in flames and the Pazzi assassination plot, for example. Leopold's story shifts the violence and drama to a central- and east-European stage, with a heretical movement and frontier warfare involving Ottoman armies, as well as battles within and among the region's Christian powers. As for "why now?" specifically, the spark seems to have been struck during a regional diet at Korneuburg at the end of 1465, where a relatively small assembly of prelates, nobility, clergy, and citizens met to complain about the emperor, whose representatives were present.[15]

14. For an overview of Friedrich-historiography, see Paul-Joachim Heinig, ed., *Kaiser Friedrich III. (1440–1493) in seiner Zeit* (Cologne: Böhlau Verlag, 1993), 7–22. On the Roman coronation, Pez, *Scriptores rerum austriacarum veteres ac genuini*, vol. 2: cols. 561–623.

15. Ludwig's suggestion of a trip to Rome in 1449 by Klosterneuburg prior Simon Heindel (d. 1465) seeking a restart of the process is dismissed by Röhrig, *Ludwig III. der Heilige*, 146.

Such querulous gatherings were nothing new. In the course of this meeting, however, John Hechtl (1465–85), the new prior of Klosterneuburg, Leopold's foundation and burial place, brought up the possibility of canonizing the long-dead margrave, thereby taking the first significant steps toward securing his sainthood. His Augustinian convent was only a few miles from Korneuburg; presumably Prior Hechtl was eager to enlarge his spiritual authority on entering his new station in life. There's little specific information about his activities at the diet, but Röhrig is convinced that it's safe to assume that, along with bishop of Passau, Ulrich von Nussdorf (d. 1479—Klosterneuburg lay within his diocese), he pushed assembly members to petition the pope to canonize the margrave. Any gathering of ecclesiastical and secular notables presented an opportunity for saint-lobbyists, who circulated amongst the members touting their candidates and soliciting supplication letters. For instance, in the late thirteenth century Richard Swinfield, bishop of Hereford, collected several letters on behalf of his predecessor Thomas Cantilupe (d. 1282, cd. 1320), whose canonization he personally desired, while attending parliaments and church councils, and in 1589 the publicist for the Polish Hyacinth (d. 1257, cd. 1594) came away from an important diet at Warsaw with a bundle of letters to take to Rome, including one from the king of Poland and another personally signed by Queen Anna.[16] Prior Hechtl, then, was doing nothing unusual in drumming up support at Korneuburg in 1465; what was unusual was his initiative and his aggressive approach, which worked.

Letters were obtained dated December 2, 10, and 12.[17] The delegates have learned, states the letter of the 10th—very likely composed by Hechtl—that the emperor has begun to urge His Holiness to canonize Leopold, pious margrave of Austria, noted for his merits and many continuing miracles.[18] Leopold would free Austria from the calamities it has suffered for many years, and still suffers. It's clear that Hechtl had brought to the diet a copy of Innocent's letter of 1358 (see above) setting up a local committee on Leopold's life and miracles. This earlier letter would have been read to or by members of the diet to emphasize the legitimacy of the cause and stimulate their interest

16. R. Finucane, *Miracles and Pilgrims: Popular Beliefs in Medieval England* (London: Dent, 1977), 175, and "Saint-Making at the End of the Sixteenth Century": 233–35.

17. The letter-date of Dec. 2 is a scribal error (presumably for Dec. 12), Ludwig, LVIII.

18. This reference to Friedrich's interest could be mere rhetoric: Röhrig, *Ludwig III. der Heilige*, 146–47, though Ludwig, LVII, has his doubts on this point.

and cooperation. Several lines of Innocent's 1358 mandate are repeated more or less verbatim, followed by a claim that the delegates at Korneuburg had "seen and read" it; in this way they were able to satisfy themselves that they weren't actually doing anything novel, merely continuing a cause already in motion. (The same modus operandi was followed in 1589 at Warsaw, when a sealed letter of 1539, brought along by Hyacinth's promoter, helped to recruit new supporters.) The Korneuburg letter concluded by asking the pope to nominate *commissarios novos* so that Leopold might be added to the catalog of saints. Several regular and secular clergy signed or sealed the supplication. Evidently Hechtl composed another letter for secular delegates, with similar wording: the supplication of December 12 is attested by about forty laymen described as city leaders, judges, consuls, and citizens of Vienna, Krems, and several other places.[19] During the diet, in a speech the bishop of Passau backed up Hechtl's efforts by drawing attention to (Bamberg) margrave Leopold's genealogical relationship to the current (Habsburg) emperor. He formally urged the assembly to petition the Holy Father to raise Leopold as a new heavenly knight, bringing Austria freedom, good fortune, and happiness.[20] As a result of these efforts, several supplications were sent to Paul II. Bishop Ulrich's own letter of January 20, 1466 (repeated in substance by Empress Leonora's of February 3), was followed by a much longer one of February 1 from Friedrich III, including many stock phrases copied from the 1358 and the December 1465 supplications. Friedrich emphasized his familial ties to Leopold, his "right by descent." The emperor sends his secretary William Forchtenauer to ask His Holiness to complete what Innocent VI had begun; Friedrich ends by calling for Leopold's sainthood to the glory of God, the honor of his saints, the augmentation of divine worship, and the dignity of Austria.[21] Although it's possible that Friedrich was interested in Leopold's canonization prior to the Korneuburg gathering of 1465, the evidence is in-

19. Ludwig, doc. IV, 5–7.

20. "[D]urch denn newn himelritter frid, glück und seligkait geben"; Bachmann, *Diplomataria et Acta*, 44, the diet on 597–606; Leopold on 605–6.

21. Ludwig, LVII–LVIII, and docs. 7–9; Bernd Rill, *Friedrich III: Habsburgs europaïscher Durchbruch* (Graz, Austria: Verlag Styria, 1987), 124, suggests that a popular patron was needed for Austria, since the available saints (Severinus, Florian, Maximilian) weren't politically useful, "nicht politisch verwendet werden." For these saints, see Pez, *Scriptores rerum austriacarum*, 1:cols. 22–93. Friedrich also followed Rudolph by confirming (in 1453) Rudolf's forgeries that asserted the duchy's special place in the empire, an attempt by Rudolph (and Friedrich) to make up for Austria's exclusion from the elite circle of the Seven Electors.

direct.[22] In any event, his undoubted involvement in the campaign materialized only after the diet, years after he had been crowned emperor in Rome.

Responding to the imperial wishes, Paul II set up a three-cardinal commission in a secret consistory of March 26, 1466. The seals of the suppliants, including the emperor and empress as well as Ulrich of Passau, were officially authenticated for the cardinals by Forchtenauer and others on 16–17 April. The committee included John Bessarion (d. 1472), Alan bishop of Palestrina (d. 1474), and Francesco Piccolomini (d. 1503).[23] Bessarion, famous Greek scholar and patron of Rome's humanists, was a highly respected member of the college. In 1449 he worked on the cause of Bernardino of Siena (canonized in 1450) and in 1459 introduced the case for Catherine of Siena (made a saint in 1461). In November 1464 Paul had appointed him to head a three-cardinal committee to come up with anti-Turkish strategies and administer a war chest.[24] Eventually (by 1468) Bessarion had become one of Paul's closest advisers. Another member of Leopold's committee, Piccolomini, was equally useful to the pope. He encouraged strong measures against Bohemia, which led to Podiebrady's deposition in a consistory of December 1466. Piccolomini, who knew German, was among the cardinals who greeted emperor Friedrich III on his visit to Rome at Christmas in 1468, and later (in 1471) was sent to the Diet of Ratisbon where he achieved nothing of substance in his anti-Turkish campaign, even though the memory of his uncle Pius II, once Friedrich's adviser, was "still warmly cherished" at the imperial court.[25]

On April 21 the committee sent a mandate to Austria appointing a five-man subcommittee to investigate Leopold's life, morals, merits, and miracles.[26] The five included the bishops of Passau (Ulrich v. Nussdorf), Gurk (Ulrich v. Hinenburg), and Piben-Petena (Michael Altkind), and the abbots

22. Ludwig, LVII. Friedrich probably would have mentioned his earlier involvement in this letter, had that been the case.

23. Bessarion, created cardinal by Eugenius IV in 1439, protector of Franciscans and Dominicans, became an extremely useful legate and patriarch of Constantinople; Alan de Coëtivy, raised to the purple in 1448, was also known as the "cardinal of Avignon"; Francisco Todeschini-Piccolomini became a cardinal thanks to his uncle Pope Pius II in 1460, and came to be called the "cardinal of Siena."

24. Pastor, *History of the Popes,* 4:83. They had plenty to do: after learning of Turkish naval preparations in May of 1465, Bessarion's committee disbursed some 60,000 ducats to Corvinus of Hungary, followed by further sums to him in April of 1466.

25. Pastor, *History of the Popes,* 4:180–81; Piccolomini was among the "pious and earnest men" of the curia (414).

26. Ludwig, doc. XI, 11–15 and 94–97.

of Vienna's Schottenstift and Klein-Mariazell.[27] The cardinals noted that since the truth would be more clearly obtained there (in Austria) than in Rome, and since pressing business at the curia prevented their personal involvement, they delegated to them their powers to investigate, with public notaries recording what was discovered. The mandate carefully set out the proper mode of interrogation: deponents were to swear as to the year, month, and day of the miracle; in whose presence; where and when and at whose invocation and in what words; the names of those among whom the miracles are said to have occurred; whether they knew the cured persons; how many days they'd seen them ill; how long they were ill; after the miracle how long they were well; and other appropriate questions. Instructed by your notarized report, the cardinals concluded, we will make our *relatio* before the pope.[28]

After this promising opening, however, little was done for more than two years. There was a visit to Germany by papal legate Lorenzo Roverella to stir up a crusade against Podiebrady. Stopping at the Klosterneuburg convent on November 7, 1467, he produced another copy of papal letters authorizing the local inquisition.[29] One cause of inactivity was the need to replace the two abbots, who had died, and the noninvolvement of the bishops—apparently, again, because of urgent business at the imperial court (Nussdorf of Passau was also the imperial chancellor). Eventually, a year later (November 1, 1468), Friedrich sent six proctors to remind Nussdorf of the cardinals' orders.[30] On December 2, 1468, Ulrich wrote to his clergy.[31] He commanded them to invite (during divine services or by publication at parish church doors) anyone from any order, rank, or grade who knew anything of Leopold's life and miracles to inform the subcommittee of what they knew, and whether they or others received health, strength of limbs, "or other graces" by invoking him. They were to testify, the letter concludes, beginning on the 22nd at Klosterneuburg. Given that the cause had languished for more

27. Röhrig, *Ludwig III. der Heilige*, 147.

28. The cardinals ordered their subdelegation, sealed or notarized, to be published by their notaries or secretaries. It was dated at Rome on April 21 (1466) in the presence of Ambrose Sleipeckh, John custode *scolastico Tridentino*, and Rudolph Vriese, Doctor, canons, specially called as witnesses. On interrogatories cf. Wetzstein, 337–53.

29. Ludwig, LXV–LXVI; in the spring of 1468 Roverella returned to Germany on the same mission, armed with indulgences: Pastor, *History of the Popes*, 4:144.

30. Ludwig, doc. XII, 14–15, and LXIV–LXV: the proctors were John [Hechtl], prior of Klosterneuburg; Wolfgang Forchtenauer; Friedrich de Castrobarko; John Rehwein, JUD; Thomas de Cilia, DD; and Kilianus Hören, with powers of substitution.

31. "Das erste Einschreiten bei den Subdelegierten"; Ludwig, LXVI–LXVIII.

than two years, this seems excessively speedy, from Friedrich's reminder of November 1 to the bishop's order of December 2 to the hearings of December 22–29, 1468; even so, some 127 witnesses testified.

Before looking at the testimony, once again we face that troublesome question, "why now?" Why did Ulrich delay more than two years after the committee ordered him to open the process? It's likely that he was preoccupied, as imperial chancellor, with Ottoman, Bohemian, and Hungarian issues, as well as internal Austrian and "German" quarrels. In addition, the usual bureaucratic inertia and Friedrich's apparent lack of enthusiasm also hindered Leopold's cause. Now, however, in December of 1468, there is a great rush to implement the cardinals' April 1466 mandate as quickly as possible. This is because, even as witnesses were being interviewed in Klosterneuburg, Emperor Friedrich, with an entourage of five hundred to seven hundred men, was approaching the gates of Rome. This pilgrimage, begun in November 1468, thus coincided with Friedrich's reviving Leopold's cause.[32] Friedrich entered the Porta del Popolo on Christmas Eve. Before emperor and pope parted on January 9, 1469, they had discussed many issues: the war with the Turks, the Hussite heretics, the Hungarian succession, and Leopold's canonization.[33] All of this suggests that during final preparations for the journey, which would have been planned months in advance, it came to imperial attention that a mandate from Rome—issued moreover at the emperor's own request—had been ignored for over two years. Hence Friedrich's naming of six proctors, followed by Ulrich's peremptory command to his clergy to start collecting witnesses. Even as the imperial caravan was trundling down through Italy, the clergy of Passau diocese were scurrying about attempting to implement what turned out to be the first significant act in Leopold's process.[34] "We can't go wrong," Ludwig suggests, in supposing that Friedrich's pilgrimage brought on the acceleration of Leopold's cause.[35] It's tempting to wonder about Leopold's future as a saint if Friedrich had stayed home.

32. The delayed pilgrimage had been vowed while the emperor was besieged in Vienna in 1462.

33. Pastor, *History of the Popes,* 4:160–69.

34. Ludwig, LXIX: "die erste Hauptverhandlung."

35. Ludwig, LXXIX: "Wir werden auch nicht fehlgehen, wenn wir annehmen, dass seine Romfahrt auch auf die in Österreich geführten Verhandlungen fördernd und befruchtend gewirkt hat."

HEARINGS AT THE TOMB

While the emperor was en route to Rome, the local (*in partibus*) inquisition, or trial, began at Klosterneuburg.[36] The three subdelegated bishops were absent as usual, presumably looking after "serious business" elsewhere—this would later be seen as a defect in procedure—so the two abbots, Matthew and John, presided. They were assisted by three notaries, two canonists from the Passau bishop's curia and Vienna's St. Stephen's cathedral, and two more St. Stephen's canons, both theologians. The witnesses were questioned from December 22 to 29. Starting things off at 9:00 AM on the 22nd, prior Hechtl prayed for divine guidance, someone preached in German, and Friedrich's proctors read out the cardinals' commissions. After this the witnesses swore on the Bible to tell the truth uninfluenced by others, unmoved by feelings of love, anger, hatred, and the like, the usual *ius commune* line found in various kinds of litigation: *prece, pretio, favore, amore, ira, odio, rancore.* They were interrogated about Leopold's life, mores, and merits (by necessity, all hearsay) and his miracles: how the witness knew of them, the year month and day they happened, who was present, and so on, as set out in the cardinals' mandate. Ludwig provides the names of 127 witnesses, from which we see that forty-two or 33% were male, and eighty-five or 67% female; of the women, twenty-one (25%) were widows. Nearly half of all the witnesses (49%) were from Klosterneuburg itself. There do not seem to have been any ecclesiastics, secular or regular, among the witnesses. This configuration, compared with lists of pilgrims at shrines and canonization witnesses in other medieval processes, is the norm for local, relatively low-level cults (in spite of occasional visits by the likes of Duke Albrecht). A typical deposition was provided by the first witness, the knight Johannes Stiklperger, about forty-eight, who stated that around March 25, 1466, his son Achacius suffered an "internal tumor" that the doctors couldn't cure. In his anxiety he vowed to take his son, along with a wax image (of the child, presumably) to blessed Leopold's tomb, praying for intercession. This done, Achacius at once awoke as if from a bad dream. He began to improve and by next day was quite well.[37]

36. For the following, see Ludwig, LXIX–LXXVIII; Pavini (*Summarium*, Pez, *Scriptores*, 1:col. 607) mentions 182 witnesses; in Pez, cols. 611 and 625–27, Pavini provides many details of the interrogations and inspection of the tomb, etc., repeated and summed up by Ludwig.

37. Ludwig, LXXI n. 1.

In addition to questioning witnesses, typically a subcommittee identified and examined the grave, along with any associated objects. Consequently, the investigators made an inventory of the suspended wax votives, candles, tablets (describing and depicting early miracles), crutches, and other offerings at Leopold's tomb. The tomb itself, in the chapel of blessed bishop Nicholas, was of stone incorporating red marble, with openings through which pilgrims could touch the margrave's sarcophagus, an arrangement shown in Canterbury's Becket windows, and in Osmund's purported tomb at Salisbury (reaching into such tombs could have unexpected results, as in the 1555 case of a woman whose hand was firmly grasped by the dead occupant).[38] The presence of candle-holders fixed to an iron lattice surrounding Leopold's grave, and an altar at the tomb's foot with five lamps burning day and night, indicates a well-established local cult. At the chapel entrance, to enhance their mood, visitors encountered a large parchment with a long prayer in fine lettering—"Oh, pious and benevolent margrave Leopold, inextinguishable light of Christianity, Oh prudent dispenser of heavenly treasures, Oh, father of orphans,... Look today upon my devotion and prayer.... I invoke you to help me, you who have aided the blind, the mute, the cripple"—and so on.[39] In addition to inspecting the tomb, the committee registered books, documents, letters, and other pertinent objects—including some of the margrave's personal possessions and liturgical vestments incorporating some of his clothing. After another stretch of inactivity, on May 7, 1469, at the insistence of the Klosterneuburg canons additional witnesses were called in by the two abbots who had overseen the earlier hearings. On May 24 and 25, twelve women and fourteen men were interrogated in the presence of imperial proctors Forchtenauer and Horner, notaries, and others.[40] This was followed by another slowdown until February of 1470. Without commenting on the lapse of more than half a year since the hearing of May 1469 or the reason the collected materials had not yet been sent to the Holy See, the Klosterneuburg register sets out another citation of witnesses dated February 14, 1470. The promoters may have hoped to make a better

38. Diego of Alcala, canonized in 1588; *MS Vat. Lat. 3517,* fol. 39v: *sensit... manum fuisse apprehensam,* which naturally evoked a screaming fit in the lady and a tug-of-war with the invisible Diego.

39. Ludwig, LXXVII–LXVIII, and Pavini in Pez, *Scriptores,* 1:cols. 625–26. As noted at the beginning of this chapter, by c. 1509 the additional visuals surrounding the tomb would have had an even greater impact on pilgrims.

40. Ludwig, LXXX–LXXXI, and doc. XIV, 16–17.

impression at the curia with testimony from people of higher social standing than the earlier batches of witnesses.[41] This seems to have worked: several *nobiles* showed up in Vienna to provide further testimony.[42] Subsequently, at a Vienna diet on the 26th, a supplication letter to Paul II was generated; about a dozen of the "upper class" who had testified a week or so earlier were also signatories to this letter.[43] Once again, a political gathering became an occasion for garnering support for a canonization. In the usual fashion the supplication claimed that a sainted Leopold would rescue Austria from the "savage treachery" of the Bohemians and other enemies, and so on, echoing the Korneuburg diet document of five years earlier.[44]

Within a week of the February 26 supplication another petition materialized, which, in Ludwig's understatement, "merits our particular attention." Written in Vienna, it came from Hungary's king and Friedrich's nemesis, Matthias Corvinus; his appearance in Friedrich's territory was unexpected, and his sudden, quick return to Hungary even more mysterious. Yet, amidst political discussions with the emperor, Corvinus found time to write to the pope (March 2, 1470) promoting Leopold.[45] This invites two questions: how did the letter come about in the first place, and what were Corvinus's motives in supporting an Austrian would-be saint? As to the first point, Corvinus was asked by Klosterneuburg's indefatigable Prior Hechtl to compose such a letter. The prior expressed the hope that the preliminary processes were drawing to a long-delayed end: it seemed time to send imperial and princely letters and the process (or processes) to Rome. This brings up the second question, motive. Perhaps Corvinus believed that it would make a good impression on Paul II, presenting himself as a true son of the Church who was prepared to support anyone who merited canonization, thus strengthening the universal faith, and ready too to battle her enemies, such as the Bohemian heretics. The king writes that while at Vienna he had been asked "by the peoples of the region" to commend Leopold's cause, which he now does. Finally, Corvinus ends with a provocative comment: "It [Leo-

41. Ludwig, LXXXI: "Vielleicht haben wir darin den einzigen Grund der Verzögerung zu erblicken, dass der Kaiser eine aktiv und recht wirksame Beteiligung des Adels wünschte."

42. Ludwig, LXXXII–LXXXIII.

43. Ludwig, doc. XV, 17–18.

44. One can identify, among the forty individuals of the first document of 1465 and thirty-three in the second of 1470, the names of fifteen men who had subscribed to both supplications.

45. For the following, Ludwig, LXXXV–LXXXVI, and docs. XVI, 18–19, CXI, 103.

pold's canonization] wouldn't be any less pleasing to me than if it should happen that one of Hungary's kings were inscribed among the saints." Röhrig sees Corvinus's purported interest in an Austrian saint in a more sinister light, as setting the stage for his planned conquest of Austrian territory.[46]

Matthias's letter was followed by yet more supplications, on March 11 and 12, 1470, from the "barons and nobles of Bohemia and Moravia," as well as the prelates and clergy of Passau diocese, gathered at the Vienna diet, and from the emperor himself. Friedrich noted that during his trip to Rome, Bishop Ulrich had been preoccupied with imperial business back home, and therefore couldn't take charge of Leopold's hearings.[47] At last, more than four years after the first supplications and some fifteen months after the first *inquisitio,* on March 18, 1470, a letter was drawn up to accompany the canonization dossier destined for Rome.[48] Probably at Bishop Ulrich's direction, the cover letter ruefully admitted that, on account of the burden of other matters, "some of us" were unable to attend all the hearings (Ulrich never did); perhaps some deficiencies had marred the cause. The writers asked the cardinals to convince His Holiness to overlook any faulty procedure and proceed to Leopold's canonization. Evidently Ulrich continued to fret about his poor performance, because two days later (March 20) he wrote in his name only to Paul II, excusing himself for nonappearance at the hearings, beginning and ending his letter with references to Turks and heretics.[49] His delinquency did, indeed, affect Leopold's cause. Meanwhile, supplications continued to be added to the bundle of documents: from Vienna university; the prior, dean, and chapter of Klosterneuburg; and the citizens of Klosterneuburg community.[50] On March 27 papal legate Bartolomeo Roverella, at imperial request, supplied a commendation for the couriers about to carry Leopold's process to Rome. On the 31st the emperor asked Bessarion to present the case to the college of cardinals, bringing it to the desired conclusion.[51] And off to Rome went the sealed, notarized, and lengthy dossier.

46. Röhrig, *Ludwig III. der Heilige,* 148.

47. Ludwig, LXXXVI–LXXXVII, and docs. XVII–XIX, 19–22.

48. Ludwig, doc. XXI, 23.

49. Ludwig, doc. XXII, 24; Ulrich includes an "interesting," as Ludwig puts it (LXXXVIII), reference to Innocent VI's being unable to proceed because of the negligence of delegated individuals.

50. Ludwig, docs. XXIII, XXIV, XXV, 25–27; again, all noting Turks and Bohemians.

51. Ludwig, docs. XXVI, 27, and XXVII and XXVIII, 27–29.

During the first three weeks of May 1470, Bessarion and his colleagues examined the package, identifying seals and formally inspecting the notarial record of the inquisition and batch of letters.[52] During the same month, however, because of the "intemperate air" of Rome, many cardinals began leaving, suspending consistories. As is still the Roman custom, many fled before the hot, muggy season arrived, an exodus that regularly retarded curial business. Apart from that, the pope's attention was diverted to an urgent matter, the Turks. Not surprisingly, many other issues—such as canonizations—tended to fade into the background. As noted above, even though Muslim authority extended over the Balkans during the later 1450s and '60s, the papal call to crusade was heeded only in Hungary. Certainly the emperor seemed dangerously unenthusiastic. Now, in June of 1470, in view of Mehmet II's great land and sea preparations for a westward attack, the pope called a consistory to discuss the issue. When news came of the brutal capture of Negropont (Euboea) on July 12, 1470, anxiety levels soared in Italy, particularly in Venice; the island had been a major moneymaker ever since the Fourth Crusade.[53] Pope Paul again attempted a general pacification of the Italian states for the sake of common defense, calling on his cardinals for advice. Eight of them, including Bessarion (on Leopold's committee), experienced in anti-Ottoman affairs, "postponing all other business," were to assemble every four days to discuss measures against the Turks, which they began to do in Bessarion's house on August 8, 1470.[54] Just a day before Bessarion's anti-Turk committee began their meetings, Paul II explained to Friedrich that the absence of some of the cardinals and others working on Leopold's case kept the pope from bringing his canonization to consistory.[55] Yet another of the cardinals on Leopold's committee, Piccolomini, was sent to a diet at Ratisbon (Regensburg) to discuss the Ottoman threat. Entering Ratisbon on May 1, the legate waited with all the other impatient members until Friedrich III's eventual appearance on

52. Ludwig, 97–98, from BAV, Vat. lat. 4023.

53. For the effect of Euboea's fall upon Italian public opinion see Margaret Meserve, "News from Negroponte: Politics, Popular Opinion, and Information Exchange in the First Decade of the Italian Press," *Renaissance Quarterly* 59, no. 2 (2006): 440–80, 446–54.

54. Pastor, *History of the Popes*, 4:174–76, 179; appendix, 497 (doc. 29, letter of 17 Jan. 1471)—Cardinal Gonzaga to his father, summing up the anti-Muslim commission's work of the previous year.

55. Ludwig, doc. XXXI, 30–31.

June 16. It soon became evident that little would be accomplished at the diet.[56] Amidst these disappointments Pope Paul II died on July 26, 1471. He had not established a unified front against the Turks; no pope ever did.

That didn't stop his successor, Sixtus IV, from trying, nor for their part did Leopold's lobbyists give up. Sixtus was elected on August 9, 1471, and within two weeks (on August 20) one of Friedrich's proctors was assuring Hechtl that he'd do all he could to resubmit the process to the new pope.[57] In December Sixtus sent five cardinals to various European leaders to stir up enthusiasm against the Turks. One of the five was Marco Barbo (d. 1491).[58] Under orders from the new pope, he left for Germany in late February 1472. In the midst of his dealing with his major charge, the Turks, Barbo received a papal brief of March 2, ordering a new inquisition into Leopold's case (in which he was to become deeply involved), since the earlier process was marred by "great negligence and deficiencies." As noted earlier, from the later thirteenth century this claim about negligence was a standard papal comment when renewing a cause. In this case, however, given Ulrich of Passau's negligence, the accusation rings true.[59] Wetzstein suggests that Barbo's orders may have come to him in the new, streamlined format, the less formal papal brief.[60] The message, in whatever form, was a setback for the Klosterneuburg canons and their prior, who had pinned their hopes on the previously accumulated materials. When Pavini wrote his *Summarium* of the case several years later, he tried to soften Sixtus's critique of the first process by claiming that it was, after all, a mere "preparatory" or general inquiry; the second inquisition (of 1472) was, in effect, a special inquiry.[61] In any event, as Röhrig notes, whatever the pope took exception to was never made explicit.[62] Barbo issued citations at various places in Austria, call-

56. Pastor, *History of the Popes,* 4:180–81.

57. Ludwig, doc. XXII, 31 (August 20, 1471); the proctor, Friedrich de Castrobarko, had been appointed by the emperor on November 1, 1468: Ludwig, doc. XII, 14–15.

58. Barbo was a nephew of Paul II, who had made him cardinal in 1467, and who became one of his uncle's closest confidants—an ambassador described him as Paul's right eye. Pastor, *History of the Popes,* 4:121–22 and n.: "è lo ochio destro del papa . . ."—a common expression.

59. "Magna . . . intervenerit negligencia et defectus," Ludwig, doc. XXXIII, 31; Vauchez, *Sainthood,* 70. Ludwig, XCIV, suggests that the inactivity of the subdelegated Ulrich of Passau was indeed the problem—"ein Haar in der Suppe." Röhrig, *Ludwig III. der Heilige,* 148, agrees.

60. Wetzstein claims this to be "eine neue Urkundenform für unsere *commissiones,*" *Heilige vor Gericht,* 375. Briefs had been used for various purposes from at least 1400.

61. Pavini claimed that the original process "sufficiens tamen fuit ut generalis et praeparatoria, licet non ut specialis," so a second inquiry was opened, Pez, *Scriptores,* 1:cols. 608–9.

62. Röhrig, *Ludwig III der Heilige,* 148: "wird nicht ausdrücklich gesagt."

ing for anyone with knowledge of Leopold and his miracles to show up at Klosterneuburg in May. Some citations could not be served because of local disturbances, arising, no doubt, from Hungarian forays. The work went on through May and June of 1472, including a new inventory of the tomb, documents, and other pertinent materials.[63] As an example of one of the many ways canonization processes could be delayed, in May 1473 the pope (at Friedrich's request, he writes) ordered Barbo to look into a second canonization candidate, the eleventh-century Emma/Hemma von Gurk.[64] Fortunately for Barbo, he was given leave to send someone else to Gurk, over 130 miles southwest of Klosterneuburg, which presumably he did. (Emma's canonization took a little longer than Leopold's, happening only in 1938.) Returning to his main charge, Barbo took further testimony about Leopold during June of 1473, bringing the total to 199 witnesses. As usual, as in Bonaventure's case, each witness was interrogated according to a list of *Articuli.* The twenty-four articles included questions derived from Geoffrey di Trani's thirteenth-century definition of a miracle, the same source—as we saw in the last chapter—used in Pavini's *relatio* for Bonaventure.[65] The papal envoy's work was not always trouble-free: on one occasion (in November 1473), when Barbo walked into his Vienna headquarters, even before taking off his shoes he realized that Hechtl wasn't there and burst out, "O holy God, where is my prior of Klosterneuburg?" In reporting this to Hechtl, Thomas List (see below) tactfully writes, "I advise you that it would be good for you to present yourself to him quickly." On another occasion (in May 1474) Prior John told Barbo that the emperor had information about the canonization, but the emperor didn't know what he was talking about. Barbo subsequently had words with John.[66] Leaving Austria, perhaps with a sense of relief, on November 15 the cardinal presented a report on his German legation in a two-hour speech in consistory.[67]

63. Pavini, *Summarium* in Pez, *Scriptores,* 1:col. 610.

64. Ludwig, docs. CXXV, and XXXV, 32–3. Emma, foundress of the church where later Gurk cathedral was built, died in June 1045; her tomb lies under an eighteenth-century altar in the crypt. See Wetzstein, *Heilige vor Gericht,* 343–44, 357–62, etc., and documentary sources for this cult on 521–22.

65. Ludwig, doc. CX, 100–102; not all that surprising, since Pavini worked on both cases.

66. Ludwig, doc. XXXVI, 33, November 24, 1473, doc. XXXVII, 33–34, May 6, 1474.

67. *Il Carteggio fra il Card. Marco Barbo e Giovanni Lorenzi (1481–1490),* ed. Pio Paschini (Vatican City: Biblioteca Apostolica Vaticana, 1948), 7, 13.

THOMAS LIST IS SENT TO ROME

About this time Thomas List, dean of the Klosterneuburg house, began his journey to the Eternal City.[68] His letters to his prior, John Hechtl, give us invaluable insights into the world of an agent lobbying for a would-be saint. List was probably the most diligent (or at least long-suffering) servant of the cause for several years at Rome, amidst sometimes severe financial hardship. The Austin canons List represented, realizing that the emperor wasn't particularly enthusiastic, became more active in the canonization campaign. Their relations with Friedrich had never been very good, anyway, though he was one of their patrons.[69]

List arrived in Rome on December 21, 1474, in pouring rain. Next day (as he wrote on December 31) Barbo, who had returned from Austria two months earlier, set aside some time for him and his party. They were well received, the cardinal asking about List's *patria.* After the pleasantrics, the cardinal said, "Recently I've done many good things for Leopold's canonization. I presented the process to our Holy Father, who ordered the principal notary of the auditors [the Rota], John Philippi, to summarize it, because it was very long." After giving assurances that he would continue his efforts "diligently" once the summary had materialized, the cardinal provided List's group with a meal. He asked if there was anything else List wanted of him, and List replied, "Not at this time." Next day List gave Barbo the emperor's and Hechtl's letters of supplication, which the cardinal received enthusiastically, remarking that he hoped for a happy conclusion to the matter. "Yet," List continues, "he didn't read them," and List couldn't tell what he might have thought about them, because the cardinal took his household off to visit the four principal churches of Rome around Christmas, the start of the 1475 Jubilee. For the time being all that List could report to his prior and fellow-canons was that a notary was working on the process. As a postscript he added that he'd like his brethren of Klosterneuburg to pray for a happy outcome—prayers that the project would need. A few days later

68. Ludwig, doc. XLI, 35, letter of November 4, 1474, from Prior John sending List to Rome. On List and his family, much based on Ludwig but with archival additions, see Richard Perger, "Thomas List: Ein Wegbereiter der Heiligsprechung St. Leopolds," *Jahrbuch des Stiftes Klosterneuburg,* Neue Folge, 13 (1985): 7–20. List died on January 25 or 26, 1493, but his burial place is unknown, 17. Various *Jarhbuch* volumes deal with specific issues of Leopold's cult.

69. Röhrig, *Ludwig III. der Heilige,* 148–49.

(January 2, 1475) he reported that another papal canonization committee of three cardinals had been constituted, of whom one was the Barbo, who had carried out the *in partibus* hearings of 1472–73. It was unusual for a person who'd conducted a local, on-site hearing to deal with the same cause at the curia. Another cardinal on Leopold's committee had been there from the start, Piccolomini (the German-speaking cardinal at the 1471 Diet of Ratisbon, later Pius III); the third member was the very wealthy vice-chancellor, Rodrigo Borgia, who had an interesting future as Alexander VI.[70]

On February 1, 1475, List reported that the process had been summarized and was ready to be reproduced so that the three cardinals, the procurator fiscal, and others could have their own copies.[71] List learned from the master of ceremonies and the proctor fiscal that Leopold's ceremony in St. Peter's would cost "around three thousand ducats, more or less." He added that since Barbo asked daily about the prior and canons of Klosterneuburg, it would be well for the prior to inform Barbo about local news: how things are between the kings of Hungary and Poland, navigation on the Danube, and relations between Friedrich and the duke of Burgundy. List then provided news of his own: the king of Hungary's party, including 110 mounts, had arrived in Rome on January 16, 1475. The royal envoy's oration before the pope pledged the submission, fidelity, and obedience of the king of Hungary and Bohemia. Sixtus's response, writes List, was in the following "or similar" words: "As much as we acknowledge the obedience, submission, and fidelity of our dear son Matthias king of Hungary and Bohemia"—here, notes List, the pope spoke the word "Bohemia" with *quadam tussitacione,* a sort of cough—"so much the more do we love him, for Matthias is as a bulwark against the great, savage Turk." That diplomatic cough represents the pope's quandary: Sixtus knew that Friedrich supported Vladislav of Poland as Bohemian king, as against Matthias's claims; but by too enthusiastically supporting Matthias against the Turks, Sixtus risked damaging relations with the emperor.[72] Concluding his letter, List noted the arrival on 28 January of King Ferrante of Naples to whom the cardinals showed great honor. Some said that he was there for the Jubilee

70. Ludwig, doc. XLII, 35–36, doc. XLIII, 36 and CXXXVII. Borgia was created cardinal by his uncle Calixtus III in 1456.

71. Ludwig, doc. XLIII, doc. XLV, 37–8, and CXXXVII.

72. Ludwig, CXXXIX and n. 2.

(planned since at least 1472), but others conjectured otherwise; subsequent events suggested that he and the pope discussed politics during his short (three-day) stay in the city, including an anti-Ottoman league.[73]

List dined again with Barbo on February 21, 1475. When he brought up Leopold's canonization, the cardinal replied that he was involved in the Turkish matter and many other difficult issues. He suggested that the emperor, his barons, prelates, and cities should send more supplicatory letters to the pope, cardinals, and others of the curia. Moreover, Barbo advised, letters from Klosterneuburg should be authenticated by a notary, "since"—List wrote—"our seals are unknown at Rome," and thus the documents were given little or no credence. The cardinal sent one of his auditors, John de Luca, with List to discuss the case with procurator fiscal Anthony de Eugubio, suggesting that Eugubio should become a proctor in Leopold's cause with an honorarium of ten ducats. This was done (although proctors fiscal usually represented—as in Bonaventure's case—the "other side" in canonizations). Then, again on Barbo's advice, the three (List, Luca, Eugubio) took the "register of the process and its summary" to another member of the committee, vice-chancellor from 1457, Cardinal Borgia (Alexander VI, 1492–1503). At first Borgia begged off, deferring to Barbo, but after Eugubio objected that Barbo had already done what he could, Borgia accepted the documents. Day after day List asked how Borgia was getting on; but the reply always was that the vice-chancellor was diligently perusing the material. "Now," List wrote with a touch of impatience, "the vice-chancellor has been absent from Rome for fully five days, and my proctor and I cannot request anything of him or find out what's going on." Twenty days later, in his last letter from Rome on this stint, List was more candid about the future pope: "I can't report a lot because the vice-chancellor is very rich, doesn't trouble himself much as to spiritual matters, and attends to acquiring one bishopric after another; he's negligent and irksome." List also noted that according to Barbo, more should be done to emphasize Leopold's fame, rather than his miracles.[74]

Apart from a few supplications, between 1475 and about 1479 Leopold's cause was in limbo.[75] Ludwig's explanations for this hiatus include imperi-

73. Ludwig, doc. XLV, 381. Pastor, *History of the Popes,* 4:278–80.

74. List claims that Borgia "non curat multum spiritualia" and was "tediosus et negligens," Ludwig, doc. XLVI, 39–40; doc. XLVII), 40–41.

75. Though the pope continued to be reminded of it, e.g., in October 1476: Ludwig, doc. L, 43.

al struggles with Burgundy, Bohemia, and especially Hungary. Papal legate Alexander of Forli had occasion to warn Friedrich that his inconsistent behavior toward Corvinus was pleasing only to the Turks. On the other hand, disregarding temporary agreements, Hungarian troops flooded into Austria as far as Krems: Corvinus occupied large swathes of the duchy, including Klosterneuburg convent (housing Leopold's grave) and town. In fact, the town was the first place in Austria to receive a confirmation of its privileges from—in exchange for homage to—its occupier Corvinus (Vienna, after a long siege, was under Hungarian authority from 1485 until Corvinus's death in 1490).[76] In Rome an outbreak of plague following yet another Tiber inundation in 1475, papal conflicts with Italian city-states and the kingdom of Naples, battles between the Colonna and Orsini, the Pazzi conspiracy of 1478 and subsequent Medici-papal conflict, all contributed to the general confusion and tumult of the '70s; and, as noted above, the capture of Otranto by the Turks in 1480 only added to the widespread anxiety and heightened sense of insecurity. Barbo, other duties set aside once again, was sent on an inspection tour of papal sites on the Adriatic in September 1480. Just ten years earlier, as we've seen, another cardinal on Leopold's committee (Bessarion) also had to suspend other business to deal with Ottoman threats.[77] In such circumstances, canonizing saints would probably have attracted less attention among papal and curial priorities.[78]

Nevertheless, the cause began to revive in early 1479. Klosterneuburg convent had Austria's Franciscan provincial general, Heinrich Collis, encourage Friedrich to push Leopold's case. However, by April Collis had bad news for Klosterneuburg: the pope had begun a process for "a certain Bonaventura."[79] As noted in the previous chapter, the canonization bull listed the emperor as one of Bonaventure's suppliants; in short, he was supporting two candidates at the same time—three including Emma von Gurk, but presumably he would have exerted more effort (such as it was) for the Austrian. Since Collis—expecting Bonaventure's canonization around Pentecost (in 1479, May 30)—was heading for Rome, the convent entrusted

76. Ferdinand Opll and Richard Perger, *Kaiser Friedrich III. Und die Wiener 1483–1485* (Vienna: Franz Deuticke, 1993), 29, Reg. 22 (May 5, 1483): Klosterneuburg was "die erste Stadt im eroberten Österreich" gaining such a confirmation.

77. *Il Carteggio*, 9.

78. Ludwig, CXLVII–CLII.

79. Ludwig, docs. LI–LIV, 44–45.

the supplications to him.[80] As we know, Bonaventure wasn't canonized until 1482; his process was held up in much the same way as Leopold's, for similar reasons. In both cases, high expectations repeatedly met with disappointment. Throughout the period covered in this book most canonization lobbyists scurrying about Rome were unsuccessful for a variety of reasons. Even if their causes reached the highest tiers, there was always a chance that popes' and cardinals' attention might be diverted: as we saw above, in 1473 Sixtus directed Barbo, already working on Leopold, to investigate Emma's cult. Certainly popes received many applications: in December 1479 a Roman curialist informed Hechtl that Sixtus was dealing with the canonization of someone from Venice.[81] In addition to Leopold, during his pontificate Sixtus was presented with at least eight other saint-candidates.[82] Given such a competitive market, energetic, constant, and long-term support of a would-be saint was crucial. A great deal depended upon the connections, status, and dedication of a candidate's Roman representative, as well as the state of Roman and curial politics; this was soon painfully obvious at the next stage of Leopold's cause.

In May 1479, a member of Barbo's German entourage encouraged the emperor to send a high-powered envoy to Rome on Leopold's behalf. However, Friedrich's choice of Andreas Zamometič turned out to be a serious mistake. We briefly encountered this Dominican archbishop of Krain in the previous chapter: he'd served the emperor for the previous three years. Andreas arrived in Rome (his fourth visit) in February 1480 with imperial instructions to promote Leopold's cause.[83] The outcome of this visit is unknown. In October Friedrich was petitioning Rome to create his protégé Zamometič a cardinal. When Sixtus procrastinated, according to the traditional interpretation Andreas began violently to attack Rome's clergy

80. Ludwig, doc. LV, 45.

81. Ludwig, doc. CXXXIX, 130 (December 6, 1479). Depositions on Catherine of Siena had been collected in Venice.

82. Di Fonzo, "Il processo di canonizzazione," 227–89, at 270. Wetzstein, *Heilige vor Gericht*, appendix 1, calendars all fifteenth-century canonization processes, most of which had no positive response, at least during that century, 514–32.

83. Jürgen Petersohn, *Kaiserlicher Gesandter und Kurienbischof: Andreas Jamometić am Hof Papst Sixtus IV. (1478–1481)* (Hannover: Hahnsche Buchhandlung, 2004). The imperial safe-conduct was issued on February 24, 1480, 164 (doc. XII). This is a reexamination of the relationship between Zamometič, pope, and curia, in which the issue of a cardinalate is subordinated to Andreas's interest in curial reform, 111–13.

and the pope, resulting in the revocation of his credentials in May, to the emperor's great annoyance and the detriment of Leopold's cause. He was clapped into Castel Sant'Angelo in mid-June of 1481, but freed thanks to imperial pressure.[84] The indignant archbishop went to Basel, where in 1482 he called for a resumption of the General Council that had vexed Eugene IV and Nicholas V from 1431 to 1449 with increasingly radical plans for conciliar reform. Though Friedrich seems to have distanced himself from Andreas, when Sixtus asked Friedrich to arrest Andreas, the emperor's tepid response suggested that he had not totally rejected his "trusty and well-beloved" archbishop, as he called him. According to chronicler Giacomo da Volterra, writing in early June 1482, in Rome "they said that Emperor Friedrich secretly favored Zamometič."[85] Finally, by imperial mandate Basel authorities locked up Andreas in December.[86] From that point forward the pope attempted to have him extradited to Rome. When Basel refused, papal emissary Angelo Geraldini, humanist bishop of Sessa/Suessa, interdicted the city.[87]

Unfortunately, List returned to Rome (May 19, 1482) just as imperial-papal wrangling about Zamometič was heating up. With him was Marquard Breisacher, an influential knight, an accomplished imperial councilor whom contemporaries, using the familiar metaphor, called "the emperor's eye."[88] In a long letter of June 7, List described their journey to the city, illustrating the many obstacles and mundane inconveniences that made travel and communication such a burden.[89] Shortly after leaving Klosterneuburg in April, List had to gather about thirty-two foot soldiers to accompany his party, because at Mautern (a few miles south of Krems) they were shot at by Hungarians. Fed up with Friedrich's confused policies, Corvinus had once again declared war (in 1481) against the emperor; and now List was suffering the consequences. In the present skirmish, he continues, "We didn't dare all move on together, but separately, one leading his horse

84. Petersohn, *Kaiserlicher Gesandter und Kurienbischof,* 29, 104–5, 128–29, 172–76 (docs. XV–XVII).

85. *Il Carteggio,* 49. The passage is "dicitur Fridericum imperatorem secreto illi assistere," *Il Diario Romano di Jacopo Gherardi da Volterra,* in Muratori, *Rerum Italicarum Scriptores,* 102.

86. James of Volterra in *Il Diario Romano di Jacopo Gherardi da Volterra,* 113: The detention was "Caesaris mandato et pontifice petente."

87. Pastor, *History of the Popes,* 4:358–63.

88. Ludwig, CLVIII, n.

89. The letter in Ludwig, doc. LIX, 47–51.

and running to escape, others remaining mounted; one way or another we got away with extreme difficulty, without harm to ourselves or our horses." Their troubles weren't over. That night they reached Emmersdorf near the famous monastery of Melk. In the morning, while List was in the middle of celebrating Mass,

> women and girls came running to the church, wailing and loudly screaming, carrying their possessions with them; no-one stayed with me at the altar, nor did any other man remain. I at once realized that the enemy was approaching, and as quickly as I could finished the Mass and hurried to my inn. We speedily jumped on our horses and left Emmersdorf. Those who had fired on us the previous day had come by night to a place nearby that we'd passed through the previous evening; in the morning they despoiled and burned everything. Had we remained there for as long as we'd planned to do, we'd have been robbed and captured.

Because of the danger, a week (skirting the enemy, presumably) was wasted. Stopping en route for some letters from the bishop of Passau to take to Rome, the party finally came via Treviso to Mestre, where they found a boat to take them the short distance (a few miles) to Venice.

At Venice, List encountered an obstacle that would plague him even after Leopold's canonization, the "cash flow" problem: how to obtain funding for daily expenses, as well as for anticipated canonization fees and living costs in Rome. He dealt with John Kopp, an agent of the Venice-based banker Ulrich Permann. Kopp was unable to hand over 500 ducats List believed the emperor had provided. Kopp promised to send the money on to Rome as soon as he'd received it. In his letter, however, List notes that "until today" (June 7, 1482) he'd heard nothing from Kopp, though he had letters of exchange from Permann himself for 1,500 ducats. Friedrich does not seem to have gone out of his way to help fund the effort, most of the cost being borne by Klosterneuburg (and, paradoxically, Matthias of Hungary). On leaving Venice, List's group stumbled into a conflict between a papal-Venetian alliance on the one side and neighboring Ferrara's Duke Ercole, backed by his father-in-law Ferrante of Naples, on the other (which also drew in Milan and Florence).[90] It was said, List reports, that Venice had some eighty thousand men in the field against Ferrara. Consequently List's party could not go by way of Padua, as they'd planned, because of innu-

90. It went on from late 1481 to the Bagnolo treaty of August 1484, by which time the pope had changed sides and interdicted Venice (May 1483).

merable rapacious mercenaries in the area. List's request for a safe conduct from Venice's doge was refused: it wasn't the Republic's custom to endanger relations with their mercenaries.[91]

Unable to pass through Padua, the party took the sea route, finding a boat to take them to Ancona for eight ducats. Day after day they asked the captain to get going, since delay was injuring their cause; but he claimed that the winds were contrary, so "with the greatest annoyance we were forced to waste time," from Sunday until Friday. Finally leaving Mestre, the party endured a week of misery on the Adriatic: the unruly horses on board (mainly Marquard's white mount) eventually smashed up some of the boat itself. Reaching the east coast and crossing into the papal states, on arrival in Rome (May 19, 1482) List immediately went to see Cardinal Barbo, who again received him amicably and invited him to dine. Following the civilities, in reply to List's queries about Leopold, Barbo replied, "Oh, you haven't come at a good time; you should have come in October, because all the cardinals have gone away due to the heat; now there's no-one to carry out the work." This is a perfect example of what had become a tradition during the thirteenth century, the evacuation of Rome by popes and cardinals from May or June until October or November.[92] List had another disappointment after his long, hard journey: as soon as he'd entered Rome he'd asked about any canonizations, and was told that Bonaventure had been made a saint a few days before List and his companions left Klosterneuburg.

List hurriedly attempted to see the pope, learning that he might have an audience in four or five days; the pope couldn't do it sooner because of his gout. Thanks to apostolic protonotary Ludwig de Agnellis, one of List's team, the pope granted an audience around Pentecost (May 26). After Agnellis summarized various documents offered by List's party, the pope handed them over to Cardinal Gonzaga (who'd been appointed to Bonaventure's committee in 1475), standing in for Piccolomini on Leopold's committee. Gonzaga suggested that they should come to the next day's public consistory, where he would put the issue before the cardinals. "We were most content with this," says List, but "as we were discussing it, a pa-

91. Ludwig, doc. LIX, 48.

92. Agostino Paravicini-Bagliani, *The Pope's Body*, trans. David S. Peterson (Chicago: University of Chicago Press, 2000), 176–79.

pal messenger came up and said to the lord of Mantua [Gonzaga], 'Most reverend lord, by mandate of His Holiness, there will be no consistory tomorrow.' Gonzaga replied, 'Very well [*bene*]; we can't do anything tomorrow; we'll see about other days.'" The days came and went, List continues, without accomplishing anything, for the response of the good fathers was always the same: nothing can be done because of the absence of the cardinals, "and they suggested that we return in October."[93] Once again List and companions turned to Barbo. Meeting a papal messenger as they were approaching his residence, they asked whether the cardinal was at home. He answered that Barbo and all the cardinals were to go to the pope immediately. Nevertheless, they went on to his house, where Breisacher explained their situation to him. The cardinal answered, "'Look, you can see that I've got to hurry to the pope; I can't do everything—write up a memo and send it to me.' Then he went to the pope. That evening at dinner," List continues, "we were told that the pope had imprisoned two cardinals, the Romans Colonna and Savelli, for treasonous association with the king of Naples; they planned to kill the pope, cardinals, protonotaries and others on the feast of Corpus Christi [in 1482, June 6]." Indeed, the pope had called a consistory on June 2, to which Barbo was hurrying earlier that day when List stopped him. The clamorous meeting of pope and cardinals lasted until that evening. Colonna and Savelli were accused, arrested, and sent to Castel Sant'Angelo. Next morning, List went to the papal palace and gave Cardinal Barbo the memo he'd asked for. "That good father said 'I'm afraid we can do nothing, yet will receive the memo and consider whether anything might be done.' And he added, 'You see how the brethren [cardinals] are: they think of nothing but the treachery of their brothers. We [i.e., Barbo] have no hope for the canonization to go forward at this time, but [rather] in October.'" Once again papal politics threatened Leopold's chances.

List concluded his letter with a reference to anxious times, and another request for the prayers of his convent—which by now must have seemed a great distance away. He certainly needed prayers, since his cause was frustrated by simultaneous conflicts on three levels: (1) There was the papal-imperial contretemps regarding Zamometič. (2) Following the Pazzi conspiracy, the pope in alliance with Venice was warring with Ferrante of Naples, Florence, Milan, and Ferrara. As noted in the previous chapter, from

93. "Ecce vos videtis, quod cogor ire festinanter ad papam," Ludwig, doc. LIX, 50.

mid-April 1482 anti-papal forces led by Lorenzo Colonna, including Turkish contingents who had captured Otranto in 1480, were attacking Rome itself. Colonna and Savelli were imprisoned because of their conspiracy and alliance with Ferrante. (3) Finally, in another but not unrelated war within Rome itself—Colonna against Orsini—the Eternal City, also from April 1482, was reduced to a confusion of factional struggles.[94] These internal and external conflicts hindered curial business and put List in an extremely awkward position. He had, indeed, come to Rome at the wrong time. On the other hand, we do well to recall that Bonaventure was canonized in the midst of this military-political chaos, on April 14, 1482.

About a month after List arrived, the cardinals and pope wrote to the emperor dismissing his envoys because nothing could be done about Leopold during the current "great troubles" and the cardinals' absence—on account of plague, Sixtus wrote. The two letters, similar in wording, suggested October as more suitable.[95] Friedrich responded in September with the expectation that in October the sainthood of Leopold, "our progenitor" would be considered.[96] But October came and went with no movement in the case. Continuing papal animosity toward both Zamometič and the emperor shows up in a letter to Barbo of December 1482. Sixtus had received a representative from Basel who, in the course of his speech, referred to "archbishop" Zamometič. The pope interrupted, saying he wasn't to be called archbishop because he'd been deprived for his evil crimes. Sixtus went on to complain of Basel's protection of the man, adding that, if this was being done out of obedience to the emperor, the people of Basel were malefactors. Two weeks later curialists were discussing how to capture Zamometič: perhaps issue him a safe-conduct, intercept him as he left Basel, and take him to Rome; the pope favored this scheme.[97] Obviously the archbishop of Krain was still a thorn in the papal side.

94. Pastor, *History of the Popes,* 4:348–57; Ludwig, CLXI–CLXIII. One could also consider List's earlier brushes with Hungarian troops another element of conflict affecting his task. Christine Shaw's work suggests that traditional views about Orsini-Colonna hostility are rather overstated: *The Political Role of the Orsini Family from Sixtus IV to Clement VII,* chap. 4, "Baroni di Roma," esp. 106, 114–16.

95. Ludwig, docs. LX, LXI, 51–52.

96. Ludwig, docs. LXII, LXIII, 52–53; Friedrich closed by asking for official (re)accreditation of his envoys, de Agnellis, Thomas List, and Marquard Breisacher, JUD, knight, member of the imperial council.

97. *Il Carteggio,* 55, 61; in March 1483 Sixtus threatened war against Basel if the emperor didn't turn Zamometič over to him, ibid., 72.

Meanwhile Agnellis, List, and Breisacher were campaigning as usual in 1483. Things seemed to be going well enough: in virtually the same words Sixtus wrote to Friedrich and the Klosterneuburg canons in June acknowledging their envoys and claiming that he and the cardinals were well-disposed to Leopold's canonization. However, the pope explained (in now familiar terms), because of intimations of plague and the absence of some of the cardinals, it didn't seem an appropriate time to deal with the matter. More positively, Sixtus announced that though he was putting off the cause, he intended to expedite it before Christmas, thus setting up another completion date, that would—again—come and go.[98] Exactly a month later, Cardinal Ferricus was reassuring the canons that everything would be ready by Christmas and that "the blessed one buried in your monastery will in short time be canonized."[99] On the same day (July 17, 1483) Borgia notified Friedrich that all was in readiness except for a *relatio*, which he, himself, would provide as quickly as possible.[100] In a now familiar pattern, all of this enthusiastic optimism was quickly squelched: the very next day, July 18, 1483, Breisacher reported to Hechtl that the long-awaited *relatio* of the three-cardinal commission, discussed in secret consistory, "was against us rather than for us": it was "slanted thoroughly and utterly against us."[101] Ludwig and Röhrig see this reversal as a result of a papal or curial realization that imperial connections made the canonization risky at a time when the eastern European political scene was particularly volatile. In any event, there were always reasons to question (or use as an excuse) Leopold's nonconformity to saintly stereotypes: he'd been married, had many children, was involved in worldly affairs, and performed no extraordinary penances or unusually pious acts.[102] Before the year's end an even stronger reason for papal reluctance surfaced.

Breisacher informed prior John that they'd met this July setback by two actions: they'd found an excellent man to rebut the negative *relatio*, acclaimed

98. Ludwig, docs. LXIV, LXV, 54.

99. Ludwig, doc. LXVI, 55: "beatum istum sepultum in vestro monasterio habituros vos esse brevi tempore canonizatum." In his *Summarium* of 1483 Pavini noted that Ferricus had been substituted for the absent Barbo, Pez, *Scriptores*, 1:col. 610.

100. Ludwig, doc. LXVII, 55; cf. also doc. CXLVI, 145.

101. Ludwig, doc. LXVIII, 56–57, "potius contra quam pro nobis"; Briesacher's choice of verb in the following suggests his suspicion of perfidy: the report "penitus ac omnino contra nos fabricata fuerat."

102. Ludwig, CLXVII–CLXVIII; Röhrig, *Ludwig III. der Heilige*, 149–50.

member of the Rota Pavini. As we saw in the previous chapter, Pavini had been deeply involved in Bonaventure's process. On Leopold's behalf he presented Sixtus with a *summarium* under ten headings: (1) A review of the many supplications; (2) explanations for delays; (3) summation of what he calls an general inquisition, followed by the same for a (4) special inquisition; (5) summation of Leopold's *vita;* (6) demonstration that everything required for canonizations had been met; (7) Leopold's *fama* and (8) popular devotion to him; (9) benefits for the Church because of his sainthood; and (10) his miracles.[103] His report reviews the Austrian documentation backing up Leopold's bid, including old chronicles, which, he adds, are trustworthy—as "I wrote in the canonization of Bonaventura."[104] (Pavini mentions his recent involvement in Bonaventure's case several times.)[105] When he comes to Leopold's *fama,* he notes that good repute continuing after thirty or forty years must indicate the real thing, and "in our case" the margrave's fame continues "even to the present times." Among the more telling aspects of his *summarium* is section nine, on benefits from the canonization. Pulling together all the reasons proffered in supplications sent to Rome over several years, Pavini gives first place to the extirpation of the deplorable Bohemian heresy. A second benefit would be peace settling upon emperor, France, German princes, Bohemia, Poland, and Hungary—in particular, Friedrich would stop battling Corvinus, which would allow a concerted effort against the Turks and the recovery of Constantinople, Macedonia, and Bosnia. (Pavini notes that if Friedrich couldn't pursue the canonization because of old age, his son Maximilian would.) Additional benefits included the building of churches, monasteries, and hospitals in Leopold's name, and, Pavini continued, using pilgrims' offerings, alms, and tithes for charitable works. In addition, the animosity of some Austrian princes against His Holiness would vanish. On the other hand, should the pope not canonize Leopold, God would be provoked against his people and their grave sins—more prevalent in these times than in earlier ages—and bring about the conquest of Italy through wars (a prescient comment) that Leopold, as a saintly intercessor, might prevent.[106] The summation did not end at this seemingly convenient point, but went on

103. *Summarium* in Pez, *Scriptores,* 1:cols. 593–672.

104. Ibid., col. 611; his reference is to Franciscan chronicles, ASV, *Congr. Riti, processus* 4216, fols. 166v–67v.

105. *Summarium,* cols. 610, 611, 668, 669, etc.

106. Ibid., col. 628–31.

to deal with Leopold's miracles. In fact, as in Bonaventure's *relatio,* more than half (about 52%) of the entire *summarium* is given over to miracles—detailing the individuals involved and their cures or other benefits, in column after overwhelming column. Pavini categorizes about four hundred wonders (with some duplications) according to type: seven raisings from the dead, such as the drowned boy whose miraculous revival was attested to by three people *de auditu,* seven *de visu;* five cures of deafness, seventeen of blindness, and so on, including plague, paralysis, fevers, demoniacs, and rescues from "adverse dangers" such as an attempt to burn down Klosterneuburg, taken from testimony at the inquisitions (with cross-referenced witness numbers). All these miracles prove that Leopold should be canonized. This section ends with a legal, theological, and philosophical discussion (citing inter alia Aristotle) of miracles—the validity of indirect proof, and so on—in which elliptical references tend to overpower the text. The *summarium* concludes with prayers composed for Leopold that Pavini based on those in Clement V's (1342–52) canonization bull of Saint Ivo of Brittany in 1347, which he suggests should be used as an exemplar for Leopold's canonization, to be carried out "as contained in the book of ceremonies." As a result of Pavini's work, Breisacher claimed, all doubts "were removed from the hearts" of the cardinal-committee, who now agreed that Leopold should be canonized.

The second beneficial action noted by Breisacher was the pope's ordering cardinal Borgia to produce a revised *relatio* to be considered in a secret consistory.[107] But things didn't go as planned: Borgia couldn't produce the required document as quickly as he'd hoped and, with the great heat and—yet again—signs of an outbreak of plague that thoroughly frightened the pope, Sixtus deferred Leopold's case until Christmas 1483 (as he'd promised the emperor a month earlier). Breisacher closed his letter by asking Hechtl for further supplications from Friedrich.

Two days later (July 20) List composed a letter for a different reason, taking us into money matters. As he'd already explained—referring to earlier letters—on May 9, 1483, he'd met Agnellis returning from the papal palace; with a pleased look he said, "Our cause is good," immediately adding, "Are you provided with money and other necessities?"[108] When List said that he

107. Ludwig, doc. LXVII, 55, July 17, 1483. Borgia informed the emperor of this by letter of 17 July 1483, so the pope must have mandated the second *Relatio* before that date.

108. Ludwig, doc. LXIX, 57–9.

could cover expenses, Agnellis asked him and Breisacher to see the master of ceremonies that very day about the financial arrangements, advising List to draw out 100 ducats *ex banco* because of the magnitude of the case. Barbo claimed that if he hadn't worked so diligently nothing would have happened: "You see how many difficulties there are"; he warned, "I urge you not to hurry things" because to canonize a man who had ruled Austria and was related to the emperor was no trifling matter. With a mention of Borgia's forthcoming *relatio,* Barbo advised List to solicit more letters from society's upper ranks. Having reported these developments, List apologized to his prior if his messages seemed contradictory, but so many changes occurred, "now one thing, now another." Given the delays and meaningless reassurances they'd received, List and Breisacher had even debated "a long time" whether to remain in Rome. List's letter then returned to finances. They'd had to sell their horses just to cover living expenses; they needed money, enough to replace their mounts and get themselves home after the canonization. Apart from having to meet these immediate needs, the ceremony itself would have to be paid for. List went into details about various sums received, pledged, or not obtained: "we will have *in banco*" 1,100 ducats put aside for the canonization—but from what the master of ceremonies said, a total of 1,300 would be needed. Without more money, List observed, the whole cause would fall through, its supporters disgraced. He closed by asking letters to be sent to him "at the inn called 'Near the Angel' in the City."[109] Nevertheless, although there were money problems, there were reasons for optimism: on the same day that List was writing, Agnellis also wrote to Hechtl: although nothing could be done now on account of the cardinals' absence *propter pestem,* the cause certainly would move on before Christmas when the cardinals had returned. Things were difficult because of bad times, but a good end was expected.

THE NEAR-DEATH OF THE CAUSE

In August 1483 Friedrich nearly ruined Leopold's chances.[110] Tension was mounting between the emperor and Sixtus over Zamometič. As we

109. Pastor, *History of the Popes,* 4:185 provides names of other Roman inns, including "ad angelum," possibly near Castel Sant'Angelo.

110. The following reconstruction and interpretation of events is based on Ludwig, docs. LXIX, LXX, LXXII, LXXIII, LXV, XCVII, 59–63, and doc. XCVII, 81–82, which is sandwiched between

saw, in December 1482 Basel authorities imprisoned him, after which Sixtus sought his extradition. The papal envoy interdicted the city for refusing to comply. As a result an imperial outburst occurred on August 24, when letters went out from Graz to several imperial cities and all subjects, and presumably to the college of cardinals but not the pope. The emperor noted that, at papal request, he'd arrested Andreas, who'd called for a (renewed) council at Basel, possibly—the emperor suggested—at the prompting of Sixtus's enemies. Only the pope and emperor, Friedrich wrote, may call such a council. While imperial and papal curialists were working on the situation, the emperor continued, a "person calling himself a commissary and papal envoy," Sessa, interdicted Basel against the emperor's express prohibition. Sessa (with papal assistance) intended to remove the prisoner from imperial jurisdiction and take him to be "finally judged in a foreign nation";[111] Friedrich is thus compelled by his duty to the empire and the German nation to reject Sessa's ban.[112] The pope should be content with Friedrich's cooperation, and do nothing until he and Sixtus agreed on a solution. Next day, in what seems a fit of tactlessness, the emperor issued four more letters, one to the college of cardinals generally, others to each of the cardinals on Leopold's commission (but, again, not to the pope), expressing Friedrich's pleasure that another *relatio* would be read in consistory at Christmas.[113] Sixtus would no doubt have heard of the imperial letters one way or another, but after they were read in consistory, the pope was livid. Breisacher later informed Hechtl (December 26, 1483) "I don't know at the suggestion of what *spiritus*," the pope had learned that because of a grievance the emperor held against him Friedrich was "unwilling to write fur-

the last letter of 1484 (December 3) and the first letter of 1485 (January 20) in Ludwig's collection; he dates it to 1483, referring to differences in contemporary styles of year-dating, doc. CXXV, 111–13; Ludwig, CLXXIV–CLXXVII; *Regesten Kaiser Friedrichs III*, ed. Paul-Joachim Heinig, Heft 4 (Vienna: Verlag Hermann Böhlaus, 1986), 422 (August 24, 1483, Graz)—Zamometič outlived Sixtus IV by three months, being found dead in his cell on November 12 or 13, 1484—an apparent ("mutmasslichen") suicide, Ludwig, CLXXVI n. 1: he was "erdrosselt," strangled or garroted, a rather unconventional way to kill oneself; and Röhrig, *Ludwig III. der Heilige*, 149.

111. "Und in fremden Nationen abgeurteilt werden."

112. "Dem Reich sowie der Deutschen Nation."

113. Ludwig, doc. CXXV, 111: "Venit quidam nuncius de Basilea, qui in causa Graynen ["Crain" was another term for Zamometič's see], ferebat literas ser.mi d. n. imperatoris ad r.mos d.nos cardinales, sed ad d. n. s. papam nullam scripturam ferebat" (undated). These letters of late August came to the pope's attention by late November, when they, or perhaps a copy of only the first one, were brought to the curia by a Basel messenger.

ther." The pope became "bitter at heart" and was indignantly "against us." His Holiness declared that nothing more would be done to canonize Leopold until the emperor sent additional supplications. Undoubtedly, papal pique arose from being snubbed in Friedrich's letters of August 25 to the college and committee, but the Zamometič letter of August 24 highlighted even more fundamental issues: it wasn't a conflict merely of personalities, but of principles.[114] Sixtus had much to object to, apart from the fact that Friedrich had blindsided him: claims that "others" had been behind the call to revive the Basel council, not Zamometič, perhaps an attempt to deflect blame; that it pertained only to pope *and* emperor ("allein dem Papst und ihm") to summon a council; that the pope himself had instigated this jurisdictional conflict; that Sixtus would be bound by what he and Friedrich might agree to, all this apart from Friedrich's negating a legate's interdiction. In short, as Friedrich and the pope fell out over inflated imperial claims and Zamometič, Leopold's cause was a victim.

Things changed almost overnight. As recently as November 25, even though List was worrying about money for the forthcoming Christmas canonization, he recorded that the pope had cheerfully promised to expedite Leopold's sainthood. "A few days later"—that is, after Sixtus learned of the Basel letters, coupled almost simultaneously with a request to the cardinals to canonize the margrave—the pope's indignation turned against Friedrich "there and then," as List heard from consistory insiders. For four or five days afterward, Sixtus allowed no audiences. Subsequently, the three-cardinal commission went privately to the pope—"I believe on St. Catherine's Day" [November 25], List wrote—to solicit Leopold's canonization. After hearing their pleas Sixtus replied with the acerbic comments that head this chapter. List and Breisacher didn't know which way to turn. They decided that Breisacher would return to Austria, leaving List in Rome. At first Breisacher couldn't gain access to Vice-chancellor Borgia to explain his departure. Finally on November 28 the cardinal summoned Breisacher, who set out his plans to leave because his efforts were a waste of time and money. Borgia tried to discourage him: the pope would no doubt canonize Leopold; he himself would produce a *relatio,* and the next day would take Breisacher to the pope. This sounded promising, but on the next day (Saturday) and

114. "Nicht so sehr persönlicher als prinzipieller Art," as Ludwig puts it.

the next, and the next, no papal audience was granted. Borgia repeatedly claimed he hadn't had time to arrange an audience. Breisacher then turned to another member of Leopold's commission, Piccolomini, with more success. On December 4, 1483, Sixtus granted an audience, and for an hour or more Breisacher discussed the canonization. The best the pope allowed was that a *relatio* could be presented in a secret consistory. Sixtus repeated what he'd said in late November, that he wouldn't proceed until Friedrich wrote to him. The pope then told Piccolomini to take Breisacher to Borgia and order him to provide a *relatio* for a secret consistory on the morning of December 12. Piccolomini conveyed this to Borgia in very serious and scolding terms. Borgia promised, "I'll do it tomorrow.... I'll shut my palace and give audience to no-one." The following Saturday Breisacher, Piccolomini, Borgia, and Barbo discussed the *relatio* for three or four hours. As they left Borgia remarked, "We've done a good job today." They agreed to meet the next Tuesday to compose the *relatio,* which was put off until Thursday (December 11). "They called me in, too," adds List, and brought him up to date. Since the document was to be read the very next day, this was blatant procrastination, especially as Borgia was told to prepare the second *relatio* in mid-July.

Surprisingly enough, given the way things had been going, the *relatio* was indeed presented in the December 12 consistory. After breakfast List asked Barbo what had happened. He learned that Borgia's presentation had been listened to by pope and cardinals with graciousness and delight, after which the college deliberated. When List asked what happened next, Barbo replied that they would vote after Christmas. Breisacher learned a little more from Borgia and Piccolomini: both of them (Borgia as usual being full of himself) agreed that the *relatio* had gone very well. Next morning (Sunday, December 13) List and Breisacher called on the vice-chancellor as he prepared to go to church. Borgia claimed that his attempt to get a vote before Christmas had failed. At an audience on December 22 Borgia and Breisacher managed with great difficulty to drag from Sixtus a promise to receive the cardinals' vote at the first consistory after Christmas, but they "should not presume to ask for more." On January 1 Sixtus left Rome on various matters but became ill, delaying the promised consistory. List's group often requested an audience, which was refused, though the pope let them know that he'd keep his word and take the vote at the new year's first consistory; they should not despair.

Finally on January 19, 1484, a vote was taken. When List asked Barbo about the results, he replied, "We cardinals did as we ought in giving our vote." The usually diplomatic List retorted, "I never get much encouragement from your lordship," only to be rebuked, "That's enough; no more." From this, List writes, "I understood that I wasn't to inquire further, as it should be a secret reserved to the pope alone."[115] Presumably the vote was positive, since next month Sixtus informed Friedrich that the canonization had been approved. However, Sixtus was still put out by the Zamometič affair; he ordered Breisacher to procure a further personal supplication from the emperor, as "required in this sort of business."[116] For more than a month Friedrich mulled over the pope's demand—as Röhrig notes, there was some justification for his hesitation: from Friedrich's point of view, a reasonable one, everything necessary for the canonization had been accomplished. By April Breisacher reported that Friedrich had agreed to cooperate.[117] The standoff ended with an imperial letter of May 3, which Breisacher obtained "with the greatest difficulty."[118] After pointedly emphasizing that the canonization had already been approved, Friedrich asked the pope to delay the ceremony no longer, and to grant a plenary indulgence for pilgrims to Leopold's grave.[119] It wasn't until August 1484 that the cause began moving again. Even under a cloud of financial uncertainty, preparations were made: a banner for the ceremony was prepared and a rough picture of Leopold sent for imperial approval, with List's promise of a better one to follow.[120]

INNOCENT VIII INHERITS THE CASE

Before he died on August 12, 1484, Sixtus fixed the canonization for the feast of All Saints (November 1, 1484).[121] With the pope's death, once again the process was suspended. Since the new pontiff, Innocent VIII (1484–92), was under no obligation to honor canonization processes instituted by Sixtus IV or any other predecessor, years of effort (and expenditure) might have been wasted.[122] A month after Innocent became pope, Hechtl was writ-

115. Secret consistories were, in theory at least, supposed to be just that—secret.

116. Ludwig, doc. LXXVI, 63.

117. Röhrig, *Ludwig III. der Heilige,* 150, Ludwig doc. LXXVII, 63–64.

118. Ludwig, doc. LXXIX, 65: "maxima cum difficultate."

119. Ludwig, doc. LXXVIII, 64–65.

120. Ludwig, docs. LXXXI–LXXXIII, 66–68.

121. Ludwig, doc. LXXXV, 69, letter of September 15, referring to an earlier report.

122. Giovanni Battista Cibò from Genoa, a cardinal in 1473, gained the tiara after agreeing to

ing a sharply worded letter to List. Nearing the end of a long reign at Klosterneuburg (from 1465) Prior Hechtl was running out of patience, and he was ill.[123] On September 13, 1484, he berated List (unfairly) for his sluggishness in not writing more often from Rome; he promised sufficient money if the canonization were to occur, but if it hadn't happened by Christmas, List was to settle his accounts and, ominously, "present yourself before us."[124] Things didn't seem promising: when Breisacher urged Innocent to complete the canonization, the pope responded that since he was new at the job he'd prefer to consult the college of cardinals.[125] But, Breisacher commented on September 15, that hadn't yet happened, since from the day Sixtus died no consistory had been held. The writer confessed that he was undecided about the whole issue: he'd spent everything on travel and other expenses, and List was broke. In the midst of these depressing circumstances Innocent finally made up his mind. On September 25, he notified the emperor that he'd learned (from Breisacher) about Sixtus's plans to canonize Leopold; he too wanted to do this, which he'd see to at Christmas.[126]

Meanwhile, it seems that List and the increasingly irascible Hechtl were falling out over finances: apparently 500 ducats destined for expenses in Rome had vanished between Venice and the city. Ulrich Permann wrote to Hechtl about this, claiming that it was List's fault. List wrote a querulous response: "The blame is in no way mine. . . . I couldn't be more amazed," he says, "how he [Permann] claims to know of something that didn't happen." List suggested that a misunderstanding arose when he'd passed through Venice (in May 1482) quickly, so as to reach Rome in time for Leopold to be canonized with Bonaventure. List had needed 2,000 ducats; he obtained

various favors for his fellow-cardinals in conclave, a hardly uncommon custom. Not known for resolute action, he increased the papal debt left by Sixtus IV by siding with Neapolitan nobles rebelling against their king, Ferrante I, 1458–94); it was the losing side. Practically his only contribution to the crusade against the Turks was to keep Djem in custody, in exchange for 40,000 ducats annually from his brother and rival, Sultan Bayezid II. Some modern critics might fault Innocent for his bull *Summis desiderantes* of December 1484, misappropriated two years later by Sprenger and especially Krämer as a preface to their witch hunters' guide *Malleus Maleficarum,* and for his shutting down Pico della Mirandola's attempt to argue nine hundred theses against all comers in Rome. The normal level of chaos that marked city life worsened when Innocent VIII's minimal oversight ended in 1492.

123. He died on June 27, 1485, and was succeeded on July 1, 1485, by James Pamperl.

124. Ludwig, doc. LXXXIV, 68.

125. "Novus in pontificatu esset"; Ludwig, CLII, mentions "many resisting" the canonization, "multis canonizacioni resistentibus," without further explanation.

126. Ludwig, doc. LXXXVI, 70.

1,500 in Venice, and the remaining 500 was supposed to be sent to him in Rome, but evidently never was. List wrote again that day, as usual begging for money, to avoid scandal to their monastery and the emperor, "in whose name especially this holy cause is pursued."[127] List mentions something that briefly illuminates another aspect of the hectic life of a proctor battling curial red tape. He asked the prior and convent for a new procuration letter. "Although the one we have is still valid," it was in a notarial hand of excessive contractions, was old and somewhat dirty from use, and, because of overly officious examination one of its seals, cracked down the middle, needed replacement. We can well imagine this to have been true, if List had been carrying around the same document since his arrival in Rome several years earlier.

By the end of October 1484, while Innocent was planning a Christmas canonization, List and Breisacher were still begging for money from Klosterneuburg.[128] Apparently Hechtl had expressed a desire for news from Rome, so List, after sharply reminding him that he couldn't discus what he didn't know, filled in the prior on recent events such as the "amazing" Orsini-Colonna battles in the city: "Many rush about in arms," and a Colonna had been tortured and beheaded in Castel Sant'Angelo.[129] In the midst of these delays and clashes, Pavini, originally engaged in mid-1483 to compose a *summarium,* continued working on Leopold's cause. He presented his *Oratio de Divo Leopoldo* in public consistory on November 20, 1484.[130] Unlike *relationes, orationes* were intended to be more persuasive in style than a "report," rhetorically praising the candidate so as to justify his canonization. In Bieler's edition the Latin transcript takes up almost fourteen pages, including nearly eight pages of posthumous miracles, ending with a reference to Borgia's earlier *relatio* (December 1483) and a supplication linking Fried-

127. Ludwig, docs. LXXXVII–LXXVIII, 70–73; "die schuld weder mein, noch meins dieners des Koppen nicht ist, sunder als wir des ain wissen haben, das solcher verczug und schuld des dechant so zu Rom ist" (18 October 1484).

128. Ludwig, docs. LXXXIX–XC, 73–75.

129. Ludwig, doc. XCI, 78; many others died as well during this January to July strife, Pastor, *History of the Popes,* 4:379–84.

130. Giovanni Francesco Pavino, *Johannes Franciscus de Pavinis, Rede auf den Heiligen Leopold (Oratio de Divo Leopoldo Austrie marchione et confessore . . .),* ed. Ludwig Bieler (Innsbruck: Tyrolia-Verlag, 1936), 13–26. Burckard writes that on this date Pavini "publice recitavit vitam et miracula beati Leopoldi, petens in fine ipsum canonizari." He terms this an *oratione. Johannis Burckardi, Liber Notarum,* vol. I, ed. E. Celini, in L. A. Muratori, *Rerum Italicarum Scriptores,* 32 (Città di Castello, 1906), 89.

rich and his son Maximilian to Hungary's king Matthias (then in process of taking over as much of Austria as he could). On the same day, List sent two reports on the *oratio,* one to his convent (in German), another to his prior (in Latin). He claimed that the speech, which he called a *relatio,* took more than an hour and a half to deliver and was heard with appreciation by pope, cardinals, prelates, ambassadors, and others, including many Germans in the crowd.[131] Hechtl subsequently described it for Corvinus, claiming that it was heard by the pope, ten cardinals, seventy archbishops, and numerous prelates, officials, and ambassadors. After reminding Matthias of his pledge of financial support, Hechtl also mentioned that the pope planned to canonize in December or on the feast of the Three Kings, January 6, 1485.[132] Master of ceremonies Burckard also made note of what he correctly terms the *oratio.*[133] At the conclusion of Pavini's speech the pope promised a vote on December 20. This consistory on the evening of the 20th was attended by the pope and nineteen cardinals (including the three working on Leopold's case) sitting on stools in a semicircle nearest the pope, with everyone else on benches according to their status: five archbishops, fifty bishops, two protonotaries, and nine other curialists (including Pavini as consistorial advocate) and Burckard, a total of eighty-seven.[134] As in January of 1484, the consistory again agreed to canonize Leopold.[135]

Conflicts between the Orsinis and the pope's favorites, the Colonnas, and other distracting issues continued to simmer, causing further delays beyond the Christmas target, while lack of funds as usual dogged List and Breisacher. On December 3 they each wrote a pathetic letter to Hechtl, the former asking for 1,800 ducats to be sent before usurious rates increased even more, the latter complaining that though they had asked for money "again and again," now—the imperial knight Breisacher continues—"I beg, I implore, I supplicate" for funds to meet canonization costs and settle debts "lest in procuring blessed Leopold's canonization I procure my own excommunication and disgrace."[136]

131. Ludwig, docs. XCII, XCIII, 77–78, both dated November 20, 1484.

132. Ludwig, doc. CXLVIII, 158, from register of letters, Klosterneuburg, n.d.

133. Johannis Burckardi, d. 1506, colleague and successor to Piccolomini, whom we met at Bonaventure's canonization, paid Sixtus 450 florins for the post in November 1483.

134. Burckard, *Liber Notarum,* 96; Ludwig, CXCIII n. 1, and see CXCI–CXCIV on the consistory.

135. As indicated in chapter 1, several consistories might be held, and votes taken, before a definitive decision to canonize was declared.

136. Ludwig, docs. CXV [*sic*—for XCV], XCVI, 80–81. Excommunication might result from

THE CANONIZATION

At last Leopold was canonized as a Confessor on Thursday, January 6, 1485, the Feast of the Three Kings (because, it was said, the margrave was of noble stock).[137] Burckard managed, and described, the ceremony. The procession entered St. Peter's, where a stage had been erected "according to what I [Burckard] wrote in my hand in the book of ceremonies" which, in fact, borrowed heavily from Patrizi Piccolomini's ceremonial for Bonaventure.[138] Participants were given candles of various weights (according to status), and after reverence was shown to the pope, the service began, as in Bonaventure's case, with a short papal "sermon or oration" on Leopold and some of his miracles. After prayers and chants Pavini arose and addressed the pope:

> Most Holy Father, I, Francis of Padua, consistorial advocate, by procuration in the name of the most serene prince and lord Friedrich, Roman Emperor eternally August, *instanter, instantius et instantissime* beg of Your Holiness that Leopold, scion of the illustrious house of Austria, be canonized and enrolled in the catalog of saints of Christ as a holy confessor.

Innocent VIII indicated his willingness to do so, pronounced the *protestatio,* declared Leopold a saint (feast day November 15), and then announced indulgences. Immediately afterward the proctor fiscal arose and commanded all the protonotaries, clergy of the *camera apostolica,* and notaries to make public instruments recording the *protestatio.* As he sat down, Pavini stood up again and in almost the same words asked for public instruments recording the canonization, and the appropriate bulls and apostolic letters. After further prayers the Mass for Epiphany was celebrated, with commemoration of Saint Leopold. At the Offertory, the gifts were brought forward. Burckard notes that these began with two unlit ten-pound candles from Borgia, followed by Breisacher (whom Burckard calls the "first envoy—*orator*—seek-

---

nonpayment of debts to Christian lenders; Breisacher seems truly desperate: "Exoro, rogo et supplico."

137. The following in Röhrig, *Ludwig III. der Heilige,* 151–55. Bull in Giusto Fontanini, *Codex constitutionum,* 195–99, and in Pez, *Scriptores,* 1:cols. 671–72. When Pavini composed his *Summarium* in 1483, he concluded with prayers and a model canonization bull that could be used for Leopold. He chose as his exemplar for both prayers and bull the canon lawyer turned parish priest, Saint Yves of Brittany (d. 1303), canonized in 1347 by Clement VI (1342–52); Pez, *Scriptores,* 1:cols. 670–72. Why not use as a model Bonaventure's bull, which Pavini, having worked on the case, would have known quite well? In any event, Pavini's suggestions were not followed.

138. For the following, see Burckard, *Liber Notarum,* 100–106, also in Ludwig, doc. CL, 162–69; *L'Oeuvre de Patrizi Piccolomini,* 238–43, for Burckard's additions to Piccolomini's work.

ing this canonization") carrying in his right hand a six-pound candle and in his left, "if I remember correctly," three live turtledoves in a gilded cage.[139] Another member of the committee presented two large loaves covered with cloth of gold and silver. Thomas List, "second envoy looking after the canonization," next approached with a six-pound candle in his right hand and in the other a silver cage with two white doves, followed by the third cardinal with two containers of fine wine (one cask plated in gold, the other in silver). A third, unnamed, "German" envoy came next, holding a candle and a multicolored cage of about six small birds. When they were all assembled before the pope, Borgia's candles were presented to Innocent, who handed them to an assistant, who in turn gave them to Burckard to put behind the altar; and all the other offerings were offered in the same way. The cardinals and orators kissed the papal knee and foot, and the pontiff completed the Mass. After the pope left, the offerings were divided up, Burckard including himself among the recipients. At least 232 pounds of candle wax and 1,420 of twisted wax and fiber for torches was consumed in the ceremony.

All of this was traditional canonization ritual, seen for instance in Bonaventure's ceremony and, even earlier, in 1391 when Brigit of Sweden attained sainthood. In that ceremony, too, as noted in the previous chapter, notaries were directed to record the pope's *protestatio* that he intended nothing harmful to the Church.[140] Piccolomini had written the same in his *Caeremoniale,* but he'd considered the protest irrelevant.[141] Therefore, Burckard's including the ritualistic *protestatio* in Leopold's ceremony was hardly an innovation. Yet someone objected. "The Reverend Cardinal [Barbo] called me [Burckard] to him afterwards, reprehending me for this sort of protestation, saying it was in no way appropriate," especially, the cardinal continued, because this case had been thoroughly examined by the cardinal-commissioners and others; since the canonization was found to be fully justified, the Church could not err. This protestation, the cardinal continued, appropriate in the past when a pope canonized without legitimate process—being somewhat compelled to do so—was not the case for Leopold. Burckard countered that the protestation was due to Piccolomini, who headed the office of ceremonies (Patrizi had

139. List copied from the register of the master of ceremonies, all the things needed for canonizing any saint; the stage, for instance, was to be a man's height, forty paces long and thirty wide. Ludwig, doc. CXXXIV, 124–25.

140. *Le Cérémonial papal de la fin du moyen âge à la renaissance,* 4:236–40.

141. *L'Oeuvre de Patrizi Piccolomini,* 123.

kept his hand in ceremonial affairs after Burckard's arrival); and "I arranged it as found in the earlier canonizations" of saints Bernardino (1450), Vincent (Ferrer, 1455/58), Catherine of Siena (1461), and Bonaventure, where it was observed. Since acts and proofs required for canonization could be false, the Church could err in this regard. "Having said this," Burckard concludes, "I dismissed the cardinal."[142] Barbo seems to have confused the ritualistic with the legalistic aspects of canonization. And, probably, because he headed the commission, with a proprietary interest and sense of pride, Barbo didn't want his work questioned; but the protestation had nothing to do with his committee.

Leopold's canonization bull opened with a long preamble based on Old Testament passages about the just ruler holding power through God.[143] The wisdom, innocence, and justice of the "Pious Margrave," whom all Germans celebrated as a saint, are praised. Readers of the bull are reminded that in our own sinful days, though the saints provide us with *exempla,* we contumaciously refuse to imitate them. In Bonaventure's bull, miracles were noted almost in passing; but in the next section of Leopold's, there is a list of cures wrought (through God) by the margrave. Paralysis, fevers, gout, infections; the blind saw, the mute spoke, the deaf heard; some were raised from the dead, others freed from captivity. At Leopold's tomb an incredible number of pilgrims left innumerable offerings. As in Bonaventure's case, the bull provides a potted history of procedural developments sometimes interrupted by wars and papal deaths, and concludes in the usual fashion.

List must have been relieved to participate in a canonization that had cost him so much worry and personal discomfort, that continued after the ceremony and celebrations were over: two weeks later List and Breisacher were begging for 1,500 to 2,000 ducats to pay off debts and allow them to return home with honor.[144] In an ironic aside List mentioned that Barbo, who'd complained about the *protestatio,* "told us that he'd been at many canonizations, yet none of them had been as honorably celebrated as this one." Some time before the end of May 1485 List wrote that he'd had several images of Leopold made, and mentioned two new biographies of the saint, one of which he'd commissioned.

142. Burckard, *Liber Notarum,* 105: "His dictis, cardinalem dimisi."

143. Fontanini, *Codex constitutionum,* 195–99 for the following; the bull is discussed in Krafft, *Papsturkunde,* 997–1002.

144. Ludwig, doc. XCVIII (January 20, 1485), 82–83.

At the time of the canonization the Klosterneuburg convent and region was under Hungarian control, and although Corvinus had supported the canons' efforts, it was unwise for imperial subjects to visit churches in enemy hands. In February and March of 1485 Innocent issued indulgences to help pay off canonization debts and restore the fabric and goods of the convent damaged in "the storms of war." Next year he authorized a translation, though this didn't occur at once.[145] After Corvinus's death in Vienna in 1490, however, the way opened up, and the cult grew. The emperor and his successor Maximilian donated a silver reliquary for the margrave's bones, and in 1493 Friedrich asked Alexander VI, who had worked (when pushed) on the process as Vice-chancellor Borgia, to renew and expand Innocent's indulgence for the war-battered convent.[146] In September 1494, over a year after Friedrich's death (August 10), Maximilian asked to have the translation delayed until he could be present. Meanwhile, money for the shrine accumulated, though pilgrim offerings themselves declined (in the first decade after the canonization they averaged 166 tal. [Pfunde] annually; in the second and third decades, 112 and 116 tal. respectively). At last, the translation was set for February 15, 1506. By then, the huge triptych-genealogy with explanatory notes hanging near the shrine was accompanied by a rich Brussels tapestry commissioned by an imperial councilor, depicting the donor, pilgrims, and votives at the tomb.[147] Yet another pope, Julius II, issued an indulgence for those attending. On the day, the bones were taken from the tomb, washed, placed in the imperial silver reliquary, and ceremoniously returned for reburial. In the procession Emperor Maximilian, to drive home his familial connection to the new saint—exemplifying the "sacred legitimation of power"—was ceremonially garbed not as emperor but as archduke of Austria.[148] The translation netted the convent 776 Pfunde.[149]

145. Ludwig, docs. C, CI, CIV, 84–88.

146. Alfred A. Strnad, "Kaiser Friedrich III und die Translatio sancti Leopoldi," *Jahrbuch des Stiftes Klosterneuburg*, Neue Folge, 7 (1971): 103–34, attempts to show Friedrich's personal interest in the translation, though the document upon which Strnad bases this conjecture (133–34) does not support him.

147. Röhrig, *Ludwig III. der Heilige*, 140–41, 153ff.

148. Maximilian also used the occasion to call a "Historikerkongress" mentioned above, in which he and his scholars discussed imperial genealogy: Röhrig, *Ludwig III. der Heilige*, 138–39, 154–55; Roberto Bizzocchi, "Church, Religion, and State in the Early Modern Period," in supplement "The Origins of the State in Italy, 1300–1600," *Journal of Modern History* 67 (Dec. 1995): S152–S165, at S165.

149. Leopold, 130–31, Prior James's account book.

Many of the obstacles to Bonaventure's canonization also affected Leopold's, excepting of course the strife that embroiled the Franciscans. Unstable political forces of attraction and repulsion that were typical of northern Italian city-states, and the Neapolitan kingdom to the south, at times created near chaos in the papacy. Conflicts within Rome itself, linked to these external issues, complicated curial policies: Colonna versus Orsini, the Colonna-Savelli conspiracy of 1482, the attack on the city by Ferrante's army in the same year. Naples and Venice formed a dangerous axis, and even before the Pazzi conspiracy of 1478 papal and Florentine political goals often clashed. Lorenzo's excommunication and the city's interdiction created problems for the papacy that were only (temporarily) resolved by 1480. Beyond Italy, imperial, Hungarian, and French rivalries contributed to the tumult surrounding the Holy See.

As suggested in the introduction, significant issues such as these very likely engaged the energies of nearly all of the resident cardinals; there were no well-established bureaus, no compartmentalized congregations, no standing committees overseeing specific areas of diplomacy, or military and political activity. When problems of great magnitude arose, the cardinals' normal work was suspended—one thinks of Barbo hurrying to the pope in the conspiracy uproar, with no time for other things. Among those things would probably have been Leopold's canonization. Barbo—a key figure on Leopold's committee—on another occasion was sent away to inspect papal fortifications. As noted in the introduction, cardinals could multitask as needed; a legate sent into Germany to deal with the Turks could also find time to discuss saint-making.

One element peculiar to Leopold's case is the lack of any sustained financial and institutional support behind the cause; whereas Bonaventure eventually had a pope and (most of) a religious order behind him, the emperor's patronage of Leopold was intermittent, due in part to political challenges and preoccupations as well as indolence. Even so, he recognized that a canonized kinsman would bring personal glory to him, his empire, and his duchy. Another element was political: in eastern Europe, Corvinus had to be supported as the "bulwark" against the Turks, whose brutal capture of Otranto in 1480 momentarily focused Italian attention. If Sixtus supported Corvinus, he would seem to slight Friedrich, whose help was also needed against Hussites as well as Turks. The emperor's support of Zamometič and his wild schemes temporarily turned an indignant Sixtus away from Friedrich and imperial causes. Personalities also mattered. Starting with the candidate himself, several cardinals claimed to have had problems with Leopold's suitability: there was little sanctity about his life, though he was a posthumous wonder-worker. Although Friedrich claimed kinship with the dead margrave, the emperor's lack of enthusiasm and (from a papal viewpoint) his arrogance hardly endeared him to His Holiness. At lower levels, personal faults might also affect ongoing business: Borgia's greater concern with benefice-collecting, according to List, than saint-making, and bishop Ulrich's neglect of duty.

Paul II, Sixtus IV, and Innocent VIII needed imperial cooperation in a troubled eastern Europe. Ineffectual though Friedrich was, he was emperor, and popes valued whatever help he might promise or provide against heretics and Turks. Sixtus reluctantly came round to this realization, and acted accordingly, accommodating (some) imperial wishes. Finally, we can't ignore the importance of pilgrimage to the margrave's tomb. When Hechtl took on the oversight of that tomb as the new prior of Klosterneuburg in 1465, one of his first acts was to attend a regional diet and obtain supplications for Leopold's canonization. If Sixtus IV was instrumental in Bonaventure's canonization, Hechtl and his canons—though working from the other end of the hierarchy—must be given similar recognition as he and they raised the prestige of their convent through Leopold. There is one more person whose work led to a successful conclusion, Thomas List. His physical stamina, dedication to the cause, and constant monitoring, reporting, and encouraging of the process come to us through his many letters. Even after being shot at, tossed about in a battered boat, shunted about by procrastinating curialists, and hounded by debt, he got the job done. Although Francis of Paola, our next saint, was sponsored by French royalty, he lacked a similar dedicated champion at the front, fighting the bureaucrats on the curial battlefield.

CHAPTER 4

The Hermit-Ambassador

Francis of Paola (c. 1416–1507, cd. 1519)

After the Minims' Calabrian hermit-founder died in France on April 2, 1507, many came to visit his corpse in a wooden coffin; for three days they paid their respects, and some even experienced miraculous cures. Meanwhile the court painter Jean Bourdichon, who had known Francis well—his workshop was a few minutes' walk from his hermitage—made a death mask "so that he could paint the true form of Francis's face."[1] The day after Easter (April 5) the body was buried in a chapel at Montils (Tours). A duchess, having learned that the chapel was periodically inundated by the river Cher, and worrying that this might quickly rot the corpse, convinced the brethren to transfer him to a stone sarcophagus above flood level.[2] The duchess was none other than Louise of Savoy, who as a teenager had visited Francis, seeking his prayers against a barren marriage. Her son born in 1494, named after the hermit, in 1515 became one of France's greatest sovereigns, Francis I.[3] Following Louise's request, Francis was disinterred ten or eleven days after inhumation, giving Bourdichon the chance to make a second death mask. The artist found the body whole, without decay or odor; another wit-

1. Pauline Matarasso, *Queen's Mate* (Ashgate: Aldershot, 2001), 251.

2. The Cher joins the Loire at Tours.

3. R. J. Knecht, *Renaissance Warrior and Patron: The Reign of Francis I* (Cambridge: Cambridge University Press, 1994), 3; Elizabeth McCartney, "The King's Mother and Royal Prerogative in Early-Sixteenth-Century France," in *Medieval Queenship*, ed. John C. Parsons (New York: St. Martin's Press, 1993), 117–41, at 118.

ness added that the corpse hadn't been eviscerated.[4] After his reburial Francis remained undisturbed until the Huguenots destroyed his tomb in April 1562, dragging the body outside and burning it, leaving only a few bones and ashes that were later reinterred. An inscription at the reburial site referred to Saint Francis as "now a martyr" in heaven, an interesting change of status in that perfect, unchanging realm. Naturally, in the process of gathering the remains, several pieces went astray, some into private hands and the parish church of Notre-Dame-la-Riche.[5] At the time of the profanation, the hermit had been a saint for more than forty years.

We'll deal with the obvious question—Why would the French nobility be concerned with a transplanted Italian hermit?—in due course; for now, the question to answer is, Who was Francis? Only the dead can be canonized, their hagiographies usually composed or rewritten after—sometimes centuries after—their deaths. In the case of Francis of Paola, however, we have an early-sixteenth-century biography possibly by Lorenzo della Chiavi, written after he joined Francis's new order, the Minims. Since this attribution isn't certain, we'll refer to this work simply as the *Vita,* which details the holy man's way of life "up to the year of the present writing, 1502."[6] It was composed, then, before Francis's death. Though it contains many hagiographical motifs, nevertheless its author's personal association with Francis in both southern Italy and France sets it apart from the general run of saints' lives; it was written some seventeen years before its subject was canonized. In much of the introductory material, below, we'll follow the *Vita*'s lead, although it is influenced by the traditional hagiographical "fiction of

4. *PT,* 280–85 (see n. 6 below); Bourdichon was the first witness examined in the Tours process.

5. Giuseppe Roberti, *S. Francesco di Paola: Storia della sua Vita,* 2nd ed. (Rome: Curia Generalizia dell'Ordine dei Minimi, 1963), chap. xix, "The Tomb of St. Francesco Profaned by the Huguenots" (631–44); his tomb was raised five feet above the floor, but only during seventeenth-century renovations. An inventory of 1808 of the Notre-Dame-la-Riche relics counted thirteen bone fragments, but a recount done in 1825 revealed only eleven. Pietro Addante, *San Francesco di Paola* (Milano: Edizioni Paoline, 1988), 279ff., a study even more hagiographically inclined than Roberti's but again, as in the latter case, useful.

6. *AASS,* April I; *Vita* on 106–20, at 107. Lorenzo has been identified as the "anonymous" biographer of Francis, though doubts about this attribution are expressed by Alessandro Galuzzi, *Origini dell'Ordine dei Minimi* (Rome: Pontificia Università Lateranense, 1967), xvi. *AASS* also contains a version of the Processus Cosentinus, 122–47, a collection of inquests taken in southern Italy, the Processus Turonensis, 147–65, and the Processus Calabricus, 165–90. Better editions (Latin and Italian) of the Tours and Cosenza processes, followed here, are by Mario M. Pinzuti, ed., *I Codici Autografi dei Processi Cosentino e Turonense per la Canonizzazione di S. Francesco di Paola* (Rome: Curia Generalizia dell'Ordine dei Minimi, 1964); Cosenza on 4–233, Tours on 237–402, hereafter *PC* and *PT.*

the well-informed witness."[7] In addition, as early as 1512 there were hearings on Francis's life and miracles, with testimony from people who knew both the living man and the dead wonder-worker, in contrast to our first two subjects, Bonaventure and Leopold.

Son of Giacomo d'Alessio and Vienna da Fuscaldo, Francis was born about 1416 in Paola, a small coastal settlement far down the western side of Italy's "boot," backing up to a wooded, hilly region within the realm of Alfonso of Aragon and (by 1459) his illegitimate son Ferrante, king of Naples. Clues in the *Vita* suggest that Francis's family were not poor, but of middling status.[8] The parents seem to have been a pious couple, especially Giacomo, who spent his nights in penitential visits to local churches. The couple had been childless for a long time, but after they invoked God and his Assisi saints, Francis and Clare, a son was born, though with an eye defect. As a remedy his mother's midwife suggested another vow. Vienna promised Saint Francis that if her son was cured, she would dress him as a Franciscan for a year or, if his piety moved him, a longer period. When the infant's eye healed, the overjoyed parents decided to call him Francis. As in the case of Bonaventure and Sixtus IV himself, a childhood miracle led to association with the Franciscan friars.

The *Vita* says little about Francis's education.[9] When he was thirteen his parents took him to the Franciscan convent at San Marco Argentano, about sixteen miles northeast of Paola. The boy fit in well, apparently, even surpassing the friars in the accustomed austerities, which suggests that the son had been affected by his father's piety. After a year, however, Francis left the friars; the Vita provides no explanation—for whatever reasons, their way of life wasn't for him. Perhaps the fact that he'd been placed with Conventuals had something to do with it; as we saw in Bonaventure's case, they were less austere than the Observants. Being released from the Franciscans' care, the teenage Francis traveled to Rome, presumably with his parents, where he is supposed to have encountered and reprimanded an unnamed cardinal for his ostentatious entourage.[10] "Audaciously," the *Vita* claims, Francis re-

7. Emore Paoli, "La santità canonizzata di Francesco di Paola," *Hagiographica* 11 (2004): 223–52, at 243, citing Delehaye.

8. *Honesta ma non ricca*, Galuzzi, *Origini*, 18.

9. There seems to be a difference of opinion among scholars as to Francis's level of literacy.

10. For the following see *AASS, Vita*, 107; D. S. Chambers, "The Economic Predicament of Renaissance Cardinals," in *Renaissance Cardinals and Their Worldly Problems* (Ashgate/Variorum,

minded him that neither Christ nor the apostles had been attended by such pomp. The cardinal replied: "Don't be scandalized, my son; for if we did otherwise, it would be despised by the people and the apostolic *ordo* [i.e., the cardinals] would be vilified one way or another." Although it's highly questionable whether a teenager from the southern hills visiting Rome for the first time would have a tête-à-tête with a cardinal, let alone complain to his face about his splendid company, this bit of invention foreshadowed Francis's later rejection of worldly riches. More generally, it reflects centuries of stereotyped criticism of the reputed wealth of popes, cardinals, and curialists. If this improbable chance encounter actually happened, interestingly, it would have occurred about the time (the 1430s) that Lapo de Castiglionchio, in *De curiae commodis,* was claiming that high prelates *ought* to be rich: "After all, who is there in this day and age who is so religious, so holy . . . that he would come up and speak to . . . a high priest [i.e., a cardinal] who, attired in a pauper's clothes, walked along with only a few companions?" Moving forward to the period just after the composition of Francis's *Vita,* a document of 1509 shows that there was an average of 154 members in each cardinal's household; and next year Paolo Cortese in *De Cardinalatu* asserted that cardinals *should* be wealthy and noble, since people admire these qualities, which cardinals—some of whom scurried about trying to rent impressive *palazzi* well beyond their budgets—ignored at their peril: Cardinal Isvalies (d. 1511) was criticized by a fellow-cardinal (Dovizi-Bibbiena) for wearing fake jewels. Many cardinals would have agreed with Juvenal; though he was writing in another era, little seems to have changed: "But here in Rome we must toe the line of fashion, living beyond our means, and often on borrowed credit: . . . To cut a long story short, nothing's for free in Rome."[11] Whether or not it actually happened, the encounter between the youthful future hermit and a rich cardinal in the streets of Rome stands for the disjunction between materiality and spirituality that was increasingly relevant as popes and cardinals became ecclesiastical princes, especially after Martin V returned to the city. Chambers sums it up: "There can be little doubt that most cardinals sincerely believed it was their duty to

1997), Essay I (from 1966), 290–93, 306; Christopher S. Celenza, *Renaissance Humanism and the Papal Curia: Lapo de Castiglionchio the Younger's De curiae commodis* (Ann Arbor: University of Michigan Press, 1999), which is an introduction to, and an edition of, "De curiae," at 75–80, 201, 203, 205, and quote from 215.

11. Satire III (d. AD 130).

follow a princely way of life." Even more so with popes: Lorenzo il Magnifico's advice to his young son Cardinal Giovanni to guard against unseemly ostentation in Rome was certainly forgotten when Giovanni became Leo X.

After this presumed Roman contretemps, Francis visited Assisi and various individuals of the region who followed "the example of Saint Antony," the original desert father. After his return to Paola, the teenager decided to become a hermit, settling into a place on his father's land about a mile and a half from town, his parents providing for his necessities. Distracted by the comings and goings of others, Francis decided to go even deeper into desolation, on land belonging to relatives. Up to this point his career resembles that of Saint Anthony, who moved progressively farther into the Egyptian desert for similar reasons. At one point the *Vita* actually claims that Francis looked like (pictures of) Saint Anthony—evidently the Paola hermit's hero, along with Saint Francis. Francis of Paola lived in a rude hut, where his parents helped him build a small oratory. His quest for contemplative solitude was facilitated by his immediate and extended family, who provided land and support. There was nothing particularly unusual about this. In addition to help from family and friends, the thick vegetation of the hills sustained many Calabrian hermits living in natural or artificial caves or huts, sometimes grouped around a church. The solitaries of Calabria—a region influenced by Greek as well as Latin traditions—provided many services to locals, especially spiritual counsel, but also medical care with herbal therapy and prayer. Some of these ascetics also voiced the discontent of local peasants, loaded with exactions by the region's powerful nobility and, occasionally, the distant royal court of Naples. Many little chapels scattered across the rugged countryside had their hermits; but, although it wasn't rare to find young men embracing the anchorite's life, they rarely persevered.[12] This, clearly, was not true of Francis. For some four years, from about age sixteen to twenty or perhaps older, he devoted himself to prayers and austerities, for instance eating nothing but uncooked herbs. As with his hero-saints, he was barefoot, never drank wine, slept little (on a wooden bed), ate no fish, and only enough vegetation to sustain life; he never cut his hair or shaved, and he wore a hair shirt. He considered money an invitation to sin—he never touched it from age fifteen, the *Vita* claimed. And

12. Galuzzi, *Origini*, 10–11, 21.

women, Francis said, were to be shunned as if they were snakes. During this same period, however, his lifestyle attracted the attention of locals (including women), many of whom visited him as well as other Calabrian hermits. Soon people of all ranks began seeking his spiritual advice. All went away consoled, according to the *Vita*. Evidently the hermit was becoming a public—even famous—figure, and some visitors asked to live with him and share his austerities, which he allowed. The men who joined him dedicated themselves to prayer, chastity, obedience, and especially poverty, with meager Lenten fare. In time this lifestyle was formalized in the Order of the Minims, "the least" of the followers of Saint Francis.

FRANCIS'S ITALIAN YEARS

Between the time that Francis decided to become a hermit, probably during the later 1430s, and his departure for France in 1483, we have few securely dated indications of how he became a "living saint" at the center of a following extending beyond Paola. During the 1450s and '60s he gained the support of Cosenza's Archbishop Caracciolo and about 1467 had a visitor from Pope Paul II.[13] After the envoy rudely observed that Francis could live an austere life only because "you are a peasant," the hermit picked up some live coals, turned to the pope's man, and responded, "It's true I'm a rustic, and if I weren't, I couldn't do this." Awed by such miraculous powers, the envoy threw himself at Francis's feet.[14] In the same year, possibly related to this visit, four cardinals provide an indulgence for those who contributed to the upkeep and repair of Francis's hermitage.[15] By the 1470s the simple hut had been transformed into a conventual establishment with kitchen, dormitory for the brethren, chapel, and presumably a space for greeting (and healing) pilgrims; by then the Caracciolos had issued the first official rec-

13. Galuzzi, *Origini*, 55; *PC*, 147–49; ibid., 48–53; on 49 n. 12 he discuses the discrepancy between testimony and chronology. Denys Hay remarks that such visitations were far from routine in Italy during this period, *The Church in Italy in the Fifteenth Century*, 51. Paul II was troubled by Fraticelli in the March of Ancona; he would have been jittery about further possibly deviant movements in other areas.

14. *PC*, 146–49, a witness present at the hermit/legate conversation; Galuzzi, *Origini*, 55.

15. Galuzzi, *Origini*, 127–28: they were cardinals Bartolomeo Roverella (papal legate in Calabria), Filippo Calandrini, Berardo Euril, and Rodrigo Borgia. The Latin of Galuzzi (on 127) suggests that the place had already been built (*ad reparationem ac conservationem edificiorum*), whereas Galuzzi's own heading for this document describes the indulgence as an aid to building it, "per aiutare la costruzione dell'eremo di Paola." Cf. also Galuzzi, *Pergamene*, codici e registri dell'Archivio generale dei Minimi (Roma: Edizioni della Curia Generalizia dei Minimi, 1970), 7.

ognition of Francis's activities in the constitution *Decet nos* and transferred oversight of the hermit's oratory/convent to Sixtus IV.[16] In 1474 Sixtus extended Francisco's privileges, assimilating them to the liberties and exemptions enjoyed by Franciscans and other mendicants.[17] This was the first of many such papal documents that eventually transformed an eremitic movement into a cenobitic institution. In 1483, at King Louis XI's "invitation," Francis left Calabria for France, never to return.

Between the 1430s and 1483 Francis transformed himself from isolated hermit on Paola's periphery to living saint at the center of a crowd of local, regional, and more distant admirers as his popularity grew around miracle-working; his first recorded wonders were associated with his building projects:[18] they involved a kitchen oven, siting of the high altar, and excavating of building stone—the holy man tamed a swarm of wasps chasing his novices—"I hid and watched," the *Vita* author confesses. Francis could immerse his hand and arm in hot oil and boiling water, and handle live coals. An oblique reference to Saint Francis involved a deer that Francis of Paola rescued from some hunters. The tamed animal used to tag along after him, even into his cell. Unlike a Saint Francis story, however, when his followers complained of hunger Francis of Paola allowed them to eat his pet, though its skin was kept "to this day" in the convent as a memento. For the pilgrims who came to his convent near Paola, the holy man usually cured with a few words and a blessing, herbs, an almond potion, or a diet of fruit (probably much more effective than a visit to the local medico). In fact, Francis's detractors "maliziosamente" nicknamed him "the herbal man," *homo herbarius.*[19] Indeed, as his fame grew, a Franciscan visitor claimed that the hermit was wrong to prescribe fruits, pears, and that sort of thing for sick people, when he should be sending them to doctors.

16. *Primo atto scritto*; the following is from Galuzzi, *Origini*, 56–60, Latin text of the archbishop's privilege on 128–130. Though Galuzzi claims that with this document the archbishop "raises" the congregation (small c) to the "'Congregazione [capital C] degli eremiti di S. Francesco d'Assisi,'" this phrase appears nowhere in the Latin text, nor is the word "Assisi" found there. Caracciolo's chancellor dates the document to Nov. 30, 1471, in the seventh year of Paul II's reign; but that pope died on July 26, 1471, in his seventh year.

17. Galuzzi, *Origini,* 130–35; the word "congregation" is not found in the text, in spite of Galuzzi's heading.

18. Paoli, "La santità canonizzata," 233; Pope Gregory I's *vita* of Saint Benedict also closely linked the building operations at Monte Cassino with the saint's miracles.

19. Galuzzi, *Origini,* 28, citing the Calabrian process.

Francis knew when a "cure" was beyond him: he sent a child injured by a pitchfork to Master Antonius, who successfully treated the wound.[20] He also incorporated physical labor—specifically, fetching construction materials for his convent—into his therapeutic repertoire. Men and women of even princely status volunteered to help, the ladies carrying stones to the sites in their silken garments. A witness testified in 1512 that about forty years earlier Francis cured a demoniac with three dried figs, then drafted him into hauling wood for the monastic fabric.[21] In 1517 another witness recalled that when a woman claimed to be too ill to carry a stone, Francis balanced one on her head, which effected a cure. Even a crippled nun was told by the holy man to "get up and carry stone for the monastic fabric"; when she complained she got the same rock-on-the-head treatment, curing her.[22] Such a stone, now memorialized as a relic, is still admired and touched by devotees at Paola. These examples might almost lead one to suspect a sense of humor in the austere hermit, which turns up again after one of his workmen fell from a height and "died." Francis took him by the hand, saying "Get up, there's nothing wrong with you"; immediately he stood and returned to work. Francis threw him a parting comment: "Don't leap like that again."[23] Not everyone accepted Francis's work-therapy: William came to him at another convent building-site, in Paterno. In 1512 he recalled the dialogue: "Father, give me a remedy; my wife is dying." Francis: "In charity, go and carry ten loads of building stone." William: "'How can I carry rocks when my wife is dying?'" and turning his back, he went off to find a doctor. Unable to locate one, he returned. This time Francis merely sent him home telling him his wife was cured; and so she was.[24] (As this example shows, Francis established other convents, discussed below.)

Wherever he was, Francis attracted crowds, which could be quite large. In one instance, a father brought his demented son, bound hand and foot. They waited "many days" but, unable to have an audience with the hermit, they went home. Francis later cured the boy. Even the nobility had to wait their turn: one of them asked someone who knew the holy man, "Could you get me an audience with brother Francis?"[25] Marchioness Polyxena, whose

20. *AASS:* April I. Lorenzo, 109; "Processus Calabricus," 177.

21. *PC*, 96.

22. *AASS*, "Processus Calabricus," 176.

23. Ibid., 177.

24. "Et cussi voltao le spalli et andao per trovare uno medico," *PC*, 159.

25. *AASS*, "Processus Calabricus," 176.

entourage included many knights, waited three days while Francis healed "a hundred" *diversas personas* before he got around to her. One assumes that delays didn't apply to emergencies: a barrel-maker lost his grip while bending a hoop that knocked out his eye. Forcing it back into the socket the sufferer went to the convent for help. After three days there, he recovered.[26]

Like many other contemporary hermits, Francis was credited with the gift of prophecy, and like others, he sometimes spoke out against the perceived injustices of local barons and Ferrante of Naples. The king, accustomed to such complainers, probably realized that he'd only injure his own reputation by silencing the now-famous hermit. By 1473, in fact, he'd taken Francis and his convent under royal protection.[27] However, this didn't prevent conflict between hermit and sovereign. From the 1470s Francis established more convents in Calabria and Sicily. He began constructing one at Castellammare di Stabbia (about a mile south of Pompeii) in 1477, but apparently without the permission of Ferrante's son Cardinal Giovanni. This led to strenuous punishment, Giovanni expelling the hermits and taking over the site for his own use. Presumably Francis's unlicensed project brought him a little too close to the royal capital; and perhaps Ferrante now recalled the hermit's earlier criticisms of himself, his wife, and his family. The upshot was a trireme arriving at Paola with armed men to arrest the hermit. When their captain saw Francis, however—according to the *Vita*—overcome, he threw himself at his feet and begged forgiveness for what he'd been sent to do. The hermit is supposed to have accepted his fate, attributing it to God's will, even providing a meal for the captain and his forty men. The *Vita* then passes immediately to a story of a demoniac woman who saw crow-devils in the forest, leaving readers to assume that Francis miraculously escaped arrest. It's likely that the locals, learning of the impending deportation of their living saint, began gathering to defend their hero, convincing the captain to take the trireme back to Naples without his prisoner. Apart from this episode, it seems that Francis was left in peace to manage an ever-growing network of convents. Perhaps he would have remained a Calabrian "founder" known to the people and Church of southern Italy, at the end of his long life being buried in their midst and becoming the center of local

26. *AASS*, "Processus Calabricus," 182.

27. See Ernesto Pontieri, *Per la Storia del Regno di Ferrante I d'Aragona Re di Napoli*, 2nd ed. (Naples: Edizioni scientifiche italiane, 1969), 423–27.

cult at Paola, where some of his relics are venerated today. However, Francis died and was buried roughly a thousand miles away, amidst a people whose language he didn't understand, revered no longer just by local peasants and rough Calabrian nobles, but by kings and queens of France.

FRANCIS IS SENT TO FRANCE

In 1483, at the request of France's Louis XI, Pope Sixtus IV commanded Francis to go to the French court. This unusual act of cooperation—the pope's agreeing to uproot a popular Italian spiritual figure and ship him off to France—is even more noteworthy in view of Franco-papal controversies that enlivened most of the 1470s. Especially after the days of Philip IV, Boniface VIII, and the Avignon papacy, relations between French kings and Roman pontiffs often were troubled. This touchy situation worsened after the councils of Constance and Basel, and the subsequent Pragmatic Sanction of Bourges of 1438 that weakened papal powers in France and strengthened the "Gallican" church. A year after his election, Sixtus IV and Louis XI (r. 1461–83) achieved a shaky *modus vivendi* in a concordat of 1472.[28] At first, king and pope got on relatively well, although quarrels soon developed: Sixtus's refusal to promote the royal relative Charles de Bourbon to the cardinalate in 1473; the king's charge of papal simony in appointing some anti-French cardinals; a misunderstanding (1474) in the pope's dealings with Milan and Venice, as against France's ally Florence; the pope's attempt at peace between Louis and Duke Charles the Bold of Burgundy seeming to favor the duke (1475). By January 1476 Louis demanded examination of all documents from Rome before publication in France, and, citing the decrees of Constance, he also called for a Church council, the proclamation for a Lyons meeting being attached to the doors of St. Peter's in March.[29] In the Pazzi conspiracy (April 1478) Louis sided with Lorenzo de'Medici against

28. Pastor, *History of the Popes,* 4:320–43. The points briefly noted here are greatly nuanced in Paul Ourliac's "The Concordat of 1472: An Essay on the Relations between Louis XI and Sixtus IV," in *The Recovery of France in the Fifteenth Century,* ed. P. S. Lewis (New York: Harper and Row, 1971), 102–84. This long article, originally published in 1942–43, deals with more than the Concordat.

29. Ourliac, "The Concordat of 1472," 119–32; see also 126: "By and large, until 1475 relations between Louis XI and Sixtus IV had not been bad." The cardinalate quarrel is on 127. Another cause of dissension in 1476 was rivalry between Charles de Bourbon, legate in Avignon, and the pope's nephew Giuliano della Rovere, who wanted that position. Their quarrel culminated in a warlike confrontation at Avignon, with victory going to Charles. However, after Giuliano met with the king in June of 1476, Louis allowed him to take over as legate in Avignon, and in December 1476 Sixtus finally elevated Charles to the cardinalate.

Sixtus. By mid-1479, this potentially dangerous situation had blown over, and in September, Louis began withdrawing support from Florence, which made its peace with Sixtus in December of the next year. By then, Otranto had fallen to the Turks (August 1480). In response to the pope's call for a crusade, Louis promised financial support on condition that other European powers also contributed. French envoys were in Rome by March 1481, and next month a crusading tithe, levied on all the European powers, was announced in France. By the time that Mehmet II's death led to the recovery of Otranto (September 1481), France and the papacy had drawn together once again, although Sixtus still wanted the Pragmatic of 1438 abrogated. The pope "never ceased to praise the goodwill of the king," sending him the golden rose, and in return Louis allowed a tithe on the French clergy.[30] This was a timely rapprochement, since both king and pope faced serious problems in 1482. For Louis, political challenges continued to require responses (e.g., to unrest in Provence), made more difficult by his own declining physical condition, and in July and August when Rome was attacked by Ferrara's ally Ferrante of Naples, the pope "in his necessity even applied to France."[31] This was about the time that King Louis first learned of Francis of Paola.

I suggested that it was "unusual" for the pope to send Francis into France. Evidently, a desire for rapprochement led Sixtus to agree to this royal request. But what had motivated King Spider to ask for this particular Calabrian holy man? When he was about fifty-six, Louis XI "began now to waxe old and sickely," as the Elizabethan translator of Commynes has it.[32] Before the end of 1481 he'd suffered at least two strokes. With Commynes's help, he carried on daily business, always fearing that his enemies would take advantage of his weakness. Settling in finally at Plessis castle (Tours), the ailing Louis kept to himself, closely guarded as if, says Commynes, he were in a frontier post. Few were allowed into the castle, which was heavily fortified and protected by crossbowmen ordered to "shoote at every man that approched neere the castell after the shutting of the gates, till they opened in the morning." Louis's doctor, the pushy Jacques Coitier, seems to have frightened the king into paying him very large fees as Louis's fear of dying became an obsession. This was well known to his courtiers, who were not to utter the word "death" in his presence.

30. Ourliac, "The Concordat of 1472," 150–55.

31. Pastor, *History of the Popes*, 4:358, n. The pope had consented to Venice's takeover of Ferrara.

32. Thomas Danett, *The History of Comines*, vol. 2 (New York: AMS Press, 1967), 85, 92.

Churches and religious houses alike benefited from the king's largesse; perhaps their torrents of prayer would fend off death.[33] Commynes writes that the king's spending spree provoked complaint from the Franciscan archbishop of Tours himself: the poor should not be taxed for the benefit of rich churches and canons. Regardless, the king sent money, gold, and silver treasures to shrines throughout Europe, including some "in the kingdom of Naples."[34] Louis's net was cast even as far as Canterbury: as early as 1478 the monks sent a token of Saint Thomas so that "he might wear it on his hat."[35] After Louis asked Sixtus for various holy relics and the pope complied in 1483, some Roman civic officials criticized the pontiff for sending them. His excuse was the king's urgent request; he was dying.[36] Even the new Turkish sultan Bayezid II (d. 1512) offered relics from Constantinople, and money, if Louis would retain custody of his brother and rival Djem (d. 1495) who'd been taken to France during 1482. The king refused the offer. Otherwise, the royal appetite for the Church's magic was insatiable. Louis wrote to the abbot of Rheims in April asking for "a little drop from the Holy Ampoule" and then, fortified with papal backing, asked (July 14, 1482) for the whole vial of the oil used for anointing French sovereigns (including himself, in 1461), which was sent to Plessis. Commynes saw it in a cupboard in the royal chamber ("there is little oil within it").[37] Another source of holy power was the ring of Florence's fifth-century Bishop Zenobius, kept by the Girolami family. Louis, having heard of this precious relic in the spring of 1482, asked Lorenzo de'Medici to borrow it for him. The ring duly arrived in May or June.[38] However, by July something was amiss: the king was writing to Lorenzo to ask whether the ring had, indeed, belonged to Saint Zenobius, what miracles it had performed, whether it had healed anyone, and how it should be worn.[39]

33. *Louis XI: Lettres Choisies,* ed. Henri Dubois (Paris: Librarie Générale Française, 1996), 509–24.

34. Philippe de Commynes, *The Life of Louis XI of France,* trans. and ed. Paul Kendall as *The Universal Spider* (London: Folio Society, 1973), 264.

35. *Christ Church Letters,* ed. J. B. Sheppard, New Series 19 (Camden Society, 1877), 37–38.

36. Charles Stinger, *The Renaissance in Rome* (Bloomington: Indiana University Press, 1998), 34. Pastor notes that Sixtus appealed to the example of Gregory the Great, who also had distributed relics, *History of the Popes,* 5:94 n.

37. *Lettres Choisies,* 524–26; Commynes, *The Universal Spider,* 272.

38. For this section see Sally J. Cornelison, "A French King and a Magic Ring: The Girolami and a Relic of St. Zenobius in Renaissance Florence," *Renaissance Quarterly* 55, no. 2 (Summer 2002): 434–69.

39. *Lettres Choisies,* 527: "Mais je désire bien savoir si c'est le même que le saint portait, pareillement quels miracles il a fait, et s'il a nuls guéri, et qui, et comment il le faut porter" (July 9, 1483).

Whatever the source of the king's doubts about the relic, they were well-founded, as it turns out that the ring was only a copy of the real thing. Consequently, Louis was asking for the (authentic) ring in November.[40] The item arrived in December 1482, brought by a teenage member of the Girolami family. Once again, however, it seems that the king developed doubts, since Lorenzo was writing to him in February 1483 to say that someone was on his way who'd witnessed the ring's miraculous powers. Louis returned the relic to Florence in a gold reliquary, and, though the king died in August 1483, the ring became the center of legal battles among the Girolamis, who were suing and counter-suing each other over a gift of money and the reliquary. The case(s) continued until at least 1486.

Louis sought help from doctors, relics, and canonized as well as unofficial saints. His father, Charles VII, had listened to prophecies from "the holy hermit" John of Ghent, a religious of the famed Burgundian monastery of Saint-Claude. In April 1482 Louis visited the monastery, and he was back in Tours by June.[41] In October he heard that John of Ghent's body, entombed in the Dominican convent of Troyes, was the site of miracles. He sent a cloth of gold to cover John's shrine. About the same time (autumn of 1482) he asked Sixtus IV to open a canonization process for *ledit ermite* who had relieved all sorts of people of their maladies. In July 1483, Louis reminded the Troyes friars that he was seeking John's canonization and asked for some of the "holy hermit's" relics.[42] At the same time as he was pushing for John of Ghent's canonization, Louis was searching for living men and women whose spiritual powers, he hoped, would prolong his life, who would "mediate between God and the king for the lengthening of the king's days. From all parts of the world the king received names of such people. To a number of them he sent messages. When some came to speak with him, he talked to them only of this lengthening of life. Most replied wisely, saying that they possessed no such power."[43] Some were lucky enough to benefit from the king's patronage, such as brother Bernardin de Doullens, who declared that Louis would enjoy a long life;[44] and the king was

40. "Je désire fort que je le puisse avoir," *Lettres Choisies,* 526 (November 14, 1482).

41. Commynes, *The Universal Spider,* 260–61; Paul M. Kendall, *Louis XI* (New York: Norton, 1971), 357.

42. *Lettres Choisies,* 527–30; John never was canonized.

43. Commynes, *The Universal Spider,* 264.

44. Pierre Champion, *Les Grands Hommes et leurs Médicins* (Lyons: Lab. CIBA, 1935), 54.

supporting at least one other hermit, "the holy man near Orléans."[45] Not all of the prophetic well-wishers who trekked to Tours hoping to please His Majesty and perhaps gain a pension or snug place at court were successful. The *Vita* notes that the king grew wary after being deceived "by several" pseudo-holy folk.[46] Apparently the skepticism with which he treated Zenobius's ring—he also ordered the two heads of Saint Lazarus investigated—carried over to living "saints."[47] However, this didn't stop the search. Consequently, when he was told about a holy Calabrian hermit, the king wanted him brought to France.

How did Louis XI come to know of Francis? Fortuitously, it seems. A witness at the 1513 hearings at Tours, John Moreau, a squire of Louis's court, testified that a Naples merchant, Matthew Coppola, happened to tell him about his barren wife who'd been delivered of an infant thanks to the prayers of a holy man in the Naples area who performed *multa miracula.*[48] In 1482, when this conversation would have occurred, commercial links between Naples and the royal residence at Tours were well established.[49] Moreau, knowing that Louis was on the lookout for such people, mentioned this to the king, who interviewed Coppola. As a result, Louis sent a legation into Calabria to fetch Francis, "if this were possible." As it turned out, it almost wasn't. Before following the fate of that legation, we should emphasize that what most interested the king was the wonder-working powers of the hermit, his thaumaturgy. This, above all, was what Louis desired—something or someone to extend his life, if not medically then miraculously. He expressed little interest in Francis's other qualities.

A party of VIPs including the master of the royal household and Moreau sailed to Calabria, where in July 1482 they met Francis; he ignored their invitations to come to France. Various reasons have been suggested for his reluctance to leave Calabria: advanced age (he would have been about sixty-six), responsibility for his growing company of followers in various convents, uncertainty about facing an intimidating king. Unable to budge

45. Ourliac, "The Concordat of 1472," 388 n. 313.

46. "A pluribus fuisset sub umbra sanctitatis deceptus," *AASS,* April I, 115.

47. *Lettres Choisies,* 518–19. On June 13, 1482, Louis ordered Jean Rolin, cardinal and bishop of Autun, to determine the matter, for some said that Lazarus's head was at Autun, others, at Avallon: the prelate is to find out in truth "où ledit chef est."

48. *PT,* 69–71.

49. Roberti, *S. Francesco di Paola;* Roberti, a Minim, is a useful source after allowances are made for a laudatory bias.

the hermit, the embassy tarried for six or seven months, appealing to Francis's temporal lord, Ferrante of Naples, whose letters and envoys to Paola also had no effect. So, for several months in 1482, a group of frustrated Frenchmen trekked between Naples and Paola, hoping to convince our Calabrian to relocate. In October Louis reminded his agents in Italy "to do as I have written concerning *le saint homme.*"[50]

Learning of Francis's resistance, Louis finally had his ambassador in Rome, Beaudricourt, turn to the pope. In two letters ("one of which I saw at Tours," the *Vita* author writes) of late 1482–early 1483, Sixtus peremptorily ordered the hermit to go to France, a command Francis could not ignore.[51] Taking along one or two companions, he made a journey that became something of a triumphal procession. Stopping in Naples in late February, Francis was fêted by Ferrante and his son; in Rome, during March over a period of several days the hermit and pope met three times for private talks with significant repercussions. Francis also found time to perform some miracles for the Romans crowding round and plucking at him for relics.[52] After the party left the city, the *Vita* reports an incident that suggests that some among the group questioned his commitment to the journey. When the hermit went off to pray in a church, "Everyone suspected that he'd taken flight; stunned, they began crying out that the king would kill them. However, the hermit was found and the party continued on their way."[53] At Marseilles, Moreau informed Louis of the hermit's approach, which so overjoyed the

50. *Lettres Choisies,* 512–13.

51. *AASS,* April I, 114; *PT,* 290–91. Roberti, after noting that the two letters no longer exist, quotes from a Vatican document that he dates to June 24, 1483, from the pope to Louis, which includes a somewhat threatening phrase: "Ipsum (Franciscum) hortati sumus, ut iter suum ad te festinaret, immo etiam sub censuris ei mandavimus, ut ne moram ullam interponeret." Roberti seems to take this as analogous to the pope's letter ordering Francis to go to France; but Roberti does not quote the rest of the sentence, in which the pope tells Louis that he has commanded Francis to do all he can to cure him: "omniaque curaret que ad incolumitatem, et sanitatem tuam . . . spectarent"; it's a command not to go, but to cure. When he wrote the letter, Sixtus knew that Francis had already arrived at the French court. Galuzzi, *Origini,* 123, quotes this letter in full, dating it to June 4, 1483.

52. *AASS,* April I, 114. One of the less salubrious of Francis's wonders involved a Roman matron who obtained some of his straw bedding, took it home, and put it on a table, where her husband saw it. Picking it up, he began laughing and calling her a stupid fool. Taking the straw into the latrine, he used it to wipe himself (disregarding his wife's pleas). The hand holding the straw adhered so tenaciously to his body that only by seeking out Francis and obtaining his blessing was "the use of his hand . . . restored." He returned home confirmed more than ever before in fear of God and his saints.

53. *AASS,* April I, 114–15.

king that "he didn't know whether he was in heaven or on earth."[54] Moreau later was amply rewarded for his efforts. In February and March Louis commanded the citizens of Lyons to provide the utmost comfort for Francis, "a man of holy life," treating him as if he were the Holy Father himself.[55] Leaving Lyons by late April, the entourage made its way to the Loire, meeting the Dauphin Charles at Amboise before entering Tours, where at last Louis XI and Francis met, in late April or early May 1483.

HERMIT AND KING FACE TO FACE

Commynes makes Louis's main concern strikingly obvious: the moment the hermit entered his presence, the king fell "downe before him, . . . desiring him to prolong his life; whereunto he answered as a wise man should."[56] "Some mocked at this hermit's comming," and there was indeed criticism of royal dependence on a simpleton who knew no French. One of the loudest critics, as we might expect, was Louis's chief physician, Coitier. Evidently he was among those who talked the king into testing the new arrival, hoping to trip him up. The king sent a golden image of the virgin, which Francis rejected. An offer of enough gold to support his convents was likewise dismissed, the hermit shunning the coins "as if they were shit" (*velut stercora*), telling Louis to return the gold to those he'd robbed. Even a simple gift of fish for Francis's companions was refused, finally convincing the king that the hermit could not be overcome by avarice, the root of all evil.[57] This stubborn Francis, in the king's eyes, was a truly holy person. Louis's main concern continued to be his own physical rather than spiritual health. Commynes: the king "continually sent to him: saying, that if it pleased him he could prolong his life."[58] However, since Francis couldn't perform the one miracle the king desired, the "vaine hope he had in this heremite" came to nothing.

The "failure" of the holy man, or rather the king's disappointment, must quickly have been communicated to Sixtus IV, since in June papal secretar-

54. *PT*, 371: *nesciebat si esset in celo vel in terra.* 55. *Lettres Choisies*, 531–32.

56. Danett, *History of Comines*, 94.

57. *Vita*, *AASS*, April I, 115, has "avaritiam, quae omnium malorum radix est," perhaps inadvertently reproducing an old anti-curial tag in which the initials could be arranged to spell out *Roma;* or, possibly the author was thinking of 1 Tim 6:10: "Radix enim omnium malorum est cupiditas."

58. Danett, *History of Comines*, 107.

ies dated two briefs to Francis enclosed in a letter to the king.[59] In the first, denoting Francis an Observant Franciscan, Sixtus writes that he's happy to have learned of his safe arrival at court. Then the pope immediately changes his tone:

Because we vehemently desire that His Majesty should feel that benefit for which he hoped from your arrival there, we desire and, enjoining upon you *in virtue of the most strict holy obedience,* we command, that you turn your attention to every care, zeal and diligence for the recovery of the health of His Majesty, in this overlooking nothing, praying God, and applying remedies that might in any way pertain to his well-being, notwithstanding whatever opinions to the contrary that others may have made to you.

Sixtus concludes by noting that he's asking God, through Francis, to keep His Highness well and healthy. At the bottom of a registered copy of this brief is: *Simile sub pena excommunicationis.* That means that a second brief to Francis was penned, but the phrase "in virtue of holy obedience" was replaced by "under penalty of excommunication," a far stronger threat should the hermit fail in his expected duties. In the king's letter enclosing the briefs the pope wrote:

We command [*mandamus,* present tense] Francis of Paola, whom we ordered to come to you, in two briefs—one in virtue of holy obedience, the other under penalty of excommunication—that he not desist from praying to God with all care, zeal and diligence, for the well-being and best condition of Your Highness, notwithstanding whatever opinions to the contrary that others may have made to him. *Therefore Your Majesty can hand over to brother Francesco either of these briefs, whichever seems best to you.* We continue to supplicate God for your health . . . [etc.], and will do what seems to you should be done.

The king gave the first version to Francis; of the second, "excommunication" brief, there is now no trace, at least in the convent's Tours archives.[60] This issue has been considered at some length because it reveals the king's and pope's attitude toward Francis. The briefs, sent so soon after his arrival, seem to have been prompted by Louis's suspicion that the Calabrian was a

59. Galuzzi, *Origini,* 122–23, prints these briefs as dated June 2, transcribed from *Registra Brevium,* ASV Arm. 39 vol. 15, where they are found together on fol. 293v; but Roberti, *S. Francesco di Paola,* 408 n. 1, transcribing from the same source (ff. 293–594), reads "II" not as Roman numeral 2, but as Arabic "11." Emphasis added.

60. Galuzzi, *Origini,* 77, emphasis added; evidently only this reference to an "excommunication letter" in the *Registra Brevium* survives in the Vatican archives; it would have been unnecessary for scribes to copy out the entire text of this second brief.

fraud, since he did no more for him than other holy men and women called to court. In addition, somewhere in the background the jealous Coitier was probably encouraging Louis's suspicions. This apparent papal subservience to Louis XI, reflected in Sixtus's reassuring letter to the monarch and reprimands to Francis, is explicable in terms of a Franco-papal rapprochement. The pope was particularly gratified by Louis's cooperation against the Venetians: on June 15, 1483—during the period Sixtus was reproaching Francis—he sent the king a copy of the bull (May 24) interdicting Venice to publish "if it seems to you it should be"—which it was.[61]

A second round of letters, also in June, reveals that pope and king were less than happy with other aspects of Francis's behavior. The pope had received His Majesty's letter stating that "that hermit" who recently arrived had spoken to the king on the pope's behalf about some tithes, and Louis suspected that he was instigated by someone else [e.g., the pope himself]. Louis wished to know the papal mind in this regard. The pope thanked his "dearest son" for his devotion to the Holy See, and continued: "as to the hermit, we urged him to hurry his journey to you—rather, we commanded under censure—that he hasten to look after you, zealously fulfilling your desire, taking care of your health and well-being." Regarding tithes, however, not a word (so the pope claims) came from us.[62] Therefore, Sixtus concluded, put your mind at rest.[63] But it didn't end there. Although the king continued to provide for Francis's comfort—for instance, in June having his finance minister in Languedoc send up some lemons, sweet oranges, and parsnips for the *saint homme* who ate neither flesh nor fish[64]—the issue came up again in another brief, of July 6, 1483. It suggests that hermit and king were still at odds over tithes. Louis had asked for certain relics, "which we [Sixtus] have freely conceded" (for which "the Roman people" upbraided the pope—see above). Moreover, once again Sixtus assured the king that he shouldn't be troubled about tithes; he is instructing "brother Francis" not to continue vexing the royal conscience. As promised, on the same day Sixtus commanded the hermit (again addressed as a Franciscan): "The very be-

61. Pastor, *History of the Popes*, 4:376 n.

62. A rather blunt "nullum a nobis verbum factum est."

63. Galuzzi, *Origini*, 123, transcribing ff. 295v–296r of ASV Arm. 39 vol. 15, dates this to IIII June 1483 (June 4), whereas Roberti, *S. Francesco di Paola*, 416, transcribing a different folio, 660 of the same ms., writes "24 iunii 1483."

64. *Lettres Choisies*, 533, June 29, 1483.

loved in Christ, our son king Louis, writes that you have troubled him over tithes; cease to do so." As for the confirmation of Francis's constitutions, which Louis supported, the pope would freely do it *only if* he took attentive care to restore His Majesty to pristine health.[65] The pope, then, was willing to approve Francis's formally establishing an order on condition that he exert himself to the utmost for the king's recovery. In August Sixtus again informed Louis that he was ready to confirm "those constitutions" Francis had prepared for his congregation; and later in the month the pope told Francis that "we will confirm" the constitutions. As it turned out, the sickly king died a few weeks later (August 30, 1483). As for those *constitutiones*, we don't know what they were or their fate, though of course a rule eventually was approved.[66]

FRANCIS AS AMBASSADOR

Traditionally, Francis's move to France has been seen as a papal gift of a famous healer. However, the pope also stood to benefit from the hermit's trip. While Francis was in Rome en route to France, during those long, repeated audiences we noted above, Sixtus assigned him the duty of maintaining good relations with the king in exchange, perhaps, for a promise of some sort of constitution for his nascent order. Among points to be settled in France was a tithe for war against the Turks. As we've seen, Louis's discomfort on this question led Sixtus to command Francis to leave it alone. Sixtus, while blaming the hermit, was exculpating himself—he may well have asked Francis to raise this very issue. As Addante puts it, this was "a diplomatic letter that didn't convey the whole truth."[67] That was true of most diplomatic exchanges: "truth" was something a good diplomat usually wished to keep in reserve. Papal envoys brought various messages to the hermit that led to Francis's influencing elements of Louis's politics, for example, the restoration of the Valentinois, and publication of the interdict against Venice in the aftermath of the Ferrara war. The political role Sixtus expected Francis to play is unmistakably evident in two letters.[68] In the first, of August 7, 1483, the pope states that his referendary and his senior house-

65. "Libenter faciemus *modop* diligentem operam prestes, ut Maiestas sua pristine incolumitati restituatur," Galuzzi, *Origini*, 123–24, emphasis added.

66. Ibid., 81–82.

67. "Una lettera diplomatica, che non diceva tutta la verità," Addante, *San Francesco di Paola*, 206.

68. Roberti, *S. Francesco di Paola*, 420–21 and nn. 1 and 2; Pastor, *History of the Popes*, 4:376–77.

hold officer "will report some matters to you in our name, to which you will give full credibility [*plenam . . . fidem*]."[69] This loosely resembles contemporary letters of credence from one political entity to another. The second letter, of August 16, emphasizes Sixtus's casting Francis in the role of papal agent. The pope, through Francis, thanks the king for publishing the bull against Venice: "It is our will that you thank him for this in our name when you'll be with His Majesty," and urges him to refuse audience to the Venetian ambassador who's said to be returning to the royal court, until papal and League representatives arrived.[70] Then the carrot: "We will confirm your constitutions; be in good heart about this." (Francis's diplomatic value, evident in papal letters, was also recognized by Ferrante of Naples in a letter of August 17, 1483.)[71] Sixtus knew that the hermit would have more intimate and continuous relations with the French king than legates or ambassadors, whose access was regulated by advisers, protocol, and the changing political climate. As Thomson writes:

> The major European power with which the popes were most deeply involved politically was France. . . . For a long time, however, the popes relied on special missions rather than creating any permanent resident nunciature. . . . In the 1470s there were various *ad hoc* embassies, with gaps between them . . . although Sixtus IV may have considered establishing a more permanent form of embassy shortly before his death in 1484.[72]

In short, in Francis the pope had a man on the inside, a valuable link to the royal mind and his private anxieties that would not have been revealed to official diplomats, whether secular or papal. For his part, as he'd grown older Louis's suspicion of envoys had increased; he was particularly wary of long-term resident ambassadors, dismissing them almost capriciously.[73] In this light, Francis's continuing presence at court becomes even more significant. The king's death, however, would seem to have made Francis's presence re-

69. Galuzzi, *Origini*, 79, dated to July 7.

70. "Volumus, ut tu nostro nomine, quando cum illius Maiestate eris . . . eamque horteris ut si orator Venetorum . . . ne audiatur . . . constitutiones vero tua confirmabimus," ibid., 125.

71. Ibid., 126.

72. John A. F. Thomson, *Popes and Princes 1417–1517* (London: George Allen and Unwin, 1980), 105.

73. Vincent Ilardi, "The First Permanent Embassy outside Italy: The Milanese Embassy at the French Court, 1464–1483," in *Politics, Religion, and Diplomacy in Early Modern Europe*, ed. Malcolm R. Thorp and Arthur J. Slavin, Sixteenth Century Essays and Studies 27 (Kirksville, Mo.: Sixteenth Century Journal Publishers, 1994), 1–18.

dundant, but instead of his returning to southern Italy, his political role extended into the next two reigns: he continued to be useful to Rome (and France).

The king's young son Charles VIII (1483–98) was at first counseled by his sister Anne, wife of Peter of Beaujeu/Bourbon. Their regency was contested by Louis of Orléans, later Louis XII.[74] As a result, civil war among the nobility marked the first five years of Charles's reign, ending with Louis's defeat in 1488. In the midst of these events, papal authority in France was again challenged. The new king was well-disposed personally toward the hermit. Although Louis XI had provided the Calabrian and a few companions with a cell at Plessis, in 1489 Charles granted Francis land and means for a proper convent just outside Tours at Montils, on the Cher. Completed by 1491, it included fourteen cells for the brethren and two prisons for delinquents. The iron fence around Plessis castle was sold to raise money for the convent.[75] At first, however, it seems that Francis took on an antiroyal stance: his efforts were directed against Gallican agitation as the French hierarchy and Estates tried to undo the fruits of cooperation (in part brokered by Francis) between Louis XI and the pope. Sixtus rightly interpreted this as a renewed attack on Rome's authority. In March of 1484 he mildly admonished the young king while praising his father.[76] Next month Francis informed Sixtus of events "in this part of France." The hermit, who included a self-congratulatory remark about his diligence in dealing with the king and his council, gave the letter to one of his followers, who on arrival in Rome would discuss complaints against His Holiness and "other secret matters."[77] Galuzzi notes that it's unfortunate that we don't have more documentation about "this side of the Hermit," a sentiment echoed by Ourliac, who muses that "one would willingly know more about the saint's diplomatic activities."[78] After Sixtus died in August of 1484, Innocent VIII (d. 1492) continued to encourage Francis's semi-clandestine diplomacy.

74. Louis was the grandson of duke Louis of Orleans (d. 1407), brother of Charles VI (d. 1422) of the Valois line.

75. Roberti, *S. Francesco di Paola,* 432–33, 438–41.

76. Ourliac, "The Concordat of 1472," 175, 391.

77. "Contra v.s. et la Sede Apostolica .... altre cosse secrete"; it was common diplomatic practice that sensitive information would be delivered orally by bearers of relatively innocuous letters, in case these should be intercepted.

78. Galuzzi, *Origini,* 80; Ourliac, "Concordat of 1472," 176. Lack of documentation didn't stop John R. Hale, in *Renaissance Europe 1480–1520,* 2nd ed. (Oxford: Blackwell, 2000), 167, from writing

Charles's attempted conquest of the kingdom of Naples raises interesting but perhaps unanswerable questions about Francis's loyalties. The king prepared to embark on his Italian adventure by reconciling with Louis of Orléans in 1491 and establishing treaties with England, Spain, and Austria in 1492 and 1493. His army's progress in 1494 is well known (about this time Francis obtained land in Rome for a Minim convent, next to which Louis XII would found the church of Trinità dei Monti). Charles arrived in Naples in February 1495 and soon was returning to France, en route engaging in the battle of Fornovo in July 1495. Denied his goals, Charles died in April 1498. What was Francis's part in the French attempt on his homeland? Galuzzi refers to an earlier commentator (Ercole, in 1932) who claimed, "maliziosamente," that Francis encouraged Charles to invade after the hermit was pressured by numerous *Regno* exiles.[79] This word, "maliciously," suggests that Galuzzi—himself a Minim—had already decided the matter, clinched by a further statement: "Knowing Francis's mind," he writes, it's difficult to attribute such an action to him and include him among the spiteful instigators of revenge.[80] One can only admire and envy brother Galuzzi for such privileged insight. Perhaps another Minim, Roberti, comes closer to the mark. Though his biography of Francis is larded with adulation, on this question Roberti is less dogmatic than Galuzzi. He writes that although it isn't possible to know Francis's thoughts on this issue for certain, nevertheless, the hermit had denounced the late Ferrante's government, and Francis may have hoped that Charles would bring stability to the *Regno* (as Savonarola hoped for Florence).[81] Guicciardini draws attention to Charles's reliance on the advice "of several very close advisers," "men of low condition," "inexperienced and vulgar men" who filled his mind with vainglorious thoughts of conquering Naples and then the Turks.[82] Could

that Francis "became heavily involved in anti-Gallican intrigues, the centre of a web of information and the sender of smuggled messages to the pope."

79. Among these, perhaps the most important was Antonello di Sanseverino, prince of Salerno: Michael Mallett, "Personalities and Pressures: Italian Involvement in the French Invasion of 1494" in David Abulafia, ed., *The French Descent into Renaissance Italy, 1494–95: Antecedents and Effects* (Aldershot: Variorum, 1995), 151–63, esp. 155–7.

80. Galuzzi, *Origini*, 85, "Conoscendo però l'animo dei Paolano." Galuzzi had used the same expressive adjective, "maliziosamente," of those who nicknamed Francis *homo herbarius*, 28. Interestingly, Pontieri used almost exactly the same phrase: "Noi...conoscendo l'anima mite di Francesco e il suo spirito alieno dalla politica," *Per la Storia del Regno di Ferrante*, 442.

81. Roberti, *S. Francesco di Paola*, 473–74.

82. Francesco Guicciardini, *The History of Italy*, trans. Sidley Alexander (New York: Macmillan,

one of these have been Francis? His own birthplace, Paola, refused to surrender to the king of Naples after Charles had withdrawn.[83] The *Vita* notes that Charles's subsequent escape from Fornovo was attributed to Francis's remaining in his cell, fasting and praying for the king's deliverance from his enemies, "Venetians, Lombards, Italians and others."[84] The *Vita* discreetly ignores the fact that one of the "others" in this anti-French Holy League was the pope, Alexander VI.

There's no doubt that Charles and Francis were close. So close, in fact, that on one occasion (a witness claimed in 1513) the hermit refused to let the king's thumping on his cell door disturb his contemplation; he refused to answer, until Charles—fearing that he'd died—prepared to force his way in. At that, "in a sad voice," Francis made it known that he was alive, but still refused to come out or say anything more. Even though this motif had already appeared in the *Vita*, it suggests a confident intimacy between king and hermit, who in October 1492 stood godfather to Charles's son, holding the king's hand while the infant was baptized by an Observant Franciscan. Francis suggested he be called "Orlando" (as a new Roland, to battle the infidel), but "Charles" was imposed on the baby when the princes of the realm objected to such an outlandish name.[85] Apart from domestic interactions, the *Vita* claims that "often" the king sought Francis's advice in more difficult matters.[86] "I have many times heard him speak before our present king, all the magnates of the realm being present.... He is still living," Commynes continues, "and therefore there could be a change, either for better or for worse, and hence I will say no more. Several people ridiculed the coming of this hermit called the Holy Man."[87]

1969), 21, 23–4, 25; for Charles's ambitions as Turkish conqueror, see David Abulafia, *The Western Mediterranean Kingdoms 1200–1500* (New York: Longman, 1997), 11, "The French Invasion of Italy, 1494–95."

83. Pietro Bembo, *History of Venice,* vol. 1, books 1–4, trans. Robert W. Ulery, Jr. (London: Harvard University Press/I Tatti Renaissance Library, 2007), 207: the town surrendered after a threatened attack by Ferrandino's men.

84. *AASS,* April I, 116; see also 115, the hermit prays (for twenty-two days) for Charles's victory in Brittany.

85. Matarasso, *Queen's Mate,* citing Th. Godefroy, *Histoire de Charles VIII, roi de France, et des choses mémorables advenues en son royaume, par Guillaume de Jaligny* [etc.] (Paris, 1684), 627. Galuzzi, *Origini,* 83–84, describes this event without mentioning the criticisms of Francis's choice of an "outlandish" name.

86. *PT,* 373; Galuzzi, *Origini,* 83; *AASS* April I, 110, 115–16: *in negotiis difficilioribus.*

87. Commynes, *The Universal Spider,* 265.

Though Charles was supportive, Francis wasn't so lucky in establishing his order with the pope. Attempts to approve a "constitution" (whatever it might have been) supported by Louis XI died with Sixtus IV. The new king tried again. In July of 1485, however, Innocent VIII turned him down: the pope preferred to adapt an already accepted rule, as in the case of brother Amadeus, a Franciscan; then "we will confirm" freely. Galuzzi suggests that on the one hand the pope, just as his predecessor, looked upon Francis as just another reformist Franciscan; and on the other that Innocent was relying on a canon of the Fourth Lateran Council prohibiting new orders.[88] As for Amadeus (Amadeo Menez da Sylva), his modified Franciscan rule had been approved in 1462 by Pius II. In 1472 he was given land on the Janiculum by Sixtus IV, whose personal confessor he was. Amadeus rebuilt a ruined monastery on the site (financed by Ferdinand and Isabella of Spain) and then retired into a cavern hollowed out beneath the cloister, where he spent his time, hermitlike, in prayer and fasting.[89] In Francis's case, it wasn't until 1493 that Alexander VI (1492–1503) approved a rule, drawn from Augustinian, Franciscan, and other sources. In 1501 the pope accepted a second version, commended by France's Louis XII (1498–1515), followed by a third iteration of 1502 and a final one in 1506 under Julius II. The Minims had finally and officially arrived, a year before their founder's death. By then there were convents in Spain, Italy, France, and Germany. French royals, such as Queen Anne of Brittany, were particularly generous patrons.[90] Occasionally Francis faced opposition, as in the early 1490s when Jean Quentin and Jean Standonck—principal of what became the fiercely regimented Collège de Montaigu—rejected his request to establish a convent near Paris. They changed their minds after meeting the holy man and being impressed by his conversation and demeanor.[91]

When Louis XII took over in 1498 after Charles died without male heirs, the aged Francis attempted to return to Italy, but was recalled by royal advisers. Perhaps they convinced Louis of his value as a respected spiritual guide and informal conduit to Rome who might be more useful or flexible

88. Galuzzi, *Origini,* 84–85, text of the brief on 125.

89. Ibid., 84 n. 12; Stinger, *Renaissance in Rome,* 186. Bramante's "Tempietto" was later built here, while Amadeus's offshoot Franciscans were absorbed into the OFM mainline by Leo X in 1517.

90. See, e.g., Roberti, *S. Francesco di Paola,* 447ff.

91. Roberti, *S. Francesco di Paola,* 449–51, dates this to 1493; Levi, to 1491: Anthony Levi, *Renaissance and Reformation: The Intellectual Genesis* (New Haven, Conn.: Yale University Press, 2002), 171.

than an orator or ambassador. As the new king confirmed and expanded the order's privileges in 1498, 1499, and 1500, Francis continued occasionally to advise on political issues.[92] Possibly he had words with Louis over the king's divorcing the unattractive Joanna of Valois (followed by Louis's marriage to Charles VIII's widow, Anne of Brittany). Francis also comforted the duke of Milan's brother Cardinal Ascanio Sforza, imprisoned at Bourges in 1500, promising him a quick restoration to liberty that finally occurred in 1502.[93] All through these years in France, Francis continued to guide his brethren while healing and consoling outsiders. His solitude must have been interrupted many times as his fame grew. Back home, in Calabria, miracles attributed to his powers continued. His thaumaturgy was noted in Rome: around 1500 he sent two of his brethren to the city on business. During their stay they went to see a demoniac from Picardy who was bound to one of the columns in St. Peter's—the "column that casts out spirits." Christ, supposedly, had been bound to that very column, in the wonderful way that space and time collapse in the universe of religious belief. The two went to her, placed Francis's rope-belt on her neck, and asked the demon to depart if Francis "was a true friend of God as we believe." The demon, which the canons of St. Peter's had been unable to expel, replied that it knew Francis well, "and intended him harm. It then left the woman."[94]

FALSE START TO THE PROCESS

During his twenty-four years in France Francis brought benefits to kings and their families through his political and spiritual counsel. His miraculous powers were just as significant. His evident piety and austerity, and the reputation that preceded him from Calabria to Tours, produced an expectant belief in his supernatural powers, including levitation (as claimed by Anne of Bourbon). There's little doubt that his miracles deeply affected the royal family. Apart from the spiritual solace he gave Louis XI in his final days, other royals enjoyed physical boons. Louis's daughter Anne of Bourbon had for some time produced no heirs until, with the help of Francis's

92. Roberti, *S. Francesco di Paola,* 510.

93. *AASS,* April I, 117–18; Roberti, *S. Francesco di Paola,* 508, 514.

94. Vita in *AASS,* April I, 117; the column and its demoniac are described by Sanuto, *I Diarii di Marino Sanuto,* ed. Rinaldo Fulin, Federico Stefani, et al. 58 vols. (Venice: F. Visentini, 1879–1903), col. 224: "la colona ove dicono esser stato legato Cristo"; see Ottavia Niccoli, *Prophecy and People in Renaissance Italy,* trans. Lydia G. Cochrane (Princeton, N.J.: Princeton University Press, 1990), 169.

prayers, she gave birth to Suzanne, who, claims the *Vita* of 1502, "still lives." (Suzanne, born in 1491, died without heirs in 1521.) Anne of Brittany, while married to Louis XII, fell ill and had no relief from medicines. She appealed to Francis, who sent her three apples. Her doctors claimed that they would complicate her stomach ailment and hasten death, but she ate them anyway and was cured.[95] When her daughter Claude, age nine, was ill with fever, Anne vowed to the dead Francis that she'd promote his canonization. During April, probably in 1508, Claude was cured.[96] Following this miracle, true to her promise Queen Anne began appealing to Rome. As well as applying to Julius II she directed the bishop of Nantes, Cardinal Robert Guibè (d. 1513), then in the city, and the procurator of the Minims, Francesco Binet, to promote Francis's cause. Binet, aware that many who had known the long-lived Francis would be dying off, was driven by a sense of urgency. However, it wasn't until May 1512 that Julius II formally initiated Francis's process. The question arises: if Anne's supplications date to around 1508, why was Julius's response delayed for some four years? The answer must lie not with the queen, but with her husband, Louis XII, regarding whom the pope is supposed to have told a French ambassador (in 1510), "I look upon your king as my personal enemy, and do not wish to hear anything more."[97]

When Julius became pope in 1503, Louis—following the lead of Charles VIII—had already (temporarily) taken Milan and Naples; his armies would disturb the peninsula for the whole of the pope's reign. Julius dedicated himself to ridding Italy of the "barbarians." In May 1510 he told a Venetian envoy that he'd spent a restless night pacing, unable to sleep, contemplating how to free Italy from the French.[98] In pursuit of this goal, by June he'd locked up one French cardinal and threatened other pro-French members of the college with a similar fate. Louis XII, meanwhile, revived some of the anti-papal provisions of the Pragmatic of 1438, about the time of Julius's remark that Louis was his personal enemy. Before the end of July 1510 Louis was planning an anti-papal council (as Louis XI had done with Sixtus IV). Countering, Julius attacked France's ally Ferrara, which once again became the scene of military conflict. His small army plodding north through September downpours elicited laughter from onlookers who, nevertheless, sup-

95. *AASS,* April I, 116.

96. Roberti, *S. Francesco di Paola,* 614–15.

97. Pastor, *History of the Popes,* 6:327.

98. For the following, ibid., 322 n.; 336; 337 n.; 339, n., 364–65; "non poteva dormer . . . . liberar Italia de'man de Francesi."

plied the papal train with provisions. Meanwhile the pope's recalcitrant cardinals Carvajal, Francisco Borgia, Briçonnet, de Prie, and Sanseverino had defected, fleeing to French Milan. En route to Ferrara, the pope fell seriously ill at Bologna. In his delirium Julius exclaimed that he preferred death to French captivity. Failing to take Ferrara, the pope returned via Bologna; by June 1511 he was back in Rome. En route he learned of the planned council of Pisa. In response Julius summoned a gathering in Rome in the spring of 1512, the Fifth Lateran Council. During October 1511, Julius completed the formation of a League with Spain, Venice, and eventually England against France, and excommunicated the "schismatic" cardinals at Pisa. In the midst of these military and spiritual conflicts, it would be highly unlikely that the pope would accommodate French royalty seeking the canonization of Francis of Paola, who had been, after all, an expatriate adviser to French kings. Julius had even more reason for anger when Louis XII defeated the pro-papal League at Ravenna in April 1512. It soon became apparent, however, that Ravenna was a Pyrrhic victory, and Julius, though forced for the moment to negotiate with France, seems to have been marking time; as he claimed, he aimed merely "to quiet down the French" before resuming their expulsion.[99] In May he opened the council, and between its first official sitting (May 10) and the second (May 17), perhaps as part of his shaky truce with France he finally responded to Queen Anne's petition, by briefs of May 13 setting up two commissions of inquiry into Francis's life, cult, and miracles, one at Tours, the other at Cosenza.[100]

With the help of Swiss troops Julius began ejecting the French in late May 1512, while the ineffective council of Pisa quietly dispersed. By the end of June, the French were gone (for now). Meanwhile Francis's local canonization inquiries went ahead. The Italian hearings (102 witnesses) ran from July 1512 to January 1513, and at Tours (57 witnesses) from July to December of 1513. An interesting aspect of these parallel processes is the requirement to investigate, inter alia, the miracles Francis performed during his lifetime.[101] Nothing is specified about posthumous miracles. Regardless, the people closest to

99. Ibid., 403, citing Sanuto.

100. For discussion and analysis of the witnesses involved in these *in partibus* inquisitions, see Cyril Polito, "Saint François de Paule: Ses rapports avec les Calabrais et les Tourangeaux," *Bollettino Ufficiale dell'Ordine dei Minimi* 47, nos. 2–3 (April–September 1999).

101. "In vita eius .... tale et tale miraculum," *PC*, 6, 12; a later copy of the papal order (on 227) has garbled this line.

Francis in time and place, that is, the witnesses who testified at Tours during 1513, just half-a-dozen years after his death, managed to get claims about his wonder-working from beyond (or rather in) the grave into the record. Many had known the hermit, in some cases for several years. He'd provided consolation as well as cures, sometimes with herbs—on occasion he stripped his garden nearly bare to load up the ladies of Louise of Savoy's court with herbs when she visited Plessis.[102] Several testified that they'd experienced or heard of posthumous miracles as well.[103] A common thaumaturgic device, widely used before and after his death, consisted of candles that he'd blessed. Particularly helpful during childbirth complications—often resulting in newborns being named after the hermit—they also quelled fires and calmed storms.[104] Sometimes, merely praying to the dead man led to a cure.[105] Just as typical of medieval cults were cures supposedly occurring at the tomb. Pilgrims came to the holy site to kneel and wait, or to thank him, for their restored health or good fortune.[106] Many left votives at or around his grave: in early December 1513, for instance, these included a "measured" candle for a cured adult, part of a woman's face, an infant, an eye, and a stomach (one-half pound in weight), all in wax.[107] Clearly, Francis followed a long-established pattern in his austerity, piety, and success as a founder as well as in miracle-working before and after death. To repeat Simon Ditchfield's succinct phrase, for the great majority of "consumers of sanctity," a saint's reputation in the sixteenth as in earlier—and, we might add, later—centuries was unquestionably linked to the power to work miracles.[108]

The period 1514–15 witnessed significant changes at the top. When the records of Francis's hearings arrived at Rome in April 1514, Julius II (d. February 1513) had been succeeded by Florence's Cardinal Giovanni de'Medici as Leo X (1513–21), who was less hostile to France. Even without formal examination of Francis's processes he cautiously approved his cult on July 7, 1513, "provided he not be considered canonized."[109] There

102. *PT,* 394.

103. Ibid., 288, 289, 292, 298, etc.

104. Ibid., 289–90, 300–301, 304–7, 316–17, 318–21, etc.

105. Ibid., 302–3, 342.

106. Ibid., 298–301, 315–16, 322–25, 333, 376, 399.

107. Ibid., 300 and 304, 303, 329, 338–39, 349 and 400.

108. Ditchfield, "Tridentine Worship and the Cult of Saints," 213.

109. Paoli, "La santità canonizzata," 224. By the seventeenth century, formal beatification procedures were in effect; until then the concept of beatus or beata was a flexible one. Simon Ditchfield has reminded me of Leo's great interest in local cults (personal communication); see below.

were also changes in France. After Louis XII died in January of 1515, Francis I, Louis's cousin and son-in-law, took the throne. Falling into line with his predecessors, the young, ambitious king moved his armies into Italy in August 1515. After some dithering, Leo joined the anti-French powers—an unfortunate choice, since in the aftermath of Francis's victory at Marignano in mid-September (with Venice as ally), Milan once again fell under French control. The pope, in a funk of regret, reportedly exclaimed to the haughty Venetian ambassador Giorgi, "We will throw ourselves into the arms of the Most Christian King, and beg his mercy."[110] In mid-October, at Viterbo (to which he'd fled in case the French continued on to Rome) Leo approved a preliminary peace agreement. Francis wished to meet the pope in person, and after consideration of various venues, Bologna was selected. Leo's entourage began moving northward, with a stop in the pope's city, Florence. En route, during November the pope had letters from the king, his wife, and his mother, Louise of Savoy, all expressing happiness at the Franco-papal peace. This Francis-Claude-Louise trio will reappear in the canonization bull as Francis's primary supporters.

The pope's entry into Florence (where anti-Mediceans were still influential) was orchestrated by local pro-Mediceans and Leo's master of ceremonies, Paris de Grassis. On December 1 the pope, his cardinals, and de Grassis discussed protocol for the forthcoming Bologna meeting. Leo's entry into that city on December 8, 1515, was as dismal as his arrival at Florence seemed jubilant. The sulky Bolognese showed scant respect for their overlord, and when de Grassis urged Leo to express outrage at their "extremely rude" behavior, the corpulent pope merely smiled and pretended not to notice. De Grassis was in his element when Leo sent him to meet Francis some three miles outside the city, to instruct the king about ceremonial arrangements, a perfect job for "the pedantic Master of Ceremonies."[111] This zealous organizer will provide interesting commentary on, as well as stage-manage, Francis's canonization. Leo and Francis finally met on December 11 in the Palazzo Publico, de Grassis leading the king by the hand as they pushed their way through the crowd toward His Holiness on a papal throne.[112] The king fervently performed the ritual *obedientia*. Leo subse-

110. Pastor, *History of the Popes*, 7:122.

111. Ibid., 7:135; Pastor used this same expression in ibid., 6:345.

112. For the following, see ibid., 7:139–45 and 8:415–33, and Edmund Bishop, "Leaves from

quently wrote to Louise to express delight at her son's behavior. For his part, the pope showed equal respect, on occasion taking the royal hand while walking with the king. After conferring for a few days behind closed doors, the two parted on the 15th, Francis taking with him a jewel-encrusted golden cross-reliquary as a gift from Leo. By December's end the king was in Milan, the pope in Florence, where, as we'll see in the next chapter, he initiated Antoninus's canonization process. He was back in Rome by the end of February 1516.

The discussions at Bologna resulted in a Franco-papal concordat, the details thrashed out by a bipartisan committee remaining behind in the city (there were alterations later on). In very broad terms the agreement gave French kings, eventually, almost complete control over the appointment of prelates and abbots within their realm, without reference to cathedral or monastic chapters or, often, the pope. For his part, Leo gained a promise of French protection for his city, Florence, and the abolition of the Pragmatic Sanction of Bourges, which, on paper, ended the threat of conciliar action and gave him a degree of freedom of election to certain French livings.[113] Francis sent drafts of the concordat to his mother; she approved. Leo's prelates and cardinals, however, did not, believing he'd given away too much. Only after six months of argument were the terms ratified and published in Rome (August 1516), and just to clinch this, Leo presented the concordat during the eleventh session of the Lateran Council in December 1516.[114] Finally, in April 1517, the pope sent official notification of these acts to the king. Apart from these issues, about this time a conspiracy to kill Leo began to come to light, which we'll discuss more fully in chapter 5 on Antoninus. Understandably, this preoccupied pope and curia to the detriment of other matters. Meanwhile, Francis was having an equally difficult time selling the concordat in his own realm. Even after a softening-up campaign starting as early as January, Parlement, the university, and the clergy resisted it. In June

---

the Diary of a Papal Master of Ceremonies" in *Liturgica Historica* (Oxford: Clarendon Press, 1918), 434–43.

113. Some of the traditional assumptions about the Concordat are raised and questioned by Robert Knecht in "The Concordat of 1516: A Reassessment," *University of Birmingham Historical Journal* 9 (1963): 16–32.

114. One of the prelates who expressed misgivings about Leo's actions—Domenico Jacobazzi—was later assigned to Francis's canonization committee. During the conflict between Julius II and Louis XII over the council of Pisa, Jacobazzi had been a staunch defender of papal authority in his tract *De Consilio* of 1512, Pastor, *History of the Popes*, 6:385.

Leo issued bulls supporting Francis and condemning such anti-concordat sentiments as contrary to the authority of both king and pope, and by the end of summer of 1518 open (but not clandestine) opposition was overcome.[115] Throughout this struggle king and pope, for the most part, worked together in a generally cordial relationship that stretched from 1516 to 1519, the year of Francis's canonization. Francis I's realm was relatively peaceful.

Soon afterward, however, the political kaleidoscope turned again. The death of Emperor Maximilian in mid-January led to Leo's supporting Friedrich the Saxon elector or the elector of Brandenburg, followed by Francis I, as counterweights to Charles king of Spain, Maximilian's grandson. In March and April 1519 the pope again made known his pro-French leanings (though actually hoping for neither Charles nor Francis to win). By the end of May, realizing that Francis could not win, Leo switched his support to Charles, which the censorious Pastor "deeply deplored."[116] Francis formally withdrew on June 26, and Charles, declared Emperor-elect Charles V on 28 June, was crowned next year at Aachen. As these portentous events were unfolding during 1518 and early 1519, at the curia there was a willingness to grant French supplications, such as requests to canonize the holy hermit of Plessis. The French royals were the principal agents behind those requests.

THE TRIAL REOPENS AND CONCLUDES

At several points in the narrative, we've mentioned the trio Francis, Claude, and the king's mother, Louise of Savoy. Louise had known the hermit and named her son after him; she exercised a certain amount of authority as regent when the king was outside the realm.[117] On May 8, 1514, Francis had married Claude, Louis XII's daughter who as a child had been miraculously cured through Francis of Paola. Perhaps at her prompting (or that of Louise, who had been concerned about the hermit's burial site), Francis I accorded privileges to the Minims on December 7, 1514. Subsequently, during 1516 and 1517 the pope received several supplications for Francis's canonization from France: three from the king, five from queen Claude, and further requests from other highly placed partisans, such as

115. For the Concordat and its effects, see Knecht, *Renaissance Warrior,* 90–103.

116. Pastor, *History of the Popes,* 7:271.

117. John F. Freeman, "Louise of Savoy: A Case of Maternal Opportunism," *Sixteenth-Century Journal* 3 (Oct. 1972): 77–98, at 83, considers the story of Francis's prediction to Louise about Francis I to be apocryphal.

Louise of Savoy and her sister Filiberta (Francis I's aunt and sister-in-law to the pope), the sister of Charles VIII Anne of Bourbon, the duke of Alençon (two requests), and the bishop of Grenoble; and fifteen places in southern Italy.[118] As a result, Leo authorized yet another series of inquiries at several sites in Calabria between 1516 and 1518 (120–130 witnesses).[119] In this so-called *Processus Calabricus,* incidentally, witnesses were asked to testify about both living as well as posthumous miracles.[120] During 1516, too, queen Claude had publicly vowed to the spirit of Francis of Paola that if she should have a male child (she'd had only girls), she'd name her son after the hermit and try to hasten his canonization, as her mother had done. Francis's cause advanced in March 1517 when the pope granted indulgences for the Minims' efforts to raise money for the anticipated canonization.[121] During the same year, in November the king "walked from Amboise to the shrine of St. Martin at Tours to pray for a son."[122] It was quite common to implore several saints for favors, as in this case. For the queen, in any event, when on February 28, 1518, she finally produced a male heir, as promised Francis received the credit: the birth of Dauphin Francis (along with the fact that Claude had herself been cured through Francis of Paola) bolstered royal support.[123]

A few more depositions about the hermit's wonders were collected in May 1518 (including the only posthumous miracle recorded in the papal bull). This was followed by the usual preliminary consistorial and rotal analyses and discussions. During this phase, a *relatio* on Francis of Paola was delivered before Leo X by Auditor of the Rota (later Cardinal) Giacomo Simoneta, occupying twenty folios of the Vatican manuscript (ASV, *Congr. Riti, processus 4216,* which also contains *relationes* for Raymund of Peñafort and Bonaventure) and twenty-eight pages in Patrizi-Accursi's edition. Francis's life is briefly set out, including the comment that some slanderers suggested that he was either insane or a fraud. His early experiences in Calabria, and

118. Pasquale Sposato, "Fonti per la storia di S. Francesco di Paola: La sua canonizzazione attraverso il 'Diarium' di Paride De Grassi prefetto delle ceremonie pontificie sotto Leone X, Introduzione," *Calabria Nobilissima* 10, nos. 31–32 (June 1956): 1–32, at 11 n. 27; hereafter Sposato, "Fonti, Intro."

119. Roberti, *S. Francesco di Paola,* 624; *AASS,* April I, 165–90.

120. "Signis in vita et post... aliis tum in vita tum etiam post obitum mirabiliter peractis," *AASS,* 180, 190.

121. Sposato, "Fonti, Intro," 10.

122. Knecht, *Renaissance Warrior,* 116.

123. Roberti, *S. Francesco di Paola,* 615–23.

his call to France, are reviewed, and his death and cult, with a summation of many miracles.[124] The next section provides reasons why Leo X should canonize Francis: his chastity, devotion to the Faith, charity, humility, patience, rule of his order, piety, prudence, sobriety, and reputation (*fama*).[125] A reference to the many suppliants is followed by a discussion of requirements for canonization, a brief review of what a miracle is, and the question of proof.[126] This seems to have especially interested Simoneta, who deals with proofs in more than three pages in the printed edition. He concludes by reviewing, in two scant paragraphs, whether miracles must occur immediately (no); whether a true miraculous cure is accompanied by pain (sometimes); whether it's still valid even though some days intervene between a vow and a cure (yes); and, finally, whether the application of physical remedies is permitted (yes). The auditor's citations range widely, from the humanists' repertoire including Sophocles, Menander, Cicero, and Vergil to the theologians' of Augustine, Jerome, Aquinas, and others as well as the Bible, several canonists, and civilians. As any historian knows who has worked through such documents, attempting to sort out precisely what authorities are cited, the process resembles an archeologist's digging through a mound of scrambled artifacts. Although several hidden or highly (even excruciatingly) elliptical citations have no doubt been missed or misattributed in Simoneta's work, I find an approximate total of at least 127 citations to fifty-five sources (taking the eleven sections of the Bible separately). Neither classical nor theological authors prevailed: the lawyers, specialists in Roman and canon law, topped the list among Simoneta's choice of authorities.[127]

124. Luigi Patrizi-Accursi, *Relazione della vita, della virtù e dei miracoli di San Francesco di Paola fatta al sommo pontefice Leone X da Giacomo Simoneta* (Rome: Libreria Pontificia di F. Pustet, 1907), 5–13.

125. Ibid., 13–22.

126. For the following, ibid., 23–32.

127. Among the canonists and civilians (forty-nine citations to twenty scholars), the most often cited individual (seven times) was "the Archdeacon" (Guido de Baysio, d. 1313, the teacher of Johannes Andreae, himself cited at least twice). Among the rest were Gregory IX's Decretals, Panormitas, Baldus de Ubaldis, and Hostiensis. Francesco Pavini's work on the canonizations of Bonaventure and Leopold was also mentioned. Thirty-one citations came from eleven sections of the Old and New Testaments, with Paul's letters being noted more than others (nine times). Among the theologians (twenty-one references to eight authors), the Latin Fathers—Ambrose, Augustine, Jerome, and Gregory—were cited, as well as Aquinas (four references). A final, "mixed" category (sixteen authorities with a total of twenty-six citations) included, from the ancient and late antique world, Sophocles, Aristotle, Menander, Cicero (twice), Tibullus, Vergil (twice), Cassiodorus, and Justinian. Averroes was also cited, once. In addition, reference was made to Antoninus of Florence's

Meanwhile the process was examined by a three-cardinal committee.[128] This included Nicholas Fieschi, cardinal bishop of Albano (c. 1456–1524), promoted by Alexander VI in 1503 at Louis XII's request. A JUD (*Juris utriusque doctor,* an expert in both canon and civil law), he seems to have headed the commission. The second member was Domenico Jacobazzi (1444–1528), also JUD, created cardinal priest of St. Bartolomeo all'Isola by Leo X in July 1517. Jacobazzi had been appointed auditor of the Rota in 1493. The third commissioner was Giovanni Salviati (1490–1553), Leo X's nephew, whom the pope named cardinal deacon of Cosmas and Damian, also in July 1517. By the early spring of 1519, the cardinals' work completed, preparations began for the final phase of the process. From here we are guided by the *Diary* of Master of Ceremonies Paris de Grassis (Paride de Grassi from Bologna, d. 1528). Paris has been unfortunate in some of his later commentators.[129] Pastor twice called the MC "pedantic," and the respected historian of western liturgy, Edmund Bishop (d. 1917), referred to him rather uncharitably as "fussy, and a flunkey born . . . simply stolid in his self-satisfaction" though full of energy and a faithful papal servant.[130] On the other hand, one has to admire a curial functionary who managed (in 1514) to get a white elephant more-or-less decorously into the center of Rome.[131] Pasquale Sposato, who produced the first complete edition of the section of the *Diary* concerning Francis, based on sound manuscript sources, is free of pejoratives, perhaps appreciating more than his predecessors the wealth of detail the meticulous, busy de Grassis has given us.[132] The following account of events leading up to Francis's canonization, and the ritual itself, will be

---

work, and even Louise, Francis I's mother, got a mention. Some authorities may have been cited more often than noted here.

128. The few final depositions of 1518 in *PC,* 227–29. Papal bull in Fontanini, *Codex constitutionum,* 208.

129. An exception is Marc Dykmans, who has dedicated a great deal of study to de Grassis: *Ephemerides Liturgicae* 96 (1982): 407–83; 99 (1985): 383–417; and 100 (1986): 270–333. See now, also, Jennifer Mara De Silva's doctoral dissertation (University of Toronto, 2007), "Ritual negotiations: Paris de'Grassi and the Office of Ceremonies under Popes Julius II & Leo X (1504–1521)." Dr. De Silva was kind enough to send me a copy of her thesis; I am most grateful to her and to Simon Ditchfield, who drew this work to my attention.

130. Bishop, "Leaves from the Diary" 435.

131. Silvio A. Bedini, *The Pope's Elephant* (New York: Penguin Group, 1997).

132. The Latin text is edited by Pasquale Sposato in "Fonti per la storia di S. Francesco di Paola: La sua canonizzazione attraverso il 'Diarium' di Paride De Grassi prefetto delle ceremonie pontificie sotto Leone X, Testo del Diario," *Calabria Nobilissima* 11, no. 33 (March 1957): 1–29, hereafter Sposato, "Fonti, Testo del Diario"; distinguished from Sposato, "Fonti, Intro."

taken from that source. Dealing as it does with practicalities, the *Diary* augments and sometimes contradicts oratorical treatments such as Pavini's *relatio* on Bonaventure and Simoneta's for Francis.

After Francis's canonization had been discussed and (conditionally) approved in secret consistories, de Grassis begins, the pope "asked me to seek out and describe what his predecessors had done in similar cases, beyond what was in the book of ceremonies."[133] Paris, claiming to have discovered many diverse opinions about the matter, did his own research into canon law and writings from various pontificates, composing a treatise for Leo. Having completed this work, he discovered that "a colleague" had stolen it; thus, he laments, he can remember only a few of the things he had written, which he now reproduces. For example, he continues, "when I remarked to the pope that the cost of a canonization was unbelievable, he asked me what it usually was. I told him that Augustino Patrizi Piccolomini and Johannus Burchard [de Grassis's immediate predecessor], then Masters of Ceremony, recorded 27,000 ducats for Bonaventure and 25,000 for Leopold. When he heard these excessive sums, almost laughing at their impossibility, the pope asked how so much money could be spent. I replied that such expenses were tolerated and in a way required by the Apostolic See so that their near impossibility or difficulty would restrain princes and people from seeking canonizations based not on a person's merits but on outside pressures arising from devotion or kinship."[134] That's the case now, continues de Grassis, with cardinal Jacobazzi (a member of Francis's committee, no less), who wants his relative Cecholella of Rome canonized; the community of Florence, seeking Antoninus's canonization; the *natio* of Germany, pushing for Benno; the doge of Venice, asking canonization for one of his ancestors; the king of Hungary, seeking the elevation of his kinsman Ladislas; and Poland's king, lobbying for his grandfather Casimir. Many others supplicate for their kin or those to whom they're devoted. Canonizing all these, Paris continues, would bring the process into contempt. Di Grassis

133. Sposato, "Fonti, Testo del Diario," 1.

134. "Cum dixissem multam esse expensam in canonizatione ordinaria faciendam preterquam credibile sit, quesivit a me papa quanta ea expensa esse soleat. . . . Quam eccessivam summam cum audiret a me pontifex et quasi illam rideret ut impossibilem factu. . . . Dixi hanc expensam sic amplam . . . a sede apostolica et a pontificibus ideo non solum tollerari sed etiam quodammodo precipi. . . . Itaque consultissime, ut opinor, sedes apostolica tantos ac tam excessivos sumptus tollerat," Sposato, "Fonti, Testo del Diario," 2.

doesn't exaggerate: Leo X was very much involved in canonization requests that included, in addition to the above and to Francis himself, the Servite Filippo Benizi of Florence, some Franciscans martyred in Africa, and John of Capistrano. A second Polish candidate di Grassis missed was Hyacinth (cd. 1594), for whom King Sigismund supplicated Leo in 1517 and 1518.[135] Furthermore, in the course of his reign he allowed limited recognition of the cults of Osanna Andreasi, Mary of Cortona, Conrad of Piacenza, Elizabeth of Portugal, John of St. Malo, Vitalis of Strasburg, Veronica of Binasco, the Carthusian Bruno, and possibly more.[136] Thus, di Grassis explained to Leo, "excessive expenses" should be tolerated to keep down this flood of applicants. Furthermore, he continued, the money usually is spent on necessities for the process, ornaments, cloth, and fur trim for all the vestments, not only for the pope but the cardinal-commissioners, and . . . Here, our diarist notes, the pope began laughing, so Paris ordered brought out from the sacristy garments that had been made by Leo's predecessors, for example, a chasuble and cope with the images of Saint Bernardino and the arms of Nicholas V, and vestments for other canonized saints. Di Grassis goes on to mention a pearl-encrusted miter, new silver candelabra, new baldachin, and all the vestments that must be provided for many people involved in the ceremony, from officiating cardinals down to papal grooms. This must have stifled papal laughter, for Leo then ordered him to write up an account of what he'd just "superficially" noted. This humorless matter of astronomical expenses, and de Grassis's comments, will be revisited in our final chapter.

The MC next claims that he examined canonizations prior to Leo's reign: Nicholas of Tolentino (1446), Bernardino of Siena (1450), Vincent Ferrer (1455), Catherine of Siena (1460, *recte* 1461), Bonaventure (1482), and Leopold of Austria (1485). Having done so, Paris concluded that Francis's process could proceed, given his way of life and miracles and the king of France's support, provided that certain issues were clarified. These included determining whether anyone other than the French king was interceding for Francis; whether the envoys specially deputed to this task were present in Rome, with their mandates; who had been local examiners (*inquisitores in partibus*) at the burial site; who'd been the auditors of the Rota

135. *Canonizationis Beati Iacinthi Poloni Ord. Praed. Relatio Trium Rotae* Auditorum (Rome, typ. Nicolai Mutii, 1597), 5.

136. Sposato, "Fonti, Intro," 20 n. 31; Krafft, *Papsturkunde,* 1013 n. 375.

"here in the City," and who the three cardinal-commissioners; whether a decision in secret consistory had been firmly agreed; when and where further consistories would occur; who would record the hearings; whether the money was sufficient; when and where the ceremony would take place, given the ruinous state of St. Peter's (being rebuilt). Prayers for the new saint, his title, feast day, and pictorial representations needed finalizing. Toward the end of his long list, de Grassis adds two items of particular interest. He writes that it was to be determined whether Leo should voice the protestation, since there was some doubt about making this statement (discussed in the previous chapter). "And finally," de Grassis notes that a decision should be made whether this ceremony is to be for Francis alone (*pro solo et unico*), or rather, "as they say," for him and Antoninus of Florence, Cecholla of Rome, Casimir of Poland, Benno of Germany, "and some others, since lawfully several could be carried out together in a single operation, as our [unnamed] doctors of canon law say."[137] This possibility of multiple canonizations was not taken up for Francis, but did occur in 1523 with our final two saints, Antoninus and Benno. The next instance of simultaneous sainthoods (five at once) took place in 1622.

After these issues were resolved (de Grassis doesn't explain when or how), a public consistory was prepared: the MC was to obtain a copy of the consistorial advocate's proposed statement, so that the pope could examine it ahead of time and prepare (i.e., have de Grassis prepare) an appropriate response; sturdy containers were to be constructed for the ceremonial offerings, which were diligently to be guarded so they wouldn't be stolen in the confusion, "as sometimes happened" in the past. If the pope makes the protestation, then both fiscal procurator and Francis's proctor were to ask for a record of this. As for the Mass, de Grassis sets out in detail how this is to proceed: prayers, offerings alternatively by cardinal-commissioners and royal orators, and so on. He spends most of this section discussing the proper colors of the vestments, suggesting that there had been confusion in the past—"I found no established tradition"—because, he claims, earlier masters of ceremony didn't understand the reasons for the different colors. He excuses them, however, since the rank of confessor, whose color, he concludes, should be white, was relatively new among the canonized. He notes,

137. Sposato, "Fonti, Testo del Diario," 5–6: "prout de iure canonico posse dicitur a doctoribus nostris," without further references; Sposato, "Fonti, Intro," 15.

too, that sometimes popes, even during a single ceremony, were vested in two (red and white), even three (red, white, violet) colors.[138] Finally, noting that the pope had often asked him to be careful in organizing this canonization, de Grassis claims "I made it my duty" to check with the brethren of the Trinity (Rome's Minim convent, Trinità dei Monti) to make sure that they had sufficient funds for the ceremony—the MC claims that he didn't want to be misled by the Minims into starting something they couldn't finish—and (again) to preview the proposed speech of the consistorial advocate, as well as the cardinals' reports summing up their own work, to be delivered in consistory.

"Finally," de Grassis writes, "on April 4 (1519) there was a public consistory on Francis."[139] Leo, 28 cardinals, and 135 prelates were present, but an important absentee was the French ambassador Guillaume Briçonnet, bishop of St. Malo.[140] "At my signal" consistorial advocate Angelo de Cesis began an hour-long oration. De Grassis had instructed him to keep his notes behind his back in case he forgot his lines, which turned out to be good advice. The pope then made a short reply authored by Paris. After the consistory, when the cardinals (as usual) applauded, "the pope turning to me said with a smile, 'Behold, master, all this praise redounds to you because you have instructed your pupil well, who did you honor.'" Afterward, the pope asked de Grassis to compose another response to the consistorial advocate for the forthcoming *semisecreto consistorio,* with an invitation to the prelates to vote. Dissatisfied with what he'd found in the book of ceremonies, or Sixtus's canonization of Bonaventure or Innocent's of Leopold, de Grassis persuaded the advocate to draw up his presentation in such a way that the pope could reply in just a few words. This pleased Leo, writes de Grassis, since he didn't want to go on and on like a hired attorney; for (the MC tactfully adds) although the pope was extremely eloquent, "it didn't seem praiseworthy to me that the pope should say as much as is set out in the ceremonial." After Passion Sunday Mass, April 10, the pope, de Grassis, and some senior cardinals met to plan further consistories. They agreed to the 13th for the next one. At this point in the *Diary,* the MC sets out what the advo-

138. Sposato, "Fonti, Testo del Diario," 9–11.

139. Ibid., 11–15 for the following.

140. Briçonnet's father, also Guillaume, who accompanied Charles VIII in the invasion, was made cardinal in January 1495. Later he would be excommunicated (1511) because of his involvement in the Council of Pisa; he was absolved by Leo X in 1514 and died several months later.

cate planned to say on that occasion. Since de Cesis summarized his "long oration" of April 4, and since that oration seems to have disappeared, this summation is useful.[141] De Cesis would remind the pope that (on April 4) he had reviewed Francis's origins, parents, kin, life, and moral conduct as well as twenty-five of his illustrious miracles in detail (*in specie*) and innumerable others in general (*in genere*), and noted supplications by the French king, his queen, his mother, and others. Given the many witnesses and work of the three cardinals, de Cesis planned to propose that the canonization go forward. Paris then gives us the response he'd prepared for Leo, to the effect that he'd be willing to canonize if he had the unanimous consent of his brethren. Finally, the MC adds some prayers he'd prepared for the canonization Mass, having rejected "inept and rather ridiculous prayers composed by the brothers of the Order of Minims."

On April 13, 1519, after a normal secret consistory, the gathering reconvened to vote on Francis; additional curialists and others entered the chamber, but again without the bishop of St. Malo.[142] In addition to the cardinals there were about seventy prelates as well as auditors, penitentiaries, proctors, and generals of the religious orders, all ranged in benches, on steps, or on the floor around the pope.[143] Advocate de Cesis delivered his rehearsed speech, to which the pope replied. Leo then asked the assembly for a vote, adding that for some time now the cardinals had indicated their support. De Grassis writes, "I had the pope say this because I knew that some were doubtful, especially the absent orator of the French king, the bishop of St. Malo [Briçonnet]." Following de Grassis's suggestion, therefore, on this occasion the pope had about a dozen of the most senior prelates expressly agree with the cardinals and give their assent to Francis's sainthood. Paris had his nephew—an assistant master of ceremonies—record these votes, as did the protonotaries at the fiscal's command. Francis I's orator for whom the pope waited in silence (and in vain) at this consistory on April 13, was Dionysio Briçonnet.[144] Prior to the 13th de Grassis had learned that he'd

141. Sposato, "Fonti, Intro," 17 n. 29, "Non si conosce il testo della relazione dell'avvocato consistoriale Angelo De Cesis."

142. For what follows, Sposato, "Fonti, Testo del Diario," 15–19.

143. For an illustration of such a gathering (in 1578), showing the different ecclesiastical orders and ranks arranged accordingly in chairs, benches, on steps and the floor, see Fernandez, "Patrimony of St. Peter," 140.

144. Sposato, "Fonti, testo del Diario," 18 n.

secretly expressed disapproval of the canonization, which (in his opinion) ought to be delayed for a hundred or at least eighty years.[145] This raises two issues: why the bishop said this, and what the pope's reaction was. St. Malo, according to de Grassis, claimed that although he'd pushed for the canonization, he'd done so as royal orator at the king's orders. As a bishop, however, who'd known Francis alive and dead, the pope was trying his conscience: he knew of no miracle that Francis had done, even after death, appropriate to saints.[146] Therefore, in conscience he didn't consider him a worthy candidate.[147] Without further explanation Sposato suggests that this reluctance stemmed from *qualche intrigo politico.*[148] Actually, at this time Franco-papal relations were comparatively good, and though "political intrigue" was constantly in the background of nearly everything that took place at the curia, it's unlikely that politics *tout court* motivated St. Malo. It could simply be that, as he stated, he didn't believe in Francis's reputation for miracle-working. This was hardly the first time that grumbling about doubtful miracles was heard within the college. A thirteenth-century cardinal responded to a promoter's account of Archbishop Edmund of Canterbury's (d. 1240, cd. 1246) wonders with "We do not believe in your miracles and we refuse to give them the approval of the Apostolic See"; furthermore, this unnamed cardinal claimed to accept Saint Martin's miracles only because the Church had endorsed them.[149] Vauchez notes that such denials may have been recorded merely to emphasize eventual acceptance; yet heartfelt skepticism (as opposed to rhetorical doubt, for effect) must have occurred in many instances as, perhaps, with St. Malo's attitude toward Francis's wonders. We'll again encounter an example of such skepticism in the next chapter, this time from a member of a canonization commission.

When de Grassis reported St. Malo's opinion to the pope, "he was very surprised and asked me what to do." A solution was the consistory of April 13, 1519, which bolstered the cardinals' decision of April 4. But since St. Malo

145. Ibid., 15: "Ego [de Grassis] intellexeram aliquos super hoc dubitare, et presertim oratorem regis Francie episcopum macloniensem qui secrete cum aliquibus sermonem habuerat quod nolebat dare votum suum . . . sed quod ipsa expeditio differetur post annos centum vel ad minus LXXX."

146. *Papa volebat gravare;* St. Malo's acts, as ambassador, cannot be attributed to orders from Francis in any case, since pope and king were closely united in hoping to stave off Charles's election as emperor in these very months, particularly during March, when St. Malo would have had ample time to receive royal directives.

147. *Ipse in conscientia sua.*

148. Sposato, "Fonti, Intro," 19.

149. Quoted in Vauchez, *Sainthood,* 481.

hadn't appeared at either meeting, Leo was "rather irritated," so next day (April 14) he asked the bishop for an explanation. The orator claimed that he'd received no notice of the consistory, nor had several other aggrieved prelates; it almost appeared, he complained, that the whole business was being kept secret. This made Leo "greatly irritated." He had his *cursores* punished for their lack of diligence (the pope had some twelve urban messengers at his disposal). De Grassis adds no further comment, but we might suspect that Leo disciplined his runners perhaps to punish them, and probably at the same time to appease the bishop, who was, after all, the French king's representative. After this meeting with St. Malo, Leo ordered his MC to send the messengers out again, this time to scour the entire city all night if needed, locating prelates who had not attended on the thirteenth. On April 15, 1519, after the usual consistory, these prelates, including Briçonnet this time, were called in. When they entered the hall, Leo was dumfounded, commenting that there were even more of them than had been at the consistory two days earlier (Paris terms this ad hoc meeting a convocation, properly distinguishing it from a consistory). The pope announced that because he was about to issue bulls claiming that he'd ascertained *all* the prelates' votes, he wanted to be able to state this truthfully, and not as a falsehood.[150] Appropriately, the bishop of St. Malo responded first, delivering a long speech excusing himself for his previous absences, noting that even now he'd not been given much information on the proceedings, and finishing by voting for the canonization. The rest of the newly rounded-up prelates, about thirty of them, also voted in favor.

There were further complications. Between April 15 and 19, Leo X heard rumors that he was about to receive letters or ambassadors from Spain, England, and Portugal asking for the simultaneous canonization of a saint (unnamed) from each of these three kingdoms, to take place along with Francis's elevation. On the nineteenth, the pope called in de Grassis to discuss what to do. Leo believed that the three *nationes* were motivated by mutual jealousies as well as anti-French animosity, although they would claim that their candidates' processes had been brewing a long time—which may have been the case. Leo believed that the requests were designed to sabotage the French campaign by inundating the curia with supplications.[151] In addition, and

150. *In veritate et non ficte.*

151. Of course, concurrently Leo had to deal diplomatically with these (and other) powers as well as France. For instance, in 1514 he had awarded the golden rose and consecrated sword and cap to Portugal's king.

no doubt behind this sudden interest in multiple sainthoods, it was precisely during these months that the crucial imperial election was still in contention, all the European powers (including England) throwing themselves into the political mêlée. The pope "urgently" consulted his MC about how quickly the hermit's canonization could be concluded, and whether there were sufficient funds. De Grassis noted that they had 1,000 ducats, which pleased Leo. Drawing on his managerial skills, the expert manipulator de Grassis had a suggestion: when the cardinals arrived in the papal chambers as usual for matins on Wednesday evening (the next day, April 20), Leo should there and then declare a convocation, call for final approval of Francis's cause, and immediately set a date for the ceremony, the Sunday after Easter (May 1). And so it all turned out: *et sic facta sunt omnia,* Paris proudly writes. At the conclusion of this evening meeting on the 20th, scarcely had the pope left the chamber when Paris was accosted by one of the three ambassadors (unnamed) asking what was going on. De Grassis told him. The ambassador questioned the rush, objecting that these matters usually took years. When the MC replied that everything was ready and the money available, the other proposed matching this sum if things could be delayed. De Grassis cut him down: "The matter isn't undecided, but concluded; the day's fixed." When he told Leo about this conversation, the MC concludes, "he smiled, content that he'd foreseen their tricks," and no doubt pleased with his own trickery.[152]

De Grassis hurriedly prepared for the ceremony.[153] He had fifty large paintings made, that were then shaped into ovoids showing at the top Francis from chest to head, crowned not with a diadem as canonized saints were, but with rays denoting a *beatus.* (The pictorial distinction between a *beatus* with rays and a *sanctus* with halo or diadem is found in the fourteenth century.)[154] In the middle was Leo X's heraldry, to the right the arms of the Church, to the left, those of the French king. At the bottom, since the Minims didn't have their own arms, the word *Charitas,* also part of Rome's heraldry, was used. These depictions on cardboard were distributed in and around St. Peter's and various places in the city, as were twelve similarly decorated banners. (Another banner was carried in the papal procession.) A wooden stage was built, about sixty-six by forty-two by six or eight

152. "Subrisit contentus quasi prevenisset cautelas illorum," Sposato, "Fonti, Testo del Diario," 19.

153. For the following, see ibid., 19–27.

154. Vauchez, *Sainthood,* 87–8.

feet high.[155] This cost 243 ducats, which also covered expenses for all other wooden structures such as benches and chairs for cardinals and officiants, two altar tables, and the like. The stage was reached by a ramp without railings, to leave an unobstructed view for the people below (also the reason for not putting backs on the cardinals' and prelates' three-tiered benches on the stage). A rope wound with garlands encircled the platform. Small supporting beams round the stage were also garlanded, with roses. De Grassis had to make a deal with the florists on account of the shortage of cash: he agreed to pay 28 ducats for labor and refreshments as they decorated the stage with flowers and created floral displays interwoven on red and green cloth (about six hundred feet of cloth was purchased, the MC keeping forty left over from the ceremony). There was a blue silk banner at each corner of the stage, with a larger version suspended from the ceiling, all with Francis's image. A new baldachin, again depicting the saint, was erected over the altar. Nothing else was put around or above the altar that might—once again de Grassis refers to this aspect—impede the people's view.[156]

De Grassis hired an "expert master of celebrations" or revels, *festaiolum expertum* (the figure who acted as onstage mediator in Renaissance plays was the *festaiuolo*), who decorated Leo's palace windows with myrtle fronds and flowers. The busy de Grassis also had to think of the papal procession preceding the ceremony, so he ordered the streets of the planned route cleaned. In case of rain, he established an alternative route under cover that went from the papal hall to the basilica entrance; this involved clearing away some of the builders' rubble. The day before the ceremony de Grassis publicized it throughout the city along with a declaration of an indulgence as well as a showing of the Face of Christ and the holy lance.[157] The MC was every-

155. De Grassis writes, "Longum cannis XI et latum 7 et altum quasi 8 pedum," Sposato, "Fonti, Testo del Diario," 19. Sposato considers these measurements to equal "lunga più di quaranta e larga più di quattordici metri," "Fonti, Intro," 22, which would give us a platform about 40 X 14 meters or 120 X 42 feet. Apart from the fact that these ratios do not follow what's given by de Grassis, if the Roman *canna* measured 1.99 meters as Zupko suggests, then the stage would have been about twenty-two by fourteen meters, or around sixty-six by forty-two feet. Ronald E. Zupko, *British Weights and Measures* (Madison: University of Wisconsin Press, 1977), 170, "Pre-Metric Weights and Measures in Western and Eastern Europe." On Sposato, "Fonti, Testo," 22, however, the height is given as *palmis VIII,* which (Zupko, 172) would make it six feet.

156. "Nihil erat quod impedire posset prospectum populi."

157. See Stinger, *Renaissance in Rome,* 39–40, for the Veronica and the holy lance, obtained by Innocent from Sultan Bajazet in 1492; it was "customarily revealed along with the Veronica from the Loggia of Benediction" on certain holy days.

where, reminding Rome's Minims to take care of expenses, arranging for a fifteen- or twenty-blast cannonade from Castel Sant'Angelo at the culmination of the ceremony, instructing two Minims to prepare and install, on the day before the event, wax tapers in the upper basilica. Some seventy of these were placed, no more, because the old church was in a state of demolition. On the day of the ceremony these two brethren were to light the tapers and keep them burning; this irritated St. Peter's clergy, who wanted to light and extinguish them when *they* pleased. Paris arranged for candles for the pope, cardinals, ambassadors, and other VIPs, kept in two chests in the upper church, to be distributed by his nephew Hippolytus, whom he calls "first master of ceremonies," meaning first assistant presumably; two more chests of candles in the lower church were to be distributed to lesser clergy and others by a "second master of ceremonies," unnamed. Processional positions of the various ambassadors had to be sorted out beforehand. A less decorous matter also had to be addressed: de Grassis arranged for the pope to order the vicar and chamberlain of St. Peter's not to seize the things brought into the church, "because I knew" he continues, that they coveted the green and rose cloth, all the banners, and many other items. The pope agreed to let them keep the stage, excluding any chairs brought in from the papal chambers, the new baldachin, and one banner to display, as a memorial. Afterward, comments our guide, "as usual they wanted to seize [more] things, but had nothing."

De Grassis notes that he had the ceremony written up for the pope in a green book, since he'd discovered that many pontiffs had wished to have their own instructions for what should be said, read, and chanted at canonizations. Perhaps this was his reply to the papally approved publication in 1516 of Patrizi Piccolomini's 1488 *Caeremoniale Romanum* (including a canonization ceremony) that is said to have incensed Paris, bringing—as he thought—liturgical mysteries down into the public domain.[158] In addition, "so that everything that needed to be done could be better foreseen and carried out," de Grassis had a *rotulus* made for his own use, an aide-mémoire, listing what he needed to remember to do. In essence, it is a mini-ceremonial: the three cardinal-commissioners are to be told about their offerings; the advocate of the cause is to be informed how, where, and what

158. Dell'Oro, *Beatificazione e Canonizzazione,* 96; on Piccolomini, *L'Oeuvre de Patrizi Piccolomini.*

he should do; places for the banners are to be selected, and so on, including how much green and red cloth is needed, where candles are to be distributed (functionaries had earlier lit and blown them out, making them easier to relight), the building of ceremonial structures (stage, baldachin, etc.), the summoning of cardinals and prelates by papal messengers, public announcements, and so on and on, for page after page, including details on the order of procession; the act of canonization itself, with ambassadorial participation; the cannonade, ringing of bells, and sounding of trumpets at the climactic moment; how the Mass should proceed, how the offerings of birds and such were to be made (gently, with a smile).[159] The Mass was to end with the pope's exhibiting the Lance and Image, to be taken from a chest on the platform. "Such was the form of my list, which I made to remind myself of things to do," de Grassis again notes, concluding, obviously after the fact, with "and everything, thank God, went well" and, he claims, was commended by the pope.

Perhaps not surprisingly, given the wealth of detail already supplied, the MC very briefly describes Francis's canonization itself. His preparations for an "internal" procession were unnecessary: although it rained all night, next morning the weather was serene. As anticipated, St. Peter's quickly filled to capacity. De Grassis gave permission for some to put up their own viewing-stands provided they weren't blocking others' views. A French visitor to Rome claimed that the ceremony lasted a good four hours, and cost him one-half ducat to watch.[160] Many were perched in the basilica's recessed windows and on its beams: "everywhere was full of people of both sexes." Before ascending the stage, Leo wanted to pray facing the high altar, but couldn't because of the mud and wet pavement. The stage itself was crammed to full capacity, even the cardinals' section so thronged by celebrities that the pope was barely able to make it to his own chair; with a smile Leo several times wondered whether it would collapse; "but I had it very well constructed," his MC smugly notes. (This was a common source of anxiety: when everyone crowded in to see the humbled cardinals of the Pisan council beg papal forgiveness in June 1512, there were fears that the floors might collapse, and in the 1513 conferral of citizenship on the two

159. "Placide, ac cum risu," Sposato, "Fonti, Testo del Diario," 26.

160. H.-R. Duthilloeul, *Voyage de Jacques le Saige de Douai,* new ed. (Douai, 1851), 26; Jacques also comments on Christ's "holy column" in St. Peter's, where he witnessed a woman's exorcism, 24.

Medici, during one of the skits "so many gentlemen had moved up to sit on the stage" that there was scarcely room for the principals.)[161] Once everyone was in place the pope began the ceremony, culminating in his declaration of Francis's sainthood, delivered with difficulty because tears stifled his words. In any case most people in the overcrowded church couldn't hear him. He spoke not in the usual papal plural, but "simply, as a man."

Referring to Bernardino of Siena, a Florentine merchant who bankrolled the immediate costs, our diarist laments that things were done on the cheap since ("as I have often said") there wasn't enough money for a proper ceremony.[162] One can only imagine what he would have done with unlimited resources. Since Leo knew that funding was a problem, he volunteered to remit his part, namely, 225 ducats. "When I learned of this I said with a smile that it didn't please me since it would affect what was due to us, the masters of ceremonies; so the pope ordered that we three masters would receive 200 ducats, that is, one hundred for me, and fifty for each of the other two." Our MC made up yet another list and had the pope sign it, setting out the fees due each person, "lest people complain to me about payment." When a household groom groused that he'd received nothing and de Grassis reported this to Leo, the pope fired him, and the same happened to a certain chamberlain, "whom the pope expelled from the palace unless he begged my forgiveness as to his comments." Besides fees already noted, de Grassis's list included one hundred ducats for each of the three cardinal commissioners, twelve for the papal messengers for three assignments, five for the keepers of the door, seventy-five for the three notaries of the process, four for the cannonists of Castel Sant'Angelo, four for the palace drummers, twenty-five in alms, and so on. There is no overall total for the entire business, the burden of which fell on French royalty.

In addition to de Grassis's narration, Sanuto copied into his *Diary* a letter of May 4, 1519, from the Venetian Marcantonio Michiel to a "dear friend" in Venice.[163] Evidently Marcantonio, a connoisseur, was sensitive to the humanists' (i.e., Ciceronian) Latin then flowing through Italy and the papal curia, for he somewhat embarrassingly warns his friend that he wrote the

161. Bonner Mitchell, *Rome in the High Renaissance: The Age of Leo* X (Norman: University of Oklahoma Press, 1973), 28, 71.

162. Sposato, "Fonti, Testo del Diario," 27–9.

163. *I Diarii di Marino Sanuto,* 27:cols. 272–77.

enclosed Latin account "for my use and recollection and not for others. After reading it, send it back since I have no other copy; don't show it to anyone unless you translate it into Italian since I wrote it hastily." After describing (in Italian) the uncomfortably crowded audience at the canonization, Michiel briefly conveys miscellaneous tidbits of Roman news: the pope prohibited the usual April 25 celebrations of Pasquino, to the great regret of the poets, who had "to scratch their itch" (*gratar la rogna*) in some other way; the ritual of Mayday morning when young men attached garlands and poems to the doors of their beloved; the duchess of Urbino's death; the great brawls among Rome's literati over Christophe de Longueil;[164] and the ceremony of cardinals and prelates showering a crowd with "little birds, fire and water" to represent the descent of the Holy Spirit upon the apostles, an activity that Partner calls a combination of folklore and hooliganism: on May 1 a feast (sponsored by the Colonnas) featured releasing animals and flocks of birds into the Basilica of the Holy Apostles, "and a pig was suspended from the roof, just above the heads of the crowd. As they struggled to get hold of it, jars of water were emptied over them from above."[165] After a few comments about Michelangelo, Raphael, and other artists, Michiel's Latin description of Francis's ceremony follows. His account complements de Grassis's and provides an "onlooker's" perspective as opposed to the MC's as privileged insider. In St. Peter's on a stage six feet high and as wide and long as that part of the church would allow, various ornaments were affixed. There were silk standards with an image of the saint, a barefoot, hooded old man in a plain garment, his tunic bound with a cord in the Franciscan manner. Holding a wooden cross, he was humbly looking at the ground, his flowing beard resting on his chest, while flickering rays glittered round his head. After again noting that people were crammed in up to the rafters, our Venetian observer described the papal procession entering the basilica. There were eleven cardinal deacons, whom he names, including Leo X's nephew Salviati, one of Francis's three commissioners; sixteen cardinal priests—also named, including Jacobazzi, another of the

164. D'Amico, *Renaissance Humanism in Papal Rome,* 110 and references; Longueil ("Longolius," d. 1522) was eventually granted Roman citizenship, the crux of the debate, Mitchell, *Rome in the High Renaissance,* 93–97.

165. Peter Partner, *Renaissance Rome, 1500–1559* (Berkeley: University of California Press, 1976), 206.

three cardinals—but only two cardinal bishops, Carvajal the Minims' protector, and Leo X's grand-nephew Raphael Riario, cardinal bishop of Ostia.[166] Michiel lists Nicolo Fieschi, third member of Francis's committee, as a cardinal-priest, though at this time he was a cardinal-bishop.[167] The other four cardinal-bishops, the letter states, were absent. Michiel continues: the crowd was so noisy that even those next to the pope could barely hear what he was saying, though people got the general impression from his gestures. Legates of the French king and queen supplicated on Francis of Paola's behalf, Leo ascribed him to the number of saints, and the Mass commenced. Offerings were made: wine, bread, one gold and two silver birdcages that Leo opened. Some of the birds flew to the roof of the basilica; others fell into the hands of the happy crowd, which bustled about catching them.

Our final witness is Leo X's bull of canonization *Excelsus Dominus.*[168] Apart from the normal summarizing of Francis's life, with a description of the committees and hearings and naming of suppliants, the bull is somewhat unusual in its extended description of his miracles, from local processes and *Vita.* As we've seen, St. Malo, and possibly others, doubted Francis's miracles. Perhaps, as we'll explore in our final chapter, this enumeration was meant as a response. In any event the extensive detail would seem to contradict Paoli's contention that miracles were merely "parenthetical" within Francis's hagiography.[169] They begin with the nobleman Jacobus de Tarsia, whose ulcerated leg doctors and surgeons couldn't cure.[170] The bull's unusually extensive details include dialogue taken from the inquisitorial process. Francis sent one of his brethren for some herbal leaves, called horse-hoof, that grew locally, and certain powders he kept in his cell.[171] After he prayed

166. Riario (d. 1521), named cardinal by Sixtus IV in 1477, was implicated in the Pazzi conspiracy in 1478, and also in the plot to poison great-uncle Leo in 1517. He participated in the 1515 meeting between the pope and Francis I at Bologna. Bernardino Lopez de Carvajal (d. 1523) was created cardinal by Alexander VI in 1493, deposed by Julius II in 1511 because of the French-inspired Council of Pisa, and restored by Leo X in 1513. Here I must express my appreciation of the work of Salvador Miranda, who has created and maintained an extremely useful Web site, a convenient and accurate source of information on the cardinalate, drawing upon scholarly bibliographical sources: http://www2.fiu.edu/~mirandas/bios1439.htm and http://www2.fiu.edu/~mirandas/consistories-xv.htm.

167. Fieschi was created cardinal-deacon in 1503, cardinal-priest in 1506, and cardinal-bishop (S. Albano) in 1518.

168. Fontanini, *Codex constitutionum,* 200–211.

169. Paoli, "La santità canonizzata," 247.

170. For the following, see Fontanini, *Codex constitutionum,* 203–6 and *PC,* 14–19, 228–29.

171. *Certos pulveres;* horsefoot, *Tussilago farfara,* is a common European weed. Among other

for the baron's health, when the materials arrived Francis made the sign of the cross and bound the powder to the ulcer with the leaves. The nobleman was cured as he rode home. Perhaps coincidentally (or for expediency?), this is the very first reported miracle in the 1512 Cosenza hearings. This is followed by a summary of eleven more *in vita* miracles, all of which occurred in or around Paola. The thirteenth miracle is the only posthumous wonder attributed to Francis, and like the first it comes from the Cosenza process with great detail, but this time is copied from the end of the inquisition, third from last among the depositions. Testifying on May 1, 1518, Julius claimed that during August 1517, while helping to transport a large cannon in the Paola area, he was saved after being tangled in the ropes of the ox-drawn cart. His colleagues, witnesses reported, began shouting "miraculo, miraculo," which in the bull becomes *miraculum acclamantes.* As noted, this is the only posthumous miracle listed; though many were recorded in the Tours process, none of these were included. In fact, no notice was taken of any "French" miracles. Mention is made of Francis's body, even after eleven days, emitting a sweet odor.[172] As a result of these wonders, the bull continues, Francis's fame reached Louis XI, who, moved by the blessed man's sanctity, asked Sixtus IV to order the hermit, in virtue of his obedience, to visit him. Sadoleto, Leo's domestic secretary who composed the bull, underplays the French king's illness.[173] Rather, after noting the favors Louis bestowed on the hermit, the bull turns to Francis's establishing the three orders of Minims (enclosed men and women, and tertiaries), with assistance from Julius II, Sixtus IV, Innocent VIII, Alexander VI, and Leo himself. Today, the bull concludes, Francis is canonized as a Confessor, whose feast day was to be April 2.

Before and after death Francis affected the lives of four French kings, their wives, and their children—and Louise of Savoy. Understandably, this Gallic elite considered themselves responsible for the Calabrian's saint-

applications, its bruised leaves are said to be remedial if applied to boils, abscesses, and suppurating ulcers, as here.

172. The first and second witnesses of the Tours process were asked if he'd been eviscerated, i.e., embalmed with aromatics; a whiff of skepticism as to the odor of sanctity?

173. Sadoleto's name appears at the end of the bull, Fontanini, *Codex constitutionum,* 211; for his career under Leo X, see Richard M. Douglas, *Jacopo Sadoleto, 1477–1547: Humanist and Reformer* (Cambridge, Mass.: Harvard University Press, 1959), 14–28.

hood. As early as May of 1483 Louis XI described himself as the "promoter, patron and protector" of Francis and his followers.[174] These somewhat inflated assertions are dwarfed by Louise of Savoy's. Just as a king emphasized his part in fostering the proto-Minims' fortunes in France, at the end of the story a king's mother made even more extravagant claims in her much-discussed and debated *Journal.*[175] Whether or not Louise wrote the words, let them stand as a fitting coda: "In the year 1519, on 5 July [*sic*], brother Francis of Paola, of the evangelical mendicant brethren, was canonized by me; in any case, I paid for it."[176]

The reasons for the elevation of a woodland hermit to royal favorite and saint, outlined in this chapter, are apparent in the narration itself. By chance, a dying king discovered Francis, plucked him from Calabrian rusticity, and set him down in the midst of one of Europe's greatest courts. Shifting politics lent this transformation a utilitarian aspect that successive popes and French kings exploited: the hermit became a useful unofficial channel between Tours and Rome as well as healer and spiritual and even political guide to French royalty *and* the papacy. Francis's ability to play these multiple roles is remarkable. Had he remained in Calabria as a prophesying hermit, perhaps—given contemporary anxieties about "living saints"—he never would have been considered for sainthood at the curia. Although the moves toward his canonization played out in irregular fashion, sometimes advancing, sometimes retreating, as in all the instances considered in this book, finally a Medici pope and Valois monarch cooperated in creating a saint whose glory could be shared by both realms. In the next chapter, Medici interests in raising another saint will be even more evident than in Francis's case.

174. *Lettres Choisies*, 532–33, to the officials of Abbeville (21 May 1483): referring to "les religieux de l'ordre des frères Minimes, duquel sommes fondateur, patron et protecteur de leurs privilèges à eux donnés par le Saint-Siège apostolique."

175. Among the many perspectives on her Journal, see Myra Dickman Orth, "Francis Du Moulin and the Journal of Louise of Savoy," *Sixteenth-Century Journal* 13 (Spring 1982): 55–66. For Orth, De Moulin, the king's tutor, was ghostwriter of the journal, composed as an astrological guide.

176. Louise of Savoy, *Journal, Collection des mémoires relatifs à l'histoire de France*, ed. C. Petitot, Petitot-Collection des memoires, serie 1, tome 16 (Paris, 1826), 401: "L'an 1519, le 5 juillet, frere François de Paule, des freres mendians Evangelistes, fut par moi canonisé; à tout le moins j'en payé la taxe."

CHAPTER 5

The Reforming Friar-Archbishop

Antoninus of Florence (1389–1459, cd. 1523)

In leaving Francis's austere cell for the noisy activity of Florence, we move from an uneducated charismatic to a self-assured archbishop, Antoninus; from rustic hero turned royal adviser to ecclesiastical boss at the heart of the premier Renaissance city. In Antoninus's Florence the cathedral with Brunelleschi's fantastic dome was consecrated by Eugenius IV, Michelozzo began the Palazzo Medici, Donatello returned from Padua to continue his sculpting, and Ghiberti's heavenly gates were finally revealed. Much of the artistic and humanistic ornament of the city—one thinks of Marsilio Ficino among many others—was due to Cosimo de'Medici, who knew Antoninus well and outlived him by about five years.

For modern historians striving to categorize saints by "type," here, surely, are good examples. However, in spite of the fact that on one level Francis and Antoninus represented Christianity in its inevitable polarities, thaumaturgic-prophetic and bureaucratic-institutional, on another level they shared many traits. Both were organizers, one commanding visitations and reports, issuing rules and regulations for his clergy and people, overseeing Dominican houses, the other planting convents first in Italy, then in France and beyond, and creating a reformed order, the Minims. Both were known personally to the popes who changed their lives: Eugenius IV, who made Antoninus Tuscany's leading prelate in 1446, and Sixtus IV, who sent

Francis off to France. Both became accustomed to moving in the most elevated circles, Antoninus in that of Cosimo de'Medici (d. 1464) and other communal leaders, Francis among France's royalty; and finally, each was determined in his own way to reform the Christians among whom he lived. For some forty-three years their lives overlapped.

Three contemporaries knew and wrote about Antoninus: Francesco da Castiglione, Vespasiano da Bisticci, and Baldovino de Baldovini. Castiglione joined the archbishop's household about 1452, where he remained until his master's death in 1459. On January 15 of that year, Antoninus conferred the title "doctor of theology" on his faithful secretary. Castiglione began his *Vita* probably in early 1460.[1] The chatty Vespasiano, well known to Renaissance scholars, was stationer to the archbishop. The two often conversed in Antoninus's San Marco convent. Vespasiano, more interested than Castiglione in the archbishop's sometimes rocky relations with the *Signoria*, is to be read with caution. Finally, Baldovini seems to have been principal notary for the prelate, whom he served for some eight years, from early 1450. Other *Vitae* were produced along the way, for example, by Leonardo ser Uberti, c. 1468, who included a list of posthumous miracles; San Marco friar and chronicler Roberto Ubaldini da Gagliano, procurator of the cause who summarized earlier biographies in 1519; and Vincent Mainard de Giminiano (Rome 1525, Paris 1527), commissioned by Clement VII, which is derivative and devotional. Further biographical information comes from scattered notarial documents, letters, ambassadorial reports, the prelate's own writings along with records of archiepiscopal income and expenses, and witnesses at canonization hearings.

ANTONINUS'S EARLY CAREER

The principal extant *Vitae* deal with Antoninus as archbishop, accounting for the final thirteen of his seventy years; his earlier life is less well known. However, enough can be pieced together to give us a general overview of the years prior to 1446. Son of Florentine notary Niccolò Pierozzi, he was born in early 1389 in a house a few paces from the Duomo. A small,

1. A principal study of Antoninus's life is Raoul Morçay's *Saint Antonin: Archevèque de Florence 1389–1459* (Tours/Paris: Lib. Gabalda 1914), source discussion in introduction, ivff. Though, as usual with many of these saints' biographies, there is more than a hint of the hagiographical, Morçay is less prone to this than others, and his work has been fully utilized in what follows; he includes useful documents in an appendix.

sickly child—he was to suffer hernia and fevers all his life—at times his survival was in doubt; of his father's seven children, only he and two sisters lived to adulthood. His youthful education is conjectural, but among the influences that affected his life were the sermons of the Dominican reformer Giovanni Dominici, a famous preacher of Florence's most prestigious convent, Santa Maria Novella. Antoninus presented himself there about 1404, hoping to join, but Dominici sent him away with a hefty study assignment, the *Decretum.*[2] Meanwhile, in 1405 Dominici received Innocent VII's approval to establish a reformed house at Fiesole. As among the Franciscans, the Order of Preachers had developed rival camps, though less extreme. Dominici sent Antoninus to Cortona for a year's novitiate, after which he was at last allowed to join the Fiesole friars in 1406. Meanwhile Dominici was called to Rome and (eventually) a cardinalate. The Fiesole Dominicans continued to follow his conservative, antihumanist teachings embodied in *Lucula Noctis,* in which he made it clear that his spiritual sons were to avoid the paganizing "contagion of humanism" exemplified, for instance, by Florence's famed chancellor Coluccio Salutati (d. 1406). Continuing his studies (emphasizing Aquinas), Antoninus, a priest from 1413, moved between Fiesole, Foligno, and Cortona, becoming vicar and prior of the last two houses along the way, and finally returning to Fiesole as prior from about 1418 to about 1424.[3] In the latter year he was sent as visitor to the Naples Dominicans, where he remained until 1428 or 1429;[4] subsequently, we find him in Rome as prior of the convent at Santa Maria sopra Minerva, one of Italy's most important Dominican communities. The basilica contains the tomb of Catherine of Siena; Antoninus oversaw the translation of her remains to a new shrine. In addition, in his *Summa* he states that during this time, under Eugenius IV (1431–47) he became a member of the

2. Castiglione claims that Dominici told him to "go memorize the *Decretum* ..." *AASS,* May I, 313–25, at 314.

3. The foregoing from Morçay, *Saint Antonin,* 13–46. See also Lorenzo Polizzotto, "The Making of a Saint: The Canonization of St. Antonino, 1516–1523," *Journal of Medieval and Renaissance Studies* 22, no. 3 (Fall 1992): 353–81, with full biographical references on 355 n. 11; this article is essentially a translation of Polizzotto's "Vicissitudini, contrasti ed esiti del processo di canonizzazione di S. Antonino," *Rivista di Ascetica e Mistica* 3–4 (July–December 1990): 363–87, arising from a conference of September 1989. Polizzotto's reconstruction is challenged by Pietschmann, below.

4. In 1429 Leonardo Bruni wrote to the vicar general of the Observant Dominicans asking that Antonino be returned from Naples to Florence "for the public good," Peter Howard, "Preaching Magnificence in Renaissance Florence," *Renaissance Quarterly* 61 (2008): 325–69, at 340.

Rota. This is an interesting claim, given the constitution of Eugenius's predecessor Martin V (1417–31), which directed that only well-known doctors of law who'd taught for at least three years after the doctorate were to be appointed to the Rota.[5]

Meanwhile, developments in Tuscany would bring Antoninus back to his native city. As early as 1435, probably at the urging of Cosimo de'Medici, Eugenius IV ordered an inquest to determine whether the Fiesole Dominicans could also take over Florence's San Marco convent, ousting the resident Silvestrines. Although an ad hoc commission found no fault with the Silvestrines, nevertheless (possibly, again, due to Medici pressure), in January 1436 Eugenius ceded San Marco to the Dominicans (each house obtaining its own prior in 1445).[6] By 1437, now residing in San Marco—then being rebuilt with Antoninus's encouragement by Michelozzo under Cosimo's patronage—Antoninus was named vicar general of Italy's Observants; a few years later, he also became prior of his convent. Not much is known of his work as prior, though in 1442 he was among a dozen Florentine leaders who established a charitable fund for the poor. In addition, he supported education, and no doubt participated in the Council of Florence of 1439. Meanwhile, he received friendly visits from his convent's patron Cosimo. Having ceded his place as prior in 1444, next year Antoninus, free to devote himself to his work as vicar general, set off for Naples.[7] He would not reach that city, being once again recalled to Florence.

After the death in August 1445 of Bartolomeo Zabarella, prelate of Florence (raised to archiepiscopal status earlier in the century), the commune sent a short list of five candidates to the pope. Eugenius ignored these and in a bull of January 10, 1446, appointed Antoninus, whose work in Rome and Florence had shown him to be an effective administrator—a quality the pope stressed.[8] Peterson suggests that the pope bypassed the other candidates, some clearly Medici partisans, because by now he'd grown hos-

5. Brundage, *The Medieval Origins of the Legal Profession,* 376–77 (the constitution was *In apostolice dignitatis specula*).

6. The details of this ejection are examined by David Spencer Peterson, "Archbishop Antoninus: Florence and the Church in the Earlier Fifteenth Century" (Ph.D. diss., Cornell University, 1985), 72–73 and nn. 117–18.

7. The foregoing from Morçay, *Saint Antonin,* 46–97.

8. David S. Peterson, "An Episcopal Election in Quattrocento Florence," in *Popes, Teachers and Canon Law in the Middle Ages,* ed. James Ross Sweeney and Stanley Chodorow (Ithaca: Cornell University Press, 1989), 300–325.

tile (for political and fiscal reasons) to the city that had sheltered him from 1434 to 1443, and also that he wanted to assert papal independence in such nominations. Morçay believed that the pope chose a non-patrician in order to give Antoninus independence from the commune's squabbling anti- and pro-Medici factions, but this may be too simple an explanation, given the complex relationships already in place between Florentine leaders of various political persuasions and the Observant Dominicans.[9] Although the Florentines claimed to praise the appointment, the new archbishop (whose first impulse, Castiglione writes, was to flee) peevishly shunned it. He finally agreed to a simple consecration ceremony at Fiesole in March 1446.[10] Quickly overcoming his earlier hesitancy—which seems to have been genuine—he revealed himself to be an activist, calling a synod in April, carrying out a diocesan visitation in August, and standing up to Cosimo and the commune, as well as his own recalcitrant clergy, on various issues. He was a very successful manipulator. As Peterson puts it, he skillfully exercised an "ability to exploit the web of competing interests surrounding his office."[11]

THE NEW ARCHBISHOP

In many ways Antoninus became a model archbishop much like Milan's Carlo Borromeo more than a century later, and, like Borromeo, he faced many challenges. It is clear that this little man of skin and bones—Castiglione's description—while conscientiously ministering to his flock, was fearless when battling clerical and lay factions within that flock.[12] For instance, in 1447, Nicholas V put him in charge of collecting a tithe ordered by Eugenius IV. The archbishop reluctantly undertook the job, agreeing that the clergy should assist the commune when necessary, though without being exploited.[13] Five years later, again assigned by Nicholas V to oversee the collection of another clerical levy to help finance Florence's wars, Antoninus had to command his suffragan at Pistoia to pay up within three days, come to some deal with the *Signoria*, or suffer interdict and additional late fees: the archbishop writes, "Every day I'm pestered by the Medici

9. Ibid., 314–16, referring to Morçay, *Saint Antonin*, 101–23.

10. Castiglione in *AASS*, 351; Peterson, "Episcopal Election," 322.

11. Peterson, "Episcopal Election," 322–24.

12. Castiglione writes that the archbishop was "statura corporis non magnus, ossibus ac nervis magis quam carne suffultus," *AASS*, May I, 314.

13. Peterson, "Archbishop Antoninus," 39.

about this."[14] After Constantinople's fall he was deeply involved in collecting funds for the crusade that never materialized, again bringing him up against both clergy and laity—in fact, to the prelate's chagrin no funds at all seem to have been sent from Florence to Rome.[15] As for dealings with Cosimo and the commune, a good example of the prelate's zeal occurred in July 1458, when he affixed to the Duomo and other churches a command (threatening excommunication) that the city's Medici-manipulated elections should take place by secret, not open, voting. Otherwise, warned Antoninus, God would punish Florence with *pestilentia* and other evils.[16] An outraged group of citizens led by Medicean factions confronted him over this, threatening to remove him from office. He's said to have replied, "For God's sake, do it." From the very start, many recognized that he preferred the *vita quieta,* as the commune had phrased it in 1446 when encouraging him to accept the job.[17] The frail but fearless prelate could also be practical and realistic in his administrative style: he and another Florentine ambassador to Rome succeeded (1455) in their petition to allow Dominican Observants to hold property and income. Antoninus justified this move away from the strict rule of poverty by noting that while the numbers of friars had increased, charitable donations from the laity had declined; times, he acknowledged, had changed.[18] This exemplifies his belief, expressed in his *Summa theologica,* that costly magnificence and holiness could coincide.[19]

Governing one of Italy's largest and wealthiest archdioceses certainly removed Antoninus from the quiet life he desired. In 1446 he carried out visitations of 149 churches in twenty-nine of his fifty-six rural parishes while overseeing the many convents, churches, and priories in the city. Several country churches were in a sorry state, with absenteeism, dilapidated fabric, and in some cases parishioners who were "virtual infidels."[20] All the more reason, then, to encourage his clergy to instruct the laity in the basic ele-

14. Morçay, *Saint Antonin,* 220–21, documents, 449–50: "Cum . . . cotidie molestemur ab istis ipsis de Medicis."

15. Ibid., 236–41, documents, 465–68.

16. Ibid., documents, 429.

17. Ibid., 439; see also Aliotti's letter to Antoninus, 440.

18. Nicolai Rubinstein, "Lay Patronage and Observant Reform in Fifteenth-century Florence," in *Christianity and the Renaissance,* ed. Timothy Verdon and John Henderson (Syracuse: Syracuse University Press, 1990), 64–82, at 67–8 on Antoninus's "apparent volte-face."

19. Howard, "Preaching Magnificence," 346, 353, and passim.

20. Peterson, "Archbishop Antoninus," 30, 590–91; his vicar continued the work into the 1450s.

ments of the faith and regularly to administer the sacraments. In his 1455 *Constitutions* of sixty articles in roughly eight sections, Antoninus stressed the practical rather than the speculative, commanding his clergy to attend more carefully to (1) church-secular relations, (2) the goods and wealth of the Church, (3) clerical administration, (4) episcopal prerogatives, (5) clerical morals, (6) concerns of the laity, (7) confraternities, and (8) the sacraments. Several of these points were typical of the injunctions issued by conscientious prelates throughout the Middle Ages. For example, Antoninus wanted to keep his clergy from mimicking the dandified idle rich of Florence, regulating hair and hat styles and gown length, and prohibiting their sporting gold or silver ornaments. This had been a problem well before the days of Innocent III, whose Lateran canons also aimed at taming priestly extravagance. Antoninus's clergy were to avoid gambling, dances, "spectacles," and taverns, and were not to play instruments or sing in "suspicious places." In spite of all his good intentions, Antoninus's Constitutions, generally ignored, were annulled in 1509.[21]

As part of his reform movement the archbishop even convinced the commune in 1454 to split the traditional Saint John Baptist procession (June 23) into two parts: on the 22nd, lay confraternities with their elaborate floats recalling "carnival vanities" (according to Antoninus) were allowed to parade through the city, but on the 23rd a religious procession took place, with confraternal and clerical participation.[22] In that year the festival began with a parade, and on the next day a procession consisting of twenty-two floats represented the biblical cycle from creation to the last judgment, with dozens of actors, and clusters of children dressed as angels. An unedifying interruption was caused by "a German . . . wearing only a loose shirt" who jumped up on the float with Octavian and the sibyl foretelling Christ's birth, grasped Octavian in his rich purple velvet and goldwork garments, and "threw him headlong onto the people in the square," but before the intruder could get to some angelic children bystanders pulled him down, beating him; he got up again but "was hit with clubs from below and from

21. Richard C. Trexler, "The Episcopal Constitutions of Antoninus of Florence," *Quellen und Forschungen aus italienischen Archiven und Bibliotheken* 59 (1979): 244–72, discusses the constitutions with an edition of the Italian text. Trexler suggests that most of Antoninus's regulations were unenforceable, inflexible, and contrary to independent communal governance.

22. Peterson, "Archbishop Antoninus," 563–80; Richard C. Trexler, *Public Life in Renaissance Florence* (Ithaca: Cornell University Press, 1980), 240–56.

above and overpowered." The account laconically continues, the "Eleventh [float was, ironically], the Temple of Peace."[23]

Antoninus contributed to the pastoral health of his clergy by composing manuals and treatises, the most important being his *Summa doctrinalis* or *Moralis* of the 1440s to 1454, sometimes called *Summa theologica.* Following the same methodical scholastic structure of logical analysis as laid down by his spiritual mentor Aquinas, Antoninus provided a practical guide for clergy rather than a theoretical treatise, dealing as he did with confession (the *Confessionale*), sin, the bible, simony, and so on. Vespasiano was involved in binding the original work, which seems to have come out in a shorter edition before 1470. Besides this, the prelate composed a *Summa historialis,* or *Chronicon,* illustrating the hand of God in history up to his own days; a copy was provided to Fiesole in 1455. In addition, there were several short works on particular subjects, as well as letters and sermons. Many of these went through several editions in the sixteenth and seventeenth centuries.[24] Although little of this corpus was particularly original—Antoninus copied chunks of Dominici's antihumanistic *Luculla Noctis* into his *Summa,* for instance—and Peterson sees in his writing a thinker "of the second order," nevertheless they became popular practical guides. A hundred years later, Cardinal Gabriele Paleotti (d. 1597) thought their vernacular versions appropriate for the parish priest's library.[25] The archbishop's writings were meant to be useful without aiming for rhetorical brilliance. His attitude toward contemporary humanists and their works was passively tolerant: he didn't go out of his way to condemn them, and yet he didn't want his clergy to be distracted or misled by "pagan" ideas. A similar conservative strain appears in his attitude toward Florentine art.[26]

There was a stern, authoritarian side to Antoninus's piety. In his *Summa theologica* he emphasized the duty of absolute obedience even, should it happen, to a morally imperfect pope.[27] Before becoming archbishop, as vicar general in Tuscany and Naples, Castiglione writes, he governed "with

23. Peter Meredith and John E. Tailby, *The Staging of Religious Drama in Europe in the Later Middle Ages: Texts and Documents in English Translation* (Kalamazoo, Mich.: Medieval Institute Publications, 1983), 240–41, from Alessandro D'Ancona, *Origini del teatro italiano,* 2 vols. (Rome, 1891), 1:228–29. In this account the parade took place on the 21st, the procession on the 22nd.

24. Stefano Orlandi, O.P., *Bibliografia Antoniniana* (Vatican City, 1961), x–xli.

25. Peterson, "Archbishop Antoninus," 17; Christopher Black, *Church, Religion and Society in Early Modern Italy* (Basingstoke: Palgrave-Macmillan, 2004), 95, 258 n. 26.

26. Creighton Gilbert, "The Archbishop on the Painters of Florence, 1450," *Art Bulletin* 41, no. 1 (March 1959): 75–87.

27. Pastor, *History of the Popes,* 5:90 n.

great diligence and severity." As Florence's spiritual leader to whom all sorts of litigation and accusations were brought, he displayed—there's that word again—"severity . . . joined with mercy."[28] (In the canonization bull this becomes "justice joined with mercy.")[29] When Antoninus discovered anything he thought improper, sinful, or unjust, he acted quickly and zealously. Vespasiano and Castiglione tell the story of the archbishop's overturning gambling tables at the Buondelmonte loggia; on another occasion he forced a priest to hand over his substantial gambling winnings to the poor.[30] Sexual vices also came under attack: Antoninus ordered the bishop of Pistoia to excommunicate a fornicating priest as well as his concubine, and he implemented Nicholas V's command (April 1452) to dissolve a Florentine convent housing two pregnant nuns.[31] A religious of the Order of Hermits delated to Antoninus's curia for many "grave crimes" was captured and tortured, after which he confessed but managed to escape from custody.[32] In another torture case the accused appealed to Rome. Bartholomew, prior of a small collegiate church, was imprisoned by the archbishop without any justification—or so Bartholomew claimed in his petition—and accused of an evil crime with a child. His hands were tied behind him and he was made to sit on a sharp "wooden horse," resulting in his confession. The archbishop deprived him of his priorate. After his release Bartholomew appealed to the pope, and in December 1455 Calixtus set up a commission to determine whether Antoninus's sentence was iniquitous or unjust.[33] Another of Antoninus's judgments was appealed by a group of foreign merchants whom he had forbidden under pain of excommunication to collect debts owed by Florentines. They took their case to Rome. In May 1455 the pope ordered an investigation into whether the archbishop's decision went beyond the bounds of justice.[34] Antoninus was equally severe when it came to fiscal matters. After his badgering the clergy of Arezzo to come up with part of a subsidy, a spokesman for the Aretines asked the pope to curb Antoninus's zeal so that he'd "go easier" on his clergy.[35] This again reminds one of Borro-

28. Castiglione, *AASS,* May I, 315 and 318; the word also implied seriousness, gravity, strictness.

29. Fontanini, *Codex constitutionum* 228.

30. *Vespasiano da Bisticci, Renaissance Princes, Popes and Prelates,* trans. W. George and E. Waters (New York: Harper, 1926, 1963, from Ital. ed. of Angelo Mai), 159; Castiglione, *AASS,* I May, 320.

31. Morçay, *Saint Antonin,* 446, 482.

32. Ibid., 469–70.

33. Ibid., 490–91.

34. Ibid., 487.

35. Peterson, "Archbishop Antoninus," 347–9: "mitius nobiscum agat; and mitius, et benignius in rebus nostris se gerat."

meo a century later, to whom a colleague wrote (in 1566), "you are too austere and rigorous."[36]

As can be expected, Antoninus was especially harsh with heretics. The very first of his sixty *Constitutions,* in fact, addressed this threat, calling for informants against anyone who questioned Church teachings.[37] The issue was more than merely theoretical, as we see in the trial of Giovanni da Montecatini (de Cani or Cavini), a doctor ("medicina, di che era maestro"), executed in 1450. The case is recorded by Antoninus's notary, Baldovini.[38] (Castiglione spends only a few lines on the event, using it to show the archbishop's greatness of spirit in the face of public disapproval of the proceedings.)[39] According to Baldovini, Giovanni was well known for his evil opinion of the Catholic faith and teachings of the Church. He was also thought to call up demons in his house in Florence's San Lorenzo parish. He and his followers resembled heretical *Fraticelli,* little sons of the devil—"figluoli del diavolo." A group of high clergy, including theologians and Antoninus's vicar, interrogated Giovanni as he lay at home in his sickbed. He claimed that Nicholas V was not the true pope and that priests consecrated by Florence's archbishop weren't true priests and couldn't consecrate the body of Christ. When asked whether he'd received communion, and where, he said, "Here, in this church." The interrogators, pointing out that his house wasn't a church, concluded that communion had been administered by *Fraticelli* priests. Giovanni refused to reply to questions about the possibility of error in the New Testament and even the truth of the Catholic faith. The attending clergy urged him to change his mind, but he was so stubborn (*tanta dura cervice*) that he neither confessed nor detested his errors. Out of compassion, Baldovini writes, Antoninus allowed him a certain term (unspecified) to think things over (not uncommon in such trials). Giovanni refused to budge. A platform was built outside the entrance to the cathedral, from which Antoninus and other prelates pronounced judgment. The heretic and invoker of demons was handed over Florence's *podestà* Niccolò Vitelli, who committed him to the flames. His books of necromancy, chiromancy, and demonic invocations were also burned. Thus Giovanni died a "martyr

36. Quoted in Black, *Church, Religion and Society,* 70.

37. Trexler, "Episcopal Constitutions," 256.

38. Morçay, *Saint Antonin,* 430–31, from a fifteenth-century ms.: Bibl. Riccardiana 1333.

39. Castiglione, *AASS,* May I, 320: "non approbantibus id multis civibus."

to the devil" as the archbishop looked on. Gene Brucker claimed that he was "the only man to die in Florence for his beliefs in the 110 years between the execution of fra Michele da Calci (1389) and Savonarola (1498)." Brucker also noted that many Florentines raised a tumult against the execution of Michele in 1389, which seems to have happened in Antoninus's 1450 case as well, if we follow Castiglione.[40] The Florentines' differences of opinion about Savonarola's death are well known.

THE ARCHBISHOP'S POSTHUMOUS CAREER BEGINS

By the time of his own death on May 2, 1459, Antoninus was widely respected (and, in some circles perhaps, feared) within and beyond Florence for his administrative abilities, great courage and integrity in dealing with political, fiscal, and spiritual issues, unblemished personal life, and conscientious pastoral care. Antoninus's first biographer and secretary of eight years, Castiglione, who knew him well enough to chide the frail archbishop on one occasion (without effect) for going out in inclement weather, composed his *Vita* around 1460, based, as he claimed, on deeds he'd seen or heard about. These included three miracles performed during his master's lifetime: one involved Antoninus's powers over nature (causing iron at a foundry to resist melting); the second, a physical cure through prayer; and the third ended a blight of sterility in Castiglione's own family, on the brink of extinction. Castiglione claimed that even before his death, Antoninus's repute as *sanctus* was acknowledged by the pope, prelates of the curia, and all the people of Italy.[41]

Sensing death approaching, Antoninus had himself moved to an archiepiscopal residence just outside Florence's walls. Meanwhile, on April 25, Pius II and his extensive entourage of a dozen cardinals and innumerable prelates arrived in the city, en route to a congress at Mantua to discuss the Turkish threat. The Florentines threw themselves into revelry to honor their august visitor: a joust in the city, a grand ball on April 30, on May 1 a

40. Gene A. Brucker, *Renaissance Florence* (Berkeley: University of California Press, 1969), 206–7.

41. "Ab omnibus Italiae populis," *AASS*, May I, 312–13. For Castiglione's place among humanist hagiographers, see Frazier, *Possible Lives*, 20–21 and chap. 2 passim; mss. and edd. on 388–89. A decade after writing his *Vita* of Antoninus (apparently taking Plutarch's *Lives* as model, with Vittorino da Feltre as the counter-life), Castiglione refused a commission to rewrite the lives of the early martyrs, questioning the value of "evidence" from such early times.

hunt staged with a variety of animals for the delight of the pope and his retinue. About the same time in the quiet suburbs Antoninus was having his last testament witnessed, and preparing himself for the end. He died on the morning of May 2, while the papal party reposed in Santa Maria Novella. The body was eviscerated, the intestines kept by a Dominican colleague in his San Marco cell.[42] When Pius learned of the prelate's passing, he ordered Cardinal Pietro Barbo (the future Paul II) to arrange a fitting funeral, which took place first in the cathedral, where a Mass was celebrated, and then in San Marco convent, where the archbishop wished to be buried.[43] While the body lay in state, people began arriving to honor Antoninus, kissing his feet and hands. The pope's grant of an indulgence for those who showed the dead prelate such honors led to even bigger crowds, people coming down from the hills and all parts of the region. Because of this popular demonstration, the body couldn't be buried for eight days—several days after the pope left Florence on May 5. Nevertheless, Castiglione reports, there was no odor about the corpse; on the contrary, it emitted a sweet smell. The archbishop looked happier in death than in life, and there was no sign of rigor in the hands or feet, all of which convinced many of the man's sanctity. No doubt the papal presence temporarily boosted Florence's population as all the worthies round about crowded into the city. This had the unintended effect of providing an expanded audience for the archbishop's funeral and subsequent exposition in San Marco. This is not to say that people wouldn't have come to honor the dead prelate; but the presence of the pope, his setting up (with the *Signoria*) of the funeral ceremonies, and his indulgence probably accelerated the formation of a cult. Nearly sixty years later, another papal visit to Florence marked the start of Antoninus's canonization process.

Antoninus's earliest posthumous wonders began at the instant of death: a certain Dominican, Constantius, while at prayer in a distant city saw him fly into the heavens, at the same time observing another Dominican, dying at the same moment, descend into purgatory. For Constantius, the saintly archbishop went to his immediate reward while an "ordinary" friar met the usual end. At the funeral a woman was cured of paralysis, and a man of his

42. *AASS*, May I, 343.

43. His remains would be translated in 1589, where his memory became associated with Florence's other patron, Zenobius: Sally J. Cornelison, "Tales of Two Bishop Saints: Zenobius and Antoninus in Florentine Renaissance Art and History," *Sixteenth Century Journal* 38, no. 3 (2007): 627–56.

fevers, by touching the body. A man whose son had fallen from a height (the doctors despaired) was made well, after which the man presented a wax image of himself at the tomb, with a smaller one of his son. A few of the archbishop's hairs delivered a noble Florentine from difficult labor. Castiglione recorded these events from the mouths of the beneficiaries themselves, such as Luisius, whose demented father was accustomed to wander the streets at night until a vow was made on his behalf. A Florentine youth was cured of apoplexy after two Dominicans prayed for him at Antoninus's tomb. In concluding his *vita et miracula,* Castiglione notes that the loss of the archbishop was (now) felt even more, in view of the calamities that had occurred since his death, particularly the Turkish threat.[44]

Castiglione's work was continued by Leonardo di ser Uberto Martini Berti, a Florentine notary who joined the San Marco Dominicans in 1458. After noting that Antoninus's merits were greater than his miracles, Leonardo claimed that Florence had had no greater shepherd since the days of Saint Zenobius. He rehearsed Antoninus's virtuous life and piety, emphasizing his chastity: he spoke with no youth or woman unless in a public place, and allowed no one under the age of twenty-five into his *famiglia.* Leonardo notes that whenever the archbishop was seen in the streets "all sorts of people ran to seek his blessing," believing that this would keep them from danger for that day—rather like the common medieval custom of carrying around a talisman for protection, or striving to glimpse an image of Saint Christopher or the Eucharist as it was elevated at Mass, which guaranteed the viewer's safety for the rest of the day. Leonardo added about sixteen or so miracles, dated to the 1460s; they included beneficiaries from Florence as well as "outsiders," women and men, simple folk and nobility. Several deal with the removal of temptation or other mental or spiritual anxieties, while others are of the usual type: toothache, broken bones, paralysis, eye problems, tumors, hernia. There were a few visions, one of heaven showing Dominic and Aquinas seated among the celestial beings, with a place reserved for Florence's spiritual hero. Wax images are mentioned, and a cure with a bit of Antoninus's clothing. Finally, another interesting report raises an issue commonly examined in canonical treatises on miracles: if medication as well as an appeal to a saint resulted in a cure, was it still

44. Castiglione, *AASS,* May I, 323–25; the *Vita* seems to have been completed in late 1461.

miraculous? A notary vowed to honor the dead prelate if cured of his fever within six days. On the fifth day, however, someone brought him medicine, which "immediately" cured him; yet the notary attributed his recovery to the holy man. "He joyfully told me this," writes Leonardo, "on 30 November 1463." The last date given in this small collection is 1468; Leonardo died of the plague in May 1481.[45] A few other wonders were recorded, perhaps by another Dominican, in the 1460s.[46] Miracles attributed to the dead Antoninus seem to have tapered off by 1471. This phenomenon has been recorded at other medieval shrines, where wonder-working saints seem to perform most of their posthumous miracles during the first decade or so after their deaths.[47] Nevertheless it's likely that pilgrims with their miracle stories continued to show up at Antoninus's tomb. In 1519 a wax-maker testified that he'd made more than 150 images, while a colleague claimed to have taken an "innumerable quantity of wax images" to the tomb over the previous forty years, going back to the late 1470s. Witnesses in 1519 also mentioned several *tabulae* depicting miracles, along with many other votives, including a pair of golden eyes.[48]

There are only a few other references to cultic activities in the 1480s. It's possible that Lorenzo *il Magnifico* was interested in promoting Antoninus's canonization during 1488, but nothing seems to have come of this.[49] In 1520, Cardinal Carvajal claimed in consistory that Leo X was following Innocent VIII's (1484–92) lead in his efforts to raise Antoninus to sainthood. Cumulatively, these notices suggest a movement of some kind favoring the prelate's canonization under way before the end of the century. Continuing recognition of Antoninus's posthumous potential is illustrated, though backhandedly, in two incidents of the 1490s. In the aftermath of Charles VIII's 1494 invasion, although Florence was spared, nevertheless rowdy French soldiers remained in the area. For whatever reasons, a group of them took Antoninus's deathbed, which had become an object of reverence in the residence where he'd died, carried it into a nearby tavern, and put it to fleshly uses, *carnium exercitium*. When an outraged admirer of Antoninus tried to buy the bed, Lawrence, the bar owner, replied, "A cancer to you and your Antoninus; what

45. Orlandi, *Bibliografia Antoniniana*, viii–ix.

46. *AASS*, May I, 334–5.

47. Polizzotto, "Making of a Saint," 357; cf. R. Finucane, *Miracles and Pilgrims*, 187.

48. Printed summary of Process in *AASS*, May I, 343–51.

49. Polizzotto, "Making of a Saint," 359.

miracles did he ever do, that you want to make him a saint?" We shouldn't be surprised to read that three days later Lawrence developed cancer of the mouth, which killed him.[50] Another eventual result of the French incursion was the rise of Savonarola, whose popularity had declined precipitously by April 7, 1498, when an ordeal by fire fizzled out, leaving anti-Savonarolans in an angry mood: next evening they laid siege to San Marco convent, threatening to burn it down. They were resisted by weapon-wielding friars and their allies who'd smuggled harquebuses and other military paraphernalia, armor, cannons, and the like into the convent.[51] At one point in the fray, some got in and destroyed many votives, throwing them down from the wooden framework at Antoninus's tomb and smashing them.[52] This destruction may have arisen from Savonarola's having recommended Antoninus as an intercessor with God, as well as his attempts to associate himself with the dead prelate while battling the Dominicans' Conventual wing.[53] Savonarola's followers will play a major role in Antoninus's process.

As the 1498 episode illustrates, much had happened to Florence, and Italy, between the archbishop's death in 1459 and 1516, when his process began. Lorenzo de'Medici's death in 1492 and Charles VIII's invasion a few years later marked the close of one era and start of another: after 1494 Italy became a battlefield between Habsburg and Valois superpowers. The Medici lost their hold in Florence after Lorenzo's son Piero, along with his brothers Giuliano and Giovanni (later Pope Leo X) fled the city, which soon fell under Savonarola's spell. From 1491, like Antoninus before him, he was prior of San Marco. By 1495 he had become very influential in the new republic's governance. His fiery sermons were so popular that the *Signoria* blatantly ignored papal attempts to muzzle him. Though removed by execution in 1498, his followers, the *piagnoni* ("snivelers") remained a weighty element in Florentine society. In 1502 republican leadership fell to Piero Soderini (d. 1522); he held it until 1512. Meanwhile Julius II's anti-French (anti-"barbarian") policy was firming up by 1510, as a Holy League was constituted against the invaders—with the notable exception of the Republic of Florence. After the French were forced to retreat after their Pyrrhic victory at Ravenna in April

50. *AASS*, May I, 350, 351.

51. Lauro Martines, *Fire in the City* (New York: Oxford University Press, 2006), ch. 17, "The Siege of San Marco."

52. *AASS*, May I, 350: "dejecerunt ad terram, & projecerunt ac confregerunt."

53. Trexler, *Public Life*, 67; Polizzotto, "Making of a Saint," 360.

1512, Julius came down heavily on the recalcitrant Republic: at the Diet of Mantua (August) the victors decided, inter alia, to punish Florence for its failure to join the League, and for acquiescence in the anti-papal Council of Pisa. The Medici were to be returned to power with the help of Spanish troops; this was accomplished after a horrific sack of Prato in late August. On September 1, 1512, Soderini fled, and Giuliano de'Medici (d. 1516) entered Florence, followed by his brother Cardinal Giovanni a few weeks later. The Republic's Great Council of 3000 was abolished a few days after that. When Giovanni became Pope Leo X in 1513 he made his cousin Giulio (later Clement VII, d. 1534) archbishop of Florence (May 1513) and cardinal (September), found a suitable marriage for his less capable brother Giuliano, and—unfortunately for his family, as it turned out—appointed his nephew, the inexperienced Lorenzo di Piero (d. 1519), de facto governor in Florence. Consequently, from 1513, both Florence and Rome were "Medicean."[54] Although many welcomed the reestablishment of the old name and old ways, resistance of the *piagnoni* coupled with Piero's arrogance and incompetence quickly ended the honeymoon. As early as February 1512 an assassination plot against Giovanni was uncovered, resulting in executions and the jailing of Machiavelli. One of the main complaints voiced at nearly all levels of Florentine society was the loss of the Great Council and imposition of high taxes, which seemed to benefit Rome (after Leo's election) rather than Florence; another was absenteeism—"the main problem" according to one scholar—as members of the Medici family emigrated to Rome and seemed to relegate Florentine governance to the back burner.[55] Apart from that, as noted, the young Lorenzo di Piero proved to be incapable of managing the Medici regime even when he was in Florence.[56] Dissatisfaction coincided with an outbreak of apocalyptic preaching in the Savonarolan vein, for example by a certain Franciscan friar Francesco, whose sermons of 1513 alarmed Piero and Cardinal Giulio de'Medici, as well as Leo X, who had the prophet arrested.[57]

54. For an overview see Rosemary Devonshire Jones, *Francesco Vettori: Florentine Citizen and Medici Servant* (London: Athlone Press, 1972), esp. ch. 5, "At the Court of Leo X (1513–15)" and ch. 6, "Florence, France and Lorenzo (1515–19)."

55. Humfrey C. Butters, *Governors and Government in Early Sixteenth-Century Florence, 1502–1519* (Oxford: Clarendon Press, 1985), 187, 219, 248, 311.

56. Ibid., 238, 240, 266–67.

57. Nelson H. Minnich, "Prophecy and the Fifth Lateran Council (1512–1517)" in *Councils of the Catholic Reformation* (Aldershot: Ashgate [*Variorum*], 2008), 8:63–88, at 76 (essay first published in 1992).

In 1515 one Fra Teodoro's anti-Medicean, anti-Roman sermons were enlivened by stories of visions featuring Savonarola himself. In February 1515 Teodoro was forced publicly to recant; on that occasion thousands in the Duomo were warned against possessing Savonarola's writings or relics. In April Leo confirmed Teodoro's condemnation, citing similarities with Savonarola's heretical opinions.[58] In March of 1515 two more preachers blasted Florence's misgovernance and Rome's vices.[59] A famous charismatic was Jerome of Siena, who lived, as Francis of Paola had done, on bread and roots, drank only water, and slept on the bare ground; he preached against the clergy to large crowds before being ousted from Milan in 1516.[60] Papal disapproval of the movement was forthcoming in the same year at the Fifth Lateran Council. It's hardly coincidental that during the eleventh session (December 19) secular and mendicant preachers were castigated, who—as "reliable report" had it—"invented miracles, new and false prophecies and other frivolities hardly distinguishable from old wives' tales . . . not sparing even those who are honored with pontifical rank and other prelates of the church." Henceforth they were not to predict the future, whether of evil times, the coming of the antichrist, or the last judgment. Nor, as noted, were they to declare anything denigrating the pope. All prophetic utterances required ecclesiastical approval before being published or preached. As Niccoli observes, however, the council's canons only partially squelched the outbreak of apocalyptic preaching during this period.[61]

Obviously, having a Florentine as Holy Father did not bring solace or the expected advantages to many in the city; if anything, it resulted in the increasing unpopularity of the Medici and their supporters, who themselves often were divided as to the best policies for Florence (and their own families). The pope's dithering diplomacy with France's Louis XII and then Francis I only added to the dissatisfaction voiced in Florence, whose merchants favored the French connection. After the victory at Marignano in September 1515, Leo agreed to negotiate with Francis at Bologna, as noted in the previous chapter. When the pope stopped in Florence in late 1515 en route to the meeting he was welcomed by the Mediceans. However, his glit-

58. Ibid., 74, 77–8.

59. Butters, *Governors and Government,* 245, 263–64.

60. Pastor, *History of the Popes,* 5:213–25, 8:445–49.

61. Niccoli, *Prophecy and People,* passim, esp. ch. 4, 89–120, including discussion of the Fifth Lateran's effect on such preaching.

tering arrival caused yet more unpopularity among the many citizens who had to take in and feed members of the papal curia: "Slogans attacking the visit were scrawled on the walls of the houses where courtiers were to stay."[62] As a Venetian ambassador reported in 1517, most Florentines disliked the power of the house of Medici.[63] On the pope's return to Florence (again causing food prices, and hostility, to rise) where he remained from December 22 to February 19, 1516, Antoninus's canonization process began. Even if, as Butters claims, the "propaganda value" of Leo's visit to Florence was small, surely it was significant for Antoninus's cause. As noted in the previous chapter, Leo supported several other processes during his reign, so a proposal regarding Antoninus, a denizen of his own city, would not have been unusual.[64] Polizzotto claims that Leo promised the canonization to the surprised San Marco friars as early as January 1516, while Pietschmann is not so convinced of this; in February, in any event, the cause was finally launched.[65]

THE CAMPAIGN BEGINS

Apparently at the conclusion of Ash Wednesday Mass on February 6, 1516, Leo was approached by his cousin Archbishop Giulio de'Medici; the prior and *gonfaloniere di giustizia* of the Republic, Piero di Niccolò Ridolfi; and the master general of the Dominicans Tommaso de Vio (Cajetan). In the names respectively of the Florentine Church, the *Signoria* and people of Florence, and the Dominican order, the trio formally requested that Leo open a process for Antoninus's canonization. The composition of this team is significant. Giulio represented spiritual authority in Florence as well as being Antoninus's successor, linking the Medici to an imagined pre-Savonarolan age when another Medici, Cosimo, had supported the archbishop (though, in fact, not always). The *gonfaloniere* was the personifica-

62. Butters, *Governors and Government,* 273.

63. Marino Giorgi's report, in *Relazione degli Ambasciatori Veneti al Senato,* ed. Eugenio Albèri, vol. 7/series 2, vol. 3 (Florence, 1846), 53: "alla più parte dei Fiorentini non piace la potenza di questa casa dei Medici."

64. Klaus Pietschmann, "Ablauf und Dimensionen der Heiligsprechung des Antonino von Florenz (1523)," *Quellen und Forschungen aus italienischen Archiven und Bibliotheken* 78 (1998): 388–463, at 388: "Zu den weniger bekannten Charakteristika" of Leo's was this openness to canonization processes.

65. Polizzotto, "Making of a Saint," 362–64; Pietschmann, "Ablauf und Dimensionen," 394 and n. 18.

tion of legality and civic order, much needed by the Medici as well as the citizenry at this time. Finally, the Dominican Cajetan's participation could be taken as a symbol of inclusion and pacification: both Antoninus and Savonarola had been priors of San Marco convent, and in 1516 there were many in the city, even including some Mediceans, who still respected the memory of the executed friar, who could now safely, if tentatively, be associated with sanctity. Cajetan himself, who knew Savonarola, believed he had "one of the best understandings of Aquinas's theology."[66] In any event, the choreographed supplication had the desired results.

Polizzotto claims that the pope, agreeing to the request, established an ad hoc investigative committee of Cardinal Lorenzo Pucci and two auditors of the Rota traveling with the pope, Giacomo Simoneta and Guglielmo Cassador.[67] It would appear, however, that the two auditors did all the work. Though Simonetta and Cassador are mentioned in the canonization bull, but Pucci is not.[68] The auditors went to work immediately—having been supplied with articles and interrogatories—beginning their hearings that Friday, a mere two days after the ostentatious Ash Wednesday ritual. The notices went out on February 8, directing potential witnesses to Simonetta's lodgings.[69] By the following Friday, in the course of gathering testimony (which Polizzotto correctly calls a *processo* in his Italian essay, but a "trial" in the English version), the auditors and their notary had taken no fewer than sixty-two depositions.[70] Clearly, this *inquisitio in partibus,* a standard preliminary, had been organized well before the suppliants' Wednesday performance. To record the testimony of so many individuals in so

66. Minnich, "Prophecy and the Fifth Lateran Council," 72.

67. Pietschmann, "Ablauf und Dimensionen," 394, and Polizzotto, "Making of a Saint," 363, date the event to February 5, but 1516 being a leap year, an alternative date would be February 6, as Orlandi reports in his study of Ubaldini's record of the case: "La canonizzazione di S. Antonio," *Memorie domenicane* 81 (1964): 85–105, 131–45, at 92, hereafter *Canonizzazione;* Pucci (1458–1531), JUD, bishop of Melfi, was one of the first four cardinals raised by Leo X on September 23, 1513, as Cardinal SS IV Coronati.

68. Fontanini, *Codex constitutionum,* 222.

69. Any person "che sappia della vita, fama e miracoli o per sè o per udita d'altri" was directed to Simonetta's residence in via de'Pandolfini to give information to the auditors, who would be there "ad ogni hora di giorno continuamente," Luca Landucci, *Diario fiorentino dal 1450 al 1516 continuata da un anonimo fino al 1542,* ed. Iodoco del Badia (Florence: Sansoni, 1883), 366, ed. N. 2, from Registro di Deliberazioni de'Signori e Collegi.

70. There seems to be no further reference to Cardinal Pucci's involvement, Pietschmann, "Ablauf und Dimensionen," 395; Polizzotto, "Making of a Saint," 364; Orlandi, *"Canonizzazione"* 92; the latter acknowledges that this process was *rapidissimo,* 93.

short a time, one week, with already prepared questions, and to add—as was done—three supplicatory letters, including one from the *Signoria* and another from the cathedral canons, indicates a well-organized, preplanned campaign. The pope and his cousin, and others, had entered into a pious conspiracy. In their letter the canons noted how cooperation between Antoninus and Cosimo de'Medici had redounded to the city's benefit, just as Antoninus's sainthood, again thanks to the Medici, would elevate that cooperation to the highest plane.

Before Leo left Florence on February 17, 1516, with his curia and auditors in tow (to the relief of many—very likely most—Florentines), a subcommittee was appointed on the 15th to continue the canonization work in the city. This group of three included Giovanni Maria Canigiani, abbot general of the Vallumbrosans and once prior of San Marco. In 1515 he had resisted Archbishop Giulio's claims of authority (emanating from Leo X) over San Marco, in an attempt to control pro-Savonarolan factions.[71] The other members were Antonio Sacramora, a cathedral canon, and the bishop of Fiesole's vicar, Lionardo Guasconi. They had their notary publish notices throughout Florence of further hearings, inviting anyone with knowledge of Antoninus's life, virtues, or miracles, to testify.[72] As a result, forty-eight people did so, between February 21 and October 30 of 1516—a far more reasonable (indeed, leisurely) pace when compared with the first hearing. These depositions, transcribed in public form, sealed with the public and private seals of the subcommissioners and the Fiesolan curia, were sent to Rome in tin boxes sealed with wax and cords. They were received, as Ubaldini (who became procurator of the cause) stated in his later summary, by auditors Cassador and Simonetta. Nine letters and the depositions of another twelve witnesses were also sent to Rome in connection with this second hearing. Among the supplicatory letters of 1516 and 1517 for Antoninus, one, dated Leipzig, October 31, 1516, was from Duke Georg of Saxony, leading force behind Benno's soon-to-be rival process.[73]

Polizzotto writes that the acts of what he terms this "second trial" (*secondo processo*)—reportage from the *in partibus* hearings—were presented at

71. Polizzotto, "Making of a Saint," 362.

72. For a later example of these printed advertisements put up in prominent places around a city, see the paper notice, about eight by twelve inches, dated December 1631, in the dossier of Marcolino di Forlì, O.P. (d. 1397), ASV, Congr. Riti, processus, 772.

73. Orlandi, *Canonizzazione,* 85–88, 94; Polizzotto, "Making of a Saint," 365.

a consistory on December 6, 1516 (December 9 in the canonization bull), but "against all expectations," the cardinals "failed to approve the canonization so dearly desired by Leo X," in part because of some cardinals' antipathy toward Leo. In addition, so as not "to humiliate the pope further," the consistory "resorted to a face-saving formula" and merely declared that sufficient evidence existed for further consideration of the proposed canonization.[74] These are arresting claims. It would have been incredible for any group of cardinals to agree, on a first review of a preliminary examination of witnesses in a newly proposed process, to "approve the canonization." Rather than contradicting "all expectations" as Polizzotto suggests, and inventing a "face-saving formula," the cardinals, inventing nothing, were proceeding along normal channels, opening the way to the next step. Pietschmann suggests that, contrary to Polizzotto, all that occurred in December 1516 was the handing over of the documentation to Cassador and Simonetta. These auditors, he asserts, presented their *relazione* a year later in consistory during December of 1517, after which Leo appointed Cardinals Bernardino Carvajal, Leonardo de Grassis della Rovere, and Bernardo di Bibbiena (soon replaced by Innocenzo Cibo) to examine the cause, on January 8, 1518.[75] Cibo was Leo's nephew, and Bibbiena a close papal adviser and protégé.

Regardless of specific chronological uncertainties, it's clear that little was done in 1517. There was a great deal on the papal mind that year. Urbino, upon which Leo had thrust his nephew Lorenzo di Piero as duke, rebelled in January, starting an expensive war that ended only in 1519. This engagement was partially funded by reluctant Florentine taxpayers and Leo's massive creation of thirty-one cardinals in July of 1517. The Urbino matter

74. Polizzotto, "Making of a Saint," 365, 369–70. Polizzotto also claims, on questionable grounds, that some anti-Mediceans "boycotted the first two trials" but testified in the third.

75. Orlandi, *Canonizzazione,* 94–95; Fontanini, *Codex constitutionum,* 222. The Spaniard Carvajal (1455–1523) was created cardinal on September 20, 1493, by Alexander VI, excommunicated for his part in the 1511 Council of Pisa by Julius II in 1511, and restored by Leo X in 1513. Julius II raised della Rovere (1464–1520) on December 1, 1505. Bibbiena (1470–1520), a close companion of Leo X before his pontificate, was made cardinal by that pope on September 23, 1513—Leo called him *alter papa.* Bibbiena, responsible for correspondence in Italian, was a prototype secretary of state; his apartment was above Leo's in the papal palace, giving him constant access to the pontiff. Cibo (1491–1550), Leo X's nephew, became cardinal on September 23, 1513. Cibo and Bibbiena, along with Pucci and Leo X's cousin Giulio de'Medici, archbishop of Florence, constituted the first cardinalate creations by the new pope; and see Pietschmann, 397–99. The other supplicatory letters came from James V of Scotland, Charles I of Spain, his brother Ferdinand, Maximilian I, Duke Joachim of Brandenburg, Georg's brother Heinrich, and Francis I of France along with his wife and mother (at this time also supporting Francesco's canonization cause).

wasn't the end of the pope's problems. As we saw in chapter 3, in June of 1482, when List went to visit Cardinal Marcus Barbo on Leopold's behalf, he was brusquely put off with an "I've got to hurry to the pope" on another matter, the arrest of Cardinals Colonna and Savelli. The members of the college being able to "think of nothing" but the conspiracy, Barbo admitted that there was no hope for a canonization "at this time." A generation later, unfortunately for Antoninus (and some cardinals), another conspiracy was uncovered, in the spring of 1517. Five cardinals and a physician and others were implicated. It was believed they intended to murder Leo by applying poison while treating the pope's anal fistulas. It should be noted that Lowe, after reviewing "substantial evidence," has her doubts, suggesting that the "spurious" conspiracy was motivated by Leo's hopes of political and financial gain.[76] The doctor and a coconspirator were executed in late June, one cardinal, the Sienese Petrucci, was strangled in Castel Sant'Angelo, and the other four were fined huge sums, with other penalties of varying severity.

By their nature, conspiracy accusations can easily spread to anyone even remotely associated with the alleged principals. In a secret consistory of June 8, 1517, when Leo demanded confessions from any among the cardinals who may have been involved, for once our stolid Paris de Grassis was flustered. "Hearing this I turned to look at my brother Cardinal [Achille] de Grassis, for fear of his being touched by any murmurs of suspicion. Achille, looking at me, silently indicated that he wasn't part of the inquiry, and [then] the pope ordered me outside for a while." When the cardinals came out of consistory, Paris noted that they seemed a gloomy lot, "and I couldn't get any information from any of them."[77] During the consistory, two more cardinals "confessed" as Leo had wished. As a result of the conspiracy it's likely that—as in the 1482 case—cardinals had little else on their minds for much of 1517. In addition to the Urbino revolt and rebellion among his cardinals, during 1517 Leo's attention was drawn to the pe-

76. Kate J. P. Lowe, "The political crime of conspiracy in fifteenth- and sixteenth-century Rome," in *Crime, Society and the Law in Renaissance Italy*, ed. Trevor Dean and K. J. P. Lowe (Cambridge: University Press, 1994), 184–203, 193–98. For similar doubts see Fabrizio Winspeare, *La Congiura dei Cardinali contro Leone X* (Florence: Olschki, 1957), cited in Mitchell, *Age of Leo X*, 109. The conspiracy question is treated at some length by Helen Hyde in *Cardinal Bendinello Sauli and Church Patronage in Sixteenth-Century Italy* (Woodbridge, UK: Boydell Press/Royal Historical Society, 2009), 131–72.

77. Pastor, *History of the Popes*, 7:463–64, quoting from Paris's *Diary*.

rennial Ottoman question, especially since the Turks seemed fully engaged in Syria and Egypt, thus leaving Constantinople ripe for Christian reconquest. A crusade was officially announced in the Lateran Council's final session (March 1517).[78] On November 4, 1517, Leo appointed a crusade committee: Cardinals Carvajal (a member of Antoninus's committee) and five other members of the college. They quickly produced a detailed memo on November 12, on tactics as well as strategy. By this time, the victorious sultan had returned to Constantinople, and Cardinal de'Medici noted that Leo was "ready to do everything in his power" against the Turk. However, the year ended without any movement of crusaders to the East. Processions and prayers had as little effect in rousing European leaders as papal begging letters and special legations. Leo continued this campaign throughout 1518, with no success.

Even after Antoninus's commission was appointed in January 1518, for the rest of the year there was little real movement in the process, which may have been due to Leo's reluctance to push the Medici candidate too hard, thus exacerbating opposition by the *piagnoni*.[79] In some quarters, however, it was believed that Antoninus's sainthood was imminent: a Dominican anti-Lutheran sermon refers to the canonization, and on December 4, 1518, a Venetian ambassador wrote that two saints were being considered in consistory, "l'uno ad instantia dil roy di Franza"—Francis of Paola, canonized, as we've seen, during 1519—"l'altro ad instantia di Firenze." Yet in the vice-chancellor's *Acta* for that week the only notice of canonization was a report on Benno's life and miracles (by Simonetta) on December 10, 1518.[80] The pace picked up next year: in February 1519 San Marco friar Ubaldini was designated proctor, working on Antoninus's behalf in Rome. A further hearing in Florence on the miracles was ordered by the cardinal commission in March, possibly as a result of skepticism in some quarters. The convent shouldered much of the cost of these processes, supported by Florence's Archbishop Cardinal de'Medici (e.g., in a letter to San Marco's prior of November 1, 1519).[81]

78. For the following, see ibid., 218ff.

79. Pietschmann, "Ablauf und Dimensionen," 419.

80. Ibid., 399–400. Georg began to express anxiety that Benno's cause would be upstaged by that of Antoninus; cf. Felician Gess, ed., *Akten und Briefe zur Kirchenpolitik Herzog Georgs von Sachsen*, Erster Band 1517–24 (Leipzig: Teubner, 1905), 107, and the next chapter of this book.

81. Pietschmann, "Ablauf und Dimensinen," 400–401.

At a secret consistory of December 19, 1519, a *relatio* of posthumous miracles was read by Cardinal della Rovere, with Carvajal also speaking on Antoninus's virtues, holiness, and *in vita* miracles. Carvajal's consistorial oration on this occasion (and on December 14, 1520, see below) displays some of his—and presumably not only his—assumptions about Antoninus's canonization in particular and, to a degree, saint-making in general during the latter part of Leo X's reign—the first years of the Reformation.[82] After his opening lines Carvajal emphasized Leo's interest in canonizations: the pope had already concluded one, Francis of Paola, and currently was involved in several other causes.[83] Carvajal then allowed himself to criticize earlier popes who'd been less involved in saint-making than Leo, perhaps because they'd reigned too briefly, or because of administrative duties, schism, wars, or—worst of all—indolence and apathy.[84] Acknowledging that determining sanctity was a difficult matter (citing inter alia Augustine and Aquinas), Carvajal recapitulated the history of canonizations from the time of Alexander III (1159–81). He noted that of the fifty-two popes from Alexander to the present (an approximately correct figure), only sixteen had canonized twenty-six saints; some pontiffs canonized several among the twenty-six. (This figure of twenty-six is too low, given that there were some forty official canonizations from c. 1200 to c. 1520; it would be interesting to know Carvajal's sources of information.) He then made a point of naming the popes who continued to reign several years after making saints, perhaps to discredit the popular belief that popes died soon after canonizing—had Leo expressed reservations about this? The orator passed to Leo's current support of Antoninus, listing the many important individuals who had supplicated the Holy See, including Spain's king, the Emperor-elect Charles; his brother Ferdinand; the chapter and commune of Florence; and the kings of France and Scotland; as well as the duke of Saxony (Georg), the Marchioness of Brandenburg and others, and in 1519 the pope's cousin Giulio, cardinal archbishop of Florence.

This led to Carvajal's summation of his own and his colleagues' part in the process: their selection as a cardinal commission and examination of two

82. The 1519 oration is in ibid., 436–47; that of 1520, 447–62.

83. Carvajal specifies Antoninus, Benno, Francesca Romana, Casimir and Hyacinth of Poland; for the last, see Finucane, "Saint-Making at the End of the Sixteenth Century," 212–15: copies of the *in partibus* process reached Rome in September of 1524, including testimony of 409 witnesses.

84. "Propter pigritiam aut desidiam."

inquisitions totaling 284 folios, which included the depositions of 110 witnesses as well as other documents, and "due historie" (biographies) of Antoninus.[85] The commission agreed, says Carvajal, that he himself would summarize the life and *in vita* miracles, his colleagues, posthumous miracles. Consequently he divided the material on the archbishop's life and virtues into fifteen propositions. "It seemed to me," says Carvajal, "best to arrange everything as Gratian did with the last compilation of decretals," that is, thematically rather than chronologically. He then launched into his explication of all fifteen headings. These included comments on Antoninus's life and rule as archbishop, including his "permitting" the burning of a heretic (who denied Mary's virginity, though the process reprinted by Morçay makes no mention of this unless it's included among the article of the faith denied by Montecatini; interesting that Carvajal should emphasize this one point). He continued by noting Antoninus's charity as well as his levitation while at prayer.[86] Interest on the part of Eugenius IV, Nicholas V, and Calixtus III is reviewed. The fifteenth *propositio* describes the archbishop's final days, death, Pius II's concern and indulgences, throngs who came to see his body, and its sweet odor. Carvajal claims that on the night of his death, three holy people saw his soul ascend to heaven. Then, as to Antoninus's *in vita* miracles, the cardinal began by noting that there would be some duplication of information within the depositions. There was a further problem, in that inconsistencies arose when different witnesses described the same wonders, and secondly in their confusing *in vita* with posthumous miracles. Again referring to the canonists, we'll deal with these repetitions, Carvajal remarks, in the same way that canon lawyers treated repetitions.[87] Carvajal will follow Gratian's system (as he did with the biographical material), *Deo dante.*[88] Af-

85. Pietschmann, "Ablauf und Dimensionen," 442–5.

86. "Elevatus a terra fere quatuor brachiis"—an accomplishment also attributed to Francis of Paola.

87. "Haberentque similitudinem iste recollectiones illis antiquis recollectionibus et compilationibus decretorum," Pietschmann, "Ablauf und Dimensionen," 446. Carvajal claims that unlike early collections arising from [Pseudo-] Isidore, which repeated a good deal of material from one synod and pontificate to the next, "que multis abundat repetitionibus." Gratian's arrangement by *distinctiones, causas et consecrationes* avoided unnecessary repetition.

88. Ibid., 446. When the Hereford canons in the early fourteenth century forwarded their list of miracles in support of bishop Thomas Cantilupe (d. 1282), they were arranged thematically under type of cure, etc.; but this was rejected, since dates were lacking. These were supplied in another, second, list arranged chronologically. A great deal of confusion and repetition resulted. Finucane, *Miracles and Pilgrims,* 102.

ter noting Thomist definitions of miracles, he continued with a discussion of Antoninus's wonders, which, according to a manuscript note, are not set out here because they are already recorded in the (two) processes.[89]

In January 1520 Leo ordered further hearings, possibly because, as Ubaldini reported, one member of the cardinalate commission, della Rovere, continued to exhibit misgivings about the posthumous miracles he was investigating. For whatever reasons, miraculously—as Mainardi claimed—his opinion changed overnight.[90] The new hearing, encouraged and supported by Cardinal Giulio de'Medici, resulted in a further 152 depositions being taken in Florence in February and March, to which ten written declarations were added.[91] Ubaldini played an important role in this third hearing, even writing out a copy of the *acta* himself "to save time and money" and eventually collecting a further thirty-four supplications.[92] Polizzotto avers that by this point, through the inclusion of *piagnoni* as witnesses, the San Marco Dominicans were attempting to hijack Antoninus's process, turning him into an emblematic Savonarolan; however, Pietschmann finds little evidence for this.[93] While letters continued to arrive in Rome, the case was thrashed out in several consistories, the three-cardinal commission going over everything again. Apparently the miracles were still being questioned, for example, in a consistory of June 13, 1520.[94] Finally, in a secret consistory of December 14, 1520, the committee, now consisting of Cardinals Achille de Grassis (della Rovere died in late 1520), Ercole de'Rangoni, and Carvajal, gave their final report, which recommended canonization.[95] It

89. Pietschmann, "Ablauf und Dimensionen," 447.

90. Ibid., 405.

91. Polizzotto, "Making of a Saint," 372–77; Pietschmann, "Ablauf und Dimensionen," 403–4; the bull notes 151 witnesses, Fontanini, *Codex Constitutionem,* 223.

92. Pietschmann, "Ablauf und Dimensionen," 404, "Um Zeit und Geld zu sparen," but also perhaps to slant the material to suit his pro-Savonarolan leanings. The thirty-four included ecclesiastical and secular petitions from Milan, Ferrara, Venice, the Camaldolese, Faenza, Siena, Fiesole, Avignon, the Carmelites, Naples, the Franciscans, Augustinians, Benedictines, king Ludwig of Hungary and Bohemia, Arezzo, the Vallumbrosans, Pistoia, and Bologna; see also Polizzotto, "Making of a Saint," 371.

93. Polizzotto, "Making of a Saint," 373–76; Pietschmann, "Ablauf und Dimensionen," 412.

94. Pietschmann, "Ablauf und Dimensionen,"405.

95. Ibid., 406. Carvajal's oration on 447ff; Fontanini, *Codex Constitutionem,* 223. The bull notes that thirty-seven cardinals voted to canonize on December 14 (Fontanini, ibid., 224); a confirmatory vote occurred on December 27. Achille de Grassis, auditor of Rota under Innocent VIII, was chaplain to Julius II in 1503, who raised him to the purple in 1511; Rangoni and his mother had greatly assisted Cardinal Giovanni de'Medici when he was captured by the French in 1512. Giovanni, as Pope Leo X, named Ercole his privy chaplain and created him cardinal in July, 1517.

seems that even without the skeptical della Rovere, questions continued to be raised as to the miracles, however: as a Mantuan ambassador wrote three days after the December 14 consistory, there were some difficulties over Antoninus's thaumaturgy.[96]

In that December 14 consistory once again Carvajal stood before pope and cardinals defending Antoninus's cause. After a very long preamble on the theme of death and the afterlife especially with regard to saints, bolstered with copious biblical and patristic references, he enunciated the traditional doctrine that canonizations are not to be rushed, but rather are carefully to proceed along the twelve steps set out by Johannes Andreae (d. 1348), following Hostiensis (d. 1271) in cap. 1 of *de reliq et ven. sanctorum.*[97] Pope Leo had been dealing with Antoninus's cause for four years. Updating to account for recent activity, Carvajal notes that three processes (with a total of 261 witnesses) have been examined, and *relationes* on them pronounced in consistories. That stage being completed, "now Your Holiness calls us to the more difficult task of consultation and decision." This was more challenging, explains Carvajal, because heretofore we've been dealing with issues of memory and recollection, that is, of writings and statements about Antoninus's life and miracles. But now, we must use another faculty, that of reason, our intellectual capacity, which—citing Aristotle's *Categories, De Anima,* and *Topics*—sets us apart from the animals with their limited memory. The problem is substantial: although miracles are very difficult to confirm, some canonists suggested that they were more open to *probatio* than a virtuous life, which could disguise secret sin.[98] (During this very period—late fifteenth and early sixteenth centuries—prophets and "living saints," especially women, attracted the special attention and suspicion of the Church and the various regional Inquisitions.)[99] Carvajal intends to base his rational analysis upon two propositions. The first is that in both civil and canon law, proof can be established by two witnesses; thus the testimony collected in the three hearings can be admitted. Broadening his commentary in a way that we might think somewhat out of place, Carvajal goes on to discuss cases in which few-

96. "Non vi sonno miracoli molto suffitienti né evidenti per li quali merita anchor di esser canonizatio," Polizzotto, "Making of a Saint," 375 n. 87.

97. Pietschmann, "Ablauf und Dimensionen," 447–50.

98. "Quia illa probare est difficillimum," ibid., 452.

99. See, for example, the many studies by Gabriella Zarri, most notably: *Le Sante Vive* (Turin: Rosenberg and Sellier, 1990) and Niccoli, *Prophecy and People,* passim.

er, and more, than two witnesses are requisite (citing inter alia the Bible, Aristotle, Aquinas, Durand *Speculator,* even Pythagoras). For instance, a cardinal-bishop can be convicted only on the testimony of seventy-two witnesses, whereas a cardinal-deacon requires a mere twenty-seven—for it's better for the Church publicly to tolerate a sinner than to depose him, unless the sin is notorious; and wills and codicils also call for different numbers of witnesses.[100]

The orator's second subdivision is presented in three parts. The first emphasizes papal authority, although councils properly established by a pope may also canonize. Secondly, canonizations are midway between ecclesiastical and secular law.[101] In matters of faith, the Church cannot err, but in temporal causes, for example involving benefices, mistakes are possible. In canonizations, however, the chance of fallibility is overcome through God's and Saint Michael's assistance. The archangel had appeared to Gregory I in the midst of a plague, Carvajal reminds his audience, saving the city from further losses; popes thenceforth looked to Michael, who, from his shrine on Mt. Gargano in the kingdom of Naples protected all of Italy.[102] Part three of Carvajal's argument interprets canonizations as situated between civil and canon law, and therefore not bound by the usual legal precepts: echoing the argument that we encountered in Pavini's *relatio* on Bonaventure, Carvajal claims that because no contention is involved, a judgment as to saints is to a degree extrajudicial.[103] Parties are not cited to contend with each other as before a court, nor need contrary opinions be heard, because the pope doesn't proceed against any party, nor does he require any particular party to appear; rather, his duty is to determine the truth of the sanctity and miracles of the candidate for sainthood, with the Lord's help. On the other hand, it's clear that some popes wished to proceed "judicially" (*iudicaliter*), as in the case of Calixtus III, who canonized Osmund, bishop of Salisbury (in 1456; Osmund died in 1099).[104]

Carvajal's argument was scholastically designed to show the pope and

100. Pietschmann, "Ablauf und Dimensionen," 453–55.

101. "Hec causa est media inter causas fidei et causas temporales."

102. Pietschmann, "Ablauf und Dimensionen," 457–58. For the shrine and cult of Michael on Gargano, see John Charles Arnold, "Arcadia Becomes Jerusalem: Angelic Caverns and Shrine Conversion at Monte Gargano," *Speculum* 75 (July, 2000): 567–88.

103. "Iudiciale non est, sed extraiudiciale."

104. Pietschmann, "Ablauf und Dimensionen," 458–59.

cardinals that everything in Antoninus's process had been executed properly, in conformity with his foregoing, basic propositions. He then moved to the business at hand: subject to correction by the Holy Father and the cardinals, "I will briefly set out what I think regarding this canonization." There is plenty of evidence of Antoninus's holy life and miracles, all proven by trustworthy means. I have set out the miracles in two *relationes*, Carvajal says; these have been summarized, printed, and distributed to the cardinals by Roberto de Ubaldini, proctor of the cause. The summaries are in two forms, following Gratian (by theme) and also by witnesses (their testimony, *seriatim*) or chronologically, as Isidore does in his decretal collection. We've seen to it, Carvajal continues, that the summaries agree with the registers. If any cardinal wishes to examine them, we have here the original registers, and it will be easy quickly to find particular passages since the places are accurately cited in the summary; therefore I won't repeat anything about them, he says. In addition to all this, he draws attention to past canonizations and the papal bulls authorizing them, which, he claims, are quasi-apostolic constitutions to be followed in future. And although comparisons are annoying, he states, yet it's not improper to examine them in facilitating Antoninus's cause, for it would seem that in the past, individuals had been canonized without as many witnesses to a saintly life, and with fewer miracles, and less holy and abundant teachings, than in the present case. There was, for example, Homobonus, canonized by Innocent III (1199), at the instance of the bishop of Cremona on the basis of testimony only of Homobonus's confessor, with merely a single miracle mentioned in the bull. (This is technically true but disingenuous on Carvajal's part, since Homobonus's bull notes that, since it would be prolix to list the miracles that occurred at the tomb, only one of them, the cure of a demoniac woman, is set out.)[105] There is no comparison, the cardinal continues, between that and the many impressive personages who have petitioned in "our cause," including Charles the emperor, the king of France, and many others; and furthermore, in the present instance, 261 witnesses have provided an abundance of testimony. Then there was Bridget of Sweden, canonized by Boniface VIII on the strength of only a few miracles, including some revelations provided in secret to the pope by her natural daughter. Sixtus IV canonized Bonaven-

105. Fontanini, *Codex constitutionem*, 35.

ture on the basis of a few miracles and for the most part individual [rather than the required two] witnesses; and Innocent VIII canonized Leopold of Austria on the basis of much hearsay testimony and single witnesses. "Your Holiness, moreover, made Francesco di Paola a saint, certainly a man of many miracles and great simplicity and humility of life—but there wasn't much learning in him, nor could he perform acts of charity and almsgiving [again rather misleading, since Carvajal himself acknowledges that mendicants weren't expected to be almsgivers]; in his *articulis* there were some single witnesses, and after Francesco's death not many miracles were noticed. Antonino, on the other hand, was eminent and holy in doctrine, as well as exhibiting simplicity, humility and charity at the highest level."[106] "Whence, Holy Father"—Carvajal concludes—"having examined earlier processes I find that a canonization is appropriate and that Antonino has for some time now been gathered to the society of the saints." The cardinal concluded by recommending canonization for the happiness of the pope "and your most noble family to which the living Antonino adhered," the prosperity of the Republic of Florence, and the felicity of the Order of Preachers that nourished and taught so noble a member of the Church.[107]

A *Summarium* of Antoninus's life and miracles was again distributed at another consistory, in December 1520; it may actually have been printed in 1519. It contained a *Vita,* outline of in-life miracles in forty-nine articles, posthumous miracles in seventy-six articles, and names of witnesses. The December consistory took about eight hours to discuss the canonization, which Polizzotto sees as an indication of resistance and doubt; Pietschmann questions this. The thirty-seven cardinals present—whom Polizzotto, without evidence, suggests had been "hand-picked for the occasion"—voted for canonization.[108] At this point, nothing would seem to have stood in the way; but, Orlandi suggests, because of wars in the Marche and Umbria, and recurrence of the plague, the matter was put off for the time being. More significantly, Leo was by now engaged in German religious issues, in January 1521 imploring Charles V to publish a bull excommunicating Luther, and at a February consistory urging his cardinals to deal with the Lutheran problem. "At that time," claimed Pastor, "the Lutheran affair occupied the

106. Pietschmann, "Ablauf und Dimensionen," 460–61.

107. Ibid., 462.

108. Polizzotto, "Making of a Saint," 378 and n. 97.

mind of the Pope almost to the exclusion of anything else": on March 28 he issued *In Coena Domini*, definitively condemning Luther; by early April Leo's "anxiety was too acute to be concealed"; and by mid-April the pope was deeply involved in rearranging his political stance regarding France and the emperor, whose help against the Saxon heretic was essential. In June 1521 Luther's picture and his writings, to Leo's great satisfaction, went up in flames in the piazza Navona.[109] In the midst of these portentous events, we find Ubaldini humbly prostrating himself before Leo X on May 18, 1521, begging him to complete Antoninus's canonization. The pope announced a consistory for the 24th in which consistorial advocate Melchior Baldassini was to present the case, but Baldassini fell seriously ill and the meeting was cancelled. Nevertheless, Leo promised to deal with Antoninus at a future time, perhaps during December. Ubaldini, sensing temporary stalemate, returned to Florence in early June. Meanwhile the pope was again drawn into the Luther problem and the contest between Valois and Habsburg over Milan and Lombardy (which the canonization bull glosses as *impedimentis*). Nothing more was done about Antoninus prior to the pope's death on December 1, 1521.[110]

ADRIAN VI CANONIZES ANTONINUS

Following his wholly unexpected election in January 1522, Cardinal Adrian of Utrecht, Charles V's lieutenant in Spain, didn't arrive in Rome until August of that year, and, even then, plague in the city prevented the full expression of Adrian VI's pontifical powers until early 1523. Adrian, like Leo, was at once pulled into temporal and spiritual conflicts: as the Bolognese ambassador wrote in January 1523, on one side were the Turks, on the other was Luther, and in the middle, the warring princes.[111] The new pope, a stranger to Italy, its regions, even Rome itself, was not well received by the Romans or cardinals, one of whom justified his negative vote in conclave because "he did not know the man, who had never been to the Curia."[112] Usually, new popes brought with them to St. Peter's an entourage of

109. Pastor, *History of the Popes*, 8:27–31, 37; Fontanini, *Codex constitutionem*, 224.

110. Orlandi, *Canonizzazione*, 102–3; Fontanini, *Codex constitutionem*, 224.

111. Pastor, *History of the Popes*, 9:171 n. 3: "[D]a uno lato et Turco, da l'altro Luttero et tra li principi tanta dissensione et rabie fanno che molti secoli sono la religione christiana non si trovò a maggior pericolo" (January 27, 1523).

112. Kasper Burmann, ed., *Hadrianus VI, sive Analecta Historica. . . .* (Trajecti ad Rhenum, 1727),

kin, friends, patrons, and dependents when they ascended the throne; Adrian chose his closest advisers from among his countrymen, who—as even a sympathetic observer noted—were slow to carry out their tasks, working as they did "in the Flemish way."[113] Adrian's shortcomings will be discussed more fully in the next chapter.

We've seen that the 1517 conspiracy to kill Leo X distracted the college of cardinals, diverting their energies from other matters. Paradoxically, another conspiracy uncovered in the spring of 1523 may have hastened Antoninus's canonization.[114] Cardinal Francesco Soderini (1453–1524), outspoken defender of French policies, was an enemy of Cardinal Giulio de'Medici, vice-chancellor and future Pope Clement VII. Letters were found implicating Soderini in a plot to invite Francis I into southern Italy, threatening papal, imperial, and Medicean interests. Adrian, who'd been friendly with Soderini up to this point, now turned to de'Medici. On the evening of April 27, 1523, Soderini was arrested and sent into Castel Sant'Angelo, where he'd remain until Adrian's death. A Venetian ambassador claimed that, in fact, de'Medici talked the pope into imprisoning the cardinal.[115] This action embroiled the cardinals in dispute during next morning's consistory. As it happened, on the morning of the 27th a supplication on behalf of Antoninus from the *Signoria* had been read in consistory, and special envoys from Florence arrived to tender obedience to the new pope. This synchronization must have been encouraging to Antoninus's lobbyists, which included Giulio de'Medici. Pastor writes, "The fall of Soderini gave at once a commanding position in the Curia to the Vice-Chancellor. . . . Henceforward Adrian himself was greatly influenced by Medici and the Imperialists saw with satisfaction a change for the better."[116] It's likely that these developments hastened Adrian's desire to please the Medici by canonizing Antoninus (and the "imperial" candidate Benno, noted in the next chapter).

Antoninus's champions continued to press their case: Ubaldini, who presented further supplications and had papal audiences on May 2 and 4,

from BAV Papi IV.XVI, Adriano VI (microfilm, 1959), 61 (Gerard Moringo's *Vita*), 109 (Paulo Giovio's *Vita*), 149 *(Conclave Hadriani Sexti)*.

113. "Tarde et difficulter more Flandrorum," Burmann, 197 (*Itinerarium* of Blasius Ortiz); on Ortiz, see Pastor, *History of the Popes*, 9:44, 71, 82ff., 121ff.

114. For the following, Lowe, *Church and Politics in Renaissance Italy*, ch. 12, "The 'Conspiracy' of 1523 and Its Aftermath"; Pastor, *History of the Popes*, 9:184–89, 191, n.

115. *Relazioni degli Ambasciatori Veneti*, 110–12.

116. Pastor, *History of the Popes*, 9:188.

claimed that Adrian was eager to canonize Antoninus, to whom, the pope said, he'd been devoted. At a public consistory on May 11, the (now recovered) Melchior Baldassini delivered an oration on Antoninus; on the 15th Adrian set the canonization for May 31.[117] (A week after the May 11 meeting, a public consistory dealt with Benno's proposed canonization.) Baldassini's two-hour delivery of May 11, according to Ubaldini, was witnessed by cardinals and ambassadors of the Empire, France, England, Hungary, Portugal, Poland, Venice, Milan, and six from the Republic of Florence. The oration, heard attentively and emotionally—claims Ubaldini—dwelt on the archbishop's life and fame, illustrated by his miracles. The pope responded with praise for Antoninus's virginity, innocence, and copious, useful teachings; he was an example not only to imitate, as with other saints, but also to admire.[118] The pope seemed ready to proceed, having heard Baldassini's oration, but some were concerned that Adrian was moving too quickly. Motivated "by what spirit, God knows," Ubaldini writes, they seem to have ignored the groundwork already carried out during Leo X's reign. Some claimed, too, that Adrian was insufficiently informed about Antoninus himself, while others blamed the Florentines for trying to kill the pope—a reference once again to the belief that popes died (within a year, some said) of canonizing saints.[119] In addition, Rome's *Conservatori,* civic counselors without much real power in the city, advised against any public ceremony since they feared that the plague season was about to open.[120] "Il povero Ubaldini," writes Orlandi, throwing himself into an effort to overcome these obstacles, composed a tract of eight folios answering these objections, gave this to the pope along with a survey of Antoninus's life and miracles and a summation of testimony, and asked Adrian to proceed regardless of objections. The pope responded that he'd always been attracted by the holy man's doctrine, and he reassured Ubaldini that his mind had been made up and could not be changed by chattering enemies, and that he was even less concerned about that superstition (popes dying after canonizations), which he'd always rejected.[121] Ubaldini, along with his colleague

117. Pietschmann, "Ablauf und Dimensionen," 408; Orlandi, *Canonizzazione,* 104–5.

118. "Esempio da imitare, come gli altri Santi," Orlandi, *Canonizzazione,* 105.

119. Kemp, *Canonisation and Authority,* 139: a belief evident from at least the 1430s.

120. Apart from one senator, Rome had three *conservatori* and a *caporione* from each city district.

121. "Chiacchere degli avversari . . . . la superstizione che abbiamo sempre condannata," Orlandi, *Canonizzazione,* 131–32.

Tommaso Strozzi, then supplicated the pope for a near date, avoiding the hot season.

About this time (it is difficult to correlate all the events in the canonization bull with Ubaldini's report) Adrian fell so seriously ill that by May 24, 1523, his doctors were in despair. (In July Emperor Charles wrote to his ambassador in Rome, Sessa, that should the pope die, he would favor Cardinal de'Medici as the next pontiff, a sentiment he repeated in October.)[122] However, after Adrian ordered almsgiving and public prayers for his health, and himself prayed to (inter alia) the Blessed Antoninus, two days later he was well enough to go in procession to the church of Santa Maria del Popolo. The pope ordered a public consistory for May 28 or 29. Everyone present had been given a compendium of Antoninus's (and possibly Benno's) life, miracles, and processes, and had listened to yet another oration by Baldassini and a second consistorial advocate. According to Blasius Ortiz, Toledo canon and Adrian's confidant, each advocate presented the case for his saint.[123] Following this, differing opinions among many of the attendees arose, objections coming in particular from a certain Bishop Diego Ramirez; but after extensive argumentation, all agreed to approve both candidates.[124]

The pope set the dual ceremony for Trinity Sunday, May 31, in St. Peter's, just as he'd done at the May 11 consistory.[125] "At the last moment," writes Orlandi, apparently referring to events of May 1523, the proceedings ran into a new set of difficulties. Ubaldini claimed that he was being dunned for fees by the papal master of ceremonies, Paris de Grassis, and other curial officials. Whether it was an excuse to fend off their demands or he actually believed it, Ubaldini objected that these curialists were asking him to commit simony: instead of buying a church office, he was being asked to pay for—in effect to buy—a saint. Ubaldini would have known that venal offices were a commonplace of Leo X's reign (according to a Venetian ambassador there were over two thousand of them); and cardinals could buy their way into the college.[126] Although the connection between simony and the popes' selling of curial offices was, as Partner puts it, "a delicate one," the issue wasn't

122. Louis-Prosper Gachard, *Correspondance de Charles-Quint et d'Adrien VI* (Brussels: M. Hayez, 1859), 192, 197.

123. "Alter quidem unius, alter vero alterius vitam, miracula & alia hujusmodi."

124. "Viros sanctos approbari," Ortiz, *Itinerarium Hadriani Sexti* in Burmann, *Hadrianus VI,* 211.

125. Orlandi, *Canonizzazione,* 132, 134–35.

126. The figure of 2,150 venal offices is given in Pastor, *History of the Popes,* 8:97.

raised until Paul III's reform commission of 1536, and even then to little effect.[127] In any event, it's likely that Ubaldini was playing a game. He took his concerns to the pope, who (as he probably foresaw) reassured him that this wasn't actually simony. Then, having made this point, the pope found the tables turned: if it wasn't simony, Ubaldini claimed, now that the cause had come under papal control, couldn't Adrian have it dealt with, that is, funded, by his chamberlain or *maestro di camera,* Alessandro Neroni. The latter, Ubaldini pointed out, was a Florentine recommended to Leo X's curia by well-placed Florentines.[128] Adrian replied that because he was unwilling to act on his own, Ubaldini should consult with Neroni and the datary. The persistent Ubaldini then remarked that Leo X had conceded to the Dominicans that the cost of Antoninus's canonization (ceremony) would be the same as for Francis of Paola, which, as bank records showed, was not in excess of 1,800 ducats, a sum the Dominicans were holding in reserve for Antoninus.

Adrian, evidently in the dark as to this claim about Francis, agreed. Ubaldini hurried to make the papal decision known to the cardinal-datary, identified as Silvio Passerini da Cortona.[129] Passerini had been Leo X's datary from January 1514 (and Leo, as Partner notes, "squeezed the system for every ducat that it was worth").[130] Ubaldini claimed that Passerini, whom Pastor describes as a "learned though self-opinionated man," as "inconsiderate as he was selfish and avaricious," insisted on 2,000 ducats. "Impossible," Ubaldini replied, "we have only 1,800."[131] The datary then told Ubaldini to go see the chamberlain and try to satisfy him. But the chamberlain, playing the old game of curial runaround, sent Ubaldini back, saying "Satisfy the Cardinal Datary."[132] Returning to the datary, Ubaldini tried to strike a deal. If 2,000 ducats or florins really was the necessary amount, this would be paid, he claimed, but it should include the publication of the bull.[133] The

127. Partner, *Renaissance Rome,* 141–42; even the Council of Trent bypassed the question.

128. Orlandi, *Canonizzazione,* 133; Pastor, *History of the Popes,* 8:105.

129. Pastor, *History of the Popes,* 9:79–80; This raises a chronological issue. One of Adrian's first acts as pope was to promote his old friend Willem van Enckevoirt to the office of datary in early 1522.

130. Pastor, *History of the Popes,* 7:203; Peter Partner, "The 'Budget' of the Roman Church in the Renaissance Period," in *Italian Renaissance Studies,* ed. E. F. Jacob (London: Faber and Faber, 1960), 256–78, at 272.

131. Pastor, *History of the Popes,* 9:425–26, VII, 203; Orlandi, *Canonizzazione* 133.

132. Orlandi, *Canonizzazione,* 133.

133. "Vi fosse compreso tutto anche la spedizione della Bolla."

Dominicans would also pay for the ceremonial hangings or vestments; however, the pope should concede a plenary indulgence and absolution of reserved cases at the saint's tomb. The datary didn't like the idea of a perpetual plenary indulgence; Ubaldini insisted that it should be granted at least once. "Good," the datary replied; "let's hope it can be done—a way will be found." Meanwhile, he advised Ubaldini to give the entire sum, or what he had available, to chamberlain Neroni, who would help him: "and he's a Florentine. Satisfy him with clinking coin [*denaro sonante*], not mere promises."[134] This time, Neroni was satisfied, and took on the job after receiving a note of exchange drawn on the Bardi bank for 1,800 florins.

On Sunday, May 31, 1523, the canonization took place, along with Benno's. (Orlandi writes that Benno's sainthood "was greatly hindered by Luther," which is not quite true—as we'll see in the next chapter.)[135] Ubaldini's version of the ceremony naturally emphasizes Antoninus, and Pietschmann believes that the Florentine did indeed receive greater ceremonial emphasis than the Saxon. A novel element seems to have involved Antoninus's (and probably Benno's) image or wooden statue: during the ceremony the stars round the head of the *beatus* were replaced with a golden diadem of the *sanctus,* apparently further developing pictorial conventions that had arisen during the fourteenth century.[136] The customary celebrations followed in the city and elsewhere. Although Benno's canonization bull issued at once, a similar bull for Antoninus was not published during Adrian's reign. It was not until November 26, 1523, the very day of his coronation, that another de'Medici, Giulio—once Florence's archbishop and one of the earliest promoters of Antoninus's cause—as Clement VII, confirmed and issued the bull. No convincing reasons have been adduced for this bureaucratic glitch.[137] Unusually for such documents, the first words of the bull refer to the fact that apostolic letters for Antoninus were not made, "which it is fitting [now] to effect." Clement VII continues by noting his own participation as cardinal in the original supplicatory triad of 1516, following this with a summation of the

134. Orlandi, *Canonizzazione,* 134.

135. Orlandi, *Canonizzazione,* 136 n. 60.

136. Pietschmann, "Ablauf und Dimensionen," 410: "eines für bisherige Kanonisationen nicht erwähnten Ritusabschnittes." Kemp, *Canonisation and Authority,* 136, refers to Malvetius, that *beati* had rays round their heads; saints, diadems. Cf. Vauchez, *Sainthood,* 87–88.

137. Polizzotto, "Making of a Saint," 378–79; Orlandi, *Canonizzazione,* 140: "Ma ci sfugge il motive"; Pietschmann, "Albauf und Dimensionen," 411: "Die Gründe sind unbekannt."

inquisitorial processes and consistorial debates up to Leo's death in December 1521. Pope Adrian then asked "us," Clement continues, to proceed with the canonization. The bull continues with a summary of Antoninus's life, death, and miracles, which are listed generically and very briefly (a treatment quite different from the papal bull for Francis of Paola), merely referring in general to resuscitations and those oppressed by diverse ailments such as lepers, the lame, deaf, dumb, blind, and demonical; no specifics are mentioned. Following this, reference is made to Adrian's consistories and the vote to canonize. Clement ends by referring once again to the delay due to Adrian's death (September 14, 1523), and commands that the present (November) bull is effective "as of 31 May": let the present letters suffice as proof of the full canonization, nor is anything more required.[138] Evidently Ubaldini had provided a draft of the bull, and later on paid about fifty ducats for an authenticated, expensively made copy for his Florentine convent.[139] The financial records of income and expenses for Antoninus's ceremony and associated costs show that just over 2,000 florins were spent, with some 200 left over, which were to go toward the embellishment of the shrine.[140]

In preparation for a translation, Antoninus's tomb was located (after some uncertainty) and opened on April 15, 1589.[141] The corpse had been dressed as a simple friar, with only a pallium to show his archiepiscopal status. Much of the substance of the body remained—some friars claimed that (even after 130 years) he looked like the images familiar to them. The corpse was cleaned with a silk cloth; it was found to have been eviscerated and sewn up, the brain removed through an incision at the back of the head, which was also resewn; there were a few white hairs on the skull. Archbishop Alessandro de'Medici (Pope Leo XI, d. 1605), who oversaw the procedure, had a bit of wax applied to the end of the nose, which had decayed a little. Alessandro ordered the body redressed not as a friar but in sumptuous archiepiscopal gear, with fine footwear and vestments of silk and satin, silver and gold ornamentation, a pectoral cross, a beautiful miter, and on

138. Fontanini, *Codex constitutionum,* 220, 232.

139. Orlandi, *Canonizzazione,* 140–41.

140. Orlandi, *Canonizzazione,* 141–4.

141. Polizzotto, "Making of a Saint," 358; for exhuming, identifying, revesting, storing, procession, and final reburial of Antoninus—where he still resides—in the Salviati chapel, see *AASS,* May I, 355–58, and May I Appendix, 766–71, based on printed edition of 1589 including notarial documents, Sixtus V's brief, etc.

the right hand a ring of sky-blue sapphire. According to custom, the friar's simple garb was retained (and hidden) under the archiepiscopal finery. Afterward, the body in a wooden box was placed in the sacristy. In this way Alessandro de'Medici used the translation to reemphasize the family connection with Antoninus 130 years after his death and 66 after his Medici-inspired canonization. Alessandro's upgrading the body by redressing it as an archbishop was intended to divert attention from his status as a San Marco friar. This was particularly significant if, as Debby has suggested, confrontation "between the supporters of Savonarola . . . and the opponents of his heritage, headed by the Medici, peaked in the years of the [Salviati] chapel's construction [1578–88]." Cochrane, on the other hand, claimed that by the "1580s . . . Savonarola's role as a prophet had been thoroughly undermined. . . . [His] role as a miracle worker had also suffered," and Archbishop Alessandro confiscated all Florence's altars dedicated to the executed San Marco prior.[142] But that would seem to suggest that the prelate felt a need to do so because of ongoing pressure from the *piagnoni*. In the end, as Debby claims, it does seem that this translation of 1589 was intended to boost "an alternative cult" to that of Savonarola.[143] In other words, Medici support of the cult in the first place, that is, from at least 1516, was stimulated by the need to quash residual Savonarolan factionalism within Florence and emphasize (contested) Medici control in the city. But there may be another reason behind the translation happening when it did. For starters, it is curious that sixty-six years elapsed between canonization and translation. More particularly, why was the unearthed body shelved for nearly three weeks? The answer seems to lie with another Medici, Grand Duke Ferdinand I, and his desire to emphasize his name and status by celebrating the translation in tandem with his marriage to Christine de Lorraine, Henry III's niece and granddaughter of Catherine de'Medici.[144] The nuptials had been agreed in October 1588 after a year's negotiation. Throughout early 1589 Florence busied itself for her grand arrival, which occurred

142. Eric Cochrane, *Italy 1530–1630*, ed. Julius Kirshner (New York: Longmans, 1988), 111.

143. Nirit Ben-Aryeh Debby, "Giambologna's Salviati Reliefs of St. Antoninus of Florence: Saintly Images and Political Manipulation," *Renaissance Studies* 22, no. 2 (2008), 197–220, at 219, 198; Debby does not take note of the resurrection of Antoninus as an archbishop; neither does Saslow (next note).

144. James M. Saslow, *The Medici Wedding of 1589: Florentine Festival as Theatrum Mundi* (New Haven, Conn.: Yale University Press, 1996), passim; Saslow suggests that Christine attended the May 9 translation but she took it in only as a window-spectator.

on April 30; Antoninus's remains had been in San Marco sacristy since the 15th of that month. On May 9, in the midst of the plays, jousts, naval battles, and other spectacles surrounding the wedding of a few days earlier, Antoninus, who'd been moved from the sacristy to a makeshift stage in San Marco church, was praised in a sermon that celebrated his life, virtues, and miracles, *and* the Most Serene family Medici. After being exhibited to a multitude of nobles, prelates, and common folk, the body was then taken up and processed through the streets of Florence, with banners showing Antoninus as archbishop; an arm bone may have been given to the cathedral en route. The procession stopped for a while so that Duchess Christine and others could view the spectacle from the windows of the Palazzo Medici. Once again, a connection is made between Antoninus, the Medici, and the fortunes of the city, newly based—it was hoped—on a French marriage alliance. Returned to San Marco, Antoninus was laid to rest in a new altar-tomb, the centerpiece of a chapel financed by the Medici-related Salviati brothers. The friars would have benefited from the huge crowds (over three thousand VIPs alone) drawn to the marriage and into the conventual church to enjoy Sixtus V's indulgence granted on April 5, 1589.

The success of this particular candidate for sainthood was the result of many overlapping and sometimes conflicting interests. Florence was in turmoil, throughout the sixteenth century suffering the wrenching effects of factionalism, in which anti-Mediceans tended to gravitate round the *piagnoni*—whose influence was felt long after Savonarola's execution. It's probably not just coincidental that while Leo was in Florence in early 1516 promoting Antoninus's process he also ordered a reexamination of Savonarola's writings.[145] Many among the elite and lesser and artisan classes were themselves uncertain as to their support of the Medici. The prospect of a new saint did not solve the factional problems. If, as several scholars have suggested, Antoninus's canonization was meant to counter the influence of the *piagnoni,* whose movement strengthened during the 1527–30 Republic and continued through the sixteenth century, the venture was not entirely successful.[146] San Marco friars continued to claim Antoninus: frescoes in

145. Minnich, "Prophecy and the Fifth Lateran Council," 79.

146. For an overview, see John M. Najemy, *A History of Florence 1200–1575* (Oxford: Blackwell Publishing, 2006), ch. 15, "The Last Republic and the Medici Duchy."

their convent showed him as a forerunner of Savonarola, and even in 1589 he was depicted (at his tomb) as a friar.[147] On the other hand, the Medici emphasized a line of archbishops of Florence who were themselves of the Medici or closely linked to the family, as with Antoninus and Cosimo: prelates such as Lorenzo the Magnificent's brother-in-law Rinaldo Orsini, and Leo X's cousin Giulio (and later on, Alessandro de'Medici). The possibility that Antoninus might become a figure around whom the city's factions could gather, perhaps smoothing the sharp edges of communal rivalry, did not materialize and may well have widened the gaps. In the end, the efforts of Giulio de'Medici and Leo X did result in the creation of a new saint, but, if we are to believe Pietschmann, "religious feelings played no large role" in the process.[148] The question of "religious feelings" playing a significant role will be raised again in our concluding example, the canonization of Benno of Meissen.

147. Pietschmann, "Ablauf und Dimensionen," 414.
148. Ibid., 417: "Auffällig ist, dass religiöse Gefühle anschienend keine grosse Rolle spielten."

CHAPTER 6

Luther's Devil-God

Benno of Meissen (c. 1040–1106; cd. 1523)

In the summer of 1524 there was a curious procession at Buchholz in electoral Saxony, led by the young men and miners of the village.[1] The revelers wore bathing caps or sieves on their heads (mocking the ecclesiastical beret) and carried gaming boards as songbooks, while an officiating "bishop" bedecked with straw sported a basket as a miter as he processed beneath a filthy canopy. Dung forks replaced candles. At an abandoned mine the revelers unearthed some "relics": a horse's head and leg bones as well as a cow's jawbone, all of which were tossed onto a dung cart and trundled to the town square. There, in a parody sermon the bishop, after praising dear Saint Benno's holy ass-bone, proclaimed an indulgence.[2] Following this the relics (along with an effigy of the pope) were dumped into a fountain or well. The participants were deliberately parodying the June translation of Benno's remains in Meissen; they knew how it had been done, and were

1. The following summary is based upon Christoph Volkmar, *Die Heiligenerhebung Bennos von Meissen (1523/24)* (Munich: Aschendorff, 2002), 172–80, who (172) emphasizes how the procession provides a rare glimpse, "einen seltenen Einblick," into grassroots anxieties. A pamphlet based on an account by Friedrich Myconius written between July and mid-August of 1524 was reprinted in Speyer and Strassburg. See discussions in, e.g., Edward Muir, *Ritual in Early Modern Europe,* 2nd ed. (Cambridge: Cambridge University Press, 2005), 105–6; Steven E. Ozment, *The Reformation in the Cities* (New Haven, Conn.: Yale University Press, 1975), 43 and ch. 2 passim; R. W. Scribner, *Popular Culture and Popular Movements in Reformation Germany* (London: Hambledon Press, 1987), 74–75 and ch. 4 passim. Myconius's letter is in J. K. Seidemann, "Schriftstücke zur Reformationsgeschichte," *Zeitschrift für die hist. Theologie* 44 (1874), 136–8.

2. "Der heilige arschbacken des liben sanct benno."

now redoing it to suit their own tastes. But why would a group of Saxon villagers be so intent upon this well-prepared ritual, inverting the celebration of a recently canonized and translated Saxon bishop? No doubt this raucous humor was inspired by anti-Benno sermons preached in May by that "other" Saxon ecclesiastic, Martin Luther. Benno's story, then, takes us finally and fully into the Reformation. But who was the unfortunate butt of this embodiment of Bosch's surrealism?

Bishop Benno of Meissen died about 1106. His life thus roughly coincided with our other "German" saint, Leopold (c. 1073–1136). In contrast to Leopold, however, practically nothing is known of Benno's life—even though two biographies exist. As David Collins has shown, the first *vita,* until recently thought to have been an early-sixteenth-century counterfeit masquerading as a late-fifteenth-century life, was composed about 1460 by a Benedictine monk named Spedel of St. Michael's monastery in Hildesheim, a center of the Bursfeld reform movement. The second *vita,* by Jerome Emser, was published in 1512 as part of the canonization campaign. The characteristics of these works, and their differences, are discussed below. For now, the generally accepted but meager facts about Benno can be summarized in short order.[3] A strong tradition has Benno entering the Benedictine monastery at Hildesheim, and then becoming a canon at Goslar.[4] From there, in 1066 Henry III appointed him bishop of Meissen, a post he held until his death forty years later. Collins notes that Benno's contemporaries recorded no "special pastoral talents or activities."[5] Be that as it may, the bishop got into trouble with emperor Henry IV, siding as he did with rebellious Saxon nobles; as a result Henry exiled him in 1075, allowing his return the next year. Evidently Benno was a strong-willed individual, being one of the few imperial prelates who supported Gregory VII in his controversy with Henry. Because of this the bishop, along with other anti-imperial prelates, was deposed in 1085 and once again sent into exile, not returning to Meissen until 1097. He died some time between 1105 and 1107, with burial in Meissen cathedral.

The geographical and political terrain on which Benno's posthumous

3. For the following, see David J. Collins, "Bursfelders, Humanists and the Rhetoric of Sainthood: The Late Medieval *Vitae* of Saint Benno," *Revue Benedictine,* Vol. 111 (2001), 508–56, including an edition of the first *vita.*

4. Though there is little historical evidence for this Hildesheim-Goslar connection, the strength of the tradition leads Collins to accept it (personal communication, May 2008).

5. Collins, "Bursfelders," 521.

career played out was anything but smooth. Emperor Charles IV's Golden Bull of 1356 listed Saxony as one of the seven imperial electorates. In 1485 the duchy was divided between Wettin brothers Ernst and Albrecht, the electoral dignity going to the Ernestine branch. The geographical partition was messy, with jigsaw-puzzle borders. Important electoral towns included Wittenberg, Zwickau, and Neustadt, while Albertine Saxony included Leipzig, Dresden, and Meissen. By c. 1500 Friedrich the Wise (d. 1525) ruled in electoral Saxony, while his cousin Georg the Bearded (1471–1539) held Albertine Saxony. Both men were imbued with Catholic zeal, though manifested in different ways: Friedrich through his enormous relic collection, which drew to its annual exposition masses of pilgrims who honored the holy remains and collected indulgences; and Georg by campaigning to reform the Church in his territory, for instance by visitations of monasteries and attempts to impose his authority in diocesan affairs, causing friction between the duke and Meissen's bishop John VI (1488–1518). (By the end of the Middle Ages, Meissen and other sees were in the palm of the Albertine duke.)[6] The cousins also supported university education, Friedrich founding the University of Wittenberg, Georg encouraging reforms at Leipzig. Benno's case offers tempting but easily misleading dichotomies because the cousins, controlling different parts of Saxony, ended up on opposite sides of the Reformation debate. One of them—Elector Friedrich—would protect the "prime" reformer, Martin Luther; the other—Duke Georg—became Luther's nemesis, supporting his enemies such as Jerome Emser while at the same time pushing for Benno's canonization. A huge pamphlet war erupted, with scurrilous attacks and counterattacks lobbed between one Saxony and the other. At first, however, the push for Benno's sainthood was uncomplicated by Reformation rhetoric. The beginnings of the canonization effort, like Benno's life itself, are not well marked in the historical record.[7]

BENNO'S PROGRESS TOWARD SAINTHOOD BEGINS

A Meissen bishop, Withego I (d. 1293), elevated Benno's remains about 1270, when some miracles occurred; the very earliest had been recorded in 1210. Withego followed up in 1285 with a forty-day indulgence for pilgrims.

6. "Fest in der Hand," Volkmar, *Die Heiligenerhebung*, 83.

7. Volkmar, *Die Heiligenerhebung*, 7: "sind nur wenige gesicherte Daten bekannt."

By the end of the fourteenth century, a Meissen canon spoke of Benno as an uncanonized saint, with a newly designed tomb and many miracles already to his credit, and in the 1450s Withego I's indulgence was renewed, with a further indulgence (one hundred days) from three cardinals: Isidore, cardinal-bishop of Sabina; Alan, cardinal-priest of St. Prassede; and cardinal-deacon Prospero Colonna.[8] Around 1460 a Hildesheim Benedictine wrote Benno's *vita,* depicting him as a model monk.[9] Three decades later Georg, while acting as regent for his absent father, Albrecht (d. 1500), was promoting Benno's cult, for reasons to be considered at the conclusion of this chapter.[10] During 1497–98 he and Naumburg and Meissen canons were pushing for curial action, and at Rome in a March consistory of 1499 Alexander VI authorized a local inquiry into Benno's miracles, naming Bishop John von Naumburg and the abbots Martin von Altzelle and Matthew von Buch to carry out a local investigation "in general, not specifically, and only as to common notoriety, not as to the truth [of claims]."[11] By advertisements posted at churches and towns throughout the dioceses of Meissen, Merseburg, and Naumburg (components of the province of Magdeburg), anyone with knowledge of Benno's miracles was directed to meet at Meissen on October 2, 1499. The 1,400-folio report prepared by Meissen canon Nicholas von Heynitz (d. 1526), who happened to be Duke Georg's chancellor, and Leipzig professor Johan von Breitenbach (d. 1507), containing some 600 sworn depositions collected between the 2nd and 10th of October, has been lost, as well as depositions taken in 1515 and 1518.[12]

After the 1499 report was received at Rome and examined in 1501, Alexander VI appointed a cardinal commission including Melchior von Meckau (d. 1509) and papal legate in Germany (1501–4) Raymund von Gurk (the French-born Raymond Pérault/Raimund Peraudi, d. 1505). On October 3,

8. Armin Kohnle, "Zur Heiligsprechung des Bischofs Benno von Meissen (1523)," in *Papstgeschichte und Landesgeschichte: Festschrift für Hermann Jakobs zum 65. Geburtstag* ed. Joachim Dahlhaus et al. (Cologne: Böhlau, 1995), 555–72, at 557–58; Volkmar, *Die Heiligenerhebung,* 25, 30–32, 42.

9. Collins, "Bursfelders," 509ff.

10. Volkmar, *Die Heiligenerhebung,* 19, discussing "die dominante Stellung Herzog Georgs" in the process. For the subordination of Meissen bishops and canons to Georg's oversight, see 81–87, 152.

11. "In genere . . . non in specie et solum quoad famam, non quoad veritatem." Kohnle, "Zur Heiligsprechung," 559; Volkmar, *Die Heiligenerhebung,* 69–70. According to an account in the consistorial archives, however, Alexander appointed "duobus episcopis et duobus abbatibus," Pastor, *History of the Popes,* 6:146 n.

12. Kohnle, "Zur Heiligsprechung," 557–60; Volkmar, *Die Heiligenerhebung,* 71–72.

1501, Georg wrote to the pope and cardinals, noting that the 1499 dossier had been sent to Rome, and seeking von Gurk's further assistance in Benno's cause.[13] Probably as a result, on November 11, 1501, von Gurk issued an indulgence for pilgrims to Benno's tomb (confirmed by Bishop John VI), as a way of defraying anticipated canonization expenses.[14] Von Gurk, sent to Germany to publicize the Jubilee indulgence, prayed at the dead bishop's tomb (January 1503) and discussed his possible sainthood with Georg (along with another candidate suggested by Georg, a certain "good Konrad von Weissensee," of whom nothing more is heard).[15] By this time conflicts over temporalities between Georg and Bishop John led to the latter's refusal to greet von Gurk in Meissen.[16] In the legate's entourage was his chaplain-secretary, Hieronymus, or Jerome, Emser (1477–1527). Emser, from a well-off Ulm family, had studied Latin, Greek, canon law, and theology at Tübingen, Basel, Erfurt, and Leipzig. During his student days, humanist currents were flowing through German universities, though unevenly; nevertheless, Emser's training would have been influenced by the new learning, as was Luther's.[17] From about 1500 he was in von Gurk's service, and in this capacity first learned of the cult of Benno of Meissen.[18] Little did Emser know how large a role that long-dead bishop would play in his life. On von Gurk's recommendation, Georg hired Emser in 1505.[19] The duke quickly took advantage of Emser's talents, having him gather information about Benno at Leipzig, Altzelle, and Meissen, and compose a panegyric on Benno for the new pope, Julius II (1503–13). This became the 1505 *Epitome ad sanctissimum dominum nostrum papam . . . super vita, miraculis et testimonia divi patris Bennonis.*[20] Georg sent Emser to Rome as Benno's advocate in the winter of

13. Otto Clemen, "Zur Kanonisation Bennos," *Neues Archiv für Sächsische Geschichte und Altertumskunde* 28, ed. H. Ermisch (1907): 115–16.

14. Volkmar, *Die Heiligenerhebung,* 73.

15. Ibid., 73 n. 261; see Felician Gess, ed., *Akten und Briefe zur Kirchenpolitik Herzog Georgs von Sachsen,* Erster Band 1517–1524, introduction, xxxiii n. 1, for a contemporary notice of this.

16. Volkmar, *Die Heiligenerhebung,* 85.

17. Charles G. Nauert, Jr., *Humanism and the Culture of Renaissance Europe* (Cambridge: Cambridge University Press, 1995), 124–36.

18. Volkmar, *Die Heiligenerhebung,* 71–74, 125–26; see also Ludwig Enders, *Luther und Emser: Ihre Streitschriften aus dem Jahre 1521* (Halle: Niemeyer, 1889), iii–v. Biographical references for Emser in Collins, "Bursfelders," 510–12 and nn. 3–6.

19. Collins, "Bursfelders," 511 n. 4. For Peraudi's letter to Georg of April 12/14, 1505, Rome, see Gess, *Akten und Briefe,* 23 #30 n. 3.

20. Volkmar, *Die Heiligenerhebung,* 75 n. 268.

1506–7, one along with at least eight others the duke commissioned at various times to promote the cause in the Holy City. Some of these representatives—including Emser, it seems—were also personally devoted to the dead bishop.[21] As for the *Epitome,* the pope didn't respond to this work (which Emser later adapted as an introduction to his longer *Divi Bennonis)* or to subsequent attempts such as another composition by the humanist Trithemius in 1506. Julius the warrior pope evidently had little time for such things: as members of the cardinal commission died off, he didn't replace them, and by 1509 the process had stalled. Nevertheless, Georg was undeterred. In 1510 he commissioned Emser to compose a proper Benno *vita,* sending him and Meissen cathedral dean Johan Hennig to examine archives outside Meissen, for instance at Hildesheim and Goslar. Emser's *Divi Bennonis Misnensis quondam episcopi vita* of 1512 was republished in the vernacular (1517, with more miracles) and again in 1521.[22] Weiss calls this work a "remarkable pastiche of scholarly guesswork and rhetorical bravado," while Collins, more kindly, refers to Emser's "biographical bricollage" that portrayed Benno as a humanist bishop, a man for all seasons and varied audiences.[23] Collins has shown how each of the two *vitae,* by Spedel and Emser, reflects the different contexts of their construction. The monk's biography turns Benno into an exemplary Benedictine, whereas the humanist Emser's Benno is a more public figure. For example, Spedel disregarded the bishop's part in the Saxon nobles' rebellion (something unsuited to a monk's life), but Emser did not; on the other hand, Emser toned down Benno's part in the investiture controversy, reluctant to portray him as anti-imperial.[24] After all, the emperor's support for the canonization could be crucial. Both *vitae* include a few miracles modeled after biblical prototypes—walking on water, turning water into wine—later mentioned in the papal bull. (Benno's missionary activity against the Slavs, also noted in the bull, lacks contemporary evidence.) Collins shows how the hagiography developed for Benno and other sixteenth-century and later saints, while humanistic in general approach, was adapted to the varying needs of anticipated audiences.[25]

21. Ibid., 92–93 and nn. 348–56 for the other proctors at Rome; n. 357 for Emser's own devotion.

22. Cf. *Divi Bennonis* in *Acta Sanctorum,* June III (Antwerp, 1701), 150–73.

23. James Michael Weiss, "Hagiography by German Humanists, 1483–1516," *Journal of Medieval and Renaissance Studies* 15 (1985): 299–316, at 311; Collins, "Bursfelders," 509, 541, 544.

24. Collins, "Bursfelders," 527, 530.

25. Collins revisits the Benno *vitae* and examines them in relation to more than three dozen

LEO X AND BENNO

Influenced by such efforts, perhaps, the Medici Leo X (1513–21) reopened the case, in late 1513 setting up a new commission of cardinals del Monte, Farnese, and Soderini. For his part, Georg named Nicholas von Schönberg (d. 1537) and Cardinal Cajetan as his proctors.[26] There were new hearings at Meissen in 1515 and 1517, the depositions being collected and sent to Rome (as in the 1499 procedure) by 1518. Supporting letters from Emperor Maximilian and Friedrich the Wise were read in consistories during May and August 1518.[27] Meanwhile, Georg's commitment to Benno's cause was evident in his fundraising, from as early as 1497; he redoubled his efforts especially from about 1518 (which Volkmar claims was the start of a critical phase in the process).[28] There was ongoing correspondence over financial backing via Jacob Fugger and the Fuggerbank, mentioning auditor of the Rota Simonetta as a payee, for instance.[29] Georg continued to support (usually with others' money) Roman proctors such as Bernard Sculteti from December 1499, though Benno's case was only one of Bernard's concerns. In February 1519 Georg published an open letter endorsing the now-deceased Sculteti's efforts on Benno's behalf.[30] The duke kept close tabs on all his agents at the curia, including Valentin Tetleben, James Gertewitz, and Dean Hennig, sending instructions and receiving reports of the latest developments. Sometimes the Meissen chapter balked at losing its members even temporarily to the Holy City to do Georg's bidding. Great emissaries weren't necessary since, the chapter misleadingly claimed, in the case of Francis of Paola the king of France used no one but a simple monk. The duke brushed aside their objections.[31]

other hagiographies by German humanists and others in *Reforming Saints: Saints' Lives and Their Authors in Germany, 1470–1530* (Oxford: Oxford University Press, 2008), esp. introduction and ch. 1. See the review by Simon Ditchfield in *Catholic Historical Review* 95, no. 2 (April 2009): 380–81; cf. also Volkmar, *Die Heiligenerhebung*, 133ff.

26. Antonio del Monte (St. Praxedis/S. Prassede); Alexander Farnese (St. Eustachius/S. Eustachio), who in August 1521 was replaced by Giovanni Salviati (Ss. Cosmus and Damian); and Francesco Soderini, replaced in March 1519 by Bernardo Carvajal (St. Crucis/S. Croce); there were no changes under Adrian VI: Volkmar, *Die Heiligenerhebung*, 76–77; for proctors, see ibid., 76 n. 273.

27. Ibid., 96.

28. Ibid., 72 n. 254 for 1497 efforts; Benno's "entscheidende Phase," 78.

29. Gess, *Akten und Briefe*, 33–34, letters #42, 43 (1518); 64–65, #79, (1519); 187, #231, 191–92, #238 (1521); Kohnle, "Zur Heiligsprechung," 563–64.

30. Gess, *Akten und Briefe*, 57, #72; 74, #94.

31. Volkmar, *Die Heiligenerhebung*, 85; Gess, *Akten und Briefe*, 104–7, #141, 142 Nov.–Dec. 1519: "wir . . . nicht wol darinnen Verenderung zu machen."

The Saxon duke also employed men closer to curial affairs, in particular the Netherlander Willem van Enckevoirt, 1464–1534/37).[32] A proctor at the curia from 1489, Enckevoirt was an apostolic secretary from 1504, protonotary, and in 1517 *orator* (ambassador) for the Habsburg Charles (later emperor) at the curia. With imperial permission he also became Georg of Saxony's proctor in the Benno cause from 1519 to 1523, during which his curial stature increased a great deal. Just two days after Adrian's election in 1522 (see below), imperial ambassador Juan Manuel (soon replaced by Luis de Cordoba, the duke of Sessa) advised the pope to appoint his compatriot Enckevoirt to the important post of datary, with influence over papal finances and the granting of benefices.[33] Adrian presented him with even more honors, granting him the bishopric of Tortosa and a cardinal's hat in 1523.[34] Under Adrian's successor Clement VII, at the emperor's initiative Enckevoirt was named bishop of Utrecht. Therefore, when this influential figure became Benno's proctor in 1519, Georg's hopes were high. He instructed his Meissen agents Gertewitz and Hennig to work in closest cooperation with Enckevoirt.

Georg sought out the great and mighty on behalf of Benno, such as his cousin Friedrich, Saxon elector, and the emperor-elect Charles. At first, Friedrich joined in the campaign: he supported proctors in the cause, and probably on August 9, 1518, for instance, his letter was among the pro-Benno supplications read in consistory. Friedrich set out three justifications for a canonization: Benno's miracles, the wishes of the German people, and his power to protect against the Hussite heretics.[35] By early 1519, however, Friedrich began to curtail his efforts.[36] Canon von Heinitz asked him to recommend Benno to the curia, and also to send one of his counselors, Hans von Minkewitz, to Rome as a lobbyist. Friedrich replied that he'd write a letter, but couldn't get along without Minkewitz. Kohnle sees

32. Volkmar, *Die Heiligenerhebung,* 79 n. 289 and 94 n. 359; Gess, *Akten und Briefe,* 107ff.

33. Gachard, *Correspondance de Charles-Quint et d'Adrien VI,* 8–9: "Del officio del datario me parece á mí que Vuestra Santidad devria proveer al protonotario Enckefort, por ser sufficiente para ello, y por lo que ha servido."

34. Ibid., 75: Adrian recommended him to Charles for the Tortosa bishopric on May 5, 1522, writing that Enckevoirt had served the emperor "muchos años sin salario ni otros provechos algunos, aunque no sin mucho travajo." It's unlikely, however, that the imperial agent received no benefits at all from this work.

35. Kohnle, "Zur Heiligsprechung," 67–68, Volkmar, *Die Heiligenerhebung,* 90.

36. Kohnle, "Zur Heiligsprechung," 568–69, 572.

this reluctance as a reflection of Friedrich's attempt to remain neutral in the increasingly significant "Luther matter."[37] In August Georg himself encouraged his cousin Friedrich to support the cause by writing again to the curia.[38] Next day Friedrich replied that he would gladly send such a letter; but on November 14 Georg had to remind him of his promise to write, a reminder repeated on November 29, when Georg somewhat querulously complained that a letter had not yet materialized—although, in fact, Friedrich had written a recommendation for Benno a week earlier.[39] Friedrich's letter was read in consistories in February and March 1520, along with ten other petitions.[40] By 1520, however, the imperial election had been decided against Leo's original choices, that is, Elector Friedrich himself, followed by the "more ecclesiastically minded" Elector Joachim of Brandenburg, and finally Francis I.[41] Thereafter the curia began critically to examine Friedrich's support not of Benno but of Luther. Perhaps as a result, by the end of 1520 Friedrich was no longer backing the dead bishop's cause, sending no more petitions to pope and curia.[42] The elector, not among the pro-Benno petitioners of 1521 and 1523, wasn't mentioned in the canonization bull.[43]

By 1520–21, on the other hand, Charles V had become more cooperative in providing supplications for Benno.[44] His was one of the letters read in the consistories of February and March 1520. This batch of eleven letters probably was put together during the winter of 1519–20.[45] Taken as a whole, they throw interesting light on Benno's circle of elite lobbyists at this particular stage. In addition to those sent by Friedrich, Emperor-elect (from June 1519) Charles, and of course Georg of Saxony and his brother Heinrich, one was from the young Elector Albrecht (1490–1545), archbishop of both Magdeburg and Mainz, created cardinal by Leo in March 1518 (he took the title of S. Pietro in Vincoli in 1521). Prior to the 1520 consistories, however, he

37. Gess, *Akten und Briefe*, 66–67, #83, 84; Kohnle, "Zur Heiligsprechung," 568–69.

38. "Mit schrifften . . . diss werg zcu fordern," Gess, *Akten und Briefe*, 96–97, #129.

39. Gess, *Akten und Briefe*, 97, #130; 103, #138; 104, #140: "so sint uns doch solche vorschrifftenoch nicht zukommon," and note.

40. Friedrich's last letter seems to have been written in November 1520, Kohnle, "Zur Heiligsprechung," 566, 569–70.

41. Pastor, *History of the Popes*, 7:259; also 272, 277.

42. Ibid., 386–87.

43. Volkmar, *Die Heiligenerhebung*, 91; as Friedrich progressively favored reformist ideas.

44. Gess, *Akten und Briefe*, 137–38, #174; 140, #176; 214–15, #263.

45. Volkmar, *Die Heiligenerhebung*, 96.

doesn't seem to have shown much interest in fostering Benno's cause, even though Meissen was within his province of Magdeburg. On the other hand, he's assured a place in history (or at least in textbooks) because of the sale of indulgences that took place in his Mainz province, which in turn helped to spark Luther's Ninety-Five Theses of 1517. His attitude toward the reformers was lenient to begin with, in contrast to that of his brother Elector Joachim I of Brandenburg (1485–1535).[46] (Joachim's was also among the supplications of early 1520.) Albrecht had been created cardinal at Joachim's request, and one suspects that he had convinced Albrecht to write a letter to accompany his own supporting Benno's. Joachim was far more active against Luther than Archbishop Albrecht, and perhaps he saw Benno as a useful anti-Luther figure even in 1519–20. In any event, in spite of Albrecht's lack of interest, he, not Joachim, was named in the canonization bull. The archbishop's unconcern continued even after the canonization: he didn't bother to come to Benno's translation. Jeffrey Smith points out that at this very time Albrecht was amassing his own huge relic collection at Halle, and probably would have seen no point in supporting possible competitors.[47]

The important figures whose letters were read to pope and cardinals in early 1520 must have bolstered Georg's hopes: surely the most powerful prelate of Germany, an elector, a second elector, and the emperor-elect himself would spur activity at the curia. But no action followed, and on several occasions Georg's optimism turned to despair. In October 1520 he directed Dean Hennig to stay close to imperial agents Juan Manuel and Enckevoirt after the latter sent a dispatch to Georg suggesting an imminent canonization, with little more remaining to do.[48] The suggestion was empty. Georg's hopes were raised more than once in 1521: Hennig (who had researched Benno's life as early as 1510) presented a short printed *Vita* with many miracles (based on Emser's work) at a secret consistory on March 20, 1521, after which the cardinals agreed to expedite the canonization.[49] Meanwhile Hen-

46. Among the seven, the electors of Brandenburg and Mainz were the last to cast votes in imperial elections.

47. Jeffrey Chipps Smith, "Salvaging Saints: The Rescue and Display of Relics in Munich during the Early Catholic Reformation," in *Art, Piety and Destruction in the Christian West,* ed. Virginia Chieffo Raguin (Aldershot: Ashgate, 2010), 23–44; and "Repatriating Sanctity" in *Repatriation,* ed. Dario Gamboni, in the *Proceedings* of the Congress of the International Committee of the History of Art (Melbourne: University of Melbourne Press, 2009), 96.

48. "Wenig in diser sach zu thun," Gess, *Akten und Briefe,* 136–37, #173, Oct. 8, 1520.

49. Volkmar, *Die Heiligenerhebung,* 78.

nig and Enckevoirt carried on with their lobbying efforts.[50] In April Georg received letters from the three-cardinal committee implying that the process was nearly completed, with nothing further than to discuss Benno's life and miracles in consistory, subject them to examination, and then celebrate a canonization Mass with the usual solemnities. The cardinals hoped that all this would occur before the upcoming hot weather shut down the curia. Again, no canonization occurred.[51] In September 1521, when it seemed yet again that Georg's efforts were about to be rewarded, the duke notified the emperor that, since things seemed to be nearing a successful conclusion, Charles should write encouragingly to his orators at the curia, especially Juan Manuel and Enckevoirt.[52] Once more, this came to nothing.

For Georg, then, 1521 was a year of repeated disappointments. It may have seemed that pope and curialists were deliberately ignoring him. Already in 1519 and 1520 his suspicions reflected an attitude widespread among his compatriots in the late fifteenth and early sixteenth centuries—that for Italians, the curia, and the popes, barbarian Germany was "Rome's cow" to be milked as needed. This seemed self-evident to Georg because other saints were being promoted or canonized, while Benno was ignored. He let Leo X himself know this, in November of 1519: although the pope had been informed of Benno's life and miracles, at the behest of the French king Francis of Paola had been canonized while "our Benno" was being ignored even though many letters and proctors had been sent to Rome.[53] In December Georg instructed the Meissen chapter to contact Enckevoirt and ask him to try to join Benno's application to Antoninus's, being shepherded through curial procedures by Cardinal Giulio de'Medici.[54] Enckevoirt, Georg adds, should also let the pope know that the king of the Romans (Charles V) was to be esteemed no less than the king of France.[55] Ironically, as early as October 1516 Georg himself had written to support Antoninus's

50. "Lobbyarbeit," ibid., 80.

51. Gess, *Akten und Briefe*, 162–63, #204 and n., April 16–19, 1521: "quod omnino speramus futurum ante vacantias proximo venturas." Volkmar, *Die Heiligenerhebung*, 100; the summary was printed on March 12.

52. Gess, *Akten und Briefe*, 189–90, #235, Sept. 9, 1521: "und sunderlich hern Johan Emanuel und hern Wilhelmen von Engkenfurth."

53. "Omisso Bennone nostro," Gess, *Akten und Briefe*, 103–4, #139.

54. Since the two were canonized together, it is possible that Enckevoirt's efforts extended beyond merely pressing Benno's cause at the curial stage; on the dual canonization, more below.

55. Gess, *Akten und Briefe*, 107–8, #143.

canonization, and Georg's agent in Rome, the Dominicans' proctor general Nicholas von Schönberg, once a member of Giulio de'Medici's chancery, was also lobbying for the Florentine candidate at the same time as he was working for Benno. This worried Georg, but when Cardinal Carvajal, presiding over Antoninus's committee from January 1518, was also appointed to Benno's committee in March of 1519, the duke's anxieties increased: would, or even could, Benno's cause be given equal treatment? Could Carvajal find enough time adequately to deal with both proceedings? Georg was realistic: the case of an obscure twelfth-century German bishop might easily be overpowered by that of a popular Florentine prelate who had died just sixty years earlier, and whose cause was supported by no less than the Florentine Cardinal de'Medici, cousin to Leo X—also Florentine. As it turned out, by 1521 at the curia Benno's cause in some ways benefited from Antoninus's progress, because it seems to have provided a useful pattern for Benno's lobbyists.[56] Yet in 1519–20, Georg saw nothing but trouble and anti-German prejudice when he considered recent and pending canonizations. He returned to this theme at least three times during 1520, his Germanic indignation on the rise: writing to his agents in Rome (Hennig and Gertewitz) in April he ordered them to finish the job or come home, since attempts on Benno's behalf weren't succeeding. He enclosed a letter, in Latin, to be seen by Enckevoirt and others at the curia, which noted that after the labors of so many of Georg's predecessors and his own, and various expenses and daily solicitations, Bennos's cause remained doubtful in spite of letters from the emperor-elect and princes of all Germany. "We are of the opinion, moreover, that our Benno is very much hindered because he is neither French nor Florentine" as the French cause had already succeeded, and now the Florentine's was advancing. Perhaps the pope favors all the princes of the world over the king of the Romans and princes of the Holy Roman Empire. "If"—the letter continues—"it seems to you [Georg's agents, but meant for other eyes as well] that the cause will be delayed perhaps for years, return the money we've invested, as we're unwilling to lose further time and effort. Though Blessed Benno might not become a saint, at least he remained blessed."[57] A month later Georg was venting his anger over this

56. Volkmar, *Die Heiligenerhebung*, 97–100.

57. "Bennonem nostrum eo potissimum impediri quod vel Gallus non sit vel Florentinus ... nolumus enim ulterius et tempus et operam perdere," Gess, *Akten und Briefe*, 119–20, #158.

issue again, in a letter to Jakob Fugger: the Rome business isn't going well, and funding will be withdrawn if nothing develops; perhaps Benno must suffer the penalty of being neither French nor Florentine.[58] Georg repeated such sentiments to Hennig in October: Benno must suffer because he's pure German born. The French king supported Francis of Paola, already canonized, and now Antoninus the Florentine was going to be canonized, even though efforts had been made for Benno for a much longer time, ever since his death.[59]

ENTER LUTHER

While all this was going on, in the background a force to which we've briefly alluded was developing that would affect Georg, Emser, and ultimately Benno. The papal response (or lack thereof) to Luther's activities from 1517 has engaged the interest of many controversialists and historians from that day to this. By 1518, however, it began seriously to be acknowledged in Rome that the "German monk"—as he was incorrectly designated—needed attending to. As for Luther's effects on Benno's case, at first (even after the 1517 Theses) apparently there was little animus between Luther and Benno's bulldog Emser. This began to change in 1518. At a dinner Emser hosted in Dresden on July 25, 1518, Luther and another guest got into an argument over the merits of scholasticism, excommunication, and indulgences; evidently Luther expressed himself with his usual candor, drawn into rash statements by the heat of the moment. Report of these comments, and other examples of Luther's opinions, some probably invented by his enemies, alarmed the aging emperor Maximilian, who passed on information about Luther's activities to Leo X. By mandate of September 11, 1518, the pope sent Cardinal Cajetan (one of Benno's proctors) to Germany to obtain Luther's recantation. Even though the Cajetan-Luther meeting in October had less than definitive results, by early 1519 Leo X—perhaps relying on optimistic reports from his inept agent Charles von Miltitz—claimed to believe that Luther was prepared to stop attacking the Church. Even as late as 1521 some cardinals imagined that Charles had quashed the

58. "Muss villeicht entgelten, das er nit ein Franzos ader ein Florentiner ist," ibid., 120, #159, May 6, 1520.

59. "Aber her ist der gbort eyn purer deutzcer gwest," ibid., 138–39, #175: "weil vor langer zceit, eyr dy verstorben."

heretical movement, congratulating Leo on his rapprochement with the emperor-elect, who, had he not snuffed out the Lutheran heresy (Panvinio, c. 1550, interpolated in this report the words "then thought quenched, now burning fervently"), the greater part of Germany would have withdrawn obedience from the Apostolic See.[60] In spite of the potential rupture in the Church, about this time the pope's interests were temporarily diverted from the northern "heretic" as the apparently more immediate problem of the imperial election came to the foreground. As successor to Maximilian I, who died on January 12, 1519, at first, as noted, Charles was at the bottom of the pope's list; even the French king was (slightly) more acceptable. These considerations affected the treatment of Leo's favored candidate Elector Friedrich and, in turn, Friedrich's subject Martin Luther. For now the "Luther business" became a secondary issue, as the pope mollified his treatment of Friedrich's potentially dangerous theologian. Papal hopes were disappointed when by June it was clear that the Habsburg Charles would be the next emperor. At the end of that month, the famous Leipzig disputation began, and Luther again attracted papal attention.

Subsequently to Cajetan's confrontation, from late June to mid-July of 1519 Luther found another forum for promoting and clarifying his opinions. At Leipzig a debate was arranged and to a great extent managed by Georg, between Luther and Karlstadt on the one side and Dominican theologian Johann Eck (d. 1543) on the other. The disputation went ahead in spite of the reluctance of the local bishop and the Leipzig university theology faculty, who, Georg complained, were ignorant cowards more devoted to drinking than debating.[61] The confrontation in the duke's castle, the Pleissenburg, was witnessed by a crowd including Georg himself, Emser, and inter alia some Bohemian Hussites. The course of events is well known: Luther, pushed to irritated extremes by Eck, ended by defending Hus.[62] This

60. Angelo Mercati, ed., *Diarii di Consistori del Pontificato di Adriano VI*, Studi e Testi 157 (1951), 83–113, at 112–13: "quam nisi sua prudentia Caesar extinxisset, magna pars Germaniae ab obedentia Sedis Apostolicae defecisset" (June 28, 1521); though included in Adrian's consistories, this entry, as Mercati notes, pertains to Leo X.

61. David Bagchi, *Luther's Earliest Opponents* (Minneapolis: Fortress Press, 1991), 234–35 and n. 82.

62. Some of the Hussites at the disputation contacted two of their spiritual leaders in Prague to convey the good news about Luther's commending Hus. These leaders, in turn, wrote to Luther, who in responding asked for a copy of Hus's *De ecclesia,* a work that confirmed Luther's conviction that the Bohemians should be included in the German reformist movement, as he stated in his

outraged Georg not only on a theological but also on a personal level because his ducal patrimony and city of Meissen had suffered depredation by the heretics during the Hussite wars. He left the disputation-hall in high indignation. Luther, ruminating on the situation more than twenty-five years later, wrote that prior to the debate, "Duke Georg was not against me. This I know for certain."[63] Whatever the case—and evidently Georg had breakfasted with Luther and Eck in the course of the Leipzig proceedings—after Leipzig, letters and pamphlets highlight Luther's and Georg's mutual, and growing, animosity.[64]

Following the debate, in August Emser wrote to John Zack, administrator of the archbishopric in Prague, assuring him that Luther's comments favoring Hus were merely rash overstatements.[65] Emser claimed that Luther would never agree with Hussite heretics. This created a dilemma for Luther: if he agreed with Emser's claims, he would seem to contradict his own Leipzig declarations, and if he disagreed he would seem—now free of argumentative emotionalism—clearly to accuse himself of heresy. This, linked with Luther's suspicion that Emser had manipulated him into self-incrimination at the Dresden dinner party a year earlier, stung Luther into publishing a response to Emser in September 1519. This was the start of an acerbic pamphlet war between the two that ran from 1519 to the end of 1521, with Luther attacking the sniveling "Goat of Leipzig" (an allusion to the goat in Emser's heraldry), Emser blasting the raging "Bull of Wittenberg."[66] Emser's promotion of Benno, however, wasn't brought into the war of words. The content of the exchanges illustrates Matheson's claim that "polemic ceased to be a heuristic tool. It became a blunt weapon."[67] In September Luther addressed a missive called "An Addition to Goat Emser," evoking Emser's "Assertion of the Goat against Luther's Hunt" in October or November of 1519. After Luther published his "Address to the Christian

"Address to the Christian Nobility." Winfried Eberhard, "Bohemia, Moravia and Austria," in *The Early Reformation in Europe,* ed. Andrew Pettegree (Cambridge: Cambridge University Press, 1992), 23–48, at 28–29.

63. Martin Luther, *Luther's Works,* vol. 34, ed. Lewis W. Spitz (Philadelphia: Muhlenberg Press, 1960), 333.

64. Bagchi, *Luther's Earliest Opponents,* 235–6.

65. Martin Luther, *Luther's Works,* vol. 39, ed. Eric W. Gritsch (Philadelphia: Fortress Press, 1970), 108.

66. Enders, *Luther und Emser,* 3ff.; Bagchi, *Luther's Earliest Opponents,* 95–96.

67. Peter Matheson, *The Rhetoric of the Reformation* (Edinburgh: T & T Clark, 1998), 187; cf. also 196.

Nobility of the German Nation" in August of 1520, Emser countered with "Against the Unchristian Book" in December 1520. Luther wrote "To the Goat in Leipzig" in early 1521, evoking Emser's "To the Bull in Wittenberg" at the end of January, 1521, which led to Luther's "Concerning the Answer of the Goat in Leipzig" in late January–early February 1521. Emser retorted with "Reply to the Answer of the Raging Bull in Wittenberg," which Luther countered in "Answer to the Hyperchristian, Hyperspiritual, and Hyperlearned Book by Goat Emser" in March. Emser's "Quadruplica to Luther's Recent Answer" followed in the spring, against which Luther fired back a sarcastic "Dr. Luther's Retraction" in October; and some time before the end of 1521, Emser got in the last word (on this round anyway) with "Reservation to Luther's First Retraction." The wrangling continued: in 1522 Leipzig authorities confiscated 1,500 copies of an anti-Emser broadsheet.[68] Next year Emser attacked Luther's translation of the Greek New Testament. Duke Georg, "single-mindedly committed to the use of propaganda," encouraged Emser's efforts.[69] In the meantime Louvain and Köln universities condemned Luther's Leipzig conclusions in late 1519, while Leo X finally promulgated the bull against the Wittenberg theologian that opened with a militant cry to the Lord to rise up against the sinful nations, *Exsurge, Domine* (Ps 9:20), in mid-June of 1520. Emser, for obvious reasons, came to be identified as a prime anti-Luther warrior: in March 1521 a Dresden printer was imprisoned (and released at Emser's own request) for defaming him, and in September of that year John Cochlaeus (1479–1552) wrote, "Will noone oppose Luther in writing besides Emser alone?" adding with similar exaggeration, "Emser alone remains unbowed" in the anti-Luther literary battle.[70] By the time he died in 1527, Emser had become, as Collins writes, "Luther's sharpest critic among the German humanists."[71]

Benno reemerges in the midst of this welter of controversy. As noted, the "Luther question," in spite of other distractions, by now engaged pope and curia. Charles's ambassador Juan Manuel even claimed in a letter of May 12, 1520, that Leo had an "extraordinary fear" of the Saxon reformer, who, about

68. Andrew Pettegree, *Reformation and the Culture of Persuasion* (Cambridge: Cambridge University Press, 2005), 104; Emser's press was based mainly in Dresden, 51.

69. Bagchi, *Luther's Earliest Opponents*, 230.

70. Ibid., 207, 210, 225 n. 41. On Emser's death in 1527, Cochlaeus succeeded him as Georg's personal chaplain.

71. Collins, "Bursfelders," 511.

the same time, had decisively identified Leo X with the Antichrist.[72] Drafts of *Exsurge, Domine,* were considered in no fewer than four consistories in May and June of 1520 before its mid-June publication.[73] About a month later Leo responded to a now-lost complaint from Georg. The pope was saddened to learn that Georg believed that Benno's cause was delayed because Georg himself was erroneously thought, at Rome, to be a Luther supporter. Leo assured Georg that he knew that the duke was the heretic's enemy, and praised his ongoing efforts against Luther and his publications. As for Benno's case itself, the pope reminded Georg that canonization was a long, arduous process, but that the cause had been examined "not negligently but prudently." Leo promised that, following the necessary cardinalate review and consistorial discussions, he would deal with the matter and if all was well, proceed to the canonization with joy, *alacri animo.*[74] Is it possible that some curialists associated the Saxons Georg and Benno with the Saxon Luther? Misinformation and misunderstandings about German princes and their policies, along with a muddled idea of German political geography, might well have led some to such a conclusion. Moreover, in October 1520 Georg had indeed acknowledged that there was some truth to Luther's denunciation of the Roman curia in his "Address to the German Nobility."[75] In any case, in spite of Leo's seeming optimism, when the pope died on December 1, 1521, Benno's canonization was still seventeen months in the future.

CANONIZATION UNDER ADRIAN VI

With Leo dead, Benno's cause once again could have ground to a halt. However, the new pope continued the process. The Netherlander Adriaan Florenzoon Dedal, Adrian VI (el. January 9, 1522, d. September 14, 1523), came from the same region that produced the Habsburg Charles. Adrian, with a doctorate in theology, became chancellor, then rector of Louvain University by 1501, and in 1507 Emperor Maximilian appointed him tutor to his grandson Charles. Being sent to represent Charles in Spain in 1515,

72. Pastor, *History of the Popes,* 8:17–18; David M. Whitford, "The Papal Antichrist: Martin Luther and the Underappreciated Influence of Lorenzo Valla," *Renaissance Quarterly* 61 (2008): 26–52, esp. 40–41.

73. Pastor, *History of the Popes,* 7:394–403; Luther was finally condemned as an excommunicated heretic in the bull *In coena domini* of March 28, 1521.

74. Gess, *Akten und Briefe,* 127–29, #164.

75. "Wy wol dennoch nicht alles unwar ist," Gess, *Akten und Briefe,* 138–39, #175, to Hennig from Dresden/Leipzig Oct. 10–15, 1520.

Adrian became bishop of Tortosa and inquisitor in Aragon and Navarre in 1516 and, at imperial request, cardinal in 1517. After Charles the new king arrived in Spain in September 1517, he appointed his old tutor inquisitor in Castile and Leon. Elected emperor in June 1519, Charles left Adrian in charge and departed for Germany in May of 1520. Almost immediately, Adrian faced a rebellion centered in Castile, mainly against Charles's appointment of about five hundred "foreigners" to Spanish offices. Several hundred of these were from the Low Countries, Adrian himself being the most conspicuous example. His inept handling of the situation foreshadows his failings as pope, which he became (thanks to the imperialist Cardinal Giulio de'Medici's scheming to block his own rivals in the conclave) in January of 1522, which stupefied all Rome. As the cardinals left the conclave, claimed a Venetian ambassador, there were cries of "Why didn't we elect one of us?" and some put up a "For Rent" sign on their houses as an indication of fear, feigned or real, that the new pope would relocate the curia to Spain.[76] Guicciardini mused that the cardinals elected him "just to waste time that morning," whereas Zimmerman notes that Adrian had "already been selected as an alternative in case of an impasse."[77] However it came about, the election decidedly alienated the Romans. On January 11, 1522, for instance, Castiglione claimed that it left him "astounded, and in such a mentally confused state that I seem to be in a new world, and that Rome no longer is where it was."[78] The emperor returned to Spain in July; the pope sailed for Italy in August without meeting him, seemingly at Charles's own request.[79]

Adrian and Charles, at first tutor and pupil, then regent and king, and finally pope and emperor, enjoyed, most of the time, an intimate and mutually beneficial relationship. Evidently Charles knew of Adrian's elevation even before the new pope did, respectively in January and February of 1522.[80]

76. Report of Luigi Gradenigo in *Relazioni degli Ambasciatori Veneti*, 74.

77. Guicciardini, *History of Italy*, 329; T. C. Price Zimmermann, *Paolo Giovio: The Historian and the Crisis of Sixteenth-Century Italy* (Princeton, N.J.: Princeton University Press, 1995), 42.

78. Quote from Stinger, *The Renaissance in Rome*, 320.

79. See Pastor, *History of the Popes*, 9:ch. II passim, and Pierre Chaunu and Michèle Escamilla, *Charles Quint* (Paris: Fayard, 2000), 9–11 for basic chronology. Gachard, *Correspondance*, 44, 66: in letters of March 9 and 29, 1522, Charles encouraged Adrian to leave for Rome as soon as possible because "la necessidad pública es tan grande, y la dilacion de su yda [departure] trae de cada dia tanto inconveniente á aquella sancta silla y á las cosas comunes de entrambos á dos."

80. Gachard, *Correspondance*, xvii, xxi.

Adrian wrote to the emperor on February 11, expressing (prophetically, as it happened) his unsuitability for such a heavy burden, which, he claimed, gave him no joy, and about a week later was urging Charles to come to Spain so that they could confer "as soon as possible."[81] (However, the two never met again.) Adrian VI's papacy would be joyless indeed. In the barely disguised irony of his *vita* of Adrian, Paolo Giovio emphasized the pope's ignorance of his new realm, as he tried to memorize the names of unfamiliar Italian towns and regions.[82] In a blistering exchange with his cardinals in consistory (March 26, 1523) Adrian claimed to owe little to the college, who had elected him to torture and imprisonment; they were executioners, *carnifices.* The pope rather heretically included the conclave-inspiring Holy Ghost in this category.[83] To begin with, however, and before Adrian reached Italy, from the emperor-elect's point of view this was a great opportunity. On March 7, 1522, using the French that he reserved for personal communications, Charles told the pope that between the two of them they could do great and good things: he would be to Adrian as a "bon filz" to a father.[84] Nevertheless, there were several occasions in 1522 and 1523 when pope and emperor would disagree, particularly regarding Adrian's attitude toward France: in the same "good son" letter the emperor warned Adrian to beware the enticing words of the French. The pope's assurance of September 30 to Charles that he "held the French king in as much amity as Your Majesty" probably was not what the emperor wanted to read.[85]

By the time Adrian died, Romans had come to caricature him as a dry, reclusive scholar who, when not ineffectually fussing about papal business, preferred to scuttle into his chambers to read and study. He never grasped

81. "En verdad no me allegro," ibid., 26: Adrian added that at his age, he should be in retirement rather than taking on such a task, "que recivir tan grandissima y cási importable carga á cuestas"; he wanted to meet Charles: "ponga por obra su venida con toda la presteza que le fuere posibile," ibid., 38.

82. *Vita Hadriani Sexti* in *Hadrianus VI, sive Analecta historica,* 122.

83. "Ad tormenta, ad carceres. . . . Spiritus Sanctus fuerat carnifex simul cum eis," Mercati, *Diarii di Consistori,* 95.

84. "Et me semble que estant le papat en votre main, et lempyre en la myenne, est pour faire par ensemble beaucop de bonnes et grandes choses." Gachard does not include this letter, which is found in *Correspondenz des Kaisers Karl V, erster Band, 1513–1532,* ed. Karl Lanz (Leipzig: F. A. Brockhaus, 1844), 59.

85. "Avons esgale amytié à nostre fils le roy de France que à Vostre Majesté," *Correspondenz,* 60; Gachard, *Correspondance,* 125–26; the emperor's letter and Adrian's reply in *Correspondenz,* 58–62, with slightly different versions in *Quellen zur Geschichte Karls V,* ed. Alfred Hohler (Darmstadt: Wissenschaftliche Buchgesellschaft, 1990), 97–100.

Italian; his Latin was bookish and "foreign," even gutterally "barbaric" to Roman ears; he was so dithery and slow that his usual response to a request for a decision came popularly to be summed up in the byword *videbimus*—"we'll see."[86] (A Venetian ambassador claimed that Leo X used the same expression when in doubt.)[87] Even Adrian's biographer, contemporary and fellow-countryman Gerhard Moring, admitted that many blamed the pope for his delays, excusing His Holiness because his job was complicated by an empty treasury, plague, Turks, *Lutheranismus* confounding all of Germany, and the pope's ignorance of the regions, cities, leaders, and affairs of Italy.[88] Apart from that, some claimed that he seemed to rely too heavily on his immediate curialists, such as Dietrich von Heeze, once his student at Louvain, and in particular his datary and countryman Willem von Enckevoirt.[89] The charge of slowness included Enckevoirt and other immediate advisers, "men of wood" (Giovio), some of whom were overwhelmed by swirling Roman, Italian, and European politics. Romans also disliked their new pope because he was determined to clean up public morals and take a reformer's broom to the sinecures and venal offices that Leo X had lavishly provided his relatives and others willing to pay the purchase price. Many lost their titles and incomes, enlarging the embittered crowd. Several of these would apply their humanistic talents to anti-papal invective. One observer noted how Rome suffered from Adrian's "extreme, rapacious avarice"; even the fact that he'd kept his own name as pope (following imperial ambassador Juan Manuel's suggestion), breaking long tradition, was criticized.[90] Pasquino (in spite of the pope's efforts to stifle him) was very busy during and immediately after this reign. To the Romans' great joy, the pope died on September 14, 1523. It's said that his physician found a notice on his door from the populace (SPQR), addressed "to the liberator of our country."[91]

86. "Tardo nelle sue operazioni"; *Relazione degli Ambasciatori Veneti,* 100, for Adrian's Latin.

87. "Vedremo": report of Marco Minio (June 1520) in *Relazione degli Ambasciatori Veneti,* 64.

88. "Ignoratio rerum Italicarum, regionum, urbium, & procerum... Vita Hadrini Sexti... auctore Gerardo Moringo," in *Hadrianus VI,* 28, 61. On Moring's work, Pastor, *History of the Popes,* 9:227: Moring's biography of 1536 experienced "little circulation."

89. "Fanno tutte le faccende e possono assai col pontefice," Gachard, *Correspondance,* lxxxix, quoting Luigi Gradenigo, Venetian ambassador to Rome; Pastor, *History of the Popes,* 9:72, 96 for Adrian's slowness.

90. Pastor, *History of the Popes,* 9:484, letter of March 21, 1523; avarice on 53; as for the pope's title, Juan Manuel had written, "Y á mi parecer deve tomar el proprio nombre que tiene, y dezir Adriano sexto," Gachard, *Correspondance,* 9.

91. Paolo Giovio, *Vita,* in *Hadrianus VI,* 136–37; cf. Pastor, *History of the Popes,* 9:222. A valiant

It must be admitted that the bookish Netherlander was thrust into a world of sometimes violent political and military change and challenges to the faith; no wonder he preferred to retreat into his study. Apart from trying to mediate between Habsburg and Valois in their Italo-European competition, attempting to control dynastic rivalries in Italy, defending his Papal States, and fencing with troublesome cardinals such as the pro-French Soderini, whom he threw into Castel Sant'Angelo, he faced the threat to Christendom posed by the Turks (who took Rhodes during his pontificate). In March and April of 1523 Ferdinand of Austria's orator openly chastised Adrian, perhaps unfairly, for his indecision about the Ottomans: whereas, he claimed, Fabius Cunctator restored the Roman Republic (through delay), by delay the pope was losing the Christian Republic.[92] Giovio remarks that the cardinals could barely suppress their laughter at the expression on Adrian's face during this diatribe.[93] In addition to all that, pope and curia had to deal with the new heresy from the north. Adrian's activities here were characteristically inept. He was well acquainted with the Luther problem. While he was still in Spain, colleagues at Adrian's old university, Louvain, sent him a copy of their condemnation of Luther's Leipzig performance. He endorsed their decision in December 1519; in April 1521 he wrote to Charles asking him to send Luther—"this evil and pestilent man"—to Leo X for proper judgment.[94] As Spain's inquisitor, also in April of 1521 he condemned the importation of Luther's books with their "heretical errors."[95] In dealing with the Lutheran threat as pope, Adrian's characteristic simplicity is unmistakable, though Pastor preferred to see it as "genuine German frankness."[96] The occasion of this naiveté was a Diet at Nuremberg (convened September 1522). Adrian sent nuncio Francesco Chieregati, charged, inter alia, with blasting Luther and his teachings and calling for the implementation of the Edict of Worms. Meanwhile the pope

---

attempt to present Adrian in a more favorable light is made by Sheryl E. Reiss, "Adrian VI, Clement VII and Art" in *The Pontificate of Clement VII,* ed. Kenneth Gouwens and S. E. Reiss (Aldershot: Ashgate, 2005), 339–62.

92. Mercati, *Diarii di Consistori,* 94–96 and in *Hadrianus VI,* "Vita" by Moring, 71.

93. Zimmermann, *Paolo Giovio,* 55.

94. "Ce mauvais et pestillent homme," Gachard, *Correspondance,* 245, letter to Charles of April 9, 1521.

95. John E. Longhurst, "Luther in Spain: 1520–1540," *Proceedings of the American Philosophical Society* 103 (1959): 66–93, at 85: "herrores hereticales y otras muchas cosas sospechosas de la fe."

96. Pastor, *History of the Popes,* 9:37–38.

wrote to Eck and other anti-Lutherans (December 1, 1522) asking what could be done to stop "this pestilential disease" and seeking written advice, admitting that "we are not sufficiently informed."[97] Chieregati addressed the diet in January 1523. Through him, the pope disingenuously confessed that Church leadership had failed: "We all, prelates and clergy, have gone astray from the right way, and for a long time no one has done well; no, not one." The pope told his nuncio to "give promises that we shall . . . before all things reform the Roman Curia, whence, perhaps, all these evils have had their origin. Thus healing will begin at the source of sickness." Such frank admission of guilt at the top, from the pope himself, astounded many Roman commentators and provided ammunition for the reformers: in Adrian's frankness, Luther saw only the simple-minded ignorance of Louvain's "crowned ass."[98] This was the pope who canonized Benno and Antoninus.

After Leo's death, as we might expect, Georg had to bring Benno to the new pope's attention. He ordered Bishop John VII of Meissen, then in Rome, to expedite matters, and especially to encourage Enckevoirt to support the cause "and our other affairs." On the same day (January 4, 1523) the duke ordered an agent to seek supplications from the VIPs at the Nuremberg Diet, who were to write to the pope, the bishop of Meissen, Enckevoirt, and others; Georg also wanted copies of all these letters.[99] As we saw in the last chapter, in consistories in May, Adrian scheduled the canonization of both Benno and Antoninus for the end of the month.[100] Knowing that Charles V was among Benno's suppliants no doubt strengthened Adrian's resolve. Just as the fall of pro-French Soderini in April 1523 helped Medici interests in Antoninus's canonization, the same may have strengthened Benno's case presented to Adrian by imperialist lobbyists. During those consistories, however, it seems that not everyone shared the pope's enthusiasm. A Mantuan observer, after reporting on a consistory for Antoninus, on May 18 turned to the other candidate: "Today there was another public consistory, dealing with Benno the German. I believe that this pope intends to make saints of the dead and to drag the desperate living to hell, especially those dealing with this curia, in which there are none but the desperate [perhaps "despera-

97. Bagchi, *Luther's Earliest Opponents,* 223.
98. Pastor, *History of the Popes,* 9:135, 142–43.
99. "Und andre unsre sachen zu fordern," Gess, *Akten und Briefe,* 421–22, 425.
100. Volkmar, *Die Heiligenerhebung,* 79–80.

dos" would be more appropriate] and malcontent."[101] As noted in Antoninus's case, some cardinals believed that Adrian was rushing things without sufficient knowledge of the candidates; there were rumors of anti-Adrianists pushing the canonizations deliberately to kill him off; and the city's leaders feared any public ceremonial gatherings at the start of the annual reign of "la pestilenza." Resistance continued to the last: even as late as May 28 or 29 "many" in consistory disagreed about the canonizations, though it's difficult to pinpoint whether Benno's or Antoninus's. The objections were led in particular by Bishop Diego Ramirez of Cuenca (Castile), referred to in the previous chapter, who—for whatever reasons—seems to have contributed most to the *longam altercationem.*[102] In the end, however, Benno's (and Antoninus's) case was accepted and at last, on May 31, 1523, the long-sought canonizations occurred.[103] Ortiz notes that because of Adrian's penny-pinching it was done on the cheap, something (he claimed) rarely seen in such ceremonies.[104] Leo X's lavish spending hadn't left Adrian with much choice; he had to be as tight-fisted as possible. Whether this extended to saving money by the two-for-one principle, in which Benno's was tacked onto Antoninus's ceremony, or it reflected a continuing denigration of "German" as opposed to "Italian" candidates, is a vexed question, considered in the next chapter. For now, note that a multiple canonization (to include Antoninus, Benno, and others) had been brought up in Francis of Paola's case, and even earlier, at the Council of Constance a synchronous triple canonization had been contemplated (but never implemented) for other would-be saints. The double ceremony may simply have been a time and money-saving device.

On the day of the canonization, Meissen's Bishop John VII was present as Georg's *nuncius et orator.* For the bishop it was a familiar situation, as he'd been active (as a Meissen canon) in Benno's cause at Rome on ear-

101. "A casa del diavolo . . . disperati e malcontenti," Pastor, *History of the Popes,* 9:142 n. 2; Pietschmann, "Ablauf und Dimensionen," 408.

102. Blasius Ortiz, *Itinerarium Hadrinai Sexti,* in *Hadrianus VI,* 211. Diego Ramirez de Fuenleal was appointed in 1518 and died in 1537. His episcopate was sandwiched between those of the apostolic administrators cardinals Rafael Sansone Riario and Alexander Cesarini.

103. Curiously, in the diaries of Adrian's consistories there are two separate notices of the canonizations: the first very briefly refers to Antoninus only, the next to both Antoninus and Benno, the latter raised to sainthood at the emperor-elect's and other German princes' entreaties, with many miracles credited to him. Not much is said of Antoninus in either entry. Mercati, *Diarii consistori,* 97.

104. Ortiz, *Itinerarium,* in *Hadrianus VI,* 212.

lier occasions. However, Enckevoirt, not the bishop, pronounced the formal request for Benno's canonization during the ceremony. After returning to Germany, Bishop John belatedly sent a copy of the papal bull to Duke Georg on July 25, also enclosing a new writing by Luther.[105] John eventually published the Office of his predecessor Benno, along with the bull, at the beginning of September 1523.[106] His apparent lack of enthusiasm—which seems counterintuitive—perhaps reflects the ongoing conflict of authority between duke and bishops, noted earlier. In 1502, a dispute had broken out between John VI and Georg over episcopal temporalities and the duke's reformist urges. In January 1503, when Cardinal von Gurk/Peraudi visited Meissen cathedral, as mentioned above, the bishop refused to attend. By the time his successor von Schleinitz became Bishop John VII, and in spite of his earlier involvement, the canonization was effectively in the hands of the cathedral chapter, which followed Georg's lead rather than the bishop's; subsequently, John was given (or took) a relatively minor role in the canonization ceremony.[107] During the second half of the fifteenth century, as Thomson points out, (Bavarian and) Saxon princes "gained control of the bishoprics," while Sixtus IV and Innocent VIII granted them rights of presentation to certain Meissen cathedral offices in 1476 and 1485.[108] Presumably insouciant John VII, having inherited this unpleasant interference, was unhappy in the role of subservient ducal agent, and let Georg know it.

In the canonization bull, *Excelsus Dominus,* Benno is, first of all, hierarchically "located," being placed with the confessors between doctors of the church and holy virgins. The bull then outlines his life and miracles, including a heroic stand against Henry IV in the investiture controversy, which—the bull claims—resulted in Benno's being taken away in chains; but by divine grace he escaped danger.[109] Miracles reputedly performed in the bishop's lifetime are mentioned, taken from the fifteenth- and sixteenth-century *vitae:* walking across the river Elbe, changing water into wine, striking the earth to produce a spring, blessing a bell that protected crops. For posthumous miracles there were encounters with two Meissen margraves, of whom one died af-

105. Gess, *Akten und Briefe,* 543–44, #538; which of Luther's writings, is not ascertainable (n. 3).

106. Volkmar, *Die Heiligenerhebung,* 104.

107. Ibid., 84–87.

108. Thomson, *Popes and Princes 1417–1517,* 153–54, concessions gained especially after, or in spite of, the Concordat of Vienna (1448).

109. Fontanini, *Codex constitutionum,* 212–14. See also *AASS,* June III, 145–231.

ter punching Benno and then, to make matters worse, ridiculing his victim's threat of retribution.[110] The second margrave lost an eye after ignoring the dead bishop's dream-warnings to restore some Meissen property.[111] The bull also notes the miraculous preservation of one of Benno's footprints, as well as the flimsy hut he lived in while converting local heathens (there is little historical evidence about Benno's missionary activities), and the wonderful state of his episcopal garb and miter "today," though removed from his grave, presumably during a translation, over two hundred years after his death. Many other miracles could be set out, including raisings of the dead and cures of various illnesses.[112] Unlike some other canonization bulls, there is little detail about his curative posthumous wonders. Having thus established Benno's credentials, the bull lists those who worked for his canonization, in this order: Charles, king of the Romans and Spain, emperor-elect (*in Imperatorem electus*—Charles would not be crowned by Clement VII until February 1530, in Bologna); Cardinal Albrecht (archbishop of Mainz and Magdeburg, whose support was not particularly enthusiastic) and Matthew; Archbishop Richard of Trier and Herman of Cologne; Ferdinand, archduke of Austria; the brothers Georg and Heinrich of Saxony—the latter would become Lutheran and witness the destruction of Benno's shrine—as well as John [VII], bishop of Meissen; and, lastly, Enckevoirt, elect of Tortosa, datary "and our domestic *praelatum*," also a representative of the saint. The bull is subscribed by A. de Castello, W. de Enckevoirt, and T. Hezius.[113] (As we saw in the previous chapter, Adrian's bull for Antoninus, canonized on the same day as Benno, wasn't published until the next pope's reign.)

THE TRANSLATION AND LUTHERAN FURY

An elevation of the new saint's remains was planned for the year following the canonization. However, Martin Luther famously turned the 1524 ceremony of Benno's translation into an anti-Catholic, anti-Georg cause célèbre, even though Luther had earlier expressed little interest in Benno.[114] For instance, he seems to have taken no notice, or at least to have written

110. "Vix ille haec verba finierat, subito consternitur . . . ac magno cum dolore & gemitu moritur."

111. Fontanini, *Codex constitutionum*, 215–16: "alterum oculum amisit."

112. Ibid., 216. As for *alia miracula*, the bull mentions only "multos . . . e mortuis excitatos constat, multos variis morbis curatos."

113. Ibid., 218–9.

114. Volkmar, *Die Heiligenerhebung*, 77–8.

nothing against, Emser's *vita* of Benno, in print from 1512. Some modern writers claim that Luther condemned Benno's canonization.[115] In fact, his wrath was aimed at the translation a year later. His attack on Benno, Georg, and Emser came as the culmination of about five years of increasing animus between Luther and the duke, who, as noted above, had by degrees become a harsh critic of Luther, eventually—according to Volkmar—turning into Luther's long-time and "most dangerous adversary," or as C. Scott Dixon puts it, "Luther's arch-nemesis."[116] Antipathy between theologian and theologically inclined duke accelerated after the 1519 Leipzig debate. Even so, until Benno's 1524 translation, and despite the fact that Benno's cause had been for many years completely identified with Georg, Luther himself admitted that he'd written nothing specifically aimed at the saint.[117]

In March 1524 announcements of the forthcoming ceremony, along with copies of the canonization bull, went out to neighboring princes and cities—including Wittenberg—setting the date for June 16. Georg wrote to his cousin Friedrich on March 21, asking him to protect the posted public notices from destruction, which, he claimed, unfortunately often happened.[118] (In Leipzig the bull *Exsurge* had been pelted with dirt and torn down, the sort of thing Georg wished to avoid; and at Wittenberg there was the well-known theatrical burning of the document by Luther and some students, with a mock procession.)[119] Finally, Luther spoke out against Benno. After facetiously remarking on the "ridiculous note" announcing the forthcoming translation in a letter to Friedrich's secretary Spalatin (April 4, 1524), in May he preached three public sermons against the Benno cult, and in early June published his first comments on the translation, a pamphlet entitled "Against the New Idol and Old Devil to be Raised in Meissen," turning Benno's translation into a highly visible Reformation controversy.[120] Luther's polemic evoked a quick response: on June 14 (two days

115. For one among many instances, Heribert Smolinsky, "Albertinisches Sachsen," in *Die Territorien des Reichs im Zeitalter der Reformation und Konfessionalisierung*, 2 (Munich: Aschendorff, 1990), 15: "Luther schrieb gegen die Kanonisation 'Wider den neuyen Abgott.'"

116. For the following, Volkmar, *Die Heiligenerhebung*, 162–63 (Georg was the "ältesten und gefährlichsten seiner Gegner"); C. Scott Dixon, *The Reformation in Germany* (Oxford: Blackwell Publishers, 2002), 119.

117. Volkmar, *Die Heiligenerhebung*, 165 n. 634: "[D]enn ich bis her nichts sonderlichs widder der heyligen ehre geschrieben habe," quoting from Luther's "Against the New Idol."

118. Gess, *Akten und Briefe*, 620–21, #621: "wie ytzt layder gewonlich geschiet."

119. Pastor, *History of the Popes*, 7:408–15.

120. Volkmar, *Die Heiligenerhebung*, 165: "[D]ie erste Schrift Luthers" against the ceremony;

before the ceremony) a Meissen cathedral preacher lauded the planned ceremony and condemned Luther's pamphlet "Against the New Idol."[121] Printers were busy, eager as usual to cash in whether their customers were pro-Lutheran or not. On April 7, 1524, the Leipzig city council petitioned duke Georg on behalf of the printers to remove restrictions: "[T]hey are not allowed to print or sell anything new that is made in Wittenberg or elsewhere. For that which one would gladly sell and for which there is demand, they are not allowed . . . to sell. But what they have in overabundance [Catholic works] . . . cannot even be given away."[122] (In fact, thanks to Luther Wittenberg rose "to the front rank of German publishing centres," overshadowing the once-dominant printing industry of Leipzig.)[123] Luther's ambiguous attitude toward the Virgin Mary and saints' cults is well known. Though he condemned excessive devotion to relics and shrines, he understood that for many people saints were useful models of holiness and sources of physical and spiritual comfort. Ironically, after his death, Luther himself generated revered "relics."[124] Even when he did criticize saint-veneration, at first Luther's approach was rather mild. For instance, in his 1520 "Address to the Christian Nobility" he blasted pilgrimages to Wilsnack, Sternberg, Trier, the Grimmenthal, "and now [the Virgin of] Regensburg, and a goodly number of others." But as for saints, he specified only "St. Antonino of Florence and certain others [who] must now be made saints and canonized . . . so that their holiness . . . may be used to bring fame and money."[125] So far, although Antoninus's and Benno's processes were more or less at the same stage in Rome, and though as noted above originally Georg supported both candidates for sainthood, in his "Address" Luther did not mention Benno.[126]

On the appointed date the June ceremony, attended by many notables

109–10: "[W]urde die Heiligenerhebung Bennos von Meissen im Frühjahr 1524 selbst zum Thema der Reformation." Gess, *Akten und Briefe*, 621 n. 2, for excerpts from Luther's letter to Spalatin.

121. Volkmar, *Die Heiligenerhebung*, 111, 161.

122. Mark U. Edwards, Jr., "Statistics on Sixteenth-Century Printing," in *The Process of Change in Early Modern Europe*, ed. Philip N. Bebb and Sherrin Marshall (Athens: Ohio University Press, 1988), 149–63 at 160, citing Gess, *Akten und Briefe*, I:641.

123. Pettegree, *Reformation and the Culture of Persuasion*, 135.

124. R. C. Scribner, "Incombustible Luther," *Past and Present* 110 (1986): 38–68.

125. Martin Luther, "To the Christian Nobility of the German Nation," in *Luther's Works*, vol. 44, ed. J. Atkinson (Philadelphia: Fortress Press, 1966), 123–217, at 185, 187.

126. Volkmar, *Die Heiligenerhebung*, 97–99, 108. Two years later, during the summer of 1522, Luther wrote a pamphlet as a contribution to a debate on the cult of saints arranged by the Erfurt authorities (in which Luther was not personally involved): Bagchi, *Luther's Earliest Opponents*, 213 n. 100.

but boycotted by representatives of electoral Saxony, went ahead without a hitch—perhaps the guards at strategic sites at the cathedral and procession route to the Augustinian church of St. Afra and back into the cathedral helped to maintain decorum. At any rate, the bishop's bones, excavated with golden shovels, were put into a glass reliquary on a cloth of gold and exhibited on the cathedral's high altar, pending relocation into a new marble tomb. Many of the Albertine Saxon elite were present, including Georg and his family, as well as many clergy, but not the archbishop of Magdeburg/Mainz, whose presence the cathedral canons had anticipated. In fact Albrecht remained in Mainz, sending only a single representative to Meissen. One interesting guest was the abbot of Goslar, who is denoted by Volkmar the only "foreign" person there, representing Benno's "Heimatstift," embodying the Goslar tradition discussed by Collins.[127] This wasn't an affair of the nobility only: there was dancing, soup, bread, and beer for everyone, including the poor.[128]

Meanwhile, even as "Against the New Idol" was being reissued, Emser, reopening the pamphlet wars, published a reply to Luther: "Answer to the Blasphemous Book against the Bishop of Meissen and the Elevation of Saints." A few other writers produced anti-Luther/pro-Benno tracts, such as Alveldt's "Against the Wittenberg Idol Martin Luther" and Bachmann's more ferociously titled "Against the Wild Clawing Boar Luther," which mimics the phrase "wild boar from the forest" in Leo's bull *Exsurge* of June 1520. But all such efforts, including Emser's, were outweighed by Luther's, whose "Against the New Idol" was reprinted ten times in 1524. By the summer and fall of that year the canonization and subsequent Meissen ceremony of June, featured in pamphlets pro and contra published in Wittenberg, Erfurt, Leipzig, Dresden, Strassburg, and Speyer, had become a subject of conversation and controversy throughout Saxony and beyond. Writing from Vienna to papal secretary Sadoleto (d. 1547) in August of 1524, legate Lorenzo Campeggio (d. 1539) mentioned Lutheran zeal against Benno's cult—"molto studio in contrario."[129] Emser, not content to issue anti-Luther pamphlets, took a page from Luther's own techniques and composed a song on Bishop Benno that not only praised the saint, but contrasted him with Luther:[130]

127. See notes 1, 2, of this chapter.

128. Volkmar, *Die Heiligenerhebung,* 111–13 and n. 430.

129. Ibid., 157–59.

130. Rebecca W. Oettinger, *Music as Propaganda in the German Reformation* (Aldershot: Ashgate,

Oh Benno, you most holy man
God has worked many wonders through
you for many people on this earth
You have interceded with Him . . .
. . .
Oh Luther, you most evil man,
what has Bishop Benno done to you
that you enjoy desecrating him so,
more than all the others?

As expected, another song—from a Luther partisan—soon appeared, against Emser:[131]

Martin has not fallen silent,
in fact, far from it!
He has not despaired of victory;
you've got to do better than that!

Goat [Emser], desist with your bleating
along with your insolence.
I advise you to be silent;
arrogance rarely does any good.

Opposition to Benno's translation was not merely literary and musical; within a month or two it was parodied in the well-known Buchholz procession described at the start of this chapter. The procession gives us a rare glimpse of grassroots attitudes.[132] Scribner draws our attention to two points, placing the parody in both more general and more specific contexts. First of all, raucous rituals of apparent blasphemy were hardly unusual, even in the Middle Ages. During the sixteenth century, he traces eleven such incidents (apart from Buchholz) between 1520 and 1524 alone. In the year prior to the anti-Benno demonstration, for instance, in Berne "a mock procession was held with an indulgence accompanied by satirical singing." Some instances of ritual degradation including iconoclasm were far more blatant, involving smearing saints' images with dung or decapitating their statues, and in a case from 1525 Saint Peter was "first hung upside down, and then disemboweled." In Reformation Germany, then, the Buchholz parade would not have

2001), 213–14; her summation of the pamphlet warfare and translation of 1524 is useful, 69ff., though with a questionable interpretation of the July 5/10, 1520, letter of Leo X to Georg on 74.

131. Ibid., 310–11, "Martinus ist nit gschwigen" (1524–27).

132. "Einen seltenen Einblick," Volkmar, *Die Heiligenerhebung*, 172.

been an isolated incident, although most inversion events occurred at carnival time—in this Buchholz was an exception.[133] In the second place, Scribner reminds us that the ex-Franciscan preacher who wrote up an account of the procession, Myconius, went to a local official because he was worried that evangelical preaching itself might be blamed for the unseemly parody. Consequently the official broke up the proceedings.[134] Moreover, the printed pamphlet claiming to reproduce Myconius's account didn't mention this appeal to the Saxon official, an example of how embellishment or suppression by printers of this era of religious propagandizing intervened, to a greater or lesser extent, between event and published report.[135]

Benno's actual relics nearly ended up as the Buchholz revelers' theatrics had described. Though attracting pilgrims through the early 1530s, his remains were sequestered at Stolpen and then Wurzen by prescient canons before a mob crowded into the cathedral to raze the shrine.[136] Duke Georg's death (April 1539) and the succession of his anti-Catholic brother Heinrich sparked this invasion. By 1572, when nearly all of Saxony was Lutheran, various Catholic German nobles as well as the archbishop of Prague coveted Benno's relics. The bidding war, overseen by Meissen's last bishop, Johann von Haugwitz (d. 1581), was won in 1576 by Bavaria's Duke Albrecht, whose agents spirited them away. (Both Ditchfield and Smith look upon this as marking the post-Reformation revival of the cult of saints rather than Diego's canonization and the founding of the Congregation of Rites in 1588.)[137] Once across the Bavarian border, a procession formed and the remains were carried triumphantly into the Wittelsbach chapel. Thus the dead, like the living who exercised the "right of emigrating" in the aftermath of the 1555 Peace of Augsburg, moved across confessional (and therefore geopolitical) boundaries. Bavaria's next duke, Wilhelm, moved the relics into Munich's Frauenkirche in 1580. Here the dead bishop (named Munich's patron saint) was honored with a redecorated shrine and huge "Benno Arch." The arch (removed in 1858) and a new Wittelsbach mausoleum be-

133. Scribner, *Popular Culture,* 73, 115, and chs. 4 ("Reformation, Carnival and the World Turned Upside-Down") and 5 ("Ritual and Reformation"), passim.

134. Myconius fled his Annaberg convent in early 1524 and became Buchholz's preacher on July 2, Volkmar, *Die Heiligenerhebung,* 174.

135. Scribner, *Popular Culture,* 74–75 and n. 15; 82 and n. 42.

136. See for the following, Chipps Smith, "Salvaging Saints," passim.

137. Ditchfield, "Thinking with Saints," 573–74; Chipps Smith, personal communication.

came, as Soergel writes, "a kind of dynastic showcase," for which Benno became a "sanctifying agent. " Through the seventeenth century the cult was boosted in and around Munich in other ways, for example, the provision of a new silver, bejeweled reliquary, a Benno confraternity, and the printing of miracle books (a straightforward listing of the saint's wonders) starting around 1600, and the first of several pilgrimage books (more expansive and apologetic than miracle books) from about 1602.[138] These efforts were moderately successful: though Benno's remained essentially a local (though in theory, as with other canonized saints, a universal) cult, some 546 miracles were recorded at the shrine by about 1700.[139]

Why was Benno canonized? One reason, obviously, was Duke Georg's being so determined a champion of the long-dead bishop, a natural inclination to honor the saintly hero of an important ducal city: Benno's canonization would have raised Meissen's prestige, just as Friedrich's collection of relics honored and periodically enriched Wittenberg. Georg's mother Zedena (Sidonia) may have played a significant role in encouraging her son's devotion to Benno—most members of the family had personally invoked the dead bishop at one time or another.[140] There is also the possibility that Georg desired a regional patron saint, a spiritual protector for his Saxon territories. Finally, Benno was enlisted in the battle against the heretics: Hussites and then, as the Reformation began to coalesce, Luther and his followers. Indeed, in the aftermath of the Council of Trent, Georg's work was remembered as an anticipation of the Counter-Reformation.[141] After reviewing possible motives, however, Volkmar concluded that perhaps Georg's personal and religious leanings and the desire for dynastic protection—from the time of Friedrich the Valiant (d. 1428) Wettins had been buried at Benno's tomb[142]—make better sense as a primary motive rather than Georg's desiring a spiritual patron for the region. Volkmar raises and

138. Philip M. Soergel, *Wondrous in His Saints: Counter-Reformation Propaganda in Bavaria* (Berkeley: University of California Press, 1993), 185 n. 51, 186, and 187 n. 53.

139. Ibid., 181–91; cf. also Soergel's "The Image of Saints in the Bavarian Counter Reformation," *Historian* 53, no. 2 (1991): 223–40, esp. 229–31.

140. Volkmar, *Die Heiligenerhebung*, 153.

141. "Vorwegnahme," ibid., 84.

142. Ibid., 90; see also 143–48; Jeffrey Chipps Smith notes that Georg built his own adjoining private chapel by the existing Fürstenkapelle in the cathedral in 1521–24 (personal communication).

then discounts another possibility, that Georg was competing with his cousin Friedrich. At first, as we've seen, the two worked together in promoting Benno, though Hallman seems to overstate the case in writing that Benno's canonization was a "project dear to the prince-elector's heart."[143] Again, there would have been little financial incentive for either in promoting the canonization, which was—as usual—a costly venture (though felt more by Meissen canons than the duke).[144] It's also likely that, in addition to personal and familial concerns, Georg's interest in Benno can be seen as an aspect of the theologically trained duke's push to reform the Church in his territories (and he sent a proctor to the Fifth Lateran Council, a further indication of his inclinations). Benno was cast in the role of reforming bishop in Emser's *vita* that the duke commissioned, differentiating it from the monkish 1460 *vita*. Perhaps, if the pope approved of Emser's Benno as an "activist" saint, Georg could interpret this, use it, in effect, as papal approval of his own reformist program. As for Benno's being promoted as a "Counter-Reformation saint," we've seen that the active canonization process began a few decades prior to Luther's Theses, and, as noted, even after that famous Wittenberg challenge to the Church and papal authority Luther paid little attention to Georg's attempts to canonize Benno. It was only after Georg and Luther had parted ways from 1519 that Benno's translation of 1524 (not his 1523 canonization) came into the crosshairs of Luther's polemic.[145] As the Reformation spread, Benno did come to be thought of as a champion of the old ("true") faith.

Adrian's one-time pupil Charles V also was essential to the eventual success of Benno's cause, seconded by his brother Ferdinand of Austria, along with various German nobles and ecclesiastics. Charles would no doubt have appreciated the utility, and the irony, of canonizing someone from Luther's own homeland. In particular, after the Diet of Worms and Luther's coming under imperial ban (as well as papal condemnation), Charles may well have thought of Benno as a special champion against Luther, a proper "anti-Reformation" saint. (As we've seen, Elector Joachim of Brandenburg may also have taken this approach as early as 1519.) Just as Saint Leopold would strengthen Austria as a bulwark against the heretics and Turks, Benno

143. Barbara McClung Hallman, "Practical Aspects of Roman Diplomacy in Germany, 1517–1541," *Journal of Medieval and Renaissance Studies* 10, no. 2 (Fall 1980): 193–206, at 195.

144. Volkmar, *Die Heiligenerhebung*, 87 n. 325.

145. Ibid., 152–56.

came to be envisioned as the iconic anti-Lutheran hero, particularly in Bavaria by the end of the sixteenth century. In addition, about the time of the canonization, during the spring of 1523 Adrian began slowly moving toward an alliance with Charles against yet another traditional enemy, the French, which may have made the pope more open to imperial requests. Even though Charles was a powerful patron of the dead bishop, it was also necessary to have help on the inside. From 1519, Georg had at his disposal the services of Enckevoirt who, from 1522—and this was a crucial point—became a close adviser to his friend and compatriot Adrian VI, who called him "my old and special friend" in a brief of February 18, 1522.[146] Volkmar, in fact, claims that Enckevoirt was the most important promoter of Benno's cause in Rome.[147] Even if he made access to the secluded pope very difficult and was himself painfully slow, and even if, as an unfriendly observer (Giovanni Maria della Porta, envoy from Urbino) claimed in September 1522, he gave the pope "much evil advice," as the man closest to the pope and representative of emperor Charles V, he was Georg's best chance for success.[148] It was widely assumed—probably with justification—that Enckevoirt and a few other favorites such as von Heeze had "great power" over Adrian.[149]

Enckevoirt's efforts on behalf of Benno, building on the work of other lobbyists such as Hennig and Gertewitz in Rome, backing by emperor Charles V, once the pope's pupil, and efforts from Saxony by Georg and his publicist Jerome Emser succeeded in impressing upon Adrian and the college of cardinals the desirability of the canonization precisely at a time when a pro-imperial, anti-Lutheran stance seemed prudent. Finally, grassroots support was also instrumental in fostering Benno's cult, manifested in pilgrimages to his grave and posthumous miracles, without which no one could be canonized. In the consistorial diaries of Adrian's reign the encouragement of Charles and other German princes appears alongside recognition of his miraculous powers.[150] The controversy between Catholics and

146. "Amicus meus antiquus et precipuus," Pastor, *History of the Popes,* 9:80 n. 2.

147. Volkmar, *Die Heiligenerhebung,* 79: He was "der wichtigste Promotor der Heiligsprechung Bennos innerhalb der Kurie."

148. Pastor, *History of the Popes,* 9:82 n. 5.

149. Chaunu, *Charles Quint,* 657. Pastor, *History of the Popes,* 9:122 and see n. 3, where the poor pope ("il povero papa") was said to be at Enckevoirt's mercy, in contrast to the views of others claiming that "questo Papa vuol vedere et intendere ogni cosa et non da auctorità a persona," 9:123 n. 1, a report from Florentine envoys.

150. "Benno episcopus Misnensis, ad preces Caroli imperatoris electi et aliorum principum

Luther highlighted by Benno's sainthood and, particularly, his translation is of some significance, considering the subsequent sixty-five-year gap in canonizations (1523–88) that some attribute to a "loss of papal nerve." This opinion, and other characteristics of saint-making between 1482 and 1523, will be considered and summed up in our final chapter.

Germanorum, expositis multis miraculis per eum factis, inter sanctos relatus est," Mercati, *Diarii di Consistori*, 97.

Conclusion

Saints were made in several interacting contexts in addition to the political in the broadest sense: the faithful had an interest in seeing the object of their devotion raised to the highest celestial level, for pious and personal reasons (as sources of thaumaturgic power, protection, and well-being as spiritual patrons, and as a guides to the next life); rival cities and towns, and the nobility mundane and ecclesiastical, benefited from the added prestige, dynastic publicity, spiritual patronage, and probably increased income that came with "possessing" a saint in their midst; the Church expressed its regulatory authority through the various canonization processes. Yet the question remains: why were certain individuals chosen rather than others? "Holy" or extremely pious individuals might be found in the smallest hamlet in a rural English parish, in the marketplace of a busy Italian commercial center, or in a tiny chapel in a Burgundian castle. As a theologian working on Bonaventure's process wrote, "Not everyone holy is worthy of canonization."[1] If that's the case, what made them worthy; in short, who made the cut, and why them? Our five individuals were successful because, having been brought to curial attention by their supporters (which presupposes a network already set up behind the push), they represented advantages to particular patrons as well as individual popes at specific points in time. In some instances the political motivation was blatant: recall the com-

1. Giambattista de'Giudici, *De canonizatione B. Bonaventurae,* Baluze, *Misc,* IV, 475.

petition between European powers to get "their" saint promoted in Francis's case, where Spain, England, and Portugal attempted to derail the French favorite; in other cases political developments played a less important role or were coincidental rather than causal.

Of our five examples, Bonaventura's is the least "political" in the traditional sense, though his posthumous career certainly was affected by ideological conflicts within his order. He eventually reached sainthood primarily because of Sixtus IV's interest in supporting an admired fellow-Franciscan who also represented, for the pope, the faction within the order that he himself favored; Sixtus vigorously cut the Gordian knot of dysfunctional infighting that had delayed sainthood for centuries. As we've seen, however, this did little to solve the Franciscans' problems. In the case of Leopold politics and heresy were more significant: imperial assistance against the Turks and Bohemian Hussites convinced Paul II, Sixtus IV, and Innocent VIII that Friedrich's goodwill was essential. During the emperor's Roman pilgrimage Paul II at the conclusion of a papal Mass prayed "that the Lord God may grant him victory over the heretical Bohemians, the Turks, and the other enemies of the Christian name."[2] During this visit, although the emperor failed to obtain approval of his succession to Hungary and Bohemia, or the transfer of Bohemia's electoral vote to Austria, he succeeded in having the pope agree in principle to further Leopold's process. On the other hand, Sixtus IV's curia was well aware of the emperor's political motives in striving for a protector-saint—who in addition was a distant relative—whose success would score prestige points against Friedrich's Hungarian rival Covinus. In several supplications, it was claimed that St. Leopold would protect and pacify Austria *and* bring honor and dignity to Friedrich and his line. Maximilian, dressing up as Austrian archduke at the translation, was merely reinforcing this dynastic linkage. Leopold also provides an excellent illustration of the intertwining of ecclesiastical and secular politics, spectacularly provided in Friedrich's and Sixtus's battle over the renegade Zamometič, which nearly wrecked Leopold's chances. Apart from that issue, with the pope "scorning" the emperor, we had an example of how a crisis within the curia itself also affected Leopold's cause: the 1482 conspiracy, with Barbo claiming that the cardinals could "think of nothing else"; therefore, as he bluntly told List, nothing could be done about the canoniza-

2. Pastor, *History of the Popes*, 4:165.

tion. In Leopold's process, sainthood and politics were very closely related.

Politics as statecraft played an equally obvious role in Francis of Paola's canonization; it was clearly linked to papal interest in cultivating good relations with ultramontane powers, this time France, even though at times popes and kings strongly disagreed on particular issues. But from the start, with Sixtus IV sending the reluctant hermit into France at Louis XI's request, a rather extravagant gift of a "living saint," to the end, with Leo X's canonization of the hermit-founder—an act encouraged by King Francis I, his wife, and his mother—Francis of Paola was an unofficial conduit for Franco-papal relations. The political aspects of the story are seen most clearly in Sixtus IV's letters to Louis XI and Francis; and, as noted, even after Louis's death, the papal curia and French court kept our Calabrian in France, where he was buried. Probably few people have combined so many careers: hermit, healer, founder of an order, royal adviser, semi-clandestine papal agent, and saint. Just as the elite circle of French royals pushed for Francis's sainthood, the equally exclusive and limited patrons of Antoninus of Florence included a Medici archbishop-cardinal (later pope), as well as a second Medici pope. Here the political elements are as visible as in Francis's canonization, though restricted to a smaller geopolitical circle—or rather axis, between Florence and Rome—than Francis's. Leo X's dynastic interests, which necessarily included the maintenance of family rule in Florence, lay behind Antoninus's elevation, which—though culminating under Adrian VI—was completed with the bull's publication by the other Medici, Clement VII, on his coronation day. A spur to Medici interest was the continuing viability of Florentine *piagnoni,* who even after the siege of Florence (1527–30) and evolution of the family into Tuscan dukes from 1532 continued to plague the ruling elite through the sixteenth century. The spectacularly famous wedding ceremonies of 1589 that recruited Antoninus as both powerful patron and anti-*piagnoni* "friend" of the Medici are evidence of this; the saint was reconstructed, literally if we recall the dressing of his corpse, as a Medici-supporting archbishop. Archduke Maximilian's participation in Leopold's translation had performed the same function. Finally, although Antoninus's life and miracles lay on the margins of living memory—some of the witnesses were in their seventies and eighties, and at least one claimed to be ninety—Benno, for all who testified about him, was a Saxon tradition, a long-dead prelate whose *fama,* as in Bonaventura's and Leopold's cases, was exploited centuries after his burial. What Vauchez wrote about Sebald of Nuremberg was in some ways true of Benno: he was "an obscure person who had lived in the eleventh century and who would, at other times, scarcely have aspired to such an honour [canonization by Martin V in 1429]."[3] Benno's canonization served many interests. He increased the prestige of his convent–burial place and its prior and canons. It also served well Duke Georg, perhaps the prime force behind the process; the archduchy of Austria; the emperors Friedrich and Maximilian; as well as the popes seeking assistance against heretics and Turks. With Benno we drift into the complex world of Luther, Dukes Friedrich and Georg, Leo X, and many other Reformation figures. Though at first religious changes didn't affect Benno's process, just a year after the canonization his translation evoked a pointed response from Luther and a burlesque parody by carnival-dressed young men and miners. Although geopolitical interests of the usual sort—popes and emperors against heretics and Turks—and portentous religious developments played important roles in Benno's sainthood, outside of Saxony (and later Bavaria) politics with a capital "P" were less evident in his canonization than with Leopold and Francis.

Ties between saints and patrons are also suggested in the rosters of supporters in canonization bulls. At various times many suppliants and lobbyists made an appearance in all of our cases; only those highlighted in the bulls are noted here (curialists and cardinals assigned to the saint are also excluded). For Bonaventura, compared with the other four, the bull sets out with great specificity, and even hierarchically arranges, the major supporters. First are emperor and kings (Friedrich, Louis XI, Ferrante, and Corvinus); then nobles and dukes (Alfonso of Calabria, John Mocenigo of Venice, Milan's Giovanni Visconti, John de Bourbon), followed by cities (Florence, Siena, Lyons, Perugia) and the saint's hometown, Bagnoregio; finally, Franciscan leaders and representatives.[4] In addition, the pope makes his personal interest unmistakably clear. This register of boosters is unrivaled by the other four in length and organization. When we turn to Leopold's canonization bull—the shortest in length of the five—the difference in patronage is striking: the slim roster of prime supporters included Friedrich and "princes and prelates of Germany."[5] The extent of Francis of Paola's sup-

3. Vauchez, *Sainthood*, 83–84.

4. Fontanini, *Corpus Constitutionem*, 189–94.

5. Ibid., 195–99.

pliants is nearly as skimpy as Leopold's: the French royals Francis I, his wife Claudia and mother Louise (recall her half-serious claim to have canonized the saint herself), along with the protector of the Minims.[6] Recognition of Antoninus's main supporters, as in Leopold's and Francis's bulls, is relatively brief and centers principally on Florence. The group includes Emperor Maximilian, "many princes and prelates," the defunct Adrian VI and the pope himself (Clement VII) as cardinal and archbishop of Florence, the Dominicans' protector, Florence's *gonfaloniere,* and the archdeacon and chapter of Florence cathedral.[7] Our final example, Benno, seems to have drawn many notables as patrons, second only to Bonaventura in numbers.[8] However, when we examine who these primary supporters were, we find a far greater localization than with Bonaventure. While the Franciscan drew monarchs from Germany, France, Sicily, and Hungary, and nobles and cities from Italy and France, Benno's circle is almost exclusively "German": the emperor-elect Charles; Cardinals Albrecht von Brandenburg and Matthias von Gurk; Archbishops Richard of Trier and Hermann of Cologne; Ferdinand, duke of Austria; Georg, duke of Saxony and his brother Heinrich; the bishop of Meissen and Adrian's man Enckevoirt, along with Klosterneuburg convent. As with Leopold, virtually no non-German "outsiders" are noted in the bull as outstanding suppliants. It is unwise to draw conclusions from so few documents, which, moreover, saw input at the drafting stage from varied sources: within the framework of "standard" phrasing, these sources included earlier bulls as well as suggestions from promoters, lawyer-advocates, papal secretaries, and popes, miracle-testimony from hearings, and *vitae* prepared by supporters.[9] However, it does appear that the more overtly "political" saints among our five (Leopold and Francis) had the shortest lists of VIP supporters, Bonaventure had the most, while Antoninus and Benno fell somewhere between the two extremes, with mainly Florentine and Saxon "names." Perhaps many European leaders were less willing to support clearly political canonizations that favored imperial and French interests. England doesn't show up in any of the bulls.

Along with differing emphases on particular groups of supporters, each

6. Ibid., 200–211.

7. Ibid., 220–32.

8. Ibid., 212–19.

9. For instance, some of Hennig's short biography found its way into Benno's bull, Volkmar, *Die Heiligenerhebung,* 100; for a discussion of the different sections of canonization bulls, see Krafft, *Papsturkunde und Heiligsprechung,* 1040ff.

bull presented varying perspectives on the saints' miracles, selected by supporters with specific representations as a goal. Naturally, in each case there was praise of the subject's holy life and virtues, emphasizing theological learning in one, activities as founder in another, and so on. More flexibility is seen in the lists of supernatural wonders. For Bonaventure the most striking aspect compared with the other four is the fact that miracles are mentioned almost in passing and in a very general sense. There is nothing whatsoever about miracles performed in life—even the leaping eucharistic particle—and only vague phrases, for example, referring to his "merits and miracles" and "many great miracles after his death," without further explanation or examples. As noted in chapter 2, lack of miracles was one of many complications in his process. It's tempting to suspect that Bonaventura's healthy list of supporters encouraged by Sixtus IV—unrivalled by the other four—was an attempt to deflect attention from his anemic thaumaturgy. When we turn to Leopold, on the other hand, after a nod to Thomistic categories of miracle, Innocent VIII's bull spends several lines on miraculous cures of fever, gout, the lame, swellings, the deaf, blind, and mute, raisings from death, and liberations from captivity, though without providing specific instances or details. However, this is followed by mention of countless memorials of miracles at the tomb, tablets and votive images, copious candles, the ill lying about awaiting cures, and the great influx of pilgrims to Klosterneuburg. Phrases such as "incredible to say," and "it would be difficult to relate how many" emphasize the magnitude of shrine-side activity continuing "even to the present day." The focus moves from Leopold's limited circle of patrons to his continuing miraculous cult that justified his canonization. It's even more the case in our other canonization heavily influenced by politics, Francis of Paola's, that a paucity of active patrons (though admittedly the few listed in the bull were royalty) was balanced by a plethora of miracles. Here, perhaps, the bishop of St. Malo's reluctance to accept his miracles may have influenced the composition of the most unusual of all five bulls in this respect. Briçonnet's doubts were well known, voiced to his friends only a month or so before the canonization. In chapter 4 we saw the good bishop remarking that he'd like the process put off for eighty or one hundred years because Francis's miracles were, in his eyes, hardly up to standard for would-be saints. Perhaps that's why Francis's supporters presented so many miracles for inclusion in the bull, which, it turns out, constituted the longest list among the five. The extensive treatment begins with Francis's ability to walk on brambles, hold red-hot objects, eject demons, and cure the sick of all kinds as well as resuscitate the dead. These general categories are followed by the longest and most detailed report of a miracle to be found in any of the bulls. The nobleman Jacobus de Tarsia suffered an apparently incurable abscess that rendered him unable to walk. The holy man sent one of his brethren to pick some herbs—we're even given its name, *Unguae cavalla,* horsefoot—that Francis used to bandage up the swelling with some powders he kept in his cell. After prayer and a blessing, en route home the nobleman felt improved, telling his wife, "It seems that I'm cured, since I don't sense the sharp pain or smell the fetid odor anymore." A little while later, to test his cure he dismounted and began walking without hindrance. All of this, dialogue included, is set out in the papal bull, whose formalism seems somewhat distorted by details about stinking ulcers. In fact, these words were taken from a miracle reported in an *inquisitio* of 1512.[10] This extended review is followed by shorter, but detailed, notices of twelve more *in vita* miracles, one posthumous wonder, and yet one more in-life miracle. The single incident attributed to Francis after his death, mentioned in chapter 4, involved a young man who nearly lost his legs in a runaway cannon-carriage accident. The dead Francis miraculously arrived to seize the thick carriage-rope and bring the rumbling caisson with its twenty oxen to a halt. Again, the bull paraphrases an incident recorded in a Cozenza inquisition of 1518.[11] In stark contrast, in Antoninus's bull there's only a short, generic list of types of cure ("diverse kinds of illness," resuscitations, the healing of lepers, the lame, deaf, mute, crippled, and blind) both before and after death, without further discussion. Apart from recalling the few miracles performed by the archbishop as he lay in state in San Marco convent, his thaumaturgy was not a noteworthy aspect. On the other hand, his pastoral leadership (through his sermons, writings, etc.) is stressed, as are the details and legitimacy of the processes themselves that led to his canonization, making this the longest of the five bulls; it's as if this particular emphasis on procedural thoroughness was a hook from which to hang the archbishop's sainthood. When it comes to our final example, Benno, canonized at the same time as Antoninus, we find a relatively short list of miracles. A half-dozen or so in-life wonders are noted, including several showing

10. *PC,* 12–17.
11. *PC,* 228–29.

his powers over nature, his bilocation, visionary appearances, and a few cases of revenge against enemies. However, "many other miracles"—raisings from the dead and various cures—are mentioned without further description. Presumably these included posthumous wonders as well. In looking at the differences in treatment of miracles, once again it seems that the most "political" of the five, Leopold and Francis, were deliberately surrounded with the greatest aura of the miraculous, at least in papal bulls. Was this a compensatory mechanism to mask the pragmatic nature of their sainthood, did it reflect greater reputations for thaumaturgy than the others, or was it mere coincidence? These few impressionistic or subjective readings can only provide suggestions—and more questions.

We're on more certain ground with another element in the canonizations: although external and curial conditions were subject to change—sometimes almost overnight as with Leopold, Friedrich III, and Sixtus IV—one constant affecting all five saints was the need to pay for the processes and canonization ceremony itself. Expenses incurred in these ceremonies (for ornaments, fixtures, and fees to participants, including popes), averaged 2,000 to 3,000 ducats—in some cases even more.[12] By way of comparison a schoolmaster's salary might be 25 to 30 ducats, while in the later sixteenth century a yearly income of between 40 and 150 ducats provided a "reasonable" living standard (the secretaries to Venice's Council of Ten, for instance, earned 100 ducats a year).[13] The minimum income suitable to a cardinal was thought to be 4,000 to 6,000 annually.[14] As for saints, in one of the few cases of careful bookkeeping, in 1487 List produced a financial statement for his new prior James Paperl, showing that the bill for Leopold came to 6,651 ducats, which undoubtedly was only a partial accounting.[15] On the whole, little can be said with certainty about the overall cost of saint-making from start to finish. Ludwig states the case succinctly: "Given the extremely long time over which a canonization process played out, to obtain complete information on its cost is impossible."[16] As we've seen, some campaigns were waged for cen-

12. For a detailed price list (Francis of Paola's canonization ceremony) see de Grassis's account in Sposato, *Fonti*, 272–79; Vauchez, *Sainthood*, 64–67, for some medieval examples.

13. Partner, *Renaissance Rome*, 134; Fernand Braudel, *The Mediterranean*, 458.

14. Thomson, *Popes and Princes 1417–1517*, 70, 86; Partner, *Renaissance Rome*, 136–37.

15. Ludwig, "Der Kanonisationsprozess," Doc. #CVI, 89, June 2, 1487; see later in this chapter for financial aspects.

16. Ludwig, "Der Kanonisationsprozess," 179: "ein Ding der Unmöglichkeit."

turies; on the face of it, it's unlikely that a running total of expenses would be kept through such long stretches of time, noting all fees for local commissioners, notaries, scribes, couriers, proctors and curialists at Rome, auditors of the Rota, cardinals, and so on, all of whom were involved at various stages. (The same holds true for sources of funding behind the causes.) Consequently, there's little reason uncritically to accept questionable traditions, for example, that Friedrich contributed 15,000 ducats to Leopold's canonization or figures recounted by de Grassis, who, as we saw, mentioned 25,000 and 27,000 ducats (attributed to Masters of Ceremony Piccolomini and Burchard) as totals for Leopold and Bonaventure. On the other hand, such figures may well reflect actual expenses. Around 1586 the Spanish ambassador made a seven-page list of eighty-six separate items for Diego's proposed canonization (of 1588) that totaled 20,954 ducats; King Philip provided 20,000.[17] Vauchez suggests that from the mid-thirteenth century high costs deterred casual or unmerited canonization applications, and, as we've seen, early in the sixteenth de Grassis blatantly claimed the same. As de'Giudici put it, apropos Bonaventure, "These days everyone wants to canonize someone."[18] About the same time canonist Malvetius claimed that an infinitely expanding number of saints would dilute devotion.[19] Whether or not the costs were deliberately kept high to hinder applicants, to encourage the rarity—thus the impact—of canonizations, or to bolster curial bank accounts (or all three), it does seem that saints became more expensive from the reign of Sixtus IV, no stranger to avarice.[20] In any event, as noted in the Introduction, funding was a constant source of anxiety for supporters. If, indeed, sainthood became more expensive, this might help to explain why fewer candidates were raised to the altar during the sixteenth century, with its price rise and economic fluctuations. However, against this argument is the fact that the greatest economic challenges were seen not in the first but in the second half of that century, when saint-making resumed with Diego (1588) and Hyacinth (1594). Though beyond the purview of this book, it would

17. L. J. Andrew Villalon, "San Diego of Alcalá and the Politics of Saint-Making in Counter-Reformation Europe," *Catholic Historical Review* 83 (1997): 691–715, at 712–13. At 707 n. 44, Villalon refers to Diego's documents in Spain, noting that he failed to turn up a copy of the process in the ASV; the documents do exist, however, in the BAV next door.

18. De'Giudici, *De canonizatione B. Bonaventurae,* 483.

19. Malvetius, "Tractatus non Infestius de sanctorum canonizatione," fols. 97r–103v at 98v:2.

20. Krafft, *Papsturkunde,* 1013.

be interesting to plot expenses for all canonizations of the seventeenth and eighteenth centuries, when Tridentine sanctity flourished and (one assumes) financial record-keeping had improved.

Related perhaps to cost-cutting or more likely expediency, it was not unheard of to open simultaneous processes, as during the Council of Constance when John XXII was supplicated for Brynolf, Nikolaus, and Ingrid as well as Peter of Luxembourg, whose cause also came before the Council of Basel.[21] At Constance a commission was set up to investigate the first three, a situation not seen again in the fifteenth century, or, probably, before.[22] In this case, of course, the schism created unusual conditions and, in any event, conciliar canonization, though known in earlier centuries, was not the norm by this time; nothing came of the attempt. Yet multiple canonizations were proposed on other occasions. In 1465 it was suggested not only that the prelates of Gurk and Salzburg team up to share costs of their candidates' (Hemma, Vitalis, and Eberhard) processes, but it would be even better, a proctor suggested, if the curia agreed to canonize all three together.[23] As for our own saints, we've seen de Grassis raising the question whether to canonize Francis alone or with several others since, he averred, (unnamed) canonists claimed that such a thing was lawful.[24] In addition, we saw English, Spanish, and Portuguese ambassadors suddenly showing up with demands to join their "saints" to Francis's cause. Though, as suggested, probably intended only to clog up the bureaucratic works to counter the French candidate, the incident does reflect a belief in the possibility of group canonizations. This possibility was not taken up for Francis, but it did occur in 1523 with Antoninus and Benno, the first, evidently, in the history of the process.[25] The next instance of simultaneous sainthoods (five at once) took place in 1622. In fact, during the planning stage for the elevation of Isidore, Ignatius Loyola, Francis Xavier, Theresa of Avila, and Neri, particular mention was made of Adrian VI's dual ceremony: Gregory XV decided it would be best "to canonize the blessed ones together and on the

21. *AASS,* July I, 605–6.

22. Wetzstein, *Heilige vor Gericht,* 381.

23. Wetzstein, *Heilige vor Gericht,* 372: "sei es gunstiger . . . alle drei Kanonisationen gleichzeitig durchführen zu lassen."

24. Sposato, "Fonti, Testo," 5–6; "Fonti, Intro," 15.

25. Krafft, *Papsturkunde,* 1019: Adrian canonized both in 1523, "wobei erstmals eine gemeinsame Heiligsprechung stattfand."

same day" and asked the Congregation of Rites to look into this possibility. Subsequently the Congregation agreed, as long as there were separate orations for each "as was done when Adrian VI canonized Sts. Benno and Antoninus on the same day."[26] The dual canonization of Antoninus and Benno might be viewed as a matter of convenience and thrift especially given Adrian's reputation for running a no-frills curia—though the expenses would have been paid by the saints' supporters; perhaps the pope also was influenced by Duke Georg's push to associate his candidate with that of the Medici camp.[27]

Apart from the great expense involved, another factor that may have lowered the rate of saint-making as defined (therefore controlled) by canonical process during the fifteenth and sixteenth centuries was the phenomenon of increasingly popular alternatives to "official" saints, manifested particularly in cults and shrines of the Virgin and of Christ.[28] This well-documented shift encouraged new expressions of piety, some of which were less welcomed by the hierarchical, "official" Church than others and, indeed, occasionally were shut down. Saints continued to attract prayers and hopes, to be honored in liturgical and paraliturgical rituals; their tombs still drew offerings of money and votives, testimonials and *tabulae,* as they had done for more than a millennium. Yet, as exemplified by the record of income at one of the most famous shrines, Becket's at Canterbury, monetary offerings—and presumably the throngs of pilgrims who brought them—had declined to nearly nothing by the end of the Middle Ages. At the same time, shrines of the Virgin and the Holy Blood rose in popularity to the

26. "Canonizare supradictos beatos simul uno eodemque die"; Congregation's opinion: "melius esse illos canonizare simul uno, eodemque die . . . ut fuit factum ab Adriano VI que eodem die canonizavit S. Bennonem et S. Antoninum," ACCS, *Regestrum Servorum Dei,* vol. 1 (1592–1654), fol. 203, January 3, 1622.

27. Gess, *Akten und Briefe,* 107–8, #143.

28. Soergel, *Wondrous in His Saints,* esp. chaps. 1–3 (Wilsnack, Niklashausen, other sites); Charles Zika, "Hosts, Processions and Pilgrimages: Controlling the Sacred in Fifteenth-Century Germany," *Past and Present* 118 (Feb. 1988): 25–64; Diarmaid MacCulloch, *The Reformation* (New York: Viking, 2003), esp. 18–22; Miri Rubin, *Corpus Christi: The Eucharist in Late Medieval Culture* (Cambridge: Cambridge University Press, 1991); Caroline Walker Bynum, *Wonderful Blood: Theology and Practice in Late Medieval Northern Germany and Beyond* (Philadelphia: University of Pennsylvania Press, 2007), stresses the "anxieties" that produced fifteenth- and early-sixteenth-century pilgrimages to blood- and host-shrines, especially Wilsnack in the fifteenth century (about which there was much debate): "No modern historian doubts that the pilgrimage was a mass phenomenon," 43. For an overview of the period see John Van Engen, "Multiple Options: The World of the Fifteenth-Century Church," *Church History* 77 (2008): 257–84.

point where they became nuisances bedeviling local town councils as well as some ecclesiastical authorities and, eventually, were targets for reformation from within and outside the Catholic Church. As with rising prices attached to sainthood, perhaps newly established Marian and Christocentric cult sites, and concomitant processions, iconography, sermons, and liturgy celebrating them, resulted in diminished cultural as well as social interest in pushing for individual canonizations of the traditional type. After all, it was a lot quicker and cheaper to hang an image of the Virgin in a cherry tree, creating a cult-site (credited with some three hundred miracles during the 1450s) than to try for a lengthy, expensive canonization of a highly admired holy individual, with uncertain results.[29] On the other hand, the saint-making process revived during the seventeenth century alongside Marian and Christological devotion. They were not necessarily disjunctive forms of piety: in fact, out in the Neapolitan countryside Sallmann noted a "low Marian presence" among the patron saints elected by some 228 communities between 1630 and 1699.[30]

Another reason for a temporary slowdown between 1523 and 1588 is proffered by Peter Burke, who sees it as a result of "a failure of papal nerve and . . . a 'crisis of canonisations.'"[31] However, during this sixty-five-year period business was proceeding as usual, although no processes came to fruition—but long delays, as we've seen, were routine. For instance, supplications continued to come in and be and acted upon, with replies from popes and the formation of various committees, for Diego and Hyacinth in 1517, 1518, 1521,

29. Becket's offerings fell from a peak figure of over £1,000 in 1220 to about £36 in 1535; similar declines were witnessed at other English shrines such as Cuthbert's, from about £35 per year in the 1380s to £16 in the 1450s, and Cantilupe's, from £178 donated by pilgrims to the fabric fund in 1291 to less that £2 in 1387, Finucane, *Miracles and Pilgrims,* 181, 193, 199. The cherry tree was in Flanders: *De codicibus hagiographicus Iohannis Gielemans* (Brussels: 1895), 526–28; burning votive candles destroyed the tree in 1459, which was replaced with a chapel including an image of the Virgin and tree.

30. David Gentilcore, review essay, "Methods and Approaches in the Social History of the Counter-Reformation in Italy," *Social History* 17, no. 1 (Jan. 1992): 73–98, at 83 n. 30, for Sallmann reference.

31. Peter Burke, "How to be a Counter-Reformation Saint," in *The Historical Anthropology of Early Modern Italy* (Cambridge: Cambridge University Press, 1987), 48–62, at 49. Burke himself notes that although twenty-four saints were canonized in the seventeenth century, there was a gap in this activity of thirty years (1629–58); and though in the eighteenth century some twenty-nine saints were raised to the altar, there was a break of forty years in these processes after 1767. Were these discontinuities also due to a "loss of nerve"? No doubt Urban VIII's changes in the requirements introduced in the 1620s and 1630 affected the fates of some would-be saints.

1523, 1524, 1526, 1530, 1563, 1564, and 1567 (listing only some of the years in which activity was registered), resulting in their canonizations in 1588 and 1594. Peñafort's case came up in 1542 when Paul III accorded Aragon's Dominicans an office in his honor "as if he were canonized";[32] Xavier's process was active in 1583; Felix Cantalice's cause was strenuously but unsuccessfully pushed in 1587 by a pope whose nerve seldom failed him, Sixtus V. Perhaps emphasis shouldn't be placed on papal anxieties but on political, economic, and religious changes that forced popes and curia to attend to a multitude of other pressing issues: for example, because of "the great turbulence that [Pius V (1566–72)] now encountered within the Christian Republic . . . though he wished, he couldn't complete" Diego's canonization, given his difficulties with France, the heretics, the Turks, and "other problems."[33] Although the 1523–88 gap undoubtedly was related to the turbulence of the Reformation, with Luther's writings and sermons reaching ever-increasing numbers of clergy and the laity after 1517, in Benno's and Antoninus 's bulls there is no special recognition of threats from beyond the Alps, only the repetition of stock phrases found in many earlier (and later) canonization bulls about the blight of infidels and heretics. The concept of "failure of papal nerve" calls for further examination.

In tracing procedures followed in our five cases, we've found differences in detail, and in the pace and rhythm of each example, but overall the process itself changed little between the thirteenth and early sixteenth centuries. Continuity outweighed change, as each set of lawyers built upon previous canonizations. This continued even after the sixty-five-year gap: aspects of Pavini's work on Bonaventura's late-fifteenth-century case, for instance, were cited in Hyacinth's process, the last canonization of the sixteenth century.[34] Many other instances of relying on precedent could be found. Even so, the Reformation and new perspectives on the supernatural eventually brought some changes to post-Tridentine processes, in addition to those introduced by Urban VIII. For instance, now witnesses were routinely asked to distinguish "miracle" (supernatural event, immediately and through God) from "grace" (supernat-

32. "Ac si esset canonizatus," ASV Congr. Riti, processus 223, fols. 2v, 15v.

33. Pietro Galesino, *Sancti Didaci Complutensis canonizatio* (Rome, 1588), 64.

34. Severinus, *Sanctissimo D N Clementi VIII . . . Cracovien. canonizationis beati Iacinthi Poloni Ord Praed. relatio trium Rotae auditorum Seraphini Olivarii Razzalii, Laurentii Blanchetti & Francisci Peniae* (Rome: Ex typ. Nicolai Mutti, 1597), 29, on old chronicles being acceptable as evidence.

ural event, not immediate, through saints).[35] Changed times were also reflected in a requirement in Hyacinth's process that a saint-candidate must be a Catholic.[36] Witnesses as well as candidates were expected to demonstrate their orthodoxy in the Reformation's wake: in 1596 the second interrogatory in Peñafort's cause was whether they'd confessed to an "approved confessor" and had communion at Easter.[37] In 1612, during a hearing for Isidore (canonized in 1622) deponents were asked whether they'd confessed and received communion "this year," and whether they'd had to respond to any *inquisitio* or been involved in crime.[38] In another change effected after the sixteenth century and especially following Urban VIII's seventeenth-century implementation of new requirements, the candidate's "heroic virtue" was regularly examined. Weinstein and Bell locate the first "truly detailed and precedent-setting examination of heroic virtue" only in 1617 in Teresa of Avila's trial[39] Vauchez contests this, tracing the concept and phrase to the fourteenth century, though admitting that it "became common" only after the Renaissance or Counter-Reformation.[40] Whatever the case, this heroism does not seem to have played a significant role in our five examples, though Vauchez finds evidence of it in Bonaventure's process. As Ditchfield writes, perhaps historians of the early modern period have "placed too much emphasis on heroic virtue," and Gentilcore draws attention to Sallmann's contention that "witnesses [in the post-Tridentine era] continually cited miracles as proof of a saint's heroic virtue, rather than stemming from it, as theologians viewed the matter."[41] Another change from earlier norms reflects increasing anxiety about the discernment of spirits, living saints, and demonology, which shows up more often in definitions of what constitutes a valid miracle. Though suspicion that de-

35. A distinction requested of witnesses in John of Capistrano's process of 1665, ASV, Congr. Riti, processus 77, fols. 27r–v, and for an early eighteenth century example, see Vidal, "Miracles, Science, and Testimony in Post-Tridentine Saint-Making," 489–90.

36. In Severinus's list of fifteen requirements for canonization, the second (the first was an authentic *vita*) was that the candidate "be a Catholic"; the third was that none of the witnesses be heretics or blasphemers, 154.

37. ASV, Congr. Riti, processus 224, fol. 94v.

38. Ibid., 3192, fol. 7v.

39. Donald Weinstein and Rudolph M. Bell, *Saints and Society* (Chicago: University of Chicago Press, 1982), 142.

40. Vauchez, *Sainthood,* 519–20, saints Yves, Catherine of Siena, and Bonaventura.

41. Simon Ditchfield, review article, "Sanctity in Early Modern Italy," in *Journal of Ecclesiastical History* 47 (January 1996): 98–112, at 104, and Gentilcore, "Methods and Approaches," 84.

monic powers could work miracles was certainly present in earlier centuries, and for example Pavini's *Relatio* of 1482 for Bonaventure adverted to diabolical tricks, by the time that Hyacinth's *Relatio* was published in 1597, the second condition for a miracle clearly prescribed that it must come "from God, not from artifice or from diabolical illusion." If done by demons, magicians, or demoniacs through natural but hidden—occult—powers, as Aquinas averred, it wasn't a miracle but a deception or illusion. The same augmentation to Geoffrey di Trani's thirteenth-century definition of a miracle is found in Angelo Rocca's 1601 treatise on canonization.[42] Around 1595 Raymund Peñafort's procurator claimed that he worked miracles neither by artifice or the power of words, but through his merits; in 1609 procurators for Philip Neri echoed this standard line, with an important addition: Neri performed miracles not from artifice or the power of words, "nor from an illicit pact with any evil spirit."[43]

Finally, by the later medieval period and sixteenth century there seems to have been an attraction to the idea that some aspects of the process were not so tightly bound to judicial *ordines* as others. We saw Pavini claiming in 1482 that canonizations (though entailing aspects of *ius commune*) could be considered in some respects extrajudicial acts, since there were no "contending parties" per se; and in 1520 Carvajal made similar comments in his defense of Antoninus. The manner in which canon and civil law applied to canonizations seems to have interested at least a few canonists throughout this period. For example, at the end of the sixteenth century, again in Hyacinth's process the appointment of a subproctor fiscal was deemed to be a new practice (*nova praxis*) and though occasionally enjoined, nevertheless it was thought unusual, unsuitable, and indecorous that a fiscal—who usually accused and punished laymen for crimes—should be involved in the sacred, purely ecclesiastical business of canonization, which the pope directs

42. An auditor of the Rota lists the four things needed for a "true" miracle; he continues, "Nam si mala arte, veluti daemonum ope fiat, non erit miraculum." These are rather, "opera mirabilia, quae quandoque vel per daemones, vel per Magos seu daemoniacos virtute aliquarum naturalium causarum occulte adhibitarum fiunt, licet quandoque vera facta sint, non tamen habent rationem veri miraculi, sed potius ista sunt, & dicuntur praestigia"; Angelo Rocca, *Opera Omnia,* Tomus Primus (Rome, 1719), 104–50, [from *De Canonizatione Sanctorum Commentarius* (1601), and in the second edition (Rome, 1610), 14]. For Aquinas on demons performing miracles see: *Summa Theol.* Pt. I, Q. 114, Art. 4.

43. Peñafort: ASV Congr. Riti, 224, fol. 10r; Neri: *Il primo processo per San Filippo Neri, Studi e Testi* 224 (1963): 14: "neque ex illicita pactione cum aliquo malo spiritu."

ex officio and extrajudicially.[44] Such sentiments may indicate that some lawyers, seeking expeditious means of bringing canonizations to term, were encouraged by political or ecclesiastical pressures to cut through the bureaucratic complexities and circumvent the usual strictures and legal delays. On the other hand, greater rather than less rule-bound "legalism" has usually been associated with sixteenth-century and later saint-making.

To sum up: although very similar procedures of investigation, examination, discussion, and voting were applied to each of our five subjects, in every case different sets of complicating factors cast doubt on a candidate's chances for sainthood. In some instances political elements were among the most significant of those factors; in others, internal problems originating with the proposers on the one hand, or with the curia on the other, or both, delayed and sometimes threatened to terminate a process. At times the principals in our story, the candidates, seem almost crushed under the weight of legal, theological, dynastic, economic, and political wrangling that touched each case in varying degrees. In the end, however, thanks to a favorable ecclesiastical-political climate, luck, perseverance, and sacrifice on the part of their supporters, they achieved sainthood. Holiness, in and of itself, was never enough.

44. "Videtur indecorum fiscalem": Hyacinth's *Relatio* (*Canonizationis Beati Iacinthi Poloni Ord. Praed. Relatio Trium Rotae Auditorum*, 1597), 17. As Pierre Delooz put it, "[T]he judicial procedure of canonization would always have to be completed by an extra-judicial decision of a political nature": "Towards a Sociological Study of Canonized Sainthood in the Catholic Church," in *Saints and Their Cults*, ed. Stephen Wilson (Cambridge: Cambridge University Press, 1983), 189-216 (at 201), an article Delooz produced in 1962 as outline for his later *Sociologie et Canonisations* (Liège, 1969).

Bibliography

PRIMARY SOURCES

Unpublished

Archivio della Congregazione per le Cause dei Santi (ACCS):
Decreta servorum Dei vol. I.
R. 53 "Documenta Autographa canonisationis B. Hyacinthi Poloni Ord. Praed."

Archivio segreto vaticano (ASV):
Congr. Riti, processi 77, 224, 772, 1681, 2177, 3192, 4216.

Biblioteca apostolica vaticana (BAV):
Vat. lat. 4015.

Bibliothèque nationale, Paris (BNP):
ms lat. 5373 A.

Exeter College, Oxford:
ms. 158.

Published

AASS. April I. 103–234.

AASS. May I. 313–51.

AASS. June III. 145–230.

AASS. July III. 811–60.

Andreae, Johannes. *In Quinque Libros Novella Commentaria*. Vol. 3. Turin, 1963.

Aquinas, Thomas. *Scriptum super libros Sententiarum magistri Peter Lombardi*. Edited by Pierre Mandonnet. Tom. 2. Paris, 1929.

Angeli Clareni Opera. Vol. 2: *Historia Septem Tribulationum Ordinis Minorum*. Edited by O. Rossini. Rome: Istituto storico italiano per il Medio Evo, 1999.

Augustinus de Ancona. *Summa de Potestate Ecclesiastica*. Rome: Ex typ. Geo. Ferrarii, 1582.

Bachmann, Adolf, ed. *Briefe und Akten*. In *Fontes Rerum Austriacarum*, zweite Abtheilung: *Diplomataria et Acta*, 42–44 Band. Vienna, 1879–85.

Bembo, Pietro. *History of Venice.* Vol. 1, books 1–4. Translated by Robert W. Ulery, Jr. London: Harvard University Press/I Tatti Renaissance Library, 2007.

Bonaventure. *Opera, Sixti V pont. max iussu diligentissime emendata.* 7 vols. Rome: Ex typ. Vaticana, 1588–96.

———. *Bonaventure: The Soul's Journey into God; The Tree of Life; The Life of St. Francis.* Edited by Ewert Cousins. New York: Paulist Press, 1978.

Bullarium Franciscanum. Nova series. Vol. 3. (1471–84). Edited by Joseph Pou y Marti. Quaracchi: Ex typ. Coll. S. Bonaventurae, 1949.

"Canonisation et politique au xive siècle. Documents inédits . . . de Charles de Blois." Edited by A. Vauchez. In *Miscellanea in onore di Monsignor Martino Giusti,* 2:381–404. Vatican City: Vatican Archive, 1978.

Canonizationis Beati Iacinthi Poloni Ord. Praed. Relatio Trium Rotae Auditorum. Rome: typ. Nicolai Mutii, 1597.

Christ Church Letters. Edited by J. B. Sheppard. New series 19. Camden Society, 1877.

Collijn, Isak ed. *Acta et Processus Canonizacionis Beate Birgitte.* Uppsala, 1924–31.

Commynes, Philippe de. *The Life of Louis XI of France.* Translated and edited by Paul Kendall as *The Universal Spider.* London: Folio Society, 1973.

Correspondenz des Kaisers Karl V, erster Band, 1513–1532. Edited by Karl Lanz. 3 vols. Leipzig: F. A. Brockhaus, 1844–46.

De'Giudici, Johannes Baptista. *De canonizatione B. Bonaventure.* In two books in *Miscellanea,* edited by E. Baluze. Lucca, 1764.

Fontanini, Giusto. *Codex constitutionum quas summi pontifices ediderunt in solemni canonizatione sanctorum a Johanne XV ad Benedictum XIII.* Rome: Ex typ. Rev. Cam. Apostolicae, 1729.

Gachard, Louis-Prosper. *Correspondance de Charles-Quint et d'Adrien VI.* Brussels: M. Hayez, 1859.

Galesino, Pietro. *Sancti Didaci Complutensis canonizatio.* Rome, 1588.

Gess, Felician, ed. *Akten und Briefe zur Kirchenpolitik Herzog Georgs von Sachsen,* Erster Band 1517–1524. Leipzig: Teubner, 1905.

Glassberger, Nicholas. *Chronica.* In *Analecta Franciscana,* vol. 2. Quaracchi: Ex typ. Collegi S. Bonaventura, 1887.

Guicciardini, Francesco. *The History of Italy.* Translated by Sidley Alexander. New York: Macmillan, 1969.

Hadrianus VI, sive Analecta Historica de Hadriano Sexto Trajectino papa romano. Edited by Kaspar Burman. Utrecht: Jacobum à Poolsum, 1727.

Il Carteggio fra il Card. Marco Barbo e Giovanni Lorenzi (1481–1490). Edited by Pio Paschini. Vatican City: Biblioteca Apostolica Vaticana, 1948.

Johannis Burckardi, Liber Notarum, vol. 1. Edited by E. Celini. In L. A. Muratori, *Rerum Italicarum Scriptores,* 32. Città di Castello, 1906.

Landucci, Luca. *Diario fiorentino dal 1450 al 1516 continuata da un anonimo fino al 1542.* Edited by Iodoco del Badia. Florence: Sansoni, 1883.

Le Cérémonial papal de la fin du moyen âge à la renaissance. Vol. 2: *De Rome en Avignon ou Le cérémonial de Jacques Stefaneschi.* Edited by Marc Dykmans. Brussels: Institut historique Belge de Rome, 1981.

Le Cérémonial papal de la fin du moyen âge à la renaissance. Vol. 4: *La retour à Rome ou le cérémonial du patriarche Pierre Ameil.* Edited by Marc Dykmans. Brussels: Institut historique Belge de Rome, 1985.

L'Oeuvre de Patrizi Piccolomini ou le Cérémonial Papal de la Première Renaissance. Edited by Marc Dykmans. 2 vols. Vatican City: Biblioteca Apostolica Vaticana, 1980–82.

Louis XI: Lettres Choisies. Edited by Henri Dubois. Paris: Librarie Générale Française, 1996.

Louise of Savoy. *Journal: Collection des mémoires relatifs à l'histoire de France.* Edited by C. Petitot. Petitot-Collection des memoires, serie 1, tome 16. Paris, 1826.

Ludwig, Vinzenz Oskar. "Der Kanonisationsprozess des Markgrafen Leopold III des Heiligen." *Jahrbuch der Stiftes Klosterneuburg* 9 (1919). Published as a stand-alone volume: Vienna/Leipzig: Braumüller.

Luther, Martin. *Luther's Works.* Vol. 34. Edited by Lewis W. Spitz. Philadelphia: Muhlenberg Press, 1960.

———. *Luther's Works.* Vol. 39. Edited by Eric W. Gritsch. Philadelphia: Fortress Press, 1970.

———. "To the Christian Nobility of the German Nation." In *Luther's Works,* vol. 44. Edited by J. Atkinson. Philadelphia: Fortress Press, 1966.

Malvetius, Troilus. "Tractatus non Infestius de sanctorum canonizatione." In *Tractatus Illustrium in utraque tum pontificii, tum Caesarei iuris facultate Iurisconsultorum,* vol. 14. Venice, 1584.

Mercati, Angelo, ed. *Diarii di Consistori del Pontificato di Adriano VI.* Studi e Testi 157. Vatican City: Biblioteca apostolica vaticana, 1951.

Muratori, Ludovico A. *Rerum Italicarum Scriptores.* 2nd ed. Vol. 22, part 3: *Il Diario Romano di Jacopo Gherardi da Volterra.* Edited by Enrico Carusi. Città di Castello, 1905.

Patrizi Piccolomini, Agostino. *Caeremoniale Romanum.* Venice, 1516; repr. Ridgewood, N.Y.: Gregg Press, 1965.

Pavino, Giovanni Francesco. *Johannes Franciscus de Pavinis, Rede auf den Heiligen Leopold (Oratio de Divo Leopoldo Austrie marchione et confessore . . .).* Edited by Ludwig Bieler. Innsbruck: Tyrolia-Verlag, 1936.

Pez, Hieronymous. *Scriptores rerum austriacarum veteres ac genuini.* 3 vols. Leipzig: J. F. Gleditschii, 1721–45.

Pinzuti, Mario M. ed. *I Codici Autografi dei Processi Cosentino e Turonense per la Canonizzazione di S. Francesco di Paola.* Rome: Curia Generalizia dell'Ordine dei Minimi, 1964.

"Procès-verbal du dernier consistoire secret préparatoire à la canonisation de Pierre Célestin." *Analecta Bollandiana* 16 (1897): 389–92, 475–87.

Processus Sixtinus Fratris Felicis a Cantalice. Edited by M. ab Altari. Vol. 10 of *Monu-*

menta Historica Ordinis Minorum Capuccinorum. Rome: Istituto storico dei frati minori cappuccini, 1964.

Quellen zur Geschichte Karls V. Edited by Alfred Hohler. Darmstadt: Wissenschaftliche Buchgesellschaft, 1990.

Regesten Kaiser Friedrichs III, Heft 4. Edited by Paul-Joachim Heinig. Vienna: Verlag Hermann Böhlaus, 1986.

[Sanuto, Marino.] *I Diarii di Marino Sanuto.* Edited by Rinaldo Fulin, Federico Stefani, et al. 58 vols. Venice: F. Visentini, 1879–1903.

Severinus. *Sanctissimo D N Clementi VIII . . . Cracovien. canonizationis beati Iacinthi Poloni Ord Praed. relatio trium Rotae auditorum Seraphini Olivarii Razzalii, Laurentii Blanchetti & Francisci Peniae.* Rome: Ex typ. Nicolai Mutti, 1597.

Spätling, Luchesius. "Tractatus pro canonizatione divi Bonaventurae a Fr. Antonio de Vercellis conscriptus." *Archivum Franciscanum Historicum* 48 (1955): 381–426; 49 (1956): 166–190.

Summa de Ordine Iudiciario. In *Quellen zur Geschichte des Römisch-Kanonischen Processes im Mittelalter,* IV Band, Heft IV. Edited by L. Wahrend. Innsbruck: Wagner, 1926.

Tolhurst, J., ed. *The Ordinale and Customary of the Benedictine Nuns of Barking Abbey.* 2 vols. Henry Bradshaw Society. London: Harrison and Sons, 1927–28.

Vespasiano da Bisticci. Renaissance Princes, Popes and Prelates. Translated by W. George and E. Waters. New York: Harper, 1926, 1963.

Wadding, Luke. *Annales Minorum seu Trium Ordinum a S. Francisco Institutorum.* 3rd ed. vol. 14. Florence: Ad Claras Aquas [Quaracchi], 1933.

Unpublished dissertations

De Silva, Jennifer Mara. "Ritual Negotiations: Paris de'Grassi and the Office of Ceremonies under Popes Julius II and Leo X (1504–1521)." Ph.D. diss., University of Toronto, 2007.

Peterson, David S. "Archbishop Antoninus: Florence and the Church in the Earlier Fifteenth Century." Ph.D. diss., Cornell University, 1985.

SECONDARY LITERATURE

Abulafia, David. *The Western Mediterranean Kingdoms 1200–1500.* New York: Longman, 1997.

Addante, Pietro. *San Francesco di Paola.* Milano: Edizioni Paoline, 1988.

Arnold, John H. *Belief and Unbelief in Medieval Europe.* London: Hodder; New York: Oxford University Press, 2005.

Arnold, John Charles. "Arcadia Becomes Jerusalem: Angelic Caverns and Shrine Conversion at Monte Gargano." *Speculum* 75 (July 2000): 567–88.

Bagchi, David. *Luther's Earliest Opponents.* Minneapolis: Fortress Press, 1991.

Bedini, Silvio A. *The Pope's Elephant.* New York: Penguin Group, 1997.

Bireley, Robert. "Early-Modern Catholicism as a Response to the Changing World of the Long Sixteenth Century." *Catholic Historical Review* 95, no. 2 (2009): 219–39.

Bishop, Edmund. "Leaves from the Diary of a Papal Master of Ceremonies." In *Liturgica Historica*, 434–43. Oxford: Clarendon Press, 1918.

Bizzocchi, Roberto. "Church, Religion, and State in the Early Modern Period." In supplement "The Origins of the State in Italy, 1300–1600." *Journal of Modern History* 67 (Dec. 1995): S152–S165.

Black, Christopher F. *Church, Religion and Society in Early Modern Italy.* Basingstoke: Palgrave-Macmillan, 2004.

Braudel, Fernand. *The Mediterranean and the Mediterranean World in the Age of Philip II.* Translated by Siân Reynolds. 2 vols. New York: Harper and Row, 1972.

Brooke, Rosalinde B. *Early Franciscan Government.* Cambridge: Cambridge University Press, 1959.

———. "St. Bonaventure as Minister General." In *San Bernardino francescano.* Centro di Studi sulla Spiritualità Medievale, Convegni, 14, October 14–17, 1973, 77–105. Todi: Accademia turdertina, 1974.

Brooks, Peter. "The Law as Narrative and Rhetoric." In *Law's Stories: Narrative and Rhetoric in the Law*, edited by Peter Brooks and Paul Gewirtz, 14–22. New Haven: Yale University Press, 1996.

Brucker, Gene A. *Renaissance Florence.* Berkeley: University of California Press, 1969.

Brundage, James A. *The Medieval Origins of the Legal Profession.* Chicago: University of Chicago Press, 2008.

———. "'My Learned Friend': Professional Etiquette in Medieval Courtrooms." In *Readers, Texts and Compilers in the Earlier Middle Ages: Studies in Medieval Canon Law in Honour of Linda Fowler-Magerl*, edited by Martin Brett and K. G. Cushing, 183–96. Aldershot: Ashgate, 2009.

Burke, Peter. *The Historical Anthropology of Early Modern Italy.* Cambridge: Cambridge University Press, 1987.

Burr, David. "John XXII and the Spirituals: Is Angelo Clareno Telling the Truth?" *Franciscan Studies* 63 (2005): 271–87.

———. *The Spiritual Franciscans: From Protest to Persecution in the Century after Saint Francis.* University Park: Pennsylvania State University Press, 2001.

Butters, Humfrey, C. *Governors and Government in Early Sixteenth-Century Florence, 1502–1519.* Oxford: Clarendon Press, 1985.

Campbell, Andrea, "A Spectacular Celebration of the Assumption in Siena." *Renaissance Quarterly* 58 (2005): 435–63.

Cambell, Jacques. "Le Sommaire de l'Enquête pour la canonisation de S. Elzear de Sabran, TOF d. 1323." *Miscellanea Franciscana* 73 (1973): 438–73.

Campagnola, Stanislao da. "Le vicende della canonizzazione di S. Bonaventura." In *San Bernardino francescano.* Centro di Studi sulla Spiritualità Medievale, Convegni, 14, October 14–17, 1973, 211–55. Todi: Accademia turdertina, 1974.

Carolus-Barré, Louis. "Consultation du Cardinal Pietro Colonna sur le IIe miracle de Saint Louis." *Bibliotheque de l'école des chartes* 117 (1959): 57–72.

Celenza, Christopher S. *Renaissance Humanism and the Papal Curia: Lapo de Castiglionchio the Younger's De curiae commodis.* Ann Arbor: University of Michigan Press, 1999.

Chambers, D. S. "The Economic Predicament of Renaissance Cardinals." In *Renaissance Cardinals and Their Worldly Problems.* Ashgate/Variorum, 1997. First published in *Medieval and Renaissance History* 3 (1966): 287–313.

Champion, Pierre. *Les Grands Hommes et leurs Médicins.* Lyons: Lab. CIBA, 1935.

Chaunu, Pierre, and Michèle Escamilla. *Charles Quint.* Paris: Fayard, 2000.

Chipps Smith, Jeffrey. "Repatriating Sanctity." In *Repatriation,* edited by Dario Gamboni, in the *Proceedings* of the Congress of the International Committee of the History of Art. Melbourne: University of Melbourne Press, 2009.

———. "Salvaging Saints: The Rescue and Display of Relics in Munich during the Early Catholic Reformation." In *Art, Piety and Destruction in the Christian West,* edited by Virginia Chieffo Raguin, 23–44. Aldershot: Ashgate, 2010.

Clemen, Otto. "Zur Kanonisation Bennos." *Neues Archiv für Sächsische Geschichte und Altertumskunde* 28. Edited by H. Ermisch (1907).

Cochrane, Eric. *Italy 1530–1630.* Edited by Julius Kirshner. New York: Longmans, 1988.

Cohen, Thomas V., and Elisabeth S. Cohen. *Words and Deeds in Renaissance Rome: Trials before the Papal Magistrates.* Toronto: University of Toronto Press, 1993.

Collins, David J. "Bursfelders, Humanists and the Rhetoric of Sainthood: The Late Medieval *Vitae* of Saint Benno." *Revue Benedictine* 111 (2001): 508–56.

———. *Reforming Saints: Saints' Lives and Their Authors in Germany, 1470–1530.* Oxford: Oxford University Press, 2008.

Cook, William R. "Fraternal and Lay Images of St. Francis in the Thirteenth Century." In *Popes, Teachers, and Canon Law in the Middle Ages,* edited by James Ross Sweeney and Stanley Chodorow, 263–89. Ithaca, N.Y.: Cornell University Press, 1989.

Cornelison, Sally J. "A French King and a Magic Ring: The Girolami and a Relic of St. Zenobius in Renaissance Florence." *Renaissance Quarterly* 55, no. 2 (Summer 2002): 434–69.

———. "Tales of Two Bishop Saints: Zenobius and Antoninus in Florentine Renaissance Art and History." *Sixteenth Century Journal* 38, no. 3 (2007): 627–56.

Daly, Patrick H. "The Process of Canonization in the Thirteenth and Early Fourteenth Centuries." In *St. Thomas Cantilupe Bishop of Hereford: Essays in His Honour,* edited by Meryl Jancey, 125–35. Hereford: Friends of the Hereford Cathedral Publications Committee for the Dean and Chapter, 1982.

D'Amico, John F. *Renaissance Humanism in Papal Rome.* Baltimore: Johns Hopkins University Press, 1983.

D'Ancona, Alessandro. *Origini del teatro italiano.* 2nd ed. 2 vols. Turin: Loescher, 1891.

Danett, Thomas. *The History of Comines.* Vol. 2. New York: AMS Press, 1967.

Daniel, E. R. "St. Bonaventura a Faithful Disciple of St. Francis? A Reexamination of the Question." In *S. Bonaventura 1274–1974,* 2:171–87. 5 vols. Grottaferrata: Collegio S. Bonaventura, 1973–74.

Debby, Nirit Ben-Aryeh. "Giambologna's Salviati Reliefs of St. Antoninus of Florence: Saintly Images and Political Manipulation." *Renaissance Studies* 22, no. 2 (2008): 197–220.

Delaborde, H. F. "Fragments de l'enquête faite a Saint-Denis en 1282 en vue de la canonisation de Saint Louis." *Mémoires de la société de l'histoire de Paris et de l'ile-de-France* 23 (1896): 1–71.

Dell'Oro, Ferdinando. *Beatificazione e Canonizzazione. «Excursus» storico-liturgico.* Rome: CLV, 1997.

Delooz, Pierre. "Towards a Sociological Study of Canonized Sainthood in the Catholic Church." In *Saints and Their Cults,* edited by Stephen Wilson, 189–216. Cambridge: Cambridge University Press, 1983.

Delumeau, Jean. *Vie Économique et Sociale de Rome dans la seconde moitié du XVIe siècle.* 2 vols. Paris: De Boccard, 1957–59.

De Silva, Jennifer Mara. "Senators or Courtiers: Negotiating Models for the College of Cardinals under Julius II and Leo X." *Renaissance Studies* 22, no. 2 (2008): 154–73.

Devonshire Jones, Rosemary. *Francesco Vettori: Florentine Citizen and Medici Servant.* London: Athlone Press, 1972.

Dienst, Heide. "Werden und Entwicklung der babenbergischen Mark." In *Österreich im Hochmittelalter (907 bis 1246),* edited by Anna M. Drabek. Vienna: Verlag der Österreichen Akad. der Wissenschaften, 1991.

Di Fonzo, Lorenzo. "Il processo di canonizzazione di S. Bonaventura da Bagnoregio, O. Min (1474–82)." *Miscellanea Francescana* 75 (1975): 227–89.

Ditchfield, Simon. *Liturgy, Sanctity and History in Tridentine Italy: Pietro Maria Campi and the Preservation of the Particular.* Cambridge: Cambridge University Press, 1995.

———. "Sanctity in Early Modern Italy." *Journal of Ecclesiastical History* 47 (January 1996): 98–112.

———. "Tridentine Worship and the Cult of Saints." In *The Cambridge History of Christianity.* Vol. 6: *Reform and Expansion 1500–1660,* edited by R. Po-chia Hsia, 201–24. Cambridge: Cambridge University Press, 2007.

———. "Thinking with Saints: Sanctity and Society in the Early Modern World." *Critical Inquiry* 35, no. 3 (2009): 552–84.

Dixon, C. Scott. *The Reformation in Germany.* Oxford: Blackwell Publishers, 2002.

Douglas, Richard M. *Jacopo Sadoleto, 1477–1547: Humanist and Reformer.* Cambridge, Mass.: Harvard University Press, 1959.

Duthilloeul, H.-R. *Voyage de Jacques le Saige de Douai.* New ed. Douai, 1851.

Eberhard, Winfried. "Bohemia, Moravia and Austria." In *The Early Reformation in*

Europe, edited by Andrew Pettegree, 23–48. Cambridge: Cambridge University Press, 1992.

Edwards, Mark U. "Statistics on Sixteenth-Century Printing." In *The Process of Change in Early Modern Europe,* edited by Philip N. Bebb and Sherrin Marshall, 149–63. Athens: Ohio University Press, 1988.

Enders, Ludwig. *Luther und Emser: Ihre Streitschriften aus dem Jahre 1521.* Halle: Niemeyer, 1889.

Fernández, Henry Dietrich. "The Patrimony of St. Peter: The Papal Court at Rome c. 1450–1700." In *The Princely Courts of Europe,* edited by John Adamson, 141–63. London: Weidenfeld and Nicolson, 1999.

Finucane, Ronald. "Authorizing the Supernatural: An Examination of Some English Miracles around 1318." In *Aspects of Power and Authority in the Middle Ages,* edited by Brenda Bolton and Christine Meek, 289–303. Turnhout: Brepols, 2007.

———. *Miracles and Pilgrims: Popular Beliefs in Medieval England.* London: Dent, 1977.

———. "Saint-Making at the End of the Sixteenth Century: How and Why Jacek of Poland (d. 1257) became St. Hyacinth in 1594." *Hagiographica* 9 (2002): 207–58.

———. "The Toddler in the Ditch: A Case of Parental Neglect?" In *Voices from the Bench: The Narratives of Lesser Folk in Medieval Trials,* edited by Michael Goodich, 127–48. New York: Palgrave Macmillan, 2006.

Fowler-Magerl, Linda. *Ordines Iudiciarii* and *Libelli de Ordine Iudiciorum.* Typologie des Sources du Moyen Âge Occidental, Fasc. 63. Turnhout: Brepols, 1994.

Fragnito, Gigliola. "Cardinals' Courts in Sixteenth-Century Rome." *Journal of Modern History* 65, no. 1 (1993): 26–56.

Frazier, Alison Knowles. *Possible Lives: Authors and Saints in Renaissance Italy.* New York: Columbia University Press, 2005.

Freeman, John F. "Louise of Savoy: A Case of Maternal Opportunism." *Sixteenth-Century Journal* 3 (Oct. 1972): 77–98.

Galuzzi, Alessandro. *Origini dell'Ordine dei Minimi.* Rome: Pontificia Università Lateranense, 1967.

———. *Pergamene: Codici e registri dell'Archivio generale dei Minimi.* Rome: Edizioni della Curia Generalizia dei Minimi, 1970.

Gentilcore, David. "Methods and Approaches in the Social History of the Counter-Reformation in Italy." *Social History* 17, no. 1 (Jan. 1992): 73–98.

Gilbert, Creighton. "The Archbishop on the Painters of Florence, 1450." *Art Bulletin* 41, no. 1 (March 1959): 75–87.

Goffen, Rona. "Friar Sixtus IV and the Sistine Chapel." *Renaissance Quarterly* 39, no. 2 (1986): 218–62.

Goodich, Michael. "The Politics of Canonization in the Thirteenth Century: Lay and Mendicant Saints." In *Saints and their Cults,* Edited by Stephen Wilson, 169–87. Cambridge: Cambridge University Press, 1983.

———. *Miracles and Wonders: The Development of the Concept of Miracle, 1150–1350.* Aldershot: Ashgate, 2007.

Hale, John R. *Renaissance Europe 1480–1520.* 2nd ed.. Oxford: Blackwell, 2000.

Hale, Matthew. *The History of the Common Law of England.* Edited by Charles M. Gray. Chicago: University of Chicago Press, 1971.

Hay, Denys. *The Church in Italy in the Fifteenth Century.* Cambridge: Cambridge University Press, 1977.

Heinig, Paul-Joachim, ed. *Kaiser Friedrich III.(1440–1493) in seiner Zeit.* Cologne: Böhlau Verlag, 1993.

Hollingsworth, Mary. *The Cardinal's Hat.* New York: Overlook Press, 2004.

Howard, Peter. "Preaching Magnificence in Renaissance Florence." *Renaissance Quarterly* 61 (2008): 325–69.

Huber, Raphael M. *A Documented History of the Franciscan Order, from the Birth of St. Francis to the Division of the Order under Leo X. 1182–1517.* Milwaukee, Wis.: Nowiny Publishing Apostolate, 1944.

Hyde, Helen. *Cardinal Bendinello Sauli and Church Patronage in Sixteenth-Century Italy.* Woodbridge, UK: Boydell Press/ Royal Historical Society, 2009.

Ilardi, Vincent. "The First Permanent Embassy outside Italy: The Milanese Embassy at the French Court, 1464–1483." In *Politics, Religion, and Diplomacy in Early Modern Europe,* edited by Malcolm R. Thorp and Arthur J. Slavin, 1–18. Sixteenth Century Essays and Studies 27. Kirksville, Mo.: Sixteenth Century Journal Publishers, 1994.

Kelly, H. A. "Inquisition and the Prosecution of Heresy: Misconceptions and Abuses." *Church History* 58, no. 4 (1989): 39–451.

———. "The Right to Remain Silent: Before and After Joan of Arc." *Speculum* 69, no. 4 (1993): 992–1026.

Kemp, Eric W. *Canonization and Authority in the Western Church.* London: Oxford University Press, 1948.

Kendall, Paul M. *Louis XI.* New York: Norton, 1971.

Kéry, Lotte, "Inquisitio—denunciatio—exceptio: Möglichkeiten der Verfahrenseinleitung im Dekretalenrecht." *Zeitschrift der Savigny-Stiftung für Rechtsgeschichte, Kanonistische Abteilung* 87 (2001): 226–68.

Kleinberg, Aviad M. "Proving Sanctity: Selection and Authentication of Saints in the Later Middle Ages." *Viator* 20 (1989): 183–205.

Knecht, Robert J. "The Concordat of 1516: A Reassessment." *University of Birmingham Historical Journal* 9 (1963): 16–32.

———. *Renaissance Warrior and Patron: The Reign of Francis I.* Cambridge: Cambridge University Press, 1994.

Kohnle, Armin. "Zur Heiligsprechung des Bischofs Benno von Meissen (1523)." In *Papstgeschichte und Landesgeschichte: Festschrift für Hermann Jakobs zum 65. Geburtstag,* edited by Joachim Dahlhaus et al., 555–72. Cologne: Böhlau, 1995.

Krafft, Otfried. *Papsturkunde und Heiligsprechung: die päpstlichen Kanonisationen vom*

Mittelalter bis zur Reformation: ein Hanbuch. Cologne: Böhlau Verlag: 2005.

Lambert, M. D. *Franciscan Poverty: the Doctrine of Absolute Poverty of Christ in the Franciscan Order, 1210–1323.* London: S.P.C.K., 1961.

Lawrence, C. H. *The Friars: Impact of the Early Mendicant Movement on Western Society.* London: Longman, 1994.

Lechner, Karl. *Die Babenberger: Markgrafen und Herzoge von Österreich 976–1246.* Vienna: Hermann Böhlaus, 1976.

Lee, Egmont. *Sixtus IV and Men of Letters.* Rome: Edizioni di storia e letteratura, 1978.

Leeper, Alexander. *A History of Medieval Austria.* Oxford: Oxford University Press, 1941.

Leff, Gordon. *Heresy in the Later Middle Ages: The Relation of Heterodoxy to Dissent c. 1250–c. 1450.* 2 vols. Manchester, UK: Manchester University Press, 1967.

Levi, Anthony. *Renaissance and Reformation: The Intellectual Genesis.* New Haven, Conn.: Yale University Press, 2002.

Longhurst, John E. "Luther in Spain: 1520–1540." *Proceedings of the American Philosophical Society* 103 (1959): 66–93.

Lowe, Kate J. P. *Church and Politics in Renaissance Italy: The Life and Career of Cardinal Francesco Soderini, 1453–1524.* Cambridge: Cambridge University Press, 1993.

———. "The Political Crime of Conspiracy in Fifteenth- and Sixteenth-Century Rome." In *Crime, Society and the Law in Renaissance Italy,* edited by K. J. P. Lowe and Trevor Dean, 184–203. Cambridge: Cambridge University Press, 1994.

Mallett, Michael. "Personalities and Pressures: Italian Involvement in the French Invasion of 1494." In *The French Descent into Renaissance Italy, 1494–95: Antecedents and Effects,* edited by David Abulafia, 151–63. Aldershot: Variorum, 1995.

Marinangeli, Bonaventura. "La canonizzazione di S. Bonaventura e il processo di Lione." *Miscellanea Francescana* 17 (1916): 65–86, 105–20, 164–74; 18 (1917): 125–35.

Martines, Lauro. *Strong Words: Writing and Social Strain in the Italian Renaissance.* Baltimore: Johns Hopkins University Press, 2001.

———. *Fire in the City: Savonarola and the Struggle for Renaissance Florence.* New York: Oxford University Press, 2006.

Matarasso, Pauline. *Queen's Mate.* Ashgate: Aldershot, 2001.

Matheson, Peter. *The Rhetoric of the Reformation.* Edinburgh: T & T Clark, 1998.

McCartney, Elizabeth. "The King's Mother and Royal Prerogative in Early-Sixteenth-Century France." In *Medieval Queenship,* edited by John C. Parsons. New York: St. Martin's Press, 1993.

McClung Hallman, Barbara. "Practical Aspects of Roman Diplomacy in Germany, 1517–1541." *Journal of Medieval and Renaissance Studies* 10, no. 2 (Fall 1980): 193–206.

Meredith, Peter, and John E. Tailby, eds. *The Staging of Religious Drama in Europe in the Later Middle Ages: Texts and Documents in English Translation.* Kalamazoo, Mich.: Medieval Institute Publications, 1983.

Meserve, Margaret. "News from Negroponte: Politics, Popular Opinion, and Information Exchange in the First Decade of the Italian Press." *Renaissance Quarterly* 59, no. 2 (2006): 440–80.

Minnich, Nelson H. "Prophecy and the Fifth Lateran Council (1512–1517)." In *Councils of the Catholic Reformation*. Aldershot: Ashgate (*Variorum*), 2008.

Mitchell, Bonner. *Rome in the High Renaissance: The Age of Leo X*. Norman: University of Oklahoma Press, 1973.

Moorman, John. *A History of the Franciscan Order from Its Origins to the Year 1517*. Oxford: Oxford University Press, 1968.

Morçay, Raoul. *Saint Antonin: Archevèque de Florence 1389–1459*. Paris: Lib. Gabalda, 1914.

Muir, Edward. *Ritual in Early Modern Europe*. 2nd ed. Cambridge: Cambridge University Press, 2005.

Najemy, John M. *A History of Florence 1200–1575*. Oxford: Blackwell Publishing, 2006.

Nauert, Charles G. Jr.. *Humanism and the Culture of Renaissance Europe*. Cambridge: Cambridge University Press, 1995.

Nehring, Karl. *Matthias Corvinus, Kaiser Friedrich III, und das Reich*. Munich: Oldenbourg Verlag, 1975.

Nemec, Jaroslav. "L'archivio della Congregazione per le Cause dei Santi." In *Miscellanea in occasione del IV centenario della Congregazione per le Cause dei Santi (1588–1988)*, 339–52. Rome: Ministero per i Beni Culturali ed Ambientali, 1988.

Niccoli, Ottavia. *Prophecy and People in Renaissance Italy*. Translated by Lydia G. Cochrane. Princeton, N.J.: Princeton University Press, 1990.

Nimmo, Duncan. *Reform and Division in the Medieval Franciscan Order: From St. Francis to the Foundation of the Capuchins*. Rome: Capuchin Historical Institute, 1987.

Nold, Patrick. *Pope John XXII and His Franciscan Cardinal: Bertrand de la Tour and the Apostolic Poverty Controversy*. Oxford: Clarendon Press, 2003.

Oettinger, Rebecca W. *Music as Propaganda in the German Reformation*. Aldershot: Ashgate, 2001.

Opll, Ferdinand, and Richard Perger. *Kaiser Friedrich III. Und die Wiener 1483–1485. Briefe und Ereignisse während der Belagerung Wiens durch König Mathias Corvinus von Hungarn*. Vienna: Franz Deuticke, 1993.

Orlandi, Stefano. *Bibliografia Antoniniana* escrizione dei manoscritti della vita e delle opere di S. Antonino O.P. Arcivescovo di Firenze, e degli studi stampati che lo riguardano. Vatican City: Tipografia poliglotta vaticana, 1961.

———. "La canonizzazione di S. Antonio." *Memorie domenicane* 81 (1964): 85–105, 131–45.

Orth, Myra Dickman. "Francis Du Moulin and the Journal of Louise of Savoy." *Sixteenth-Century Journal* 13 (Spring 1982): 55–66.

Ourliac, Paul. "The Concordat of 1472: An Essay on the Relations between Louis XI and Sixtus IV." In *The Recovery of France in the Fifteenth Century*, edited by P. S. Lewis, 102–84. New York: Harper and Row, 1971.

Ozment, Steven E. *The Reformation in the Cities.* New Haven, Conn.: Yale University Press, 1975.

Paciocco, Roberto. *Canonizzazioni e culto dei santi nella christianitas (1198–1302).* Assisi: Edizioni Porziuncola/Società internazionale di studi francescani, 2006.

———. *Da Francesco ai "Catalogi Sanctorum": livelli istituzionali e immagini agiografiche nel ordine Francescano (secoli 13–14).* Collectio Assisiensis 20. Assisi: Porziuncola,1990.

Paoli, Emore. "La santità canonizzata di Francesco di Paola." *Hagiographica* 11 (2004): 223–52.

Papa, Giovanni. *Le cause di canonizzazione nel primo periodo della Congregazione dei Riti (1588–1634).* Città del Vaticano: Urbaniana University Press, 2001.

Paravicini-Bagliani, Agostino. *The Pope's Body.* Translated by David S. Peterson. Chicago: University of Chicago Press, 2000.

Partner, Peter. "The 'Budget' of the Roman Church in the Renaissance Period." In *Italian Renaissance Studies,* edited by E. F. Jacob, 256–78. London: Faber and Faber, 1960.

———. *Renaissance Rome, 1500–1559: Portrait of a Society.* Berkeley: University of California Press, 1976.

Pastor, Ludwig von. *The History of the Popes from the Close of the Middle Ages.* Translated by F. Antrobus. 40 vols. London: Kegan Paul, 1899–1953.

Patrizi-Accursi, Luigi. *Relazione della vita, della virtù e dei miracoli di San Francesco di Paola fatta al sommo pontefice Leone X da Giacomo Simoneta.* Rome: Libreria Pontificia di F. Pustet, 1907.

Pellegrini, Marco. *Ascanio Maria Sforza* [d. 1505]: *La parabola politica di un cardinal-principe del rinascimento.* 2 vols. Rome: Istituto storico italiano per il medio evo, 2002.

———. "An Episcopal Election in Quattrocento Florence." In *Popes, Teachers and Canon Law in the Middle Ages,* edited by James Ross Sweeney and Stanley Chodorow, 300–325. Ithaca, N.Y.: Cornell University Press, 1989.

———. "A Turning-Point in the History of the Factional System in the Sacred College: The Power of Pope and Cardinals in the Age of Alexander VI." In *Court and Politics in Papal Rome, 1492–1700,* edited by Gianvittorio Signorotto and Maria Antonietta Visceglia, 8–30. Cambridge: Cambridge University Press, 2002.

Perger, Richard. "Thomas List: Ein Wegbereiter der Heiligsprechung St. Leopolds." *Jahrbuch des Stiftes Klosterneuburg,* Neue Folge, 13 (1985): 7–20.

Petersohn, Jürgen. *Kaiserlicher Gesandter und Kurienbischof: Andreas Jamometić am Hof Papst Sixtus' IV. (1478–1481).* Hannover: Hahnsche Buchhandlung, 2004.

Peterson, David S. "An Episcopal Election in Quattrocento Florence." In *Popes, Teachers, and Canon Law in the Middle Ages,* edited by James Ross Sweeney and Stanley Chodorow, 300–325. Ithaca, N.Y.: Cornell University Press, 1989.

Pettegree, Andrew. *Reformation and the Culture of Persuasion.* Cambridge: Cambridge University Press, 2005.

Piana, C. "I processi de canonizzazione su la vita di S. Bernardino da Siena." *Archivum Franciscanum Historicum* 44 (1951): 87–160, 383–435.

Pietschmann, Klaus. "Ablauf und Dimensionen der Heiligsprechung des Antonino von Florenz (1523)." *Quellen und Forschungen aus italienischen Archiven und Bibliotheken* 78 (1998): 388–463.

Polito, Cyril. "Saint François de Paule: Ses rapports avec les Calabrais et les Tourangeaux." *Bollettino Ufficiale dell'Ordine dei Minimi* 47, nos. 2–3 (April–September, 1999).

Polizzotto, Lorenzo. "The Making of a Saint: The Canonization of St. Antonino, 1516–1523." *Journal of Medieval and Renaissance Studies* 22, no. 3 (1992): 353–81.

Pomata, Giovanna. "Malpighi and the Holy Body: Medical Experts and Miraculous Evidence in Seventeenth-Century Italy." *Renaissance Studies* 21 (2007): 568–86.

Pontieri, Ernesto. *Per la Storia del Regno di Ferrante I d'Aragona Re di Napoli.* 2nd ed. Naples: Edizioni scientifiche italiane, 1969.

Prodi, Paolo. *The Papal Prince.* Translated by Susan Haskins. Cambridge: Cambridge University Press, 1987.

Quaglioni, Diego. "La prova del miracolo spunti dalla dottrina di diritto comune." In *Notai, Miracoli e Culto dei Santi,* edited by Raimondo Michetti, 99–114. Milan: Giuffré, 2004.

Rashdall, Hastings. *The Universities of Europe in the Middle Ages.* Edited by F. M. Powicke and A. B. Emden. Vol. 1. Oxford: Oxford University Press, 1936.

Reiss, Sheryl E. "Adrian VI, Clement VII and Art." In *The Pontificate of Clement VII,* edited by Kenneth Gouwens and S. E. Reiss, 339–62. Aldershot: Ashgate, 2005.

Rill, Bernd. *Friedrich III: Habsburgs europaïscher Durchbruch.* Graz, Austria: Verlag Styria, 1987.

Roberti, Giuseppe. *S. Francesco di Paola: Storia della sua Vita.* 2nd ed. Rome: Curia Generalizia dell'Ordine dei Minimi, 1963.

Robson, Michael. *The Franciscans in the Middle Ages.* Woodbridge, UK: Boydell Press, 2006.

Röhrig, Floridus. *Leopold III. der Heilige: Markgraf von Österreich.* Vienna: Herold Verlag, 1985.

Rubinstein, Nicholai. "Lay Patronage and Observant Reform in Fifteenth-century Florence." In *Christianity and the Renaissance,* edited by Timothy Verdon and John Henderson, 64–82. Syracuse: Syracuse University Press, 1990.

Samerski, Stefan. *"Wie im Himmel, so auf Erden"?: Selig- und Heiligsprechung in der Katholischen Kirche 1740 bis 1870.* Stuttgart: Kohlhammer, 2002.

Saslow, James M. *The Medici Wedding of 1589: Florentine Festival as Theatrum Mundi.* New Haven, Conn.: Yale University Press, 1996.

Schimmelpfennig, Bernard. *Die Zeremonienbücher der römischen Kurie im Mittelalter.* Tübingen: M. Niemeyer, 1973.

Schulte, J. F. von. *Die Geschichte der Quellen und Literatur des Canonischen Rechts.* 3 vols. Stuttgart: F. Enke, 1875–80.

Scribner, R. W. "Incombustible Luther." *Past and Present* 110 (1986): 38–68.

———. *Popular Culture and Popular Movements in Reformation Germany.* London: Hambledon Press, 1987.

Seidemann, J. K. "Schriftstücke zur Reformationsgeschichte." *Zeitschrift für die hist. Theologie* 44 (1874): 136–38.

Seppelt, Franz Xavier. *Monumenta Coelestiniana: Quellen zur Geschichte des Papstes Coelestin V.* Paderborn, Germany: F. Schöningh, 1921.

Shaw, Christine. *The Political Role of the Orsini Family from Sixtus IV to Clement VII: Barons and Factions in the Papal States.* Rome: Istituto storico italiano per il medio evo, 2007.

Soergel, Philip M. "The Image of Saints in the Bavarian Counter Reformation." *Historian* 53, no. 2 (1991): 223–40.

———. *Wondrous in His Saints: Counter-Reformation Propaganda in Bavaria.* Berkeley: University of California Press, 1993.

Smolinsky, Heribert. "Albertinisches Sachsen." In *Die Territorien des Reichs im Zeitalter der Reformation und Konfessionalisierung,* vol. 2. Munich: Aschendorff, 1990.

Sposato, Pasquale. "Fonti per la storia di S. Francesco di Paola: La sua canonizzazione attraverso il 'Diarium' di Paride De Grassi prefetto delle ceremonie pontificie sotto Leone X, Introduzione." *Calabria Nobilissima* 10, nos. 31–32 (June 1956): 1–32.

———. "Fonti per la storia di S. Francesco di Paola: La sua canonizzazione attraverso il 'Diarium' di Paride De Grassi prefetto delle ceremonie pontificie sotto Leone X, Testo del Diario." *Calabria Nobilissima* 11, no. 33 (March 1957): 1–29.

Stinger, Charles. *The Renaissance in Rome.* Bloomington: Indiana University Press, 1998.

Strnad, Alfred A. "Kaiser Friedrich III und die Translatio sancti Leopoldi." *Jahrbuch des Stiftes Klosterneuburg,* Neue Folge, 7 (1971): 103–34.

Thomson, John A. F. *Popes and Princes 1417–1517.* London: George Allen and Unwin, 1980.

Toynbee, Margaret R. *S. Louis of Toulouse and the Process of Canonisation in the Fourteenth Century.* Manchester, UK: University Press, 1929.

Trexler, Richard C. "The Episcopal Constitutions of Antoninus of Florence." *Quellen und Forschungen aus italienischen Archiven und Bibliotheken* 59 (1979): 244–72.

———. *Public Life in Renaissance Florence.* Ithaca, N.Y.: Cornell University Press, 1980.

Turley, Thomas. "John XXII and the Franciscans: A Reappraisal." In *Popes, Teachers, and Canon Law in the Middle Ages,* edited by James Ross Sweeney and Stanley Chodorow, 74–88. Ithaca, N.Y.: Cornell University Press, 1989.

Van Engen, John. "Multiple Options: The World of the Fifteenth-Century Church." *Church History* 77 (2008): 257–84.

Vauchez, André. *Sainthood in the Later Middle Ages.* Translated by Jean Birrell. Cambridge: Cambridge University Press, 1997.

Vidal, Fernando. "Miracles, Science, and Testimony in Post-Tridentine Saint-Making." *Science in Context* 20 (2007): 481–508.

Villalon, L. J. Andrew. "San Diego of Alcalá and the Politics of Saint-Making in Counter-Reformation Europe." *Catholic Historical Review* 83 (1997): 691–715.

Volkmar, Christoph. *Die Heiligenerhebung Bennos von Meissen (1523/24)*. Munich: Aschendorff, 2002.

Walsh, Barbara. "Keys to Success: Propriety and Promotion of Miraculous Images by Roman Confraternities." In *The Miraculous Image in the Late Middle Ages and Renaissance*, edited by Erik Thunø and Gerhard Wolf, 161–84. Analecta romana instituti danici, supplementum 35. Rome: "L'Erma" di Bretschneider, 2004.

Weinstein, Donald, and Rudolph M. Bell. *Saints and Society*. Chicago: University of Chicago Press, 1982.

Weiss, James Michael. "Hagiography by German Humanists, 1483–1516." *Journal of Medieval and Renaissance Studies* 15 (1985): 299–316.

Wetzstein, Thomas. *Heilige vor Gericht: Das Kanonisationsverfahren im europäischen Spätmittelalter.* Cologne: Böhlau Verlag, 2005.

———. "*Virtus morum et virtus signorum?* Zur Bedeutung der Mirakel in den Kanonisationsprozessen des 15. Jahrhunderts." In *Mirkel im Mittelalter: Konzeption, Erscheinungsformen, Deutungen*, edited by Martin Heinzelmann et al., 351–76. Beiträge zur Hagiographie 3. Stuttgart: Franz Steiner Verlag, 2002.

Whitford, David M. "The Papal Antichrist: Martin Luther and the Underappreciated Influence of Lorenzo Valla." *Renaissance Quarterly* 61 (2008): 26–52.

Wilson, Stephen, ed. *Saints and their Cults*. Cambridge: Cambridge University Press, 1983.

Woodward, Kenneth L. *Making Saints: How the Catholic Church Determines Who Becomes a Saint, Who Doesn't, and Why*. New York: Simon and Schuster, 1990.

Ziegler, Joseph. "Practitioners and Saints: Medical Men in Canonization Processes in the Thirteenth to Fifteenth Centuries." *Society for the Social History of Medicine* 12 (1999): 191–225.

Zimmermann, T. C. Price. *Paolo Giovio: The Historian and the Crisis of Sixteenth-Century Italy*. Princeton, N.J.: Princeton University Press, 1995.

Index